Contemporary Issues in Criminal Justice Policy
Policy Proposals from the American Society of Criminology Conference

Natasha A. Frost

Northeastern University

Joshua D. Freilich

John Jay College of Criminal Justice

Todd R. Clear

John Jay College of Criminal Justice and American Society of Criminology, President

WADSWORTH
CENGAGE Learning

Australia • Brazil • Japan • Korea • Mexico • Singapore • Spain • United Kingdom • United States

WADSWORTH
CENGAGE Learning

Contemporary Issues in Criminal Justice Policy: Policy Proposals from the American Society of Criminology Conference
By Natasha P. Frost, Joshua D. Freilich, and Todd R. Clear

Senior Publisher:
Linda Schreiber

Senior Acquisitions Editor:
Carolyn Henderson Meier

Assistant Editor:
Erin Abney

Editorial Assistant:
John Chell

Media Editor:
Ting Jian Yap

Senior Marketing Manager:
Michelle Williams

Marketing Assistant:
Jillian Myers

Senior Marketing
Communications Manager:
Tami Strang

Content Project Manager:
Christy Frame

Creative Director:
Rob Hugel

Senior Art Director:
Maria Epes

Print Buyer:
Linda Hsu

Cover Designer:
Bartay Studio

Compositor:
Pre-PressPMG

For product information and technology assistance, contact us at
Cengage Learning Customer & Sales Support, 1-800-354-9706.

For permission to use material from this text or product,
submit all requests online at
www.cengage.com/permissions.
Further permissions questions can be e-mailed to
permissionrequest@cengage.com.

ISBN-13: 978-0-495-91109-8
ISBN-10: 0-495-91109-7

Wadsworth
20 Davis Drive
Belmont, CA 94002-3098
USA

Cengage Learning is a leading provider of customized learning solutions with office locations around the globe, including Singapore, the United Kingdom, Australia, Mexico, Brazil, and Japan. Locate your local office at: **www.cengage.com/global**.

Cengage Learning products are represented in Canada by Nelson Education, Ltd.

To learn more about Wadsworth, visit
www.cengage.com/wadsworth

Purchase any of our products at your local college store or at our preferred online store **www.ichapters.com**.

Printed in the United States of America
1 2 3 4 5 6 7 13 12 11 10 09

CONTENTS

CRIMINOLOGY & CRIMINAL JUSTICE POLICY

JUSTICE POLICY

DRUG & ALCOHOL POLICY

TERRORISM POLICY

IMMIGRATION POLICY

POLICING POLICY

ACKNOWLEDGMENTS

The editors would like to thank the eight distinguished scholars who volunteered their time to serve as area chairs for policy essay submissions and who in the process helped shape the sessions and the contents of this book. The policy session area chairs were: Alfred Blumstein, Jack Greene, Karen Heimer, Mark Kleiman, Gary LaFree, Daniel Nagin, Cathy Spatz-Widom, and Michael Tonry. The editors would also like to thank Seokhee Yoon for her tireless work as the program assistant for the 2009 annual meeting and for her help in cross-checking references for this book.

EDITORS

Natasha A. Frost is Assistant Professor in the College of Criminal Justice at Northeastern University. Natasha's primary research and teaching interests are in the areas of punitiveness, formal and informal social control, and the effects of incarceration and reentry on individuals, families, and communities. Natasha was co-chair of the 2009 program committee for the American Society of Criminology's annual conference in Philadelphia.

Joshua D. Freilich is Associate Professor in the Criminal Justice department at John Jay College of Criminal Justice and the Deputy Executive Officer of the Criminal Justice Ph.D. Program at the Graduate Center/John Jay College, CUNY. He is a lead investigator for the National Consortium for the Study of Terrorism and Responses to Terrorism (START), a Center of Excellence of the U.S. Department of Homeland Security (DHS). Josh was co-chair of the 2009 program committee for the American Society of Criminology's annual conference in Philadelphia.

Todd R. Clear is Distinguished Professor, John Jay College of Criminal Justice, City University of New York. He has authored 11 books and over 100 articles and book chapters. His most recent book, *Imprisoning Communities: How Mass Incarceration Makes Disadvantaged Neighborhoods Worse*, was published by Oxford University Press in 2007. Todd Clear was President of the American Society of Criminology in 2008-2009.

CONTRIBUTORS

Geoffrey P. Alpert is a Professor of Criminology and Criminal Justice at the University of South Carolina.

James Austin is the President of the JFA Institute, a position he has held since 2003.

David Bayley is Distinguished Professor in the School of Criminal Justice, State University of New York at Albany.

Joanne Belknap is a Professor of Sociology at the University of Colorado, Boulder.

Thomas G. Blomberg is Dean and Sheldon L. Messinger Professor of Criminology at Florida State University's College of Criminology and Criminal Justice.

Alfred Blumstein is the J. Erik Jonsson University Professor of Urban Systems and Operations Research and former dean at the Heinz College of Carnegie Mellon University.

Anthony A. Braga is a Senior Research Associate and Lecturer in Public Policy at Harvard University's John F. Kennedy School of Government and a Senior Research Fellow at the Berkeley Center for Criminal Justice, University of California, Berkeley.

Sandra Bucerius is an Assistant Professor of Criminology at the Centre of Criminology, University of Toronto.

David Caspi is a full-time faculty member in the Department of Law and Police Science at John Jay College of Criminal Justice.

Scott Chenault is a doctoral student at the University of Nebraska Omaha.

Steven Chermak is a Professor in the School of Criminal Justice at Michigan State University.

Johnna Christian is an Assistant Professor in the School of Criminal Justice at Rutgers University.

Valerie A. Clark is a doctoral candidate in Crime, Law, and Justice at the Pennsylvania State University.

Obie Clayton is a Professor of sociology at Morehouse College and Director of the College's Sponsored Research program and Executive Director of the Morehouse Research Institute.

Roger Clegg is President and General Counsel of the Center for Equal Opportunity.

Philip J. Cook is ITT/Sanford Professor of Public Policy, and Professor of Economics and Sociology, at Duke University.

Gary Cordner is a Professor in the Department of Criminal Justice at Kutztown University of Pennsylvania.

Martha Crenshaw is a Senior Fellow in the Center for International Security and Cooperation and the Freeman Spogli Institute, and Professor of Political Science by courtesy, at Stanford University.

Kelly Damphousse serves as Associate Dean in the College of Arts and Sciences and Presidential Professor of Sociology at the University of Oklahoma.

Meredith Dank is a Research Associate at the Urban Institute in Washington, D.C.

Scott H. Decker is Professor and Director in the School of Criminology and Criminal Justice at Arizona State University.

Nora V. Demleitner is Dean and Professor of law at Hofstra University School of Law.

Laura Dugan is an Associate Professor in the Department of Criminology and Criminal Justice at the University of Maryland.

Godfried Engbersen is Full Professor in Sociology at the Erasmus University in Rotterdam.

Patricia Erickson has been a Senior Scientist with the Centre for Addiction and Mental Health, and before that the Addiction Research Foundation, for over 30 years.

Barry C. Feld is Centennial Professor of Law at the University of Minnesota Law School.

Thomas E. Feucht is Executive Senior Science Advisor at the National Institute of Justice, U.S. Department of Justice.

Eric Garland is a Doctoral Candidate at the University of North Carolina - Chapel Hill School of Social Work.

James C. Hendrickson is a doctoral student at the Department of Criminology at the University of Maryland at College Park.

Elaine Hyshka recently completed a Certificate in Addiction Studies and a Master of Arts in Sociology at the University of Toronto.

Michelle Inderbitzin is an Associate Professor of Sociology at Oregon State University.

Christopher A. Innes is Chief of Research and Evaluation at the National Institute of Corrections.

Leslie W. Kennedy is a University Professor at Rutgers University and Director of the Rutgers Center on Public Security.

Mark A.R. Kleiman is Professor of Public Policy at UCLA and the editor of the *Journal of Drug Policy Analysis*.

Gary LaFree is director of the National Consortium for the Study of Terrorism and Responses to Terrorism (START) and Professor of Criminology at the University of Maryland.

Arjen Leerkes is Assistant Professor in Sociology at the Erasmus University in Rotterdam and researcher at the Scientific and Documentation Centre of the Dutch Ministry of Justice.

Richard Legault is a Post-Doctoral Research Fellow and Co-Director of the Terrorism and Preparedness Data Resource Center.

Alan Lizotte is Interim Dean and Professor in the School of Criminal Justice, The University at Albany and Executive Director of the Hindelang Criminal Justice Research Center.

Cynthia Lum is an Assistant Professor in the Administration of Justice Department at George Mason University.

Doris Layton MacKenzie is Professor of Criminology and Criminal Justice at the University of Maryland.

Edward R. Maguire is Associate Professor of Justice, Law, and Society in the School of Public Affairs at American University.

Ramiro Martinez, Jr. is an Associate Professor of Criminal Justice at Florida International University.

Shadd Maruna is Professor of Justice Studies and Human Development at the School of Law, Queen's University Belfast and Director of the Institute of Criminology and Criminal Justice.

Michael Massoglia is Assistant Professor of Sociology at Penn State University.

Stephen Mastrofski is University Professor in the Department of Administration of Justice and Director of the Center for Justice Leadership and Management at George Mason University.

Candace McCoy is a member of the faculty of the Graduate Center of the City University of New York and teaches in the doctoral program of the John Jay College of Criminal Justice.

Dario Melossi is Professor of Criminology at the School of Law of the University of Bologna.

Kiminori Nakamura is a doctoral student at the Heinz College, Carnegie Mellon University.

Brian Nussbaum currently works as an Intelligence Analyst; however, beginning in 2010 he will be an Assistant Professor of Criminal Justice at Bridgewater State College in Massachusetts.

William Oliver is an Associate Professor in the Department of Criminal Justice.

Hal Pepinsky retired from Indiana University January 1, 2009, after 39 years full-time of professing criminal justice at several state universities.

Carrie Pettus-Davis is currently a doctoral student at the School of Social Work, University of North Carolina at Chapel Hill.

Liz Ressler is a graduate student at New York University and a research assistant at the Prisoner Reentry Institute at John Jay College.

Richard Rosenfeld is Curators Professor of Criminology and Criminal Justice at the University of Missouri-St. Louis and President of the American Society of Criminology in 2009-2010.

R. Barry Ruback is Professor of Crime, Law, and Justice, and Sociology at the Pennsylvania State University.

Jason Schnittker is Associate Professor of Sociology at the University of Pennsylvania.

Tracy Siska is a Ph.D. student at the University of Illinois at Chicago in the Department of Criminology, Law, & Justice.

Ralph B. Taylor teaches and researches in the Department of Criminal Justice at Temple University.

Faye S. Taxman is a University Professor in the Administration of Justice Department, co-Director of the Network for Justice Health, and Director of the research program in Evidence-based Corrections and Treatment at George Mason University.

Karen Terry is a Professor in the Department of Criminal Justice at John Jay College of Criminal Justice.

Douglas Thomson is a Professor of criminal justice and sociology at Chicago State University.

Susan Turner is a Professor in the Department of Criminology, Law and Society at the University of California's Irvine campus.

Chris Uggen is Distinguished McKnight Professor and Chair of Sociology at the University of Minnesota.

Bert Useem is a Professor of sociology at Purdue University.

Bill Wakefield is a Professor in the School of Criminology and Criminal Justice at the University of Nebraska at Omaha.

Vincent J. Webb is Dean and Director of College of Criminal Justice and the George Beto Criminal Justice Center at Sam Houston State University.

Charles Wellford is a Professor in the Department of Criminology and Criminal Justice at the University of Maryland.

David Weisburd is Distinguished Professor of Administration of Justice and Director of the Center for Evidence Based Crime Policy at George Mason University and Walter E. Meyer Professor of Law and Criminal Justice and Director of the Institute of Criminology at the Hebrew University Faculty of Law.

Linda M. Williams is Professor of Criminal Justice and Criminology, at the University of Massachusetts Lowell.

Sue-Ming Yang is an Assistant Professor in the Department of Criminal Justice at Georgia State University.

Joseph Young received his Ph.D. from Florida State University in 2008.

Franklin E. Zimring is the William G. Simon Professor of Law and chair of the Criminal Justice Research Program at the University of California, Berkeley.

FOREWARD

TODD R. CLEAR

The book you now hold in your hands is at once a new idea and a well established one.

Consonant with the theme of the conference: *Criminology and Criminal Justice Policy*, this volume offers 23 essays on crime policy, written by some of the country's leading criminologists, accompanied by commentary by similarly well-known leaders in our field. The volume contains all of the policy papers presented in 2009 Annual Conference Thematic Panel series. Each paper proposes a policy strategy in crime and justice, providing the empirical justification for the policy.

The volume is new, in that this is the first time that the American Society of Criminology has ever published a proceedings of its annual meetings. We thank Cengage Pubishing Company for their willingness to produce this volume, and to make it available free-of-charge to every registered conferee. We also hope that the idea of a proceedings, made available at the outset of the meeting, proves a successful enough way to give life to the theme of the conference that future program committees will offer a similar version of this idea.

The volume is well-established in two ways. First, the format for these essays—short empirical arguments with responses—was honed by the then-new ASC journal, *Criminology & Public Policy*, and was a format used for one of the more popular issues in its first six volumes. We hope this book will prove similarly useful as a teaching and policy guide.

But second, and just as important, this volume is not new because it reflects a growing interest of academic criminology in the policy arena. Here, we provide a collection of scholarly arguments in favor of change in crime and justice; scholarship buttressed by evidence. The energetic interest in shaping crime and justice policy on the part of scholarly criminology is a wholesome development, not wholly new (as Charles Wellford's points out in his essay) but perhaps never before as important, given the several public statements of the Justice Department that seem to usher in a new era of "evidence-based crime policy." To the extent we find ourselves at the beginning of a new, empirically-based era in crime and justice policy, this volume shows that the field is up to the challenge.

Putting this volume together was a substantial effort on the part of the Program Chairs and the policy essay sub-area chairs. It also reflects a belief on the part of the publisher that policy is an important new frontier for criminology, and a volume such as this will be an important contribution to the debates ahead.

No doubt there will be controversy about some of these essays—policy work provokes strong opinion. But I hope there will be no disagreement that by moving the ASC and its academic tradition squarely into the policy arena, both the field of criminology and the real-world of crime and justice practice will benefit.

ADVANCING JUSTICE POLICY

NATASHA A. FROST
JOSHUA D. FREILICH

Late in 2007, when President-Elect Todd Clear approached us about potentially co-chairing the 2009 American Society of Criminology (ASC) conference in Philadelphia, we enthusiastically accepted. Although in hindsight, our enthusiasm was more than a bit naïve, we remain grateful for the opportunity and, despite all of the work, deeply value the experience. The conference, we are confident, will be memorable. This edited volume, which has been designed to allow for more seamless integration of policy discussions in the classroom setting, we hope will further efforts to overcome the traditional knowledge divide between practice and empirical knowledge related to criminal justice issues.

This volume has a history that we will briefly recount to develop a context for the book. Part of what drove our initial excitement around chairing the 2009 program was the ability to shape the program and make it our own. The 2007 Atlanta meetings had recently concluded and Todd and Natasha had just edited their final issue of Criminology & Public Policy (CPP) together (Volume 6, Issue 4). The November 2007 issue of CPP was exclusively devoted to an array of criminologists making concise policy arguments on the basis of accumulated evidence. The issue contained no original empirical research, but rather was filled with these targeted policy prescriptions written in language that non-specialists could readily understand. To accompany the release of the issue, a series of special Criminology & Public Policy sponsored sessions featuring authors of the policy essays was offered during the 2007 Atlanta meetings. The November 2007 issue and the accompanying CPP sessions were incredibly well-received. To this day, people suggest that the special November 2007 issue of CPP was perhaps the best we ever published and the sessions drew large crowds (quite a few conference attendees could be found at every single CPP session). So, when we took on the burden that would become the 2009 ASC program, we knew that we wanted to somehow replicate that 2007 success on a grander scale.

For the 2009 conference, we solicited the usual individual presentations, complete thematic panels, roundtable papers and sessions, and posters, but also put in a new type of submission – policy proposals. Those interested in presenting policy proposals needed to submit an abstract by the regular deadline and a full draft of the essay just two months later (and almost six months ahead of the actual conference). The program chairs, Todd Clear, and eight Policy Area Chairs[1] then vetted the proposals in a mini-peer-review process that was designed primarily to

1

ensure the submission met the criteria required of a policy proposal. The author needed to articulate and then defend a policy proposal relying on a body of empirical evidence. We were not looking for a theoretical or empirical paper with some policy recommendations in the final paragraphs, but rather for an essay that would put the policy recommendation front and center. The call for papers indicated that two discussants – selected by the committee – would respond to each of the policy proposals.

When we put out the call for papers, we had no idea what the response to the policy proposal sessions would look like. After all, the prospect of such a session might be intimidating – particularly for young scholars. We were determined though to be as inclusive as possible and therefore tried to not judge proposals on their merit per se (e.g. did we agree with the policy or not, etc.), but rather on the author's ability to make a policy argument supported by evidence. We were confident that the discussants would challenge the proposal's merits where necessary. We ultimately received over 35 initial abstract submissions, and 23 essays that met the criteria for inclusion in a policy session were submitted by the deadline.

The deadlines had to be strictly enforced because we had secured the agreement of Cengage/Wadsworth to publish these essays in the book that you are now holding. In a unique arrangement, Cengage agreed to publish this book in advance of the conference and make a complimentary copy available to every conference attendee.

As mentioned above, for the conference sessions, we were recruiting two discussants to debate and discuss the merits of the proposed policy. As we proceeded, we realized the book would be a more useful pedagogical tool if we included some of the responses here as well – laying the foundation for extended policy discussions. Policy respondents, who were also serving as discussants for the sessions had just two weeks to craft a response for inclusion in this collection. Of the 46 discussants who signed on for the sessions, an impressive 30 submitted a response essay under this aggressive timeline.

As a testament to the inclusive nature of the process, this book includes original contributions from distinguished professors, internationally renowned scholars, up-and-coming junior faculty, and even a few doctoral students. The respondents are among the most respected criminologists in their respective areas. The final collection includes a total of 53 essays - 23 lead policy proposals and 30 response essays.

The book is organized thematically and fittingly opens with a contribution from long-time Department of Justice employees Thomas Feucht (NIJ) and Chris Innes (NIC) who argue that. if we want to effectively advance policy and practice, we need to build genuine researcher-practitioner partnerships that more fully draw on the strengths of all contributing parties.[2] We open with this essay because it reminds us that we need to do more than simply improve the way in which we communicate research findings to policy-makers and practitioners.

To kick of the debates, Charles Wellford – a scholar well-known for his policy-relevant work and particularly his work with the National Academy of Sciences – argues that criminologists need to stop complaining about their lack of influence on policy and practice. The responses to this provocative essay come from the current Editor of CPP, Tom Blomberg and the incoming (2009-2010) President of the ASC, Rick Rosenfeld.

These opening contributions are followed by policy proposals that we have grouped into eight thematic policy areas. We open with the broadest of the areas: justice policy proposals (a policy area that was added late in the process to capture those proposals that did not fit neatly into one of the other seven areas). The proposals in the justice policy area range from extending the vote to non-incarcerated felons to eliminating disparities in economic sanctions. Here some of the nation's leading scholars engage issues of equity, fairness, forgiveness and redemption that are often at the heart of justice debates. The justice policy essays are followed by a pair of essays related to drug and alcohol policy – here both policies call for a relaxing of prohibitions related to alcohol (drinking age) and drugs (marijuana regulation).

Although the terrorism policy proposals are unique and varied, all conclude that harsh unilateral responses do not make for effective policy. LaFree et al. call for international cooperation and Legault and Hendrickson offer an assessment of competing policies for addressing terrorists' access to firearms. Both Chermak et al. and Dugan and Young endorse policies that reach out to involve extremists in the political system, so as to avoid backlash and other effects that contribute to political violence. Similarly, all three lead authors of the immigration policy essays endorse more inclusive (and less exclusionary) policies around immigration and migration. We were pleased that here a number of the contributors were international scholars.

There are two quite distinct policing policy essays. While Gary Cordner's proposal for a national policy university was quite well-received by two of the nation's leading policing scholars (Geoff Alpert and David Bayley), Mastrofski and colleagues' proposal for the widespread adoption of hot-spots policing was met with cautious optimism by Ed Maguire and quite strident opposition from Ralph Taylor. The same pattern emerged in the area of juvenile justice, where one policy proposal (to stop arresting and prosecuting sexually exploited teens) proved difficult to disagree with and the other (to ban juvenile transfer and adopt blended sentencing) raised some concerns for Barry Feld, one of the country's leading scholars of juvenile justice policy.

The book concludes with a series of proposals that touch on some of the most pressing issues in correctional policy. In a time when many have been arguing for a return to the rehabilitative orientation, in the first proposal Taxman and Ressler argue that simply reaffirming rehabilitation is not enough, and posit that public health needs to be at the heart of the correctional mission. With its emphasis on radicalization, the second correctional policy essay could have fit equally well in the terrorism section and indeed was initially submitted in the terrorism area. We put it with the correctional policy essays because it argues that prison is not the site for rampant radicalization that many have suggested it might be. In the third correctional policy essay, Doug Thomson takes on mass incarceration arguing that a re-orientation in sentencing, with an emphasis on community well-being, would go a long way to reducing our over-reliance on incarceration. James Austin offers a thoughtful response and identifies one of the fundamental impediments to substantial policy change around mass incarceration when he points out that "the same 'community' that makes the laws and funds the legislators and other public officials are from a very different 'community' from those who are arrested and sentenced by the courts on a daily basis. The upper class community believes that the current criminal justice system is functioning just fine and is cost-effective." In the final essay, of this section and of the book, William Oliver argues that, in the planning for ex-offender reintegration, a crucial component has been left out of the reentry discussion. He argues that more attention needs to be paid to family reunification generally and domestic violence issues specifically to help ensure that the transition home is a smooth one for both the offender and for his family.

Although this collection of policy proposals is certainly impressive in both its breadth and its depth, as we edited the complete volume, we were struck by the following observation: If they were to be categorized ideologically, the majority of the policy proposals (and most of the responses) could definitely be characterized as left of center. In some cases, the proposals or responses are quite radically left. Indeed, there were some policy proposals for which we struggled to find a respondent who would argue an opposing viewpoint. It is, for example, hard to find a criminologist still willing to argue that we need more incarceration. In other areas, the task of identifying oppositional voices was much less daunting. Obviously, each essay stands alone, and the empirical knowledge provides some – if not strong - support for each policy proposal.[3] Nonetheless, such a skew to one side of the ideological fence could reinforce the skepticism some conservative politicians have to academic proposals that they already tend to view with "ideological suspicion." Moreover, as recent elections have demonstrated, about half of the country identifies as conservative and the reality of public policy is that those elected to office are unlikely to endorse policies that are not palatable to their constituents. There are certainly strategies for overcoming the oft-made accusation of "liberal-bias" in academia and producing high-quality social science evidence is certainly one of them. Nonetheless, those who engage in policy work need to recognize that their policy prescriptions, which are often so well-received in academic circles, are likely to face much tougher audiences outside of those circles. While it is beyond the scope of this introduction to delve more deeply into this issue, we felt it an important point to mention and one that could be explored further elsewhere.

Although some of the proposed policies might be met with skepticism and others will surely spark quite animated debate, we feel privileged to be able to contribute to a more informed dialogue and we hope that this book becomes a valuable teaching tool for those looking to make criminal justice policy a more integral part of their criminology curriculum.

ENDNOTES

[1] The policy area chairs were: Alfred Blumstein (Penal Policy), Jack Greene (Policing Policy), Karen Heimer (Justice Policy), Mark A.R. Kleiman (Drug Policy), Gary LaFree (Terrorism Policy), Daniel Nagin (Crime Policy), Cathy Spatz–Widom (Domestic Violence Policy), and Michael Tonry (Immigration Policy). As program chairs, we sincerely thank all of the policy area chairs for their assistance in putting together this aspect of the 2009 program - we are confident it will be the highlight.

[2] It was the National Institute of Justice (NIJ), under the leadership of then director Jeremy Travis, that first conceived of a journal more explicitly devoted to criminal justice policy. In fact for its first three years in print, NIJ fully funded the publication and distribution of CPP.

[3] Clearly the strength of the empirical evidence in support of the proposal also varied across policy issues.

CREATING RESEARCH EVIDENCE: WORK TO ENHANCE THE CAPACITY OF JUSTICE AGENCIES FOR GENERATING EVIDENCE[i]

THOMAS E. FEUCHT
CHRISTOPHER A. INNES

More and more, like so many other sciences, including psychology, medicine, and a host of "precise" (i.e., natural) sciences, criminology seeks to build and sustain effective pathways that link research findings into the work of practitioners and the decisions of policy makers. Recent calls for "evidence-based practice" and policy in criminal justice are only the latest version of this (See for example Chemers & Reed, 2005; Daniels, 2004; Lipsey, 2005; and Mears, 2007). Often, this issue is framed merely as a problem of communication or the need for more effective transmission of research results from researchers to practitioners. In order for practice to change in response to evidence, according to this argument, research findings only have to be made available to practitioners to be incorporated into practice.

Effectively transmitting evidence to practitioners is challenging enough for most researchers, but focusing only on transmitting findings to practitioners prevents researchers from capitalizing on the full potential of practitioners and falls short of what researcher-practitioner partnerships can accomplish. The one-way "transmission of results" approach creates a reliance on the relatively narrow experiences and skill set of the researcher, underestimates researchers' own biases, and misses opportunities to conduct research in ways that are more fruitful and effective. The solution, we argue below, is not to turn researchers into practitioners or vice versa; it is to develop partnerships that honor and exploit the strengths of each of the partners.

As in other disciplines of an applied nature, criminologists are familiar with the notion of working in "partnership" with practitioners. Being partners suggests equal roles, but an over-emphasis on the research craft – the methods and tools of research – often creates a dysfunctional imbalance in these partnerships. An effective partnership, on the other hand, should cultivate in the practitioner partner a capacity and shared responsibility for the actual work of generating research knowledge while promoting in the researcher partner an appreciation of and respect for the practitioner's point of view.

A primary obstacle to more effective partnerships lies in the roles traditionally assigned, particularly the role of researcher. The classic role of the researcher emphasizes objectivity and a sort of intellectual disengagement from the object of the research; it incorporates notions of the researcher's unique capability for generating evidence. In this paper, we outline the potential contribution of the practitioner to the essential work of research, including their distinctive ways of accumulating and validating evidence. We also describe two sorts of research partnership activities that, in our experience, have shown great promise and would be fruitful for further exploration.

A recent paper coauthored by one of the authors (Innes & Everett, 2008) discussed the contrast between the different ways researchers and practitioners think and talk about experience. Drawing on the insight by John Dewey (1925) that in ordinary language the concept of "experience" has a dual meaning, the authors noted the distinction between experience of something, as when we observe the world around us and experience with something, which is participatory. When we have observational experiences, including when they are systematic as in scientific research, it produces evidence. When we have participatory experiences, we develop skills. The relative emphasis which researchers place on the first meaning of experience, as opposed to practitioners' greater faith in experience in the second sense, underlies much of the gap between the two communities. For example, when researchers talk about what works, they usually are talking about an expected sequence of events based on a causal explanation. When practitioners talk about what works, they are more often discussing how they can actually do something.

This distinction, in and of itself, would not necessarily cause much grief, were it not for the all-too-human habit of assuming that one's own particular way of knowing is somehow superior. Researchers tend to believe that knowledge developed through inferential reasoning from objective facts is simply better than knowledge gleaned in other ways. Practitioners' so-called "knowledge," in the view of some researchers, is merely anecdotal. In their interactions with practitioners, researchers seem to seldom realize that practitioners often think of researchers as introducing their own brand of bias. Many practitioners often view researcher evidence as a sort of second-hand knowledge and a poor substitute for "real knowledge" garnered through direct experience. Practitioners, on the other hand, place enormous trust in the insights they have gained through extensive hands-on experience by themselves and their colleagues. Although practitioners are usually too polite to say so when research contradicts their experience-based understanding of the way things really are, their first instinct is often to ask "what went wrong with the research?" Many a potential partnership has floundered at the point when a researcher in turn has dismissed such questions as evidence of the practitioner's limited – and likely biased – anecdotal way of knowing.

Aside from such obvious faux pas, the research community many times adds to the problem by continuing to cultivate a heroic self image. The social sciences in the United States arose alongside the Progressive movement, and still embedded in their core is a pervasive faith in the power of science to solve social problems. The cult of the expert and his or her central role in the information age rests on this fundamental Enlightenment ideal. This routinely is translated into the self-assigned role of the researcher as having a more objective, arms-length relationship to the subject of study, i.e. to practitioners and what they do. At its worst, this can shade into a belief that practitioners themselves are a potential contaminating influence on the researcher's own objectivity. As many applied researchers have learned, however, it is possible to work in close and productive partnerships with practitioners while still maintaining clear boundaries (Welsh & Zajac, 2004). Mutual respect and appreciation, not hubris on either side, is the essential basis for these partnerships.

Perhaps the most difficult circumstance in which to envision researchers and practitioners engaged in the shared partnership work of knowledge-building is in the special knowledge enterprise of program evaluation. In the world of determining "what works," vigorous advocates emphasize the role of the independent evaluator-researcher as the necessary means to ensure objectivity, validity, and faithful execution of rigorous (and often complex) evaluation methods. Indeed, efforts to persuade practitioners to incorporate into practice evidence from researchers of "what works" are often buttressed by claims of the strength of evidence that a detached "arms length" researcher lends to the findings. That is, practitioners should trust the findings of researchers precisely because they are not – and are not anything like – practitioners.

We, however, are persuaded by another perspective. In 2001, Fetterman described a 21st-century vision for evaluation. He describes the overarching, shared aim of client and evaluator: "to understand, improve, and create a better life" in whatever domain they work. Truth is sought without presuming that the evaluator somehow holds a unique claim to it. In Fetterman's 21st century, "Clients and 'evaluators' will work as partners with a shared vision of the task at hand," with the evaluator "more of a collaborator... than an external, distanced expert with no vested interest in the program's future" (Fetterman, 2001).

Fetterman's view of the researcher-evaluator will be immediately dismissed by some as hopelessly naïve and perhaps even ethically flawed. His hope of transforming evaluation into a collaborative effort involving evaluators and "clients" touches a nerve that reaches to the core of research. It is particularly sensitive in the context of research that aims to provide knowledge with practical and policy applications, including program evaluation. Claims about collaborative evaluation methods like participatory evaluation, with an emphasis on the production of shared knowledge leading to more extensive use of research by practitioners (see Jackson and Kassam (1998) for a rich discussion of this evaluation method), are met with dire warning about the loss of objectivity and compromised study validity as a result of role-blending between evaluator and stakeholder/partner. (See, for example, Scriven, 1997)

At least two other research communities not unrelated to criminal justice – psychology and medicine – have wrestled with binding together more closely the external evidence brought to practice through research and the practitioner's own way of knowing. A 2005 American Psychological

Association (APA) Task Force on Evidence-Based Practice developed a policy statement that was adopted by the APA Council of Representatives (APA Presidential Task Force on Evidence-Based Practice, 2006). In its policy recommendation, the Task Force established the definition of evidence-based practice as "the integration of the best available research with clinical expertise in the context of patient characteristics, culture, and preferences" (emphasis added). The blending of external evidence with "clinical expertise" as the base of evidence-based practice was presaged in a BMJ editorial several years earlier: "The practice of evidence-based medicine means integrating individual clinical expertise with the best available external clinical evidence from systematic research" (Sackett et al., 1996, emphasis added). This means, the editorial continues, that "evidence-based medicine is not 'cookbook' medicine." While external evidence is essential and individual patient care should be informed by it, it cannot replace individual clinical expertise.

The APA Task Force goes on to name a key ingredient for clinical expertise that is typically missing among criminal justice practitioners: psychologists, unlike most criminal justice practitioners, "are trained as scientists as well as practitioners," and this fosters "a clinical expertise that is informed by scientific expertise," allowing the practitioner to draw more effectively on external evidence but also "to frame and test hypotheses and interventions in practice as a 'local clinical scientist'" (p275-6).

We acknowledge that this does not (yet) accurately portray criminal justice practice. We see it, nonetheless, as the goal of joining research and practice – not as two professions marked primarily by their distinct skills and different knowledge paradigms, but as professions whose knowledge-building acumen and evidence-using habits are becoming increasingly merged and overlapping. We describe two activities below that have already made significant contributions to this merging.

THE TRANSFORMATION OF CRIMINAL JUSTICE KNOWLEDGE-BUILDING: TWO (OF MANY POTENTIAL) PATHWAYS

What are the pathways to a more effective collaboration between researchers and practitioners in building evidence through applied research? A concerted commitment to the goal of real partnerships, where each partner acknowledges and values the other's way of knowing, is sure to identify several promising strategies. Drawing on our experiences, we describe two strategies: one focused on cultivating clinical expertise among criminal justice practitioners, and one which involves practitioners more directly in the work of program evaluation. Imaginative researchers and practitioners, working together toward a shared skill set for building knowledge, will certainly find other equally promising avenues.

Cultivating clinical expertise among criminal justice practitioners: The National Institute of Corrections is a federal agency focused on the intersection of research and practice. Its tendency is toward an emphasis on the improvement of practice in corrections and the use of research evidence as an important resource toward that end. One mechanism through which NIC works is its sponsored "networks" of practitioners who share some key aspect of practice. NIC has sponsored networks for large and small jails, supports a State prison administrators association, and has created a number of networks in Community Corrections. These networks serve several goals, including serving as a conduit for information, much of it research based; soliciting feedback from the field; building a stronger infrastructure within particular sectors of corrections; and serving as a "sounding board" for the agency.

Two of its newer networks capitalize on the growing research capacity of practice agencies. One is the Institutional Corrections Research Network (ICRN) made up of researchers working within state-level correctional agencies. A similar effort, co-sponsored with NIJ, is the Community Corrections Research Network (CCRN) composed of researchers working in pretrial, probation and parole agencies. These in-house researchers often have a limited role of simply "running the numbers" on their organization, tracking populations and basic measures of performance, or other routine reporting functions. Only a few have the time and resources for more ambitious research projects. In part through NIC and NIJ's leadership, the agencies in the ICRN and CCRN are assuming greater responsibility for corrections research within their agencies and across the field of corrections. By combining these practitioner-researchers with more traditional types of researchers, the networks are building the infrastructure within the field that is as necessary prerequisite for the kinds of partnerships we are advocating

There is nothing complicated about these research network efforts; yet they are largely unduplicated in other fields of criminal justice practice. They embrace a few key principles. First, it is all about improving practice. Second, it provides practicing agencies with important information about the tools, strategies, and knowledge base of the research enterprise. Finally, it encourages a network of practitioners to take ownership of the goals and the means of empirical research. In this way, the networks are building the kind of clinical expertise that prepares the field of practice for the work of research.

Research partnerships by design: The demonstration field experiment: Consider the practical question of how best to solve a burglary. On average, what investigative and forensic strategies are most likely to identify and bring to conviction the burglar? Consider within this fairly broad research question a more specific hypothesis: Is the bother and cost of trying to collect DNA evidence from a burglary crime scene worth it compared to "business-as-usual" investigative and forensic strategies used for burglaries, in terms of higher rates of perpetrator identification and successful prosecution? The precise way in which we specify this hypothesis suggests the need for an experiment; this is in fact the way in which the question was answered by researchers and practitioners working collaboratively in five communities.

In June, 2008, the National Institute of Justice (NIJ) released the findings from its 5-site DNA field experiment on solving property crimes. The results of the experiment were very impressive. (Roman et al., 2008). Rarely does a single criminal justice intervention achieve two-fold (or better) rates of success as this experiment demonstrated: twice as many offenders were identified through DNA compared to fingerprints; and three times as many suspects were arrested in cases where DNA was used. But the process of researchers and practitioners working together to design and implement the field experiment is, in some ways, the more dramatic story.

A few key features of the demonstration field experiment define the heightened sense of partnership cultivated between researchers and practitioners. In its inception, the intervention – and the experiment to test it – was not conceived by either the researchers or the practitioners alone. Each made substantive contributions to how DNA would be collected at crime scenes, how randomization would be achieved, and how subsequent process, implementation, and analysis issues would be resolved (NIJ, 2008).[ii]

One other feature distinguishes this demonstration field experiment from more ordinary program evaluation: the implementation work to be performed by the practitioners (and evaluated by the researchers) is invented and contrived explicitly for the purpose of learning something, for testing a hypothesis. More ordinary program evaluation often takes as its starting point a pre-existing "program" in which practitioners are invested and to which the evaluator-researcher alone can bring the necessary skepticism.

Clearly, there are existing practices which will form the basis even for a new experimental intervention. (The five DNA demonstration sites, for instance, already had in place some established procedures for processing burglary crime scenes as well as some policies or practices for gathering and using DNA evidence.) And between the extremes of evaluation of an existing program and the invention of a new intervention for the explicit purpose of demonstration, there is a range of blending that can occur. The essence, however, is that researchers and practitioners begin the demonstration field experiment together as partners, with joint intellectual ownership of the process and the outcomes and a shared commitment to and responsibility for the knowledge enterprise. It is one promising variation on what Liberman has described as "evidence-generating policy," where policies or programs are implemented with the explicit goal of learning something (Liberman, 2009). This kind of program implementation undoubtedly would be a new undertaking for many practitioners; engaging with practitioners willing and able to do so is probably equally novel for researchers.

CONCLUSION

Our short essay has touched only briefly on an issue we believe is central to any effort to advance our science and promote the use of evidence to solve the real-world problems of crime and public safety. We are aware of work by others who are wrestling with these same issues and reaching recommendations not unlike our own (Shepherd, 2007; Weisburd & Neyroud, forthcoming). We know there are likely many other promising pathways to create effective, balanced partnerships between researcher and practitioner. (We follow with great interest, for example, the work in crime prevention that draws extensively on a model of action research, where the researcher's responsibility for generating and testing evidence is shared with practitioners or an even larger group of stakeholders. See Kennedy (2009) for an example of this type of knowledge-building collaboration.)

We know our notions about shared responsibility between researchers and practitioners for the work of generating evidence is at odds with more traditional approaches to the work of criminology and criminal justice research. We are convinced, however, that criminologists and criminal justice researchers must better equip themselves for a future that demands a more nimble way of thinking about and organizing evidence. An important first step for researchers would be to establish a more refined "taxonomy of evidence" – and to develop it in closer collaboration with practitioners and policy makers. This taxonomy should anticipate the work of a broader range of researcher-practitioners who possess the clinical expertise to bring to the evidence-generating enterprise a distinctive and legitimate way of knowing and of generating and testing evidence.

The work of research is rooted in the skill set, professional identity, and culture of the research profession. The spreading branches of research work, however, already reach well beyond the ranks of researchers, particularly where the goal is knowledge to inform practice and policy. Criminal justice practitioners are already preparing for a more earnest partnership with researchers in building the knowledge needed to create a criminal justice system that is just, effective and humane in its practices and promotes public safety and healthy communities in its outcomes. What researchers must do, we believe, is to share with practitioners the best part of their professional identity: their commitment to excellence in evidence, their zeal for precision, and their persistent skepticism of the taken-for-granted world. In our vision of the 21st century, researcher will be known not only for their unique skills, but by the way they have encouraged and aided others in becoming what Stricker (2006) refers to as "local clinical scientists." Working in partnership with practitioners, helping them to be more knowledgeable in the work of research, equally committed to the principles of scientific skepticism, and as respectful of the researchers' way of knowing as researchers are of theirs, would be criminology's best gift toward ensuring more effective criminal justice policies and practices in the 21st century.

REFERENCES

American Psychological Association Presidential Task Force on Evidence-Based Practice. (2006). Evidence-based practice in psychology. *American Psychologist, 61,* 271-285.

Chemers, B. & Reed, W. (2005). Increasing the evidence-based programs in criminal and juvenile justice: A report from the front lines. *European Journal on Criminal Policy and Research, 11,* 259-274.

Daniels, D.J. (2004). Remarks of the Honorable Deborah J. Daniels, Assistant Attorney General, Office of Justice Programs. Annual Conference on Criminal Justice Research and Evaluation, July 19, Washington, DC.

Dewey, J. (1925). *Experience and Nature.* Chicago: University of Chicago Press.

Fetterman, D.M. (2001). The transformation of evaluation into a collaboration: A vision of evaluation in the 21st century. *American Journal of Evaluation, 22,* 381-385.

Innes, C.A. & Everett, R.S. (2008). Factors and conditions influencing the use of research by the criminal justice system. *Western Criminology Review, 9,* 49-58.

Jackson, E.T. & Kassam, Y. (1998). *Knowledge Shared: Participatory Evaluation in Development Cooperation.* West Hartford, Ottawa: IDRC/Kumarian Press.

Kennedy, D. (2009). Drugs, race, and common ground: Reflections on the High Point Intervention. *NIJ Journal, 262,* 12-17.

Liberman, A. (2009). Advocating evidence-generating policies: A role for the ASC. *The Criminologist, 34,* 1-5.

Lipsey, M.W. (Ed.). (2005). *Improving Evaluation of Anticrime Programs.* Washington, DC: National Research Council.

Mears, D. (2007). Toward rational and evidence-based crime policy. *Journal of Criminal Justice, 35,* 667-682.

National Institute of Justice. (2008). *DNA and Property Crime.* Washington, D.C.: U.S. Department of Justice.

Roman, J.K., Reid, S., Reid, J., Chalfin, A., Adam, W. & Knight, C. (2008). *The DNA Field Experiment: Cost-effectiveness Analysis of the Use of DNA in the Investigation of High-volume Crimes.* Washington, D.C. Urban Institute.

Sackett, D.L., Rosenberg, W., Gray, J.M., Haynes, R.B. & Richardson, S. (1996). Evidence-based medicine: what it is and what it isn't. *BMJ, 312,* 71-72.

Scriven, M. (1997). Truth and objectivity in evaluation. In E. Chelimsky and W.R. Shadish (Eds.), *Evaluation for the 21st Century* (pp. 477-500). Thousand Oaks: Sage.

Shepherd, J. (2007). The production and management of evidence for public service reform. *Evidence and Policy, 3,* 231-251.

Stricker, G. (2006). The local clinical scientist, evidence-based practice, and personality assessment. *Journal of Personality Assessment, 86,* 4-9.

Welsh, W. & Zajac, G. (2004). Building an effective research partnership between a university and a state correctional agency: Assessment of drug treatment in Pennsylvania prisons. *Prison Journal, 84,* 143-170.

Weisburd, D. & Neyroud, P. (Forthcoming). *Police Science: Toward a New Paradigm.* Kennedy School of Government and the National Institute of Justice.

ENDNOTES

[i] Findings and conclusions reported here are those of the authors and do not necessarily reflect the official positions or policies of the U.S. Department of Justice.

[ii] It helps, we believe, to have a neutral third party to facilitate the researcher-practitioner partnership. In the case of the DNA demonstration field experiment, this role was provided by NIJ, the funding agent for the project.

CRIMINOLOGISTS SHOULD STOP WHINING ABOUT THEIR IMPACT ON POLICY AND PRACTICE

CHARLES F. WELLFORD

In recent years we have seen a variety of efforts by criminologists to increase the impact of criminology on public crime and justice policy and practice. This panel and others like it at this and previous meetings; special issues of *Criminology and Public Policy* and the creation of the journal itself; and the pronouncements and actions of ASC leaders to secure representation in Washington D.C. are examples of a growing call for more impact on policy and practice. A related set of issues is the call for more funding for crime and justice research and improvements in our research agencies – a set of issues I do not address in these remarks. Needless to say I support all of these efforts, especially those calling for more and better support for research. What I find troubling, and hence the intentionally provocative title of this paper, is the relatively uncritical way in which the call for more impact of criminology on public policy and practice is made. Usually before we suggest a solution we define and characterize the dimensions of the problem we are trying to solve. In these remarks I want to try to do that and then argue that there may be too much influence rather than too little. I do this with the hope that future discussions of the impact of criminological research will be grounded in the kind of empirical science we seek to apply to others. I also do this from the perspective of one who believes that criminology should have an impact on policy and practice. In fact, I hope to demonstrate that it is inevitable – encouraging us to move beyond the tired debate about science and values.[i]

THE ISSUE

To determine the relationship between criminological research and policy[ii] we need measures of the both concepts, a way to measure their relationship, and a testable theory of the relationship. None of these tasks are developed in the literature on this topic. Reviews that are discussed below often rely on ad hoc definitions or "obvious" measures of each concept and their relationship. Explanations of the relationship are at best also ad hoc. At the core of this issue are two proportions that need to be estimated: 1) the proportion of polices that are adopted with substantial input from criminological research; and, 2) the proportion of criminological research that impacts policy. Neither of these is easily estimated. At a minimum their calculation requires a count of adopted policies and a count of criminological research outputs. Number 1 above is the ratio of research to polices; number 2 above is the ration of policies to research. In part because we cannot count all polices the discussion tends to focus on recently adopted major policies (e.g., "mass" incarceration; hot spots policing; sentencing reforms). Similarly, the focus on the research side is relatively recent empirical research.

Those who contend that criminology has minimal impact assert that most policy is not research driven and that most research is ignored by policy makers; while those who argue that criminology has had substantial impact find most policies are research informed and that even weak research results have impacts – sometimes substantial impacts. Both sides seem to believe that policy should be informed by research and that most research should consider policy implications. This is one of the characteristics that sets criminology apart from most other social sciences. From the beginning our field has included improving criminal justice as a primary goal.   While other social sciences have been characterized as including "a growing withdrawal... behind curtains of theory and modeling" (Newsom, 1995/96), criminology has, as a discipline, sought from its beginning to influence crime and justice policy.

THE EVIDENCE

Policies influenced by research. Fortunately there have been others who have addressed the extent to which contemporary crime and justice policies are influenced by criminological research. This point seems so obvious to me that I will offer the assessments of others and trust the reader accepts their conclusions. In 1987, Joan Petersilia (one of those criminologists most concerned with this issue and most anxious to see a greater influence of criminology) sought to determine the influence of "criminal justice" research. In acknowledging how difficult it is to determine influence, she observes that the impact of social sciences can only be measured over a long period of time. When considering criminal justice policy and practice over two decades Petersilia concludes there is "convincing evidence that research has influenced both". Does this mean that research has determined policy and practice? Petersilia concludes that "the concepts and conclusions of some research studies have, in fact, been so thoroughly assimilated in policy and practice that some of the people interviewed in this study had forgotten where they had originated"(1987, p.vi).

Twenty years later this conclusion seems even more descriptive of the influence of the research done by some criminologists.   Consider the following from one of the leading theory textbooks in our field:

> *Today, both liberals and conservatives increasingly rely on criminological theory and research to support their recommendations about crime and policy... to some extent*

> *criminological theory and research are superseding political ideology*
> *as the source of crime policy... In the future, criminological theory*
> *and research, rather than political ideology, will be the major source*
> *of crime policy* (Bernard, Snipes & Gerould, 2010).

As criminological research achieves knowledge that meets the test of science it can be safely predicted that it will continue to, as have other sciences, influence areas of public life to which it is addressed.

The critic of this position may argue that research is just used to reinforce ideology and that research that conflicts with political ideology will be ignored. This may be true at the national level of debate about crime policies (and was truly generally during the early 2000's) but at the level where policies are developed and implemented (state and local) the overwhelming mantra is "What Works" -- and in crime and justice issues the answer must be research based.

But you say what about DARE? What about right to carry laws? Where is the influence of research? My response is: 1) remember that both of these were presented as research based and sold as such; 2) dueling studies do not do much to inform policy; in fact they give greater value to ideology; and 3) in highly politicized areas especially when research has not been accepted fully by the research community, it is very difficult for research to trump ideology (e.g., global warming and stem cell policies of the Bush administration).

So, criminologists do not claim that our work does not influence policy. Study when it does; why it does not; and what we can do to make sure research results are presented clearly, fairly and effectively to policymakers.

Research influences policy. A far more difficult task awaits those who want to determine the extent to which criminological research influences policy for here the essential issue is when something does not happen – research is produced that could or should influence policy but does not (or maybe more precisely does not in a accepted time frame). Addressing this issue requires reviewing and assessing all research, determining if it could influence policy, and if it did. This is made easier in publications like *Criminology and Public Policy (CPP)* where the research results and the policy implications are clearly summarized. However, beyond that outlet it is difficult to identify all criminological research and to determine if the research could have and did influence someone other than other researchers. While I cannot do this systematically, for illustrative purposes, lets consider the most recent issues (at the time I am writing this paper) of *CPP* (2009) and *Criminology* (2009).

The February issue of *CPP* contains papers of the "prison boom", the police use of force, and risk assessment for women. Any assessment of these topics would conclude that they concern issues of importance for policy makers and practitioners. The lead article by William Spelman seeks to explain the rise in imprisonment in the United States since 1977. After a careful analysis of this increase, Spelman offers the following policy implication:

> *The availability of publicly acceptable alternatives to incarceration may not be sufficient to reverse course. Federal funding of alternatives – but not prisons – would provide states with the financial incentive to reduce prison populations.*

I am sure many criminologists would agree with this policy. Unfortunately, in this instance there is nothing in the research reported by Spelman that directly supports this "policy implication." It may be logically connected to the research results but it is not research based. The paper helps us understand the increase in prison populations but it does nothing to provide an empirical basis for an alternative policy. Of course, as you might expect, the commentaries on the paper question whether we can learn anything from it about the sources of the prison increase. The reviewers ask: is the model complete; are the estimates stable; and, is the interpretation reasonable given the limitations faced by the researcher? Good research but not perfect; policy recommendations without research – what do we expect a policy maker to do? This work like much of criminological research identifies what is wrong with current policy but offers little empirical guidance on what alternative policy can be implemented.

The paper on police use of force is even more flawed and it offers a policy recommendation that lacks credible research support and does little to advance our understanding of what the Supreme Court meant when it found that judgments about use of force must be based on the "judgment from the perspective of a reasonable officer on the scene". The risk assessment paper demonstrates that the LSI-R works about as well for women as it does for men. The policy implication is to use this risk assessment instrument of female offenders. Good research; reasonable policy recommendation; probably not findings that will convince anyone of the value of criminological research but undoubtedly someone has already implemented the recommendation.

Shifting to the articles in *Criminology*, we find eight articles. Leaving aside the question of the rigor of each paper, not one of the papers suggests that the research supports any particular policy and none of them unambiguously lead to any particular recommendations for practitioners. These are research papers that contribute to the development of theory and to the better understanding of crime and justice issues but they do not yet lead one to specific policy recommendations. I do not think these papers should be faulted for not doing so. My point is that most criminological research, like most other social science research, is not developed enough to, by itself, convincingly suggest policy. Any policy impact of the research reported in this issue of our leading journal would be accidental, unintended, and most likely wrong[iii]. For this issue, and I suspect many others, the denominator in our "impact ratio" would be zero. It is difficult to argue that research has no impact if the authors of that research do not think it is ready for such use and/or if the policy implications suggested by the authors have little or no research basis.

A NEW POLICY FOR ASC

Rather than argue that no one uses our research and that therefore we need more funding and greater organizational independence for the national crime and justice research funding agency – I am sure others see the contradiction in these positions – I suggest our leadership adopt the following positions:

1. Identify and celebrate the contributions criminological research has and continues to make to crime and justice policy and practice. Hot spots policing, problem oriented policing, sentencing guidelines, correctional management and programming, parole release, crime prevention through environmental design, are just a few of the current policies and practices that have been largely determined by the research, theories, and methods of criminological research. Our basic measure of crime, the National Crime Victimization Survey, and our basic measure of law enforcement agencies, LEMAS, were created by and have been largely advanced by criminologists. The Blueprints effort and the Campbell Coalition have identified empirically sound programs for crime prevention and control. These examples and many more should be used to demonstrate our profound impact. Even, when the impacts are the result of research that is later called into question (e.g., right to carry laws, scared straight, and three strikes laws) we should acknowledge their impact and learn from these instances to avoid such premature or misguided uses of research to change policy in the future. Recently, while reading a history of the depression, I came across the name Raymond Moley who served in Franklin Roosevelt's "brain trust", may have created the phrase "new deal", certainly was a major contributor to those programs, and later wrote one of the most widely cited critiques of the Roosevelt administration. Moley is described as an "expert in criminal justice reform" but I doubt anyone in this room knows of his works on courts and prosecution and the fact that he helped create the most fundamental changes in government policy of this century and then developed a still quoted critique of many of those programs. A better understanding of our history will show how important reform on criminal justice has been to our field and how many "criminologists" have contributed to those reforms.

2. Do more to advance the study of criminology as a science. Rather than only focus on people (the series ASC sponsored on great criminologists) or organizations (the ASC webpage has a section on history but it is of ASC not criminology), we should encourage scholarship on the development of our field, the forces that influence it, and the ways it has impacted crime and justice. By recognizing this as an important area of scholarship, the ASC can move us beyond anecdotes (as in this paper) to the application of the tools we use to evaluate others to criminology.

3. Recognize that money follows influence. Federal science funding lags developments in fields of science. It is only when we become convinced that an area of science has value do we see increases in funding. As long as we argue that no one listens to us no one will understand just how much criminal justice practitioners do listen. Until practitioners become our advocates we will not have the political support needed to elevate crime and justice research at the federal level and increase levels of funding for this work. Our acceptance of our role in policy reform will help practitioners see the value of supporting our growth

CONCLUSION

The foundations of criminology (a term not used for over 100 years after the usual date used for the beginning of classical criminology) are in improving criminal justice policy. Beccaria sought to make justice more rational and to do so with "geometric precision" -- science would provide an alternative to ideology (i.e., religion) as the foundation for justice (1963, p.10). We know that this work not only profoundly influenced notions of justice throughout the Western world but it also influenced the leaders of the American and French revolutions. It is difficult to find a major criminologist since Beccaria who has not also influenced crime and justice policies in the United States. Yet as a field we have not documented and celebrated this fact and we have not sought to understand when and why criminology has these impacts. In fact some, in a misguided effort to make our field appear scientific, have argued against criminology acknowledging the impact of the field on policy.

Rather than complaining about no one using our research I have suggested that we celebrate its use. Rather than ignoring scholarship directed at our field we should encourage it and make it a central element in our meetings and journals. Rather than seeking additional research funding on the promise of contributions we should seek increased funding from a position of carefully documenting what the meager investments in our field have already realized. Rather than argue that research that is not perfect is of no value recognize that what our even limited research offers is more informative than ideology alone. In sum, let us accept the role science, including the science of crime and justice, has had since it emerged as a new way to understand the world – to alleviate the miseries of mankind (Bacon, 1620).

REFERENCES

Bacon, F. (1620). The Great Instauration. Available online: http://www.constitution.org/bacon/instauration

Beccaria, C. (1963). *Essays on Crime and Punishment.* Indianapolis, Indiana: Bobbs Merrill.

Bernard, T., Snipes, J. & Gerould, A. (2010). *Theoretical Criminology.* New York: Oxford University Press.

Newsom, D. (1995-96). Foreign policy and academia. *Foreign Policy, Winter,* 62-74.

Petersilia, J. (1987). *The Influence of Criminal Justice Research.* Santa Monica, CA: RAND Corporation.

Weber, M. (1946). Science as a vocation. In H. Geth and C. Mills (Trans.), *Essays from Max Weber.* New York: Oxford University Press.

ENDNOTES

[i] Of course science should be as "value free" as possible. However, especially, the social sciences cannot be divorced from value issues. This is especially true for criminology where, as Weber (1946) observed, much of what we do is to make those in power better understand the consequences of their actions.

[ii] From now on in this paper I refer to policy to cover both policies and practices, unless the distinction is necessary to elaborate on differences associated with each of these types of impact. Usually this is a distinction without a difference.

[iii] I am reminded of an instance when Doug Smith published a paper that showed the importance of intact families on delinquency. Members of the conservative, family movement latched on to it as demonstration that their policies on families were supported by this research. Doug had a good laugh at their uncritical and inappropriate use of his research.

ADVANCING CRIMINOLOGY IN POLICY AND PRACTICE[*]

THOMAS G. BLOMBERG

Charles Wellford's "provocatively" titled essay, "Criminologists Should Stop Whining about Their Impact on Policy and Practice," claims that criminologists have and are continuing to pursue an uncritical path in their call for more influence upon policy and practice. The essay acknowledges that, although it is difficult to establish precisely how often and in what ways criminology has actually influenced policy and practice, there might have been far too much criminological influence rather than too little given criminology's limited stage of scientific development. To support this argument, the essay provides a brief review of the 1987 report by Petersilia; the 2010 text by Bernard, Snipes, and Gerould; and the most recent issues of Criminology & Public Policy (Volume 8 Issue 1, 2009) and Criminology (Volume 47 Issue 1, 2009). It concludes that, although there have been instances of criminological research being assimilated into policy and practice, the more general problem is that criminological research has not been sufficiently established as a science to inform policy and practice responsibly. Consequently, criminological research has not been as influential as many would like. The essay recommends that instead of whining for more influence upon policy and practice, criminologists should (1) identify and celebrate past contributions of criminological research to crime and justice policy and practice, (2) do more to advance the study of criminology as a science, and (3) recognize that money will follow criminology as it becomes more scientifically advanced. In sum, accept the status quo of the criminological profession and be happy.

SOME RESPONSES

After reading the essay, I was left wondering about its exact purpose. To elaborate, I do not believe that criminologists who advocate for more criminological influence on policy and practice would seriously disagree about past instances in which criminological research informed policy and practice in some way, nor would they take exception to the fact that such contributions are difficult to accurately measure. Rather, I believe that a growing number of criminologists are no longer content to merely conduct and publish research; instead, many of us are critically exploring ways in which our profession and ourselves can play a more meaningful role in

[*] Thanks to Karen Mann and Shanna Van Slyke for their helpful comments and suggestions.

applying criminological research to policy and practice, where appropriate. In recent years, it has become evident that many criminologists and the American Society of Criminology (ASC) leadership believe that it is appropriate to consider various strategies aimed at increasing criminology's functions and influence in policy and practice. Thus—for many criminologists—it is not about whining but quite the opposite: It is about not being content to whine and instead being motivated to identify, assess, pursue, and evaluate new and refined strategies that are designed to responsibly increase criminology's policy and practice influence while the discipline simultaneously advances its scientific foundations.

It is widely acknowledged in the field of criminology that our science is continuously evolving.   However, policy and practice decisions are necessarily being made now and they will not wait until our discipline reaches some future ideal level of scientific development. The notion of waiting until we evolve into a more scientifically strong discipline before influencing policy and practice brings to mind examples of human diseases such as cancer and HIV/AIDs and evolving experimental drugs for these diseases. Today, while we know much about cancer and HIV/AIDs, we do not have a scientifically proven cure for these diseases. Yet we have a series of experimental drugs developed from our ever-increasing research on these diseases that have made positive and often-life-and-death differences for afflicted individuals. Would any of us seriously question or criticize the medical profession for actively applying and testing these experimental drugs in the effort to combat such deadly diseases? Moreover, should we not, as criminologists, follow a similar ethic in our efforts to reduce the pain and suffering of crime; namely, sharing exactly what we do and what we do not know in the ongoing effort to advance crime and justice policy and practice? It is not an all or nothing proposition but rather making policy and practice progress with what we know.

So, the question that arises is whether we, as members of a developing scientific profession, should be content to wait for our science to evolve more before exploring ways to apply our research and knowledge to policy and practice. As research criminologists, we know that our discipline's scientific advancement should and must be continuous thus bringing into question at what precise point criminology will be sufficiently advanced to influence policy and practice. Is it not prudent to critically assess and explore how best to move forward with still evolving and incomplete research knowledge?   Or, as Wellford recommends, should we devote scarce resources to the careful examination of us as a discipline and identify and publicize our past contributions to society? In much of the current critical discussion on advancing criminology's policy and practice influence, we have blamed the discipline itself—this is the whining Wellford discourages—rather than complaining about an ill-informed public, ideologically driven policymakers, or the more general politicized policymaking process itself. At the same time, national, state and local policymakers are pleading for the best information available to inform their pressing policy and practice issues and questions. Most of us are aware that we have not faired well in advancing our discipline's policy and practice role and so we are searching for better ways to do just this, particularly given these increasing requests by policymakers for research inputs into policy. In terms of relevant personal experiences at the local, state, and national levels, I have received numerous requests for various outcome estimates related to a series of pending crime and justice policy decisions. The question is should I wait until better research is available or provide the best information now for the pending policies decisions? I believe that the answer is clear: provide the best information that is now available thereby facilitating more informed policy decisions.

A PERSPECTIVE ON CRIMINOLOGY AND POLICY AND PRACTICE

What is occurring in criminology and sociology is an unprecedented recognition of the importance of confronting important policy and practice issues with more accessible empirical research. Although not all criminologists or sociologists agree that we should assume any policy or practice role whatsoever, there is a growing number of scholars who are no longer content to sit back and instead are now actively pursuing a more proactive policy and practice role (Clear and Frost, 2001; Burawoy, 2005). In sum, the traditional divide between research and policy and practice is being seriously questioned by many criminologists in the ultimate attempt to guide, temper, and understand what appears to be a potentially ominous future for crime and justice policy and practice. The question is not only, What works? but also, What kind of future do we seek and at what price?

Certainly, pursuing an increased policy and practice role creates tension for criminologists. For example, this pursuit requires criminologists to be accessible and to confront immediate issues reflected in today's headlines, journalists' questions, and urgent e-mail inquiries— while simultaneously being comprehensive, reflexive, and objective. Moreover, as many of us in the discipline know from personal experience, it is not easy to go in front of congressional bodies to deliver compelling research and policy arguments in the often-restricted time limit of 5 minutes. But we are learning in the process and, further, these lessons are being passed on to our students. Clearly, objectivity requires scholarly work to be nuanced, which often renders it impenetrable to larger public, legislative and policymaking bodies. Beyond immediacy and accessibility, moreover, are the issues of commitment and values. Committed scholarship involves a delicate balance: It is not so much a matter of identifying and advocating a particular policy or practice; rather, it consists of explaining what choices and likely consequences are involved in various policy and practice options. Mere advocacy or the "taking of sides" for some specific policy or practice should never trump careful and objective analysis. Surely our field's research is sufficiently developed in a number of areas (e.g., incarceration and reentry, educational achievement during incarceration and recidivism, drug treatment and aftercare, hot-spots policing) to enable a presentation of the likely consequences associated with the various policy and practice options being considered.

As evidenced by the theme of this year's ASC meeting—namely, "Criminology and Criminal Justice Policy"—the question of the appropriate policy and practice role for criminology is generating dialogue, reflection, and disciplinary change. Further, ASC's decision to publish the journal Criminology & Public Policy in 2001 demonstrated its desire to facilitate and responsibly promote the relationship between state-of-the-art research and timely criminal justice policy and practice questions. Far from lamenting criminology's ineffectiveness in the policy and practice arena, the ASC acted and the journal's wide audience reflects the field's interest in bridging the gap between research and reality.

Returning to Wellford's essay, his fundamental claim is that criminological research has not developed scientifically enough by itself to responsibly guide policy and practice. The immediate concern that arises from this claim is that the criminal justice policy and practice process will not wait until criminology evolves more scientifically. As we all know, in the absence of research input, the policy process will move forward with available information and political and ideological inputs. So, should criminologists sit back and wait? It is important to recognize that, neither our research nor the policy process itself is fully developed. It is important to recognize that not only is criminology's research still developing but also so is the policy process itself. Whether at the local, state, or national levels, policymaking is often hurried, rash, reactive, and shortsighted. For example, the Florida legislative session allows 60 days for debate, amendment, voting, and re-amendment of hundreds of legislation pieces— far too often with no consideration of research evidence. Would not the presentation of relevant research findings, with full disclosure of the methodological limitations, be preferable to hurried policy and practice decisions with no link to research?

CONCLUSION

Wellford's essay is reflective of the dialogue that continues over the appropriate policy and practice role for criminologists and other social scientists. Like Wellford, some criminologists and social scientists argue that we know far too little to make meaningful contributions to policy and practice. Others maintain that they are researchers without policy-related training to enable them to contribute effectively to crime and justice policy.

But a growing number of criminologists argue that criminology is an applied discipline and that working toward establishing a more meaningful research and policy and practice link is a necessary and integral part of their professional roles.

The sort of policy and practice role that will emerge for criminology from this discourse and related initiatives is unknown. Yet I suspect that, in the future, criminologists will increasingly be involved in efforts to link their research to applicable policy and practice. The process will be incremental and will necessarily involve overcoming various knowledge limitations and policy and practice process impediments. Further, the blurring of professional role boundaries and the confrontation between political ideology and available research evidence will not easily be accomplished. But the alternative is far worse—namely, crime and justice policy and practice largely determined by politics and ideology or mere convenience.

Let me conclude by agreeing with Wellford's claim that there have indeed been some bright spots when criminology has influenced policy and practice. However, while being cautiously optimistic, I remain concerned about the future. My concern is due to the lack of any institutionalized mechanism for linking criminological research and policy at any level. As Mears (2009) suggested, "One could expect bright spots, but the norm by far would be a huge disjuncture, one caused not by any one party but, again, by a lack of an institutional foundation for integrating research and policy." As a result of this disjuncture, some could suggest that we should simply relax and be optimistic; after all, the bar is so low that it would take very little to improve policy, even with modest steps toward institutionalizing a research–policy link. Fortunately, however, many of us are not satisfied with waiting for these modest steps, nor are we content to merely accept the status quo. A large and growing number of us are already and will continue to actively pursue and evaluate various strategies for linking our research to policy and practice. And shame on us if there is some professional disagreement during this process!

REFERENCES

Bernard, T., Snipes, J., and Gerould, A. (2010). *Theoretical Criminology.* New York: Oxford University Press.

Burawoy, M. (2005). 2004 ASA Presidential Address: For public sociology. *American Sociology Review, 70,* 4–28.

Clear, T.R. & Frost, N.A. (2001). Criminology and Public Policy: A New Journal of the American Society of Criminology. *Criminology & Public Policy, 1,* 1–3.

Criminology. 2009. Volume 47 Issue 1.

Criminology & Public Policy. 2009. Volume 8 Issue 1.

Mears, D.P. (2009). Personal correspondence.

Petersilia, J. (1987). *The Influence of Criminal Justice Research.* Santa Monica, CA: RAND.

RAISING THE LEVEL OF PUBLIC DEBATE: ANOTHER VIEW OF CRIMINOLOGY'S POLICY RELEVANCE

RICHARD ROSENFELD

Charles Wellford's provocative essay serves as an important reminder that criminology has both an empirical and normative connection to crime and justice policy. He and others have documented the factual connection and I endorse Professor Wellford's call for a more systematic appraisal of the size and scope of criminology's policy impact. I want to spend a few moments discussing the normative connection. What kind of impact *should* criminology have on criminal justice policy and practice? There are multiple answers to this question and each calls attention to a different aspect of the field's contribution to the alleviation of human misery (Bacon's challenge) and the public role of the criminologist.

Current discussions of criminology's policy relevance, including Professor Wellford's, focus primarily on a single dimension of impact: the role of research in demonstrating whether a given policy or practice achieves its intended outcome. Does DARE reduce student drug use? Does hot spots policing reduce crime? Does this or that corrections program reduce recidivism? We might call this the "what works" orientation to criminology's influence. It is a critically important contribution, but it does not exhaust the influence criminology does and should have on policy. To the degree we focus on what works in criminal justice policy and practice, we risk losing sight of a broader kind of impact that we should seek to strengthen: the role of criminology in, to use what now seems a quaint phrase, *raising the level of public debate*. Let's call this the "consciousness-raising" orientation to criminology's influence on policy (another old-fashioned expression). Not only is it a broader conception of criminology's relationship to public policy, I suggest that it largely subsumes the "what works" orientation. And for good reasons.

MAKING CONNECTIONS

What does it mean to raise public consciousness of crime and justice policy? First and foremost consciousness-raising involves uncovering and clarifying connections among events, processes, or actions that are conventionally viewed as separate and distinct. In the late 20th century feminist movement, consciousness-raising meant connecting the personal and political, that is, locating the origins of personal troubles in political oppression and seeking personal liberation in political action. My vision of consciousness-raising with respect to criminal justice policy is hardly as

31

momentous, but it does entail promoting public awareness of the impact of policy on the lives of individuals who may appear to be far removed from its effects. An obvious connection is the sheer cost of criminal justice policies. Soaring corrections budgets, for example, impose significant opportunity costs on other public outlays, including those for crime prevention programs of proven effectiveness. Hiring more police means cutting back on other city services, especially when municipal budgets are strapped by reduced revenues. Using the death penalty as punishment for crime greatly increases case-processing costs to meet Constitutional requirements for fairness and to minimize errors (Fagan et al. 2004).

But the collateral effects of criminal justice policies extend beyond public budgets. Denying felons the right to vote may influence election outcomes (Manza and Uggen 2006). The constant "churning" of young men from disadvantaged communities to prison and back may further destabilize and deplete social capital in the affected areas (Clear 2007). Long delays in the release of crime statistics impede criminal justice planning and response (Rosenfeld 2007). The point is that criminal justice policy has latent consequences for persons who are not themselves its immediate or direct targets. Clarifying these connections should be regarded as one of criminology's chief contributions to policy debate.

Not all of the putative collateral effects of criminal justice policy may hold up under close inspection and, of course, not all such consequences need be harmful or costly, especially when weighed against demonstrable benefits. And some connections between policy and personal safety, encouraged by policymakers, may be spurious. That may be true of sex offender registration and notifications laws (Bray and Sample 2006; Zimring 2004). These are matters for research of the kind Professor Wellford proposes. But I would caution against a narrow "what works" orientation to policy evaluation. We need to show not only whether a given policy or program achieves its intended objectives, but *why* it succeeds or fails. That requires digging beneath its surface to disclose the underlying principles at work that connect the given instance to the general class of relevant actions and processes. No evaluation should be considered complete until it produces or invokes an *idea*, what we like to call "theory," that situates the success or failure of the extant policy or program in the context of other initiatives based on the same operating principles. Otherwise, our evaluations will remain disjointed and ad hoc and will have little lasting influence, casualties of abstracted empiricism (Mills 1959).

THE ROLE OF IDEAS

A good example of evaluation research that does connect the results of discrete studies to general principles is Gottfredson's and colleagues' research on delinquency and the social organization of schools (Gottfredson, Wilson, and Najaka 2002; Payne, Gottfredson, and Gottfredson 2003). The animating idea in this research is that *communal school organization*, the combination of shared values and goals with active and collaborative leadership, reduces delinquency. As the researchers point out, this idea is closely related to the concept of *collective efficacy* in research on crime and neighborhood social organization (Payne, Gottfredson, and Gottfredson 2003: 751-2; Sampson, Raudenbush, and Earls 1997). The idea that collective efficacy reduces crime has outlived the particulars of the research that produced it and entered into broader public discourse (e.g., Butterfield, 1997; Press, 2007). Gottfredson's work on the schools also has been highlighted in policy and practitioner forums (Gottfredson, 2007; 2008).

When it comes to increasing public consciousness of criminal justice policy and its effects, what matters are organizing ideas, not disconnected research findings. Collective efficacy, broken windows, stigma, total institutions, tipping points, hot spots, mass incarceration, prisoner reentry, code of the street, white collar crime – such ideas shape public debate over the premises and consequences of crime and justice policy. I do not mean to denigrate the role of empirical research. Research disciplines ideas. The best research specifies an idea's scope of application and reveals its unanticipated consequences. On occasion research overthrows a prominent idea but only when it demonstrates that a competing idea makes better sense of existing research findings and offers novel directions for future inquiry (Kuhn, 1996). The influence of research on policy, then, is indirect; research devoid of ideas has no policy relevance.

If it is true that criminology affects public debate and policy through its ideas and only indirectly through research, we must ask whether our ideas are up to the task. What makes for a policy-relevant idea? According to Wellford, we should not expect our ideas to be taken seriously by policymakers when criminologists themselves cannot agree on them. "Dueling studies," he argues, "do not do much to inform policy." But neither do unified research findings guarantee policy impact. The bulk of criminological research, for example, indicates that the death penalty fails to deter homicide, but most states retain capital punishment. The broken windows thesis, on the other hand, invites lively debate among criminologists, yet it remains a popular idea in influential policing circles. And conflicting research results, at a minimum, convey important information to policymakers about the fragility or weakness of policy effects. That is the import of the National Academy of Science's review of research on whether permitting individuals to carry concealed firearms deters violent crime (Wellford, Pepper, and Petrie 2004). Scientific consensus is neither a necessary nor sufficient condition for policy impact.

META-THEORY AND PUBLIC COMMUNICATION

Nothing we can do as criminologists, of course, guarantees that our work will influence public policy. But we stand a better chance of affecting the terms of debate, I have argued, when our research results are distilled in cogent ideas that transcend distinct policy domains, reveal underlying connections among seemingly disparate results, and highlight the collateral consequences of crime and justice policy. By what means can we augment the policy relevance of our ideas? I suggest that we strengthen two aspects of our scientific and professional practice: theory explication and public communication.

The "what works" paradigm in criminology has been greatly enhanced in recent years by meta-analysis, the systematic evaluation of research methods and results (e.g., Lipsey 2009; Lipsey and Cullen 2007). We should encourage equivalent improvements in what might be termed *meta-theory*, the identification of assimilating ideas that make sense of research results within and across distinct substantive areas. I have proposed something along these lines for connecting the results of discrete program evaluations to aggregate crime rates (Rosenfeld 2006). Such work does not entail the invention of new theories or theory integration as currently practiced. Rather, it requires distilling pertinent concepts and propositions from existing theories to explain a more general class of phenomena. The resulting ideas – systematic in formulation, fundamental in purpose, global in scope – readies research results for public consumption.

Once prepared, ideas must be effectively communicated beyond the borders of the scientific community if they are to have any chance of informing policy debate. This was the rationale for the creation of the ASC's policy journal, *Criminology & Public Policy*. How effective it has been in influencing policy is an empirical question that should be addressed in the research agenda that Professor Wellford sets forth. But, even though the word "policy" is in the title and its articles contain policy summaries, *CPP* remains an "academic" journal.

We should consider creating broader and more accessible forums for communicating our work in plain language that focuses on ideas, not research results. *Contexts*, the American Sociological Association's opinion magazine, might be a model for such an effort, although its print readership does not extend much beyond the ASA membership.[i] Crime and punishment are staples of popular culture. In principle, a magazine devoted to the serious, non-technical exploration of our subject matter should have broad appeal. And it would only have to reach .1% of the audience for *Law and Order* or *CSI* to be viable. As ASC President, I will ask the publications committee to explore the possibilities and challenges of developing such a publication in criminology.

CONCLUSION

Enhancing criminology's policy relevance involves more than ensuring that policy is informed by research, no matter how scientifically sound. It also requires identifying and communicating the ideas that make sense of research results. If we want policymakers to pay more attention to our research, we must devote greater attention to the production and dissemination of our ideas. Some of our work has little or no policy relevance, as Professor Wellford points out, but most of it does, or could if we extracted from it the theoretical principles that explain why a given policy or program is effective, why others are not, and how to tell the difference between them so that past mistakes are not endlessly repeated. I have called this our consciousness-raising contribution to public policy but why not call it education? Most criminologists are required to teach, do research, and engage in service to make a living. That's a not a bad job description for the kind of policy relevance I have in mind.

REFERENCES

Bray, T.M. & Sample, L.L. (2006). Are sex offenders dangerous? *Criminology & Public Policy 3,* 59-82.

Butterfield, F. (1997). Study links violence rate to cohesion in community. *New York Times* (August 17), 27.

Clear, T.R. (2007). *Imprisoning Communities: How Mass Incarceration Makes Disadvantaged Neighborhoods Worse.* New York: Oxford University Press.

Fagan, J., Liebman, J.S., West, V., Gelman, A., Kiss, A. & Davies, G. (2004). *Getting to Death: Fairness and Efficiency in the Processing and Conclusion in Death Penalty Cases After Furman.* Report to the National Institute of Justice. Washington, DC: National Criminal Justice Reference Service.

Gottfredson, D.C. (2007). Improving school safety: Lessons from research. Presentation to the Task Force on School Safety, Annapolis, MD (May).

Gottfredson, D.C. (2008). Schools and delinquency. Invited address presented at the Protective School Revisited conference, University of Arizona (October).

Gottfredson, D.C., Wilson, D.B., & Najaka, S.S. (2002). The schools. In J.Q. Wilson & J. Petersilia (Eds.), *Crime: Public Policies for Crime Control. Second edition.* San Francisco: ICS Press.

Kuhn, T.S. (1996). *The Structure of Scientific Revolutions.* Third edition. Chicago: University of Chicago Press.

Manza, J. & Uggen C. (2006). *Locked Out: Felon Disenfranchisement and American Democracy.* New York: Oxford University Press.

Lipsey, M.W. (2009). The primary factors that characterize effective interventions with juvenile offenders: A meta-analytic overview. *Victims and Offenders, 4,* 124-47.

Lipsey, M.W. & Cullen, F.T. (2007). The effectiveness of correctional rehabilitation: A review of systematic reviews. *Annual Review of Law and Social Science, 3,* 297-320.

Payne, A.A., Gottfredson, D.C., & Gottfredson, G.D. (2003). schools as communities: the relationship among communal school organization, student bonding, and school disorder. *Criminology 41,* 749-778.

Press, E. (2007). Can Block Clubs Block Despair? *American Prospect* (May 16).

Rosenfeld, R. (2006). Connecting the dots: Crime rates and criminal justice evaluation research. *Journal of Experimental Criminology 2*, 309-319.

Rosenfeld, R. (2007). Transfer the Uniform Crime Reporting Program from the FBI to the Bureau of Justice Statistics. *Criminology and Public Policy, 6*, 825-834.

Sampson, R., Raudenbush, S.W., & Earls, F. (1997). Neighborhoods and violent crime: A multilevel study of collective efficacy. *Scienc, 277*, 918-924.

Wellford, C.F., Pepper, J.V., & Petrie, C.V. (2004). *Firearms and Violence: A Critical Review.* Washington, DC: National Academies Press.

Zimring, F.E. (2004). *An American Travesty: Legal Responses to Adolescent Sexual Offending.* Chicago: University of Chicago Press.

ENDNOTES

[i] *Context*'s on-line audience is substantially larger (Chris Uggen, personal communication, June 22, 2009.)

Processes of Redemption Should be Built into the Use of Criminal-History Records for Background Checking[i]

Alfred Blumstein
Kiminori Nakamura

Problem of Redemption

Many people have made mistakes in their youthful past, but have since turned themselves around and live a respectful life. We define redemption as the process of "going straight" and being released from bearing the mark of crime. Two important trends make the problem of redemption a growing public concern: 1) there has been an increasing demand for background checks for a wide variety of purposes, most importantly for employment assessment, and 2) a growing number of individual criminal records have accumulated and are becoming easily accessible electronically. With the rapid advancement in information technology, individuals with a criminal record are not only haunted by the question about their criminal background on job applications, but also faced with computerized criminal background checks upon which employers increasingly rely.[ii]

The concern is evidenced by the report from the Attorney General sent to Congress in June, 2006 on criminal history background checks (U.S. Department of Justice, 2006). In the report, there is a recommendation for time limits on the relevancy of criminal records, which reflects the fact that the potentially lasting effect of criminal records is a common concern among many governmental and legal entities that have a say in this issue. Such entities include the U.S. Equal Employment Opportunity Commission (EEOC), which is concerned about discrimination based on criminal records because those with criminal records are disproportionally racial/ethnic minorities.[iii] The American Bar Association (ABA) is also concerned about the negative lasting effect of criminal records in employment settings. Both organizations are taking an initiative to broaden the discussion about the problem of redemption and to address how to alleviate the negative consequences of criminal records, including a time limit on their relevancy.[iv]

Ubiquity of Background Checking and Criminal Records

Employers conduct background checks on job applicants for several different reasons. One may be to verify their moral character. Another reason, more directly related to the context of criminal-history background checks, may be the desire to assess their risk of committing crimes that could cause physical, financial, and reputational damage to the organization. With the recent advances in information technology and the Internet, individuals' criminal records have never been more easily accessible (Barada, 1998; Munro, 2002; SEARCH, 2005). A recent survey of firms from multiple cities in the U.S. reveals that about 50 percent check the criminal background of job applicants (Holzer, Raphael & Stoll, 2004). Another survey finds that 80 percent of the large employers in the U.S. now run criminal background checks on their prospective employees (Society for Human Resources Management, 2004).

Some employers conduct criminal background checks on job applicants voluntarily to identify those who may commit criminal acts in the workplace in order to minimize loss and legal liability of negligent hiring that could result from such acts (Bushway, 1998; Scott, 1987). For some job positions involving vulnerable populations, such as children and the elderly, laws require employers to conduct such background checks (Hahn, 1991). Also, occupational licensing laws could disqualify many individuals based on the requirement of "good moral character" (Harris & Keller, 2005; May, 1995).[v] Many employers show considerable reluctance to hire individuals with criminal records (Holzer, et al., 2004; Holzer, Raphael & Stoll, 2003; Pager, 2003; Schwartz & Skolnick, 1962);[vi] other research has shown the relationship between criminal records and poorer employment prospects (e.g., Bushway, 1998; Grogger, 1995).

The ubiquity of background checking is matched by the growing prevalence of criminal-history information. In 2007, the UCR reports that law enforcement agencies across the U.S. made over 14 million arrests. In 2006, over 81 million criminal-history records were in the state criminal-history repositories, 91 percent of which were automated (Bureau of Justice Statistics, 2008). Prior research suggests that the general public's chance of being arrested in their life time is rather high. Over forty years ago, it was estimated that fifty percent of the U.S. male population would be arrested for a non-traffic offense in their lifetime (Christensen, 1967). Among those who have an arrest record, some have an isolated record that was acquired years ago and have maintained a clean record since then, but the evidence of contact with the criminal justice system, even if it was in the distant past, could remain in the repositories forever.

RELEVANCE OF CRIMINAL HISTORY

One rationale behind the practice of checking the criminal background of job applicants is that the employers recognize the strong positive relationship between past and future criminal offending. The continuity in criminal behavior has been well established (Piquero, Farrington & Blumstein, 2003). While these studies lend support to employers who would avoid any potential employees with a criminal-history record, these employers would also be well advised by some interlinked lines of research in criminology, which present equally strong evidence of desistance from crime in a subpopulation of those with past offenses. Also, the age-crime curve demonstrates a steady decline in criminal activity after a peak in the late teens and young-adult period, and aging is one of the most powerful explanations of desistance (Farrington, 1986; Hirschi & Gottfredson, 1983; Sampson & Laub, 1993).

Most importantly, time clean since the last offense strongly affects the relationship between past and future offending behavior. Studies on recidivism consistently demonstrate that those who have offended in the past will have the highest probability of reoffending within several years, and the probability will decline steadily afterwards (e.g., Gottfredson, 1999; Hoffman & Stone-Meierhoefer, 1979; Maltz, 1984; Schmidt & Witte, 1988). Two BJS studies that tracked released U.S. prisoners show that of all those who were rearrested in the first 3 years, approximately two-thirds were arrested in the first year, indicating the declining recidivism rate over time (Beck & Shipley, 1997; Langan & Levin, 2002). Despite the abundance of evidence that recidivism occurs relatively quickly, little attention has been paid to the smaller population of ex-offenders who stay crime-free for an extended period of time.

ESTIMATION OF REDEMPTION TIMES

While past wrongdoings are a useful sign of future trouble, this information has decreasing value over time because the risk of recidivism decreases monotonically with time clean, and there can come a point where we can be confident that the risk of reoffending has subsided to the level of a reasonable comparison group. The problem here is that there has been very little empirical information that can help to establish that point. The absence of reliable empirical guidelines has left employers no choice but to set their own arbitrarily selected cut-off points based on some intuitive sense of how long is long enough, inevitably with a conservative bias.[vii] Given the importance of this issue, particularly for those individuals with other employment vulnerabilities, it becomes important to develop empirical estimates of a reasonable point of redemption.

Recent papers by Kurlychek and her colleagues have shed some light on the population characterized by long-time avoidance of crime (Kurlychek, Brame & Bushway, 2006; 2007). Examining the hazard, which is the probability of reoffending at a given time conditioned on having stayed clean until that time, they show that the risk of offending for those with criminal records converges toward the risk for those without a record as substantial time passes. They used the longitudinal data from the Second Philadelphia Birth Cohort Study (Tracy, Wolfgang & Riglio, 1990) and the 1942 Racine birth cohort study (Shannon, 1982). They estimated that after approximately 7 years of crime-free time, the reoffending risk of those with criminal records is similar to those without a criminal record (Kurlychek et al., 2006; 2007). While the advantage of such longitudinal cohort data is the opportunity to compare those with and those without criminal records, it is worth noting that there are limitations, such as relatively smaller geographical coverage and the limited follow-up.

In contrast to conventional recidivism studies, where most recidivism can be observed in the 3-5 year follow-up time, the estimation of redemption times requires a much longer interval, sufficient for the recidivism probability to become small enough. This requires reasonably large initial samples so that we can estimate the recidivism probability with sufficient precision after the large majority of any initial cohort has already recidivated. Furthermore, in order to aid in shaping policies on redemption in the face of widespread background checking, it is important to develop estimates of redemption times based on criminal-history records from official repositories. Blumstein and Nakamura (2009; hereafter BN-2009) estimated redemption times based on criminal-history records from the New York repository. The records contain over 88,000 individuals, who experienced their first arrest in 1980 in New York State. They allow 27 years of follow-up time. This provided a large enough population to disaggregate into a reasonable number of important variables reflecting crime type and age at first arrest, and still have an adequate number of individuals who have remained clean of crime 10 and 20 years later. In BN-2009, we estimated two time points when redemption is reached. One point, which we denote as T*, is where the recidivism risk, which is quantified as hazard function, declines and crosses the age-crime curve, the arrest level of the general population of the same age, and so can serve as a point of redemption. This can help an employer who has selected a job applicant for a position and wants to compare that individual's risk of arrest with someone of the same age from the general population. The cross-over occurs because the general population includes people who have no criminal records as well as people who have multiple arrests.

Another perspective considers employers who have multiple job applicants for a position, on all of whom a background check is run. Those with no prior record (whom we designate as the "never-arrested") are inherently less risky than those with a prior record, but that difference can diminish with the time the individual with a prior arrest stays clean. This provides another point of redemption: when the recidivism risk of an individual with a criminal record is "sufficiently close" to one without, and we designate that point as T**. T** should be larger than T* because the comparison group (the never-arrested) are less risky than the general population.

Our analysis of T* focused on three ages at first arrest: 16, 18 and 20, [viii] three types of first offenses: robbery, burglary, and aggravated assault. The analysis of T** uses two broader categories of crime types, violent and property.[ix] Table 1 provides the values of T* by age and crime type at first arrest. Younger offenders and those who have a criminal record of robbery tend to have larger values of T*, indicating that they need to stay clean longer.

Similarly for T**, younger and violent offenders need to say clean longer to be deemed comparable to those without a criminal record (9.4 years for age 18 violent, 6.9 years for 18 property, 3.8 years for age 20 property).[x]

Table 1. Values of T* by C_1 and A_1
(arrest probability at T* in brackets)

First Offense	Age at First Arrest		
	16	18	20
Robbery	8.5 (.103)	7.7 (.096)	4.4 (.086)
Burglary	4.9 (.105)	3.8 (.097)	3.2 (.086)
Aggravated Assault	4.9 (.105)	4.3 (.098)	3.3 (.086)

NEED OF FURTHER ROBUSTNESS TESTS

We believe that the accumulated findings about redemption times represent a significant step forward in an area where so little is known empirically about the redemption process. As usual, however, some important efforts remain. The estimates of redemption times in BN-2009 are based on individuals who stayed clean in New York, but they could have been arrested in another state. Based on some prior work and our own review of a small sample of New York arrestees, we anticipate a correction in the order of 10 percent.

There is a possibility that conditions in one state are distinctively different from other states or that offenders first arrested in a particular year (e.g., 1980) were different from those arrested in other years with different levels of crime (Blumstein & Wallman, 2006), so it is important that we generate robustness tests of the findings. That will include collecting data from multiple states to examine how patterns of redemption vary across the states. This will provide an opportunity to look across the states to see if their offending patterns or their arrest patterns differ. Examining multiple cohorts of arrestees will also allow us to generate information on time trends in arrest patterns and in recidivism patterns as well as information on any period effect.

POLICY IMPLEMENTATIONS

The problem of redemption is old and new. In the 1960s and the 1970s, law reformers advocated for a legal system that limits the various negative consequences of carrying a criminal record and helps facilitate the reintegration of ex-offenders into the society (Love, 2003). In 1956, the Attorney General of the United States called the National Conference on Parole, which was sponsored jointly by the United States Board of Parole and the National Council on Crime and Delinquency. The conference recommended the abolition of laws that restrict the rights of those with criminal records and the adoption of laws to expunge the record of conviction and disposition (Bell, 1957; Love, 2003). The National Council on Crime and Delinquency (NCCD) published a model statute that provides discretionary power to the judge of the sentencing court to annul convictions and in effect authorizes an individual with an annulled conviction to say "in testifying or in filling out applications of various kinds, that he had not been convicted" (NCCD, 1962). In the same year as the NCCD released the model act, the American Law Institute (ALI) proposed the Model Penal Code in which the sentencing court would be empowered to remove the disqualification disability as a result of the conviction after the sentence is complete, and "vacate" the judgment of conviction after an additional period of good behavior (5 years) (ALI, 1985). It is notable that the proposal does not justify the removal of the conviction record but in spirit acknowledges the rehabilitation process by considering the length of good behavior.[xi]

After the reform movements in the '60s through the '70s came the two decades of retribution-focused, "tough on crime" policies. Many barriers were enforced to prevent those with criminal records from pursuing employment opportunities, while limiting the means available for them to restore their rights and status. The computerized criminal background checks and the increasing concern of negligent hiring liability among employers brought about a situation where criminal records can be a lifetime handicap. The findings of redemption times will be of considerable value in enhancing redemption opportunities and consequent employment opportunities for individuals who made a mistake in the past but have since lived a lawful life.

Despite the good intention, past reforms that are designed to relieve the handicapping effect of criminal records suffer from a limitation of lack of empirical support. For example, to the best of our knowledge the ALI's 5-year period of good behavior to vacate a conviction is not based on reliable empirical evidence. The knowledge of T^* and T^{**} along with the consideration of various conditions put forth (age at first arrest, crime types, risk tolerance, etc) could provide the empirical evidence to formulate reasonable redemption policies.[xii] Discussed below are ways in which the information about redemption times could be used by various pertinent parties to facilitate the redemption process.

For Users of Criminal Records.

Employers who run background checks on job applicants should be given a brief document informing them of the diminished value of records older than T* or T** years for risk assessment purposes.[xiii] Since employers have a strong concern about liability suits, states should consider passing a statute that could protect employers from such due-diligence vulnerability in case they hire someone whose last arrest was longer ago than T* or T**.[xiv] This would be a relief for employers who are otherwise willing to hire individuals with criminal records, and would add to the existing incentives such as Work Opportunity Tax Credit (WOTC) and Federal Bonding Program (FBP). Such liability-protection statutes could also be applicable to employers that ask applicants about their criminal background, but would limit their inquiries to criminal involvements that occur within the last T* or T** years. This would be relevant to the concerns of the "ban the box" movement, but would stop short of prohibiting the "box".[xv]

The governor of each state is empowered to grant a pardon as an act of clemency and forgiveness. Most typically, a pardon board reviews relevant information about the individual seeking clemency and makes a recommendation to the governor. Although the length of the law-abiding period is considered one of the most important factors in pardon applications, pardon boards should use research on redemption times in establishing how long a law-abiding period is long enough for the individual to be deemed appropriate for pardon.[xvi]

For Distributors of Criminal Records

State record repositories could adopt a policy not to disseminate criminal record information older than T* or T** years. This could apply specifically to the states that make their criminal-history information publicly available on the Internet.[xvii] States are clearly moving in the direction of making individual criminal records more publicly accessible (Jacobs, 2006). However, given the lasting consequence of disseminated records on a large number of individuals, finding means to limit the dissemination would be a realistic approach to the problem.[xviii] States should consider a policy to seal repository records of events older than T* or T** years in response to a request from a non-criminal justice agency. Such sealed records could still be accessible for criminal justice purposes.

A more aggressive approach would be to expunge records older than T* or T** years. A record being expunged does not necessarily mean that the record is literally destroyed; rather, the expunged records "almost always remain available for use by law enforcement agencies and the courts, and in some states they may be accessible to other public agencies and even to private investigative services hired to perform criminal background checks for employers" (Love, 2003).

Despite these criticisms, concealment and denial of criminal records after some "rehabilitation period" are common in many countries. For instance, in the UK, according to the Rehabilitation of Offenders Act 1974, those who are convicted of certain crimes, after specified rehabilitation periods, are treated as though the crime never happened, and are not obligated to reveal the record when asked at employment settings.[xix] There are similar systems of sealing and expungement of criminal records in the European Union and countries such as Canada and Australia (Lam & Harcourt, 2003; Loucks, Lyner & Sullivan, 1998; Ruddell & Winfree, 2006).

Since many employers rely on background-check services provided by commercial vendors of criminal records, if states seal or expunge records older than T^* or T^{**} years, this should be accompanied by a process of requiring those old records also to be erased from commercial databases.[xx]

The main criticisms of sealing and expungement include the compromise of governmental transparency (Franklin & Johnsen, 1981; Kogon & Loughery, 1970) as well as the possible adverse effect on non-offenders due to statistical discrimination. Certificates of rehabilitation and other similar means can circumvent the problem. Certificates of rehabilitation are designed to remove certain collateral consequences for eligible ex-offenders and can potentially enhance their employment prospects.[xxi] The certificates reward good behavior of ex-offenders by explicitly acknowledging them as being rehabilitated rather than erasing the record of their contact with the criminal justice system. Thus, they are similar to pardons in spirit, but are relatively more accessible than pardons. Currently, only a handful of states issue such certificates (Love & Frazier, 2006; Samuels & Mukamal, 2004), but they could be used more widely by taking advantage of the empirical evidence of T^* and T^{**}.[xxii]

Next Steps

Undoubtedly, one of the main reasons that there has been very little progress on limiting the restrictions on the availability of criminal-history records has been the lack of empirical estimates of when such redemption properly occurs. As a result of our work, we have now identified redemption times based on the two criteria comparing a redemption candidate with the general population and the never arrested as a function of age and crime type at first arrest. This information provides both users like employers and distributors like repositories to make informed judgments about when redemption is appropriate based on their own local values and to make decisions about how redemption opportunities should be implemented. Legislatures could aid the process by protecting employers from "due-diligence" liability claims if they adhere to reasonably established redemption times. But it remains important that action be taken in this direction because of the large and growing number of people who are inappropriately being denied opportunities that should be available to them.

REFERENCES

American Law Institute. (1985). Model Penal Code: Official Draft and Explanatory Notes. Complete text of Model Penal Code as Adopted at the 1962 Annual Meeting of The American Law Institute at Washington, D.C., May 24, 1962. Philadelphia, PA: The American Law Institute.

Barada, P.W. (1998, November). Exploding the court check myth. *HR Magazine, 43,* 16-19.

Beck, A.J. & Shipley, B.E. (1997). *Recidivism of Prisoners Released in 1983. Washington,* DC: Bureau of Justice Statistics.

Bell, M. (1957). *Parole in Principle and Practice: A Manual and Report.* New York: National Probation and Parole Association.

Blumstein, A. & Nakamura, K. (2009). Redemption in the presence of widespread criminal background checks. *Criminology, 47,* 327-359.

Blumstein, A. & Wallman, J. (2006). The recent rise and fall of American violence. In A. Blumstein and J. Wallman (Eds.), *The Crime Drop in America* (pp.1-12). New York: Cambridge University Press.

Bureau of Justice Statistics. (2008). *Survey of State Criminal History Information Systems, 2006.* Washington, DC: Bureau of Justice Statistics.

Bushway, S.D. (1998). The impact of an arrest on the job stability of young white American men. *Journal of Research in Crime and Delinquency, 35,* 454-479.

Bushway, S.D. (2004). Labor market effects of permitting employer access to criminal history records. *Journal of Contemporary Criminal Justice, 20,* 276-291.

Bushway, S.D., Briggs, B., Taxman, F., Thanner, M. & Van Brakle, M. (2007). Private providers of criminal history records: Do you get what you pay for? In S. Bushway, M.A. Stoll, and D.F. Weiman (Eds.), *Barriers to Reentry? The Labor Market for Released Prisoners in Post-Industrial America,* (pp. 174-200). New York: Russell Sage Foundation.

Bushway, S.D. & Sweeten, G. (2007). Abolish lifetime bans for ex-felons. *Criminology & Public Policy, 6,* 697-706.

Carey, C. (2004). *No Second Chance: People With Criminal Records Denied Access to Public Housing.* New York: Human Rights Watch.

Christensen, R. (1967). Projected percentage of U.S. population with criminal arrest and conviction records. In *Task Force Report: Science and Technology* (pp. 216-228). Report to The President's Commission on Law Enforcement and Administration of Justice, prepared by the Institute for Defense Analysis. Washington, DC: U.S. Government Printing Office.

Fahey, J., Roberts, C. & Engel, L. (2006). *Employment of Ex-Offenders: Employer Perspectives.* Boston, MA: Crime and Justice Institute.

Farrington, D.P. (1986). Age and crime. In M. Tonry and N. Morris (Eds.), *Crime and Justice: An Annual Review of Research* (pp. 189-250). Chicago, IL: University of Chicago Press.

Finlay, K. Forthcoming. Effect of employer access to criminal history data on the labor market outcomes of ex-offenders and non-offenders. In D. Autor (Ed.). *Studies of Labor Market Intermediation.* Chicago, IL: University of Chicago Press.

Franklin, M.A. & Johnsen, D. (1981). Expunging criminal records: Concealment and dishonesty in an open society. *Hofstra Law Review, 9,* 733-774.

Freeman, R. (2008). Incarceration, criminal background checks, and employment in a low(er) crime society. *Criminology & Public Policy, 7,* 405-412.

Gardiner, Lord (Chairman). (1972). *Living It Down: The Problem of Old Convictions.* The Report of a Committee set up by JUSTICE, The Howard League for Penal Reform, and the National Association for the Care and Resettlement of Offenders. London, UK: Stevens.

Gottfredson, D.M. (1999). *Effects of Judges' Sentencing Decisions on Criminal Careers.* Washington, DC: U.S. Department of Justice.

Grogger, J. (1995). The effect of arrests on the employment and earnings of young men. *Quarterly Journal of Economics, 110,* 51-71.

Hahn, J.M. (1991). Pre-employment information services: Employers beware? *Employee Relations Law Journal, 17,* 45-69.

Harris, P.M. & Keller, K.S. (2005). Ex-offenders need not apply: The criminal background check in hiring decisions. *Journal of Contemporary Criminal Justice, 21,* 6-30.

Henry, J.S. & Jacobs, J.B. (2007). Ban the box to promote ex-offender employment. *Criminology & Public Policy, 6,* 755-762.

Hirschi, T. & Gottfredson, M. (1983). Age and the explanation of crime. *American Journal of Sociology, 89,* 552-584.

Hoffman, P.B. & Stone-Meierhoefer, B. (1979). Post release arrest experiences of federal prisoners: A six-year follow-up. *Journal of Criminal Justice, 7,* 193-216.

Holzer, H.J., Raphael, S. & Stoll, M.A. (2003, March). Employer Demand for Ex-offenders: Recent Evidence from Los Angeles. Paper presented at the Urban Institute Roundtable on Offender Re-Entry, New York.

Holzer, H.J., Raphael, S. & Stoll, M.A. (2004). Will employers hire former offenders?: Employer preferences, background checks, and their determinants. In M. Patillo, D.F. Weiman, & B. Western (Eds.), *Imprisoning America: The Social Effects of Mass Incarceration* (pp. 205-246). New York: Russell Sage Foundation.

Holzer, H.J., Raphael, S. & Stoll, M.A. (2006). Perceived criminality, criminal background checks, and the racial hiring practices of employers. *Journal of Law and Economics, 49,* 451-480.

Jacobs, J.B. (2006). Mass incarceration and the proliferation of criminal records. *University of St. Thomas Law Journal, 3,* 387-420.

Jacobs, J.B. & Crepet, T. (2008). The expanding scope, use, and availability of criminal records. *Journal of Legislation and Public Policy, 11,* 177-213.

Kethineni, S. & Falcone, D.N. (2007). Employment and ex-offenders in the United States: Effects of legal and extra legal factors. *Probation Journal, 54,* 36-51.

Kogon, B. & Loughery, D.L. Jr. (1970). Sealing and expungement of criminal records – The big lie. *The Journal of Criminal Law, Criminology and Police Science, 61,* 378-392.

Kurlychek M.C., Brame, R. & Bushway, S.D. (2006). Scarlet letters and recidivism: Does an old criminal record predict future offending? *Criminology & Public Policy, 5,* 483-504.

Kurlychek M.C., Brame, R. & Bushway, S.D. (2007). Enduring risk? Old criminal records and predictions of future criminal involvement. *Crime & Delinquency, 53,* 64-83.

Lam, H. & Harcourt, M. (2003). The use of criminal record in employment decisions: The rights of ex-offenders, employers and the public. *Journal of Business Ethics, 47,* 237-252.

Langan, P.A. & Levin, D.J. (2002). *Recidivism of Prisoners Released in 1994.* Washington, DC: Bureau of Justice Statistics.

Loucks, N., Lyner, O. & Sullivan, T. (1998). The employment of people with criminal records in the European Union. *European Journal of Criminal Policy and Research, 6,* 195-210.

Love, M.C. (2003). Starting over with a clean slate: In praise of a forgotten section of the model penal code. *Fordham Urban Law Journal, 30,* 1705-1741.

Love, M.C. & Frazier, A. (2006). Certificates of rehabilitation and other forms of relief from the collateral consequences of conviction: A survey of state laws. In American Bar Association Commission on Effective Criminal Sanctions (Ed.), *Second Chances in the Criminal Justice System: Alternatives to Incarceration and Reentry Strategies* (pp. 50-55). Washington DC: American Bar Association.

Maltz, M.D. (1976). Privacy, criminal records, and information systems. In S.H. Brounstein & M. Kamrass (Eds.), *Operations Research in Law Enforcement, Justice, and Societal Security.* Lexington, MA: D.C. Heath and Company.

Maltz, M.D. (1984). *Recidivism.* Orlando, FL: Academic Press.

May, B.E. (1995). The character component of occupational licensing laws: A continuing barrier to the ex-felon's employment opportunities. *North Dakota Law Review, 71,* 187-210.

Munro, N. (2002). The ever-expanding network of local and federal databases. *Communication of the ACM, 45,* 17-19.

Nagin, D.S. (1998). Criminal deterrence research at the outset of the twenty-first century. In M. Tonry (Ed.), *Crime and Justice: An Annual Review of Research, Vol. 23,* (pp. 1-42). Chicago, IL: University of Chicago Press.

National Council on Crime and Delinquency. (1962). Annulment of a conviction of crime: A model act. *Crime and Delinquency, 8,* 97-102

National Employment Law Project. (2008). Major U.S. Cities Adopt New Hiring Policies Removing Unfair Barriers to Employment of

People with Criminal Records. Available online: http://www.nelp.org/
nwp/second_chance_labor_project/citypolicies.cfm

Pager, D. (2003). The mark of a criminal record. *American Journal of Sociology, 108,* 937-975.

Pager, D. (2007). *Marked: Race, Crime, and Finding Work in an Era of Mass Incarceration.* Chicago, IL: University of Chicago Press.

Pennsylvania Board of Pardons. (2005). Factors Considered by the Board of Pardons in Evaluating Pardon /Commutation Requests. Pennsylvania Board of Pardons, Commonwealth of Pennsylvania.

Petersilia, J. (2003). *When Prisoners Come Home: Parole and Prisoner Reentry.* New York: Oxford University Press.

Piquero, A.R., Farrington, D.P. & Blumstein, A. (2003). The criminal career paradigm: Background and recent developments. In M. Tonry (Ed.), *Crime and Justice: A review of research, Vol. 30,* (pp. 359-506). Chicago, IL: University of Chicago Press.

Raphael, S. (2006). Should criminal history records be universally available? *Criminology & Public Policy, 5,* 515-522.

Ruddell, R. & Winfree, R. Jr. (2006). Setting aside criminal convictions in Canada: A successful approach to offender reintegration. *The Prison Journal, 86,* 452-469.

Sampson, R.J. & Laub, J.H. (1993). *Crime in the Making: Pathways and Turning Points Through Life.* Cambridge, MA: Harvard University Press.

Samuels, P. & Mukamal, D. (2004). *After Prison: Roadblocks to Reentry.* New York: Legal Action Center.

Schmidt, P. & Witte, A.D. (1988). *Predicting Recidivism Using Survival Models.* New York: Springer-Verlag.

Schwartz, R.D. & Skolnick, J.H. (1962). Two studies of legal stigma. *Social Problems, 10,* 133-142.

Scott, C.R. (1987, October). Negligent hiring: Guilty by association. *Personnel Administrator,* 32-34.

SEARCH Group, Incorporated. (2001, April). Survey of Which States Provide Public Access to Their Criminal History Records Through the Internet. Sacramento, CA: SEARCH Group, Inc.

SEARCH Group, Incorporated. (2005). Report of the National Task Force on the Commercial Sale of Criminal Justice Information. Sacramento, CA: SEARCH Group, Inc.

Shannon, L.W. (1982). *Assessing the Relationship of Adult Criminal Careers to Juvenile Careers.* Washington, DC: U.S. Department of Justice.

Society for Human Resources Management. (2004, January). SHRM finds employers are increasingly conducting background checks to ensure workplace safety – Press Release. Available online: http://www.shrm.org/press_published/CMS_007126.asp

Stoll, M.A. & Bushway, S.D. (2008). The effect of criminal background checks on hiring ex-offenders. *Criminology & Public Policy, 7,* 371–404.

Tracy, P.E., Wolfgang, M.E. & Figlio, R.M. (1990). *Delinquency Careers in Two Birth Cohorts.* New York: Plenum.

Transportation Security Administration. (n.d.) *Disqualifiers – HAZMAT Endorsement Threat Assessment Program.* U.S. Department of Homeland Security, Transportation Security Administration.

Travis, J. (2002). Invisible punishment: An instrument of social exclusion. In M. Mauer and M. Chesney-Lind (Eds.), *Invisible Punishment: The Collateral Consequences of Mass Imprisonment,* (pp. 1-36). New York: The New Press.

U.S. Department of Justice. (2006). *The Attorney General's Report on Criminal History Background Checks.* Washington, DC: U.S. Department of Justice.

Westin, A.F. & Baker, M.A. (1972). *DATABANKS in a Free Society: Computers, Record-Keeping and Privacy.* New York: Quadrangle Books.

Wheelock, D. (2005). Collateral consequences and racial inequality: Felon status restrictions as a system of disadvantage. Journal of Contemporary *Criminal Justice, 21,* 82-90.

ENDNOTES

[i] Much of the text here draws from Blumstein and Nakamura (2009), referred to henceforth as BN-2009.

[ii] The concern has been raised at least since the 1970s (Maltz, 1976; Westin and Baker, 1972).

[iii] For example, see here:
http://www.eeoc.gov/abouteeoc/meetings/11-20-08/index.html.

[iv] For example, see here:
http://www.abanet.org/abanet/media/release/news_release.cfm?releasei d=234

[v] Restrictions on rights and opportunities of individuals who have contact with the criminal justice system (i.e. arrests, convictions), that are not part of the sentence imposed, are broadly termed "collateral consequences" or "invisible punishment" (Travis, 2002). They include restrictions on professional and occupational licensing, which are possibly important means for ex-offenders to increase their employment opportunities. The occupations that are affected by the restrictions range from health care, nursing, and education, to plumbing and barbering. Collateral consequences could also include denial of governmental benefits, such as welfare and public housing, termination of parental rights, and revocation or suspension of driver's licenses (Kethineni & Falcone, 2007; May, 1995; Petersilia, 2003; Samuels & Mukamal, 2004; Wheelock, 2005).

[vi] Some evidence suggests that the negative effect of criminal background checks on the hiring of ex-offenders is strongest for employers who are legally required to conduct such background checks (Stoll & Bushway, 2008).

[vii] Although 7 years seems to be a common restorative period (e.g., Transportation Security Administration, n.d.), perhaps due to a view that 5

years is too short and 10 years is too long, there is some evidence that the cut-off points set by users of criminal records could be much larger or could be "indefinite" (Carey, 2004: 50).

viii In contrast to most other jurisdictions, New York considers 16-year-olds to be "adults".

ix Broader crime categories provide larger sample sizes that are needed to generate the desired precision in estimating hazard as the time clean becomes large.

x Our previous analysis estimated T* as a point of redemption by comparing people with a prior record who have stayed clean with members of the general population of the same age. In contrast to T*, which can be calculated as an intersection of two curves, comparison with the never-arrested inherently involves more complex choices. Since the risk of rearrest for a redemption candidate might be expected to approach, but not cross, the risk of arrest for the never-arrested, it becomes a matter of having to assess when the two curves are "close enough." That assessment is similar to that of T*, but requires an estimate of "risk tolerance" to establish when the hazard for those with a prior arrest is "close enough" to those without.

xi An order to vacate the judgment of conviction "does not preclude proof of the conviction as evidence of the commission of the crime" (ALI, 1985: 259).

xii The current political climate seems more supportive of such empirical evidence: for example President Obama's agenda includes "Reduce Crime Recidivism by Providing Ex-Offender Supports" (http://www.whitehouse.gov/agenda/urban_policy/).

xiii Users of background checks should base their decision not only on the information about criminal history but also on information about other important factors (such as employment history, marriage, and educational attainment).

xiv While such legal protections would most likely be welcomed by employers, their concern over possible damage to the organization's reputation would not be eliminated (Fahey, Roberts & Engel, 2006).

xv The "box" refers to a question on job applications that asks prospective employee whether they have ever been convicted of a crime. So far, the movements to "ban the box" have been largely limited to employment for city governments (Henry & Jacobs, 2007; National Employment Law Project, 2008).

xvi For example, in Pennsylvania, the Board of Pardons (2005: 1) publicly states that the length of time free of crime after the offense is one of the best indicators of rehabilitation that the applicant can demonstrate.

xvii In 2001, 13 states (out of the 38 that responded to the survey) provide public access to criminal history records through the Internet (SEARCH, 2001). Samuels and Mukamal (2004) report that 28 states allow Internet access to criminal records).

xviii Some employers might "statistically discriminate" based on correlating individual characteristics of a job applicant with generic covariates of criminal activity such as race and ethnicity. As a result, limiting employers' access to criminal records could possibly have an adverse consequence for those without criminal records (Bushway, 2004; Finlay, forthcoming; Freeman, 2008; Holzer, Raphael & Stoll, 2006; Pager, 2003; Raphael, 2006).

xix The Rehabilitation of Offenders Act of 1974 followed a report called *Living It Down: The Problem of Old Convictions*, a report of a committee chaired by Lord Gardiner (1972). The report shows that the longer a convicted person remains crime-free, the less likely that the person will commit another crime.

xx Given the discrepancy between the records from official sources (state repositories) and the records from commercial databases (Bushway et al., 2007), it is important that any update (i.e., sealing or expungement) that takes place on the official records is reflected on the records in the commercial sources. Jacobs and Crepet (2008) highlight the difficulty in forcing vendors to make such changes because their right to access the criminal records would be protected by the First Amendment of the Constitution.

xxi Criminal history records are regarded as "negative credentials" or a scarlet letter "A" (Kurlychek et al., 2006; Nagin, 1998) that signify "social stigma and generalized assumptions of untrustworthiness or undesirability" (Pager, 2007: 33; see also Jacobs, 2006 and Jacobs & Crepet, 2008), whereas certificates of rehabilitation attempt to emphasize the progress made by the ex-offender. Regarding more fair representation of riskiness by taking into account the positive factors, Bushway and colleagues (2007) mention that it is conceivable for the government to devise some score (like a credit score) that indicates the risk of offending, which can be affected by positive factors such as the length of crime-free time, completion of a drug treatment program, and vocational training, as well as negative factors such as committing a further crime (for a similar approach see Freeman, 2008).

xxii Bushway and Sweeten (2007) discuss policy implications regarding the diminished value of old criminal records in the context of collateral consequences.

"Virtue's Door Unsealed Is Never Sealed Again": Redeeming Redemption and the Seven-Year Itch

Shadd Maruna

Blumstein and Nakamura's policy essay "Processes of Redemption Should Be Built into the Use of Criminal-History Records for Background Checking" is ground-breaking in many ways. The innovative and rigorous data analysis makes a considerable contribution in addressing a crucial social issue. The policy options outlined – pardons, certificates of rehabilitation, The Rehabilitation of Offenders Act in the United Kingdom – are badly under-discussed in US criminology, and augment the wider literature around ex-prisoner reentry. The authors' primary contribution, however, may be their daring use of the hugely important concept of "redemption" in both their title and the body of this work.

Redemption is something of an elephant in criminology's living room. Outside of criminology, redemption is a ubiquitous concept (see McAdams, 2006). As a *New York Times* critic put it: "There is no public narrative more potent in America today -- or throughout history -- than the one about redemption" (Kakutani, 2001). As consumers of literature and popular fiction, Americans in particular almost insist upon a redemptive arc for our main characters (see Nellis, 2009)[i], and of course redemption features as a central (even *the* central) concept of almost all the major religious traditions.

The need for redemption in society is obvious: "There has to be a way to restore people to good standing so that they'll be motivated to return to cooperation with all of the other cooperators in the population" (McCullough, 2008, p. 109). Without the chance of redemption, "every failure results in guilt from which there is no exit." (Smith, 1971, p. 206). Hannah Arendt (1958, p. 213) talks about this as the "burden of irreversibility" in *The Human Condition*:

> Without being forgiven, released from the consequences of what we have done, our capacity to act would, as it were, be confined to one single deed from which we could never recover; we would remain the victim of its consequences forever, not unlike the sorcerer's apprentice who lacked the magic formula to break the spell.

With some notable examples (e.g., Bazemore, 1998; Braithwaite, 1989; Cullen, 2007; Travis, 2002), criminology has not addressed the question of how those who have been punished for wrongdoing can redeem themselves and reseal "virtue's door." When I have used the term redemption in the past (e.g., Maruna, 2001), I have been told (by both secularists and the

53

faithful) that I am incorrectly co-opting a religious term that has no relevance to a social scientific study of crime. One colleague told me to "Leave redemption to God." Another said that he stopped reading a draft I sent him when he got to the words "redemption" and "forgiveness" (which was particularly unfortunate because I used those words in the title of the paper). He said the paper sounded too "church-y" for his tastes. This is quite an irony. After all, could there be anything more "church-y" than sin, punishment, damnation, an "eye for an eye?" Historical work on the origins of the prison clearly demonstrates that religious thought and religious movements "were not simply contributing factors but provided one of the primary sources of motivation and direction for the creation of the new U.S. penal system in the late eighteenth century" (O'Connor, Duncan & Quillard, 2006). In other words, the "too church-y" ship has sailed long ago for the study of "corrections" whether we choose to admit it or not. So, if we are going to have secular damnation, surely we also need to have some form of secular redemption to restore such persons civil status. One of the remarkable contributions of this paper by Blumstein and Nakamura is not only to recognize this, but also to apply the same scientific rigor to the question of redemption that criminologists have long utilized in the study of penology.

At the same time, legitimate concerns could be raised about the way that redemption is defined by Blumstein and Nakamura and their application of criminological science to the issue. I am in the process of writing a book about redemption at the moment and have been staggered at the lack of clear definition for the term in both the theological and secular literatures. As such, Blumstein and Nakamura do the literature a service by providing a working definition for the concept in their paper. However, their definition – "the process of 'going straight' and being released from bearing the mark of crime" – suffers from its compound, two-part nature. Essentially, they argue that redemption involves two, related, but clearly separable processes. The first is what is commonly called "desistance" in the criminological literature – although this is a term that is not without its own definition difficulties (cf. Laub & Sampson, 2001; Maruna, LeBel & Immarigeon, 2004). The second might be thought of as official forgiveness, de-stigmatization or de-labeling by the state.

Pairing these two processes together into a single definition makes some sense and is consistent with popular usage of the word redemption in English. One says, "I have redeemed myself" or the White Sox "redeemed themselves this season after last year's terrible performance." In other words, we do typically think of redemption as involving an intentional change in behavior on the part of an actor or actors. Yet, Blumstein and Nakamura are right that redemption is more than *just* behavioral change (hence, more than "reform" or "rehabilitation"); it also "requires ratification by others" (Hieronymi, 2001, p. 550). That is, one says "I redeemed myself *in the eyes of* my family" or else the White Sox have "redeemed themselves *in the eyes of* their fans." It is the "eyes" that matter here with redemption. In a theological context, the eyes belong to one's god; in a secular context, presumably it is the eyes of the State that matter. Berkeley legal scholar Meir Dan-Cohen (2007, p. 117) refers to practices such as forgiveness and pardon as "revisionary practices" – all "perform the same function: the cessation of a range of appropriate negative responses triggered by a wrongful action." What does one have to do to earn the state's official forgiveness?

It is on this crucial issue that I worry about the assumptions underpinning Blumstein and Nakamura's definition and their empirical model. Desistance (the first part of their two-part definition) is explicitly passive, by definition. That is, the word refers to an absence of some behavior (in this case, crime). Typically, when one thinks about redeeming oneself, we think of doing something to "make amends," or "make good" on some debt. Imagine that you get drunk and publicly insult someone at a conference. You could redeem yourself by not insulting the person in the next seven or eight times you see them. Eventually, by behaving professionally over a long period of time, you can disabuse even those with very thin skin that you are a complete jerk. On the other hand, you could also expedite this whole process considerably by apologizing, making some gesture of reparation (offering to help edit a manuscript, buying them a drink). Both processes get to the same result (proving to others that you are not an irredeemable bully), but the passive strategy takes a good deal longer than the active strategy.

In both their definition of redemption and their empirical model, Blumstein and Nakamura opt for the slow strategy of redemption and seem to shut the door on expedited models, which I find puzzling. Blumstein and Nakamura's phrase "estimation of redemption times" sounds awkward precisely because redemption is not commonly understood as the passive passage of time. It usually involves doing something. An individual who has made a mistake does not usually redeem himself simply by not making another mistake for a period of time.

Likewise, according to Blumstein and Nakamura's model, "Redemption has been reached" when "the risk of reoffending has subsided to the level of a reasonable comparison group." Here the authors appear to change their definition of redemption to refer to some estimated change in a person's likelihood of re-offending. Risk and redemption are not concepts that are commonly associated with one another, but the idea appears to be that people should be officially forgiven when it is safe to do so from an empirical standpoint (when their pattern of behavior makes their risk level similar to the rest of us). Yet, risk is not an "internal" characteristic of persons. Although there is certainly a role for agency in the desistance process (see Laub & Sampson, 2003; LeBel, et al., 2008), structural and social forces also play a substantial role in desistance as well. As has long been recognized, reintegration is a "two-way street" involving not just changes and adjustments on the part of the person returning from prison, but also on the part of the community and society welcoming him or her.

As such, there is something of a "catch-22" involved in Blumstein and Nakamura's risk-based model of redemption. In order to be officially forgiven, in this model, an individual has to successfully desist from crime for a substantial period of time. Yet, it can be awfully difficult to successfully desist if a person cannot get a decent, straight job, qualify for loans or housing assistance, or even rent a room[ii] because of a criminal conviction (see e.g., Archer and Williams, 2006; Gerlach, 2006; Holzer, Raphael & Stoll, 2006; Lucken & Ponte, 2008; Thacher, 2008; Travis, 2002). Although former prisoners no longer face "civil death," it is difficult to avoid the conclusion that with the growing number of obstacles before them the "released offender confronts a situation at release that virtually ensures his failure" (McArthur, 1974, p. 1). Likewise, if someone *has* managed to desist from crime for a half-decade or more, they most likely have been reintegrated and are comfortably employed. In such cases, the opportunity to expunge one's criminal conviction may be symbolically meaningful, but have little impact on recidivism.[iii]

Desistance is both a cause and a consequence of reintegration. The two processes occur simultaneously and the one reinforces the other. Blumstein and Nakamura appear to recognize this problem in other parts of their paper. At one point, for instance, they argue that "The findings of redemption times will be of considerable value in enhancing redemption opportunities and consequent employment opportunities." Here, "redemption opportunities" presumably refer to the things typically thought of as comprising of reintegration (jobs, housing, social networks), but of course, all of these things would be enhanced by official forgiveness and the opportunity to move one from one's past mistakes.

There is, therefore, something problematic about using empirical data based on other ex-prisoners' past experiences of desistance as guides for the future treatment of ex-prisoners. One runs the clear risk of reifying existing experiences, as if there were something magical -- or rather "internal" or biological -- about these patterns of behavior. So, for example, if empirical research suggests that that it takes people born into Cohort X around 7 years before their risk levels are the same as individuals who do not have a record, then employers might (justifiably) interpret this by not hiring someone in Cohort Y who has only 3 or 5 years desistance since a conviction. Yet, this behavior on the part of employers, presumably, will then add to the difficulties such people face and could conceivably lead to a self-fulfilling prophesy.[iv] After all, we know from reliable empirical research that Cohort X faced considerable discrimination in attempting to reintegrate and desist from crime (many of which were caused by their criminal records). If Cohort Y were treated differently (i.e. had fewer obstacles in their path to reintegration), presumably their "time to redemption" (or dynamic risk score) would be different as well (Western, 2002).

Consider this. There is another use of the term "redemption" in common parlance that is neglected in Blumstein and Nakamura's paper: the idea of "redeeming lost souls." Typically, this means reaching out to others who have not changed their behavior, who have not desisted or made amends, but still sending the message that they have intrinsic value. The idea behind this sort of redemption, which Arendt refers to as "Christian charity," is that by extending such messages of hope to individuals, they will then change their behavior. This use of the term essentially reverses the chronology from Blumstein and Nakamura's model: providing unconditional forgiveness first, then expecting desistance to follow. It is doubtful that the state could ever act as a "redeemer" in this sense of the word (although it is not uncommon for former prisoners to credit prison or probation employees for taking it upon themselves to make such efforts to reach out to "lost" prisoners). Yet, at the same time, as Blumstein and Nakamura themselves suggest, gradual "redemption opportunities" could be made available to those in the early stages of desistance (even before the "seven year itch"). That is, if long periods of desistance from crime (and the low risk scores that accompany such patterns) is society's desired outcome, it may make sense to experiment with forgiveness even before T* or T** years.

In conclusion, Blumstein and Nakamura are absolutely right that criminological discussions of redemption "should be based on reliable empirical evidence." Yet, as an aspect of the justice process, redemption (like its sibling concept "punishment") requires a normative analysis as well. That is, a system of pardoning offences (like a sentencing framework) needs to be based not just on empirical grounds (of "what is"), but also on normative grounds of what ought to be (what is right, fair and just). In this regard, the expansive literature on restorative justice provides an ideal model. Future normative research might address questions about what is required for an individual to be forgiven of various crimes (Can individuals "speed up" the redemption process? Can they "earn" forgiveness through acts of reparation, restitution and community service? Or is discrimination on the basis of a criminal record ever even legitimate?), as well as empirical questions such as what impact these forms of forgiveness (pardons, rituals of reintegration, certificates of rehabilitation) have on patterns of desistance. To be sure, more research is needed on these issues and the field is therefore deeply in debt to Blumstein and Nakamura for this remarkable, pioneering analysis of a crucial topic. I hope it generates considerable debate.

REFERENCES

Archer, D. & Williams, K.S. (2006). Making America 'The Land of Second Chances': Restoring socioeconomic rights for ex-offenders. *New York University Review of Law and Social Change, 30,* 527-584.

Arendt, H. (1958). *The Human Condition.* Chicago: University of Chicago.

Bazemore, G.(1998). Restorative justice and earned redemption: Communities, victims, and offender reintegration. *American Behavioral Scientist, 41,* 768-813.

Braithwaite, J. (1989). *Crime, Shame and Reintegration.* Cambridge, UK: Cambridge University Press.

Cullen, F.T. (2007). Make rehabilitation corrections' guiding paradigm. *Criminology & Public Policy, 6(4),* 717-728.

Dan-Cohen, M. (2007). Revising the past: On the metaphysics of repentance, forgiveness, and pardon. In A. Sarat & N. Hussain (Eds). *Forgiveness, Clemency & Mercy,* (pp. 117-137). Stanford: Stanford University Press.

Gerlach, E. (2006). The background check balancing act: Protecting applicants with criminal convictions while encouraging criminal background checks in hiring. *University of Pennsylvania Journal of Labor & Employment Law, 8,* 981-1000.

Hieronymi, P. (2001). Articulating an uncompromising forgiveness. *Philosophy and Phenomenological Research, LXII,* 529-555.

Holzer, H.J., Raphael, S. & Stoll, M.A. (2006). Perceived criminality, criminal background checks, and the racial hiring practices of employers. *Journal of Law and Economics, 49,* 451-480.

Kakutani, M. (2001, Feb 4). Faith Base: As American As Second Acts and Apple Pie. *New York Times,* p. D1.

Kurlychek M.C., Brame, R., & Bushway, S.D. (2006). Scarlet letters and recidivism: Does an old criminal record predict future offending? *Criminology & Public Policy, 5,* 483-504.

Laub, J. & Sampson, R. (2001). Understanding desistance from crime. *Crime and Justice: A Review of Research, 28,* 1-70.

Laub, J. & Sampson, R. (2003). *Shared Beginnings, Divergent Lives: Delinquent Boys to Age 70.* Cambridge, Mass.: Harvard University Press.

LeBel, T.P., Burnett, R, Maruna, S., & Bushway, S. (2008). The chicken or the egg of subjective and social factors in desistance. *European Journal of Criminology, 5,* 131-159.

Lucken, Karol & Ponte, Lucille, M. (2008). A just measure of forgiveness: Reforming occupational licensing regulations for ex-offenders using BFOQ Analysis. *Law & Policy, 30,* 46-72.

Maruna, S., Immarigeon, R., & LeBel, T.P. (2004). Ex-Offender Reintegration: Theory and Practice. In S. Maruna and R. Immarigeon (Eds.) *After Crime and Punishment: Pathways to Ex-Offender Reintegration,* (pp. 1-25). Cullompton: Willan.

Maruna, S. (2001). *Making Good: How Ex-Convicts Reform and Rebuild Their Lives.* Washington, DC: American Psychological Association Books.

McAdams, D.P. (2006). *The Redemptive Self: Stories Americans Live By.* New York: Oxford.

McArthur, A.V. (1974). *Coming Out Cold: Community Reentry from a State Reformatory.* Lexington, MA: Lexington Books.

McCullough, M.E. (2008). *Beyond Revenge: The Evolution of the Forgiveness Instinct.* San Francisco: Jossey-Bass.

Nellis, M. (2009). The Aesthetics of Redemption: Released Prisoners in American Film and Literature. *Theoretical Criminology, 13,* 129-146.

O'Connor, T.P., Duncan, J. & Quillard, F. (2006). Criminology and religion: The shape of an authentic dialogue. *Criminology & Public Policy, 5,* 559-570, p. 561.

Petersilia, J. (2003). *When Prisoners Come Home: Parole and Prisoner Reentry.* New York: Oxford University Press.

Ruddell, R. & Winfree Jr., T. (2006). Setting aside criminal convictions in Canada: A successful approach to offender reintegration. *The Prison Journal, 86,* 452-469.

Smith, R.W. (1971). Redemption and politics. *Political Science Quarterly, 86,* 205-231.

Thacher, D.(2008). The rise of criminal background screening in rental housing. *Law & Social Inquiry, 33,* 5-30.

Travis, J. (2002). Invisible punishment: An instrument of social exclusion. In M. Mauer and M. Chesney-Lind (Eds.), *Invisible Punishment: The Collateral Consequences of Mass Imprisonment.* New York: The New Press.

Western, B. (2002). The impact of incarceration on wage mobility and inequality. *American Sociological Review, 67,* 526-546.

ENDNOTES

i As just one example: To the shock and dismay of some film critics, popular surveys routinely find that the decidedly average *The Shawshank Redemption* is currently America's "all-time favorite" film, see http://www.imdb.com/chart/top.

ii In a systematic study of ex-prisoners without housing, Bradley and colleagues (2001, p. 8) found that "discrimination due to a criminal record" was the most frequently cited reason for homelessness.

iii Some evidence for this argument might be found in the low take-up rate of application-based system of pardons in Canada. In Canada, former prisoners are eligible to apply for pardons after remaining crime-free over a specified waiting period, and almost all applicants are successful, yet only a tiny fraction actually apply. Ruddell and Winfree (2008) estimate the take-up at less than 5 percent of those convicted between 1996 and 2002.

iv Here it is notable that the authors point out that seven years seems to be a common restorative period for states and national associations at the moment due to the arbitrary view that "5 years is too short and 10 years is too long." It is somewhat ironic, then, that seven years also turned out to be the length of time identified by Kurlychek and colleagues (2006) in their research as the magic number for the leveling of aggregate risk scores. This could be coincidence or it could be the arbitrary rule of thumb of a society has itself become a sort of self-fulfilling prophesy.

THE PRICE AND THE PROMISE OF CITIZENSHIP: EXTENDING THE VOTE TO NON-INCARCERATED FELONS[*]

CHRISTOPHER UGGEN
MICHELLE INDERBITZIN

With numerous potential benefits and very low risk to the general public, we argue that every U.S. state should follow current international practices and extend voting rights to parolees and felony probationers. The clear majority of disenfranchised felons are currently living and working in communities beside us, yet they have no voice in the laws that govern themselves and their families. As the rate and number of disenfranchised citizens continues to rise, this is a critical moment to reevaluate and reverse such policies.

In this essay we discuss six reasons to extend the vote to non-incarcerated felons. Re-enfranchising parolees and probationers would: (1) extend democracy; (2) reduce racial disparities in access to the ballot box; (3) enhance public safety (as probationers and parolees who vote have significantly lower recidivism rates than those who do not); (4) be responsive to public sentiment; (5) accord with international standards and practices; and, (6) be consistent with the re-integrative goals of community corrections, offering felons a chance to participate as stakeholders in their communities.

1. Extending democracy

Felon disenfranchisement today bars more than 5 million U.S. citizens from the ballot box (Manza & Uggen, 2006). The practice is at the center of an ongoing battle between the ideals of democracy and the reality of unequal access to and ownership of the full rights of citizenship (Keyssar, 2000).

The United States has a long history of denying the vote to prisoners, as well as those on probation, parole, and even former felons no longer under supervision. U.S. felon disenfranchisement laws are state-based, and each of the 50 states maintains different laws concerning a felon or ex-felon's right to vote. Currently, 34 states deny felony parolees the right to vote and 30 states deny felony probationers the right to vote (Manza & Uggen, 2006; Sentencing Project, 2008). Although a general trend toward re-enfranchisement is evident in recent decades (Behrens, Uggen & Manza 2003), the power of inertia (Becker, 1995) retains a strong hold in many states.

---

[*] We thank the Sentencing Project and Paul Bellatty of the Oregon Department of Corrections for their generous support and assistance and Heather McLaughlin for helpful comments.

While many states have pared back their restrictions, three decades of correctional population growth has increased the total number disenfranchised -- from about 1.2 million in 1976 to 5.2 million in 2004 (Manza & Uggen, 2006). A full 74 percent of those disenfranchised are *non-incarcerated* probationers, persons on supervised release, and ex-felons no longer under supervision -- and a disproportionate number of them are racial minorities.

Figure 1. The number of disenfranchised felons in the U.S. has risen dramatically since the 1970s.

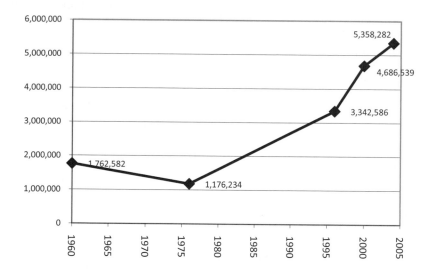

2. Reducing racial disparities in access to the ballot box

Passage of U.S. felon disenfranchisement provisions has been linked to the racial threat posed by newly-freed slaves (Behrens et al., 2003), while the contemporary period is marked by stark racial disparities in the impact of these laws. After weighing the evidence, Wacquant (2005) has gone so far as to characterize race or, more precisely, blackness, as "America's *primeval civic felony*" (p. 136). The movement to restore the voting rights of felons has thus emerged as a powerful civil rights issue.

Felon disenfranchisement policies disproportionately impact African Americans in the United States, with 1 in 12 ineligible to vote in 2004 due to felony convictions – a rate that is almost 5 times higher than non-black rates (King, 2006). Nationally, about 2.4 percent of the adult population is disenfranchised by virtue of a felony conviction, though this figure rises to over 8 percent for African Americans (Manza & Uggen, 2006).

Many states are today considering rescinding their disenfranchisement provisions for probationers and parolees, in part because these laws dilute the voting strength of communities of color. Even in a low-incarceration state like Minnesota, for example, about 10 percent of the otherwise eligible African American voting-age population (and almost 17 percent of otherwise eligible voting-age African American males) were disenfranchised in 2007. If a proposed bill to restore the vote to non-incarcerated felons succeeds in that state, these rates would drop by two-thirds.

Figure 2. Reenfranchising probationers and parolees would reduce racial disparities in Minnesota and elsewhere.

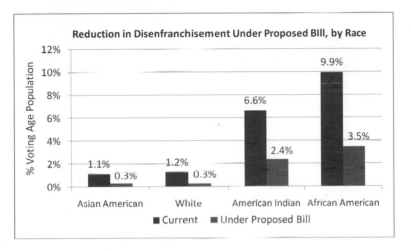

3. Enhancing public safety

While it is difficult to make strong causal claims on the basis of available data, it is clearly the case that voters are less likely than non-voters to commit new crimes. For example, a Minnesota study finds that voters in the 1996 elections were significantly less likely than non-voters to be rearrested from 1997 to 2000; about 16 percent of non-voters were rearrested, relative to only 5 percent of voters (Uggen & Manza, 2004).

As for those currently under supervision, Oregon is one state that permits probationers and parolees to vote. We matched Oregon voting and crime records and found that probationers and parolees did vote when given the chance; turnout rates were nontrivial and increased over time off supervision (Uggen, Inderbitzin & Vuolo 2007). Perhaps more importantly, we found that probationers and parolees who exercise their right to vote have significantly lower recidivism rates than those who do not. Oregon is an unusual case in that all voting is done by mail; as such, the effect of civic participation may be even stronger in states where voting is a more visible community event and neighbors come together at the polls on election day.

Figure 3. Probationers and parolees who vote in Oregon have significantly lower recidivism rates than those who do not vote.

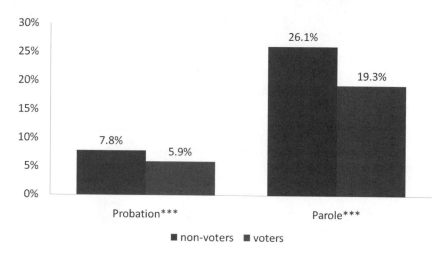

Probation***   Parole***

■ non-voters   ■ voters

4. Responding to public sentiment

Arguments that felon disenfranchisement policies reflect the will of the American public are simply not supported by public opinion data. Based on a national public opinion poll conducted by the Harris organization, Manza, Brooks, and Uggen (2004) found that 80 percent of Americans support re-enfranchising those who have completed their sentences, 68 percent support voting rights for probationers, and 60 percent support voting rights for parolees.

Figure 4. The general public supports voting rights for former felons, probationers, and parolees, but not prisoners.

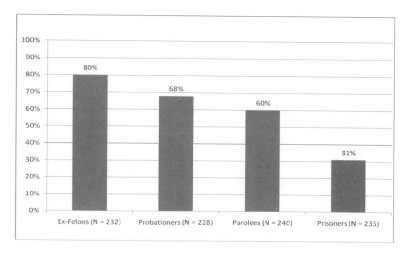

This suggests that the 34 states that disenfranchise parolees and the 30 states that deny probationers the right to vote are at odds with public opinion. Public support only drops below 50 percent at the prison gate, as only 31 percent of U.S. residents favor re-enfranchising current prison inmates.

5. Consistency with international practices

America is virtually alone in the world in extending disenfranchisement to those who are not currently incarcerated. Internationally, there is a move toward re-enfranchising current prison inmates (Ewald & Rottinghaus 2009; Ispahani 2006).

Figure 5. While non-incarcerated felons may vote in almost every nation but the United States, even current prisoners retain voting rights In at least 40 nations.

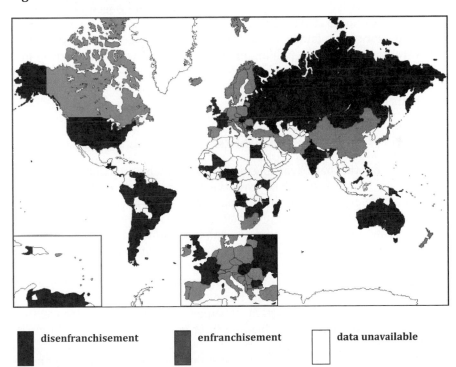

　　■ disenfranchisement　　　　■ enfranchisement　　　　□ data unavailable

A recent survey of 105 nations finds that 65 maintained a general disenfranchisement provision for currently incarcerated *prisoners*, while 40 generally permitted even prisoners to vote (Uggen, Van Brakle & McLaughlin 2009). The United States is clearly an outlier on the international scene, both for the broad scope of its disenfranchisement laws and for the large number of U.S. citizens affected by these provisions.

6. Helping to reintegrate felons

Debate around disenfranchisement often contrasts people categorized as felons with those we consider citizens, yet felons are *themselves* citizens, taking on roles as taxpayers, homeowners, volunteers, and voters (Uggen & Manza, 2005: 65). As they work to build and rebuild lives in the community and to "develop a coherent pro-social identity for themselves" (Maruna, 2001: 7), felony probationers and parolees face challenges in three important domains: work, family, and community. While socioeconomic and family reintegration are obviously pressing issues for felons under supervision (Laub & Sampson, 2003; Uggen, 2000), civic participation is another area where good intentions and fragile bonds can either be strengthened or can fall to pieces.

In our view, voting may facilitate reintegration for felons under supervision, serving as a "deviant decertification" process (Braithwaite & Mugford, 1994; Erikson, 1964; Maruna, 2001) in which they rejoin their community as citizens in good standing. As Manza and Uggen (2006) point out: "Though political participation likely plays a small role relative to pressing work and family needs, the right to vote remains the most powerful symbol of stake-holding in our democracy" (p.163). Offering this chance for probationers and parolees to take political action and to conceive of themselves as stakeholders in their communities comes with low costs and rich potential benefits.

POLICY RECOMMENDATION

Based on the best available empirical evidence, including our own research in Minnesota and Oregon, we believe states should act to re-enfranchise felony probationers and parolees. As we have shown, restoring the vote to those under community supervision would expand democracy, reduce racial disparities at the polls, enhance public safety, comport with national public sentiment and international standards, and foster the re-integrative mission of community corrections. The Oregon data show clearly that some probationers and parolees can and do exercise their right to vote. Perhaps more importantly, we found a positive correlation between voting and successful completion of supervision, with no evidence that extending the franchise to probationers or parolees poses any threat to public safety.

While we understand that politicians must both lead and be responsive to their constituents and that "revolutions may go backwards" (Inderbitzin, Fawcett, Uggen & Bates, 2007), we urge policy makers to follow President Obama's admonition to "choose our better history" (Obama, 2009) in this matter. Extending voting rights to non-incarcerated felons would not simply extend a privilege to a stigmatized group – it would also encourage former offenders to live up to their responsibilities as citizens.

Nationally, the trend over the past decade has been toward more inclusive legislation. Since 1997, 19 states have amended their felon disenfranchisement policies to expand voter eligibility. As a result of those reforms, more than 700,000 individuals have regained the right to vote (King, 2008). More specifically, in 2001 Connecticut restored voting rights to persons on felony probation and in 2006 Rhode Island restored voting rights to persons on felony probation and parole (King, 2008).

Re-enfranchising probationer and parolees appears to be a positive step for all involved. By extending the franchise to the approximately 1.8 million citizens denied the vote while on probation or parole (Manza & Uggen, 2004), it brings us closer to the ideal of a truly democratic society. Civic reintegration can become a reality in such an inclusive democracy, enhancing both public safety for the community and quality of life for the individuals and families involved. Extending voting rights encourages non-incarcerated felons to view themselves as real stakeholders in their communities, while realizing both the price and the promise of citizenship.

REFERENCES

Becker, H. (1995). The power of inertia. *Qualitative Sociology, 18,* 301-09.

Behrens, A., Uggen, C. & Manza, J. (2003). Ballot manipulation and the 'menace of negro domination': Racial threat and felon disenfranchisement in the United States, 1850-2002. *American Journal of Sociology, 109,* 559-605.

Braithwaite, J. & Mugford, S. (1994). Conditions of successful reintegration ceremonies: Dealing with juvenile offenders. *British Journal of Criminology, 34,* 139-71.

Erikson, K. (1964). Notes on the Sociology of Deviance. In H.S. Becker (Ed.), *The Other Side* (pp. 9-22). New York: The Free Press.

Ewald, A. & Rottinghaus, B. (2009). *Criminal Disenfranchisement in an International Perspective.* Cambridge: Cambridge University Press.

Inderbitzin, M., Fawcett, K., Uggen, C. & Bates, K.A. (2007). 'Revolutions may go backwards': The persistence of voter disenfranchisement in the United States. In K.A. Bates and R.S. Swan (Eds.), *Through the Eye of Katrina: Social Justice in the United States* (pp. 37-53). Durham: Carolina Academic Press.

Ispahani, L. (2006). *Out of Step with the World: An Analysis of Felony Disenfranchisement in the U.S. and Other Democracies.* New York: American Civil Liberties Union.

Keyssar, A. (2000). *The Right to Vote: The Contested History of Democracy in the United States.* New York: Basic Books.

King, R. (2006). *A Decade of Reform: Felony Disenfranchisement Policy in the United States.* Washington, DC: The Sentencing Project.

King, R. (2008). *Expanding the Vote: State Felony Disenfranchisement Reform, 1997-2008.* Washington, DC: The Sentencing Project.

Laub, J. & Sampson, R. (2003). *Shared Beginnings, Divergent Lives: Delinquent Boys to Age 70.* Cambridge, MA: Harvard University Press.

Manza, J., Brooks, C. & Uggen, C. (2004). Public attitudes toward felon disenfranchisement in the United States. *Public Opinion Quarterly, 68,* 276-87.

Manza, J. & Uggen, C. (2004). Punishment and democracy: The disenfranchisement of nonincarcerated felons in the United States. *Perspectives on Politics, 2,* 491-505.

Manza, J. & Uggen, C. (2006). *Locked Out: Felon Disenfranchisement and American Democracy.* New York: Oxford University Press.

Maruna, S. (2001). *Making Good: How Ex-Convicts Reform and Rebuild Their Lives.* Washington, DC: American Psychological Association.

Obama, B. (2009, January 20). Transcript: Barak Obama's inaugural address. *The New York Times.*

Sentencing Project. (2008). *Felony Disenfranchisement Laws in the United States.* Washington, D.C.: The Sentencing Project.

Uggen. C. (2000). Work as a turning point in the life course of criminals: A duration model of age, employment, and recidivism. *American Sociological Review, 677,* 529-46.

Uggen, C., Inderbitzin, M. & Vuolo, M. (2007). What Happens When Probationers and Parolees Vote? Community Supervision and Civic Reintegration. Paper presented at the annual American Society of Criminology meeting, Atlanta, Georgia.

Uggen, C. & Manza, J. (2004). Voting and subsequent crime and arrest: Evidence from a community sample. *Columbia Human Rights Law Review, 36,* 193-215.

Uggen, C. & Manza, J. (2005). Disenfranchisement and the civic reintegration of convicted felons. In C. Mele and T. Miller (Eds.), *Civil Penalties, Social Consequences* (pp. 67-84). New York: Routledge.

Uggen, C., Van Brakle, M. & McLaughlin, H. (2009). Punishment and social exclusion: National differences in prisoner disenfranchisement. In A. Ewald and B. Rottinghaus (Eds.), *Criminal Disenfranchisement in an International Perspective* (pp. 59-78). Cambridge: Cambridge University Press.

Wacquant, L. (2005). Race as civic felony. *International Social Science Journal, 57,* 127-142.

Felons Should Not Have An Automatic Right To Vote

Roger Clegg

In their policy essay, Professors Uggen and Inderbitzin "discuss six main rationales for extending the vote to non-incarcerated felons" (p. 2). My response will discuss why none of these rationales is persuasive on it own terms, but I want to begin briefly with a more fundamental criticism of the essay.

This more fundamental criticism is that the essay does not address the reason why felons, non-incarcerated and otherwise, are not allowed to vote in the first place. This is a rather damning omission.

Consider: One could, no doubt, adduce rationales similar to the essay's for extending the vote to the three other groups generally not allowed to vote in the United States. Allowing children to vote would, I suppose, "extend democracy," allowing noncitizens to vote would reduce national-origin "disparities in access to the ballot box" in many parts of the country, allowing the mentally impaired to vote may well help "to integrate" them into the larger society, and so forth. But such arguments would be unpersuasive unless the reasons we have for disenfranchising these groups of individuals were not also addressed.

And, indeed, there are good reasons for not allowing felons to vote. It makes sense to argue that you don't have a right to make the laws if you aren't willing to follow them yourself. When you vote, you are making the law—either directly, in the case of referenda and the like, or indirectly, through the selection of lawmakers. To participate in self-government, you must be willing to accept the rule of law. As noted above, we don't let everyone vote--not children, not noncitizens, not the mentally incompetent. There are certain minimum and objective standards of trustworthiness, loyalty, and responsibility, and those who have committed serious crimes against their fellow citizens don't meet those standards. As Uggen & Inderbitzin obliquely acknowledge, the practice of disenfranchising felons has been around for quite a while—thousands of years actually, as even opponents to the policy have noted.

In sum, a call to overturn this policy must make some effort to address the reasons for keeping it. The essay makes no attempt to do this.

I now turn to the arguments made by Uggen & Inderbitzin—but remember, even if you find my refutations less than completely persuasive, it is necessary to weigh the purported benefits of felon voting against the costs just discussed but not mentioned in the essay.

Uggen & Inderbitzin first argue that allowing non-incarcerated felons to vote will "extend democracy." Well, if we define "democracy" simply as "allowing people to vote," then it is certainly true—indeed, it is a tautology—that allowing more people to vote will "extend democracy." But, as noted above, that would mean that allowing four-year-olds to vote would extend democracy, too. If democracy means something more than that— something about the quality of a government and not just the number of people voting—it needs to be explained, and it needs to be explained how allowing these particular people to vote would improve the government's quality. In this section, Uggen & Inderbitzin refer to the "power of inertia," but of course conservatives do not assume that, when it comes to governance, inertia is necessarily a bad thing.

Uggen & Inderbitzin next argue that their proposal will "reduce racial disparities at the ballot box." This is necessarily true so long as some racial groups have a higher (or lower) percentage of convicted felons than their share of the general population, and one suspects this will always be the case to some degree. Uggen & Inderbitzin focus on African Americans here, and they are correct that this particular group is "overrepresented" among convicted felons, but of course there are other racial and ethnic minorities among whom this may not be true.

In all events, the fact that a disenfranchisement policy has a disparate impact on the basis of race does not mean that it is an unwise policy. As suggested earlier, allowing only citizens to vote has a disparate impact on Latinos today in many states. Nor does it make the policy racist: Men are "overrepresented" in prison compared to women, but it is not suggested that felon disenfranchisement laws are sexist. (Uggen & Inderbitzin state, "Passage of U.S. felon disenfranchisement provisions has been linked to the racial threat posed by newly-freed slaves" (p. 4), but those laws are no longer on the books, and would be unconstitutional if they were; rather, these laws have ancient roots, and were adopted in the United States almost always without an eye on race. See, in addition to what I've written on this subject—appended at the end of this response—John Dinan's "The Adoption of Criminal Disenfranchisement Provisions in the United States: Lessons from the State Constitutional Convention Debates," *Journal of Policy History*, vol. 19, No. 3, 2007, pp.282-312).

Uggen & Inderbitzin next argue that their proposal will "enhance public safety (as probationers and parolees who vote have significantly lower recidivism rates than those who do not)." They acknowledge, however, that "it is difficult to make strong causal claims on the basis of available data," and rightly so, since this assertion almost surely confuses cause and effect. That is, one suspects it is more accurate to say that felons who vote are those who have already turned over a new leaf, rather than that the act of voting somehow has helped them turn over that leaf.

Uggen & Inderbitzin then suggest that polling data suggest that most Americans agree with their proposal. I am sure that I could frame questions in this area that yield different results ("Do you think that a murderer should be able to vote the day he is released on parole?"). In all events, if the public is so supportive, then why is it "that the 35 states that disenfranchise parolees and the 30 states that deny probationers the right to vote cling to these punitive policies"? Perhaps, like those who cling to religion and guns (Uggen & Inderbitzin could have quoted President Obama here, too), they see a good--indeed nonpunitive reason--for these policies, at least when the issue is seriously confronted.

Uggen & Inderbitzin then argue that their proposal would "better fit international practices." But American exceptionalism is not new, and often has much to recommend it. Our economy has, heretofore at least, been less regulated; Americans are more religious than most Europeans; and so forth. I am sure that there are many things that the United States does that most countries do not do, but that Professors Uggen & Inderbitzin support. For example, we allow freer speech than most other countries.

Finally, Uggen & Inderbitzin argue that their proposal would "be consistent with the reintegrative goals of community corrections, offering felons a chance to participate as stakeholders in their communities." Here I actually am in sympathy with the general sentiment, but I think it is best served on a case-by-case basis, *after* the individual felon has shown that he is no longer a threat to the community, but has been giving something back to it. At that time, I would be all in favor of a formal ceremony—similar to a naturalization ceremony—where the right to vote is restored.

Let me also note that, in their conclusion, Uggen & Inderbitzin refer to felons as "a stigmatized group." Well, yes, those who commit serious crimes against their fellow citizens are indeed stigmatized—and rightly so. Uggen & Inderbitzin also note that many states recently have expanded voter eligibility to more felons, but of course most have not, and some (Utah, Kansas, Massachusetts) have moved in the other direction.

FELON DISENFRANCHISEMENT

The relevant part of the website of the Center for Equal Opportunity [link: http://www.ceousa.org/content/blogcategory/64/93/] includes, among other things, a list of what I've written in this area (appended below), along with the following questions-and-answers that focus on some common arguments in favor of felon enfranchisement.

Why should felons not be allowed to vote?
Because you don't have a right to make the laws if you aren't willing to follow them yourself. To participate in self-government, you must be willing to accept the rule of law. We don't let everyone vote--not children, not noncitizens, not the mentally incompetent. There are certain minimum and objective standards of trustworthiness, loyalty, and responsibility, and those who have committed serious crimes against their fellow citizens don't meet those standards.

Shouldn't some felons be allowed to vote?
Yes, and some shouldn't. The decision to restore the right to vote should not be made automatically. It should be made carefully, on a case-by-case basis, weighing the seriousness of the crime, how long ago it was committed, and whether there is a pattern of crime.

Haven't felons paid their debt to society?
They've paid enough of their debt to be allowed out of prison, but that doesn't mean there aren't continuing consequences. We don't let felons possess firearms or serve on juries, for instance. By the way, most of the groups that want felons to be able to vote want them to be able to vote when they are still in prison, so this "paid their debt to society" argument is a red herring.

Aren't these laws racist?
No. They have a disproportionate impact on some racial groups, because at any point in time there are always going be some groups that commit more crimes than others, but that doesn't make the laws racist--just as the fact that more crimes are committed by men doesn't make criminal laws sexist. The people whose voting rights will be diluted the most if criminals are allowed to vote are the law-abiding people in high-crime areas, who are themselves disproportionately black and Latino.

But, historically, weren't these laws passed to keep African Americans from voting?
A few southern states did so a hundred years ago, but those statutes are no longer on the books, and they would be unconstitutional if they were. Today's laws have their roots in ancient Greece and Rome, came to the American colonies from England, and are found in nearly every state in the country, where they were adopted without any racist intent at all and have never been applied discriminatorily.

Don't these laws keep felons from rejoining society?
Two out of three felons who are released from prison commit another crime, but it is ridiculous to assert that the reason they do so is that they can't vote. If a felon shows that he or she really has turned over a new leaf and is no longer a threat to the community but is giving something back to it, there should be a formal ceremony that restores the right to vote to that individual. But it should not be done automatically.

Do these laws violate the Constitution and the Voting Rights Act?
No. The Supreme Court has ruled that they do not violate the Constitution, and indeed the Constitution itself contains language approving of felon disenfranchisement. Similarly, the history of the Voting Rights Act makes clear that it was not intended to require letting criminals vote.

REFERENCES

Clegg, R. (2008, July 24). Commentary – should felons have the right to vote? – NO: Felon disenfranchisement is actually a good idea. Examiner.com. Available online: www.examiner.com

Clegg, R. (2007, November 30). Voting rights on a slippery slope. Pajamas Media. Available online:
http://pajamasmedia.com/blog/get_out_the_vote_who_shouldnt/

Clegg, R. (2006, August 26). Franchise protection. *Wall Street Journal*, A11.

Clegg, R., Conway III, G.T., & Lee K.K. (2006). The bullet and the ballot? The case for felon disenfranchisement statutes. *Journal of Gender, Social Policy & the Law, 14,* 1-26.

Clegg, R., Conway III, G.T., & Lee, K.K. (2008). The case against felon voting. *University of St. Thomas Journal of Law & Public Policy, 2,* 1.

Clegg, R. (2004, October 18). Perps and politics: Why felons can't vote. *National Review Online.*

Clegg, R. (2001, Fall). Who should vote? *Texas Review of Law & Politics, 6(1),* 159-71.

Testimony of Todd Gaziano and Roger Clegg before the House Judiciary Committee's Subcommittee on the Constitution (Oct. 21, 1999).

REDUCE DISPARITY IN ECONOMIC SANCTIONS

R. BARRY RUBACK
VALERIE A. CLARK

Offenders convicted of the same crime and having the same criminal record should receive the same punishment. If they do not, then this disparity raises questions not only of fairness but of due process and equal protection. In the criminal justice system, issues of disparity usually arise in connection with whether and how long a convicted offender must spend in jail or prison. But that exclusive focus is not justified, given that there are more than 4.2 million individuals currently on probation (Glaze & Bonczar, 2007), compared to about 1.6 million prisoners (Sabol, Couture & Harrison, 2007). These nonincarcerated offenders are restricted and punished in other ways, among the most common of which are economic sanctions. We argue here that there is disparity in how these sanctions are imposed and that this disparity should be reduced.

Economic sanctions, which refer to court-imposed penalties requiring offenders to pay money or forfeit property, can be of three types: fines, costs and fees, and restitution. Fines are monetary penalties for crime. Costs and fees refer to court-imposed orders to reimburse the jurisdiction (local, county, state) for the administrative cost of operating the criminal justice system. Restitution refers to a payment by the offender to the victim for financial losses. All three types of sanctions can be used to serve one or more purposes of sentencing, including punishment, deterrence, rehabilitation, and restoration of justice. Typically, economic sanctions in the United States are additional penalties rather than sole sanctions, as they are in Europe (Hillsman, 1990).

Economic sanctions have been criticized because they have little effect on wealthy offenders, can pose a severe hardship for poor offenders, and raise constitutional questions regarding imprisoning individuals for nonpayment of debt. However, for three reasons, their use is likely to increase (Ruback & Bergstrom, 2006). First, the costs of the criminal justice system have risen substantially. One way to reduce the burden on taxpayers is to make offenders pay for at least part of those costs. Second, there are increasing pressures for intermediate sanctions, that is, those sanctions that are more severe than mere probation but less severe (and less expensive) than incarceration. Third, because of increasing concern for victims (Office for Victims of Crime, 1998), restitution awards are likely to be imposed more frequently. Economic sanctions have become more common worldwide. For example, criminal fines are imposed in 77% of cases in England and Wales (Moxon, Sutton & Hedderman, 1990) and in

42% of courts of general jurisdiction and 86% of cases in courts of limited jurisdiction in the United States (Weisburd, Einat & Kowalski, 2008).

   Problem of setting amount of sanctions. The single biggest problem regarding setting of economic sanctions is that judges lack complete information about offenders' economic circumstances, including employment income (net of taxes), other sources of income (e.g., welfare, unemployment), residence expenses, and number of dependents (Hillsman & Greene, 1992). One of the most important questions regarding economic sanctions relates to the imposition of multiple economic sanctions. Thus, consistent with the idea that judges believe there is a total amount of economic sanctions that is fair, an increase in one type of economic sanction seems to lower the amounts of other types of economic sanctions (Olson & Ramker, 2001; Ruback, Ruth & Shaffer, 2005; Ruback, Shaffer & Logue, 2004).

   Evidence suggests that economic sanctions tend to be imposed unequally. In particular, research indicates that they are imposed differently with respect to location (rural versus urban areas; Olson & Ramker, 2001; Ruback et al., 2005), type of crime (Gordon & Glaser, 1991), and offender characteristics (Ruback & Shaffer, 2005).

   In this paper, we examine the imposition in Pennsylvania, which has one of the most complete data collection systems in the country, including a record of virtually all economic sanctions imposed in criminal courts of general jurisdiction. We describe the current use of fines and costs/fees to show two effects: (a) there is disparity in their use between individuals and between counties, and (b) there is inconsistency in their use, in that mandatory fines are not always imposed. We then argue that this disparity in the imposition of economic sanctions should be reduced.

METHOD

   We used three sets of data to characterize the current use of economic sanctions in Pennsylvania: (1) data from the Pennsylvania Commission on Sentencing (PCS) on cases sentenced in the years 2006 and 2007; (2) data from the Administrative Office of Pennsylvania Courts (AOPC) on cases adjudicated in the years 2006 and 2007; and (3) contextual information at the county level derived primarily from the U.S. Bureau of the Census. For individual sentences, we combined the case information from the PCS data with the detailed information on economic sanctions from the AOPC data.

PCS Data
   Under Pennsylvania law, judges are required to submit a computerized Guideline Sentencing Form for most felony and misdemeanor convictions in the state. This form contains information about the offender (race, gender, age), about the offender's prior convictions, about the conviction offenses

(offense type, offense severity as measured by the Offense Gravity Scale of the Guidelines), the mode of disposition (guilty plea or trial), and about the sentence imposed (incarceration in jail or in prison or not incarcerated, length of sentence). The PCS data for 2006 and 2007 contained a total of 275,258 offenses.

AOPC Data

The AOPC data for the combined years of 2006 and 2007 totaled 1,584,264 cases, of which there were 517,160 guilty pleas or guilty verdicts. There were a total of 677,453 sentences and 5,607,263 economic sanctions imposed. Of these 5.6 million economic sanctions, 15 categories accounted for 55% of the total.

These 5.6 million economic sanctions were imposed from 2,629 different types of sanctions as coded by the AOPC. We reviewed the 2,629 different types of sanctions and recoded them into one of three categories: costs/fees, fines, and restitution. We further divided costs/fees and fines by whether they were assessed by the state or county.

Census Data

We collected several basic county-level characteristics and economic indicators for our contextual analysis, which came primarily from the 2000 U.S. Census. We included the population of the county, the percentage urban population within each county, the percentage of the population living below the poverty level, and the percentage of males 15-24 within each county. These variables were included in order to test whether the size of the county, the degree of urbanization in a county, the economic climate of the county, and the number of individuals most prone to engaging in crime were related to how economic sanctions are imposed. As a measure of political conservatism, we included the percentage of county voters who voted for the Republican candidate in the 2002 gubernatorial election. This measure of conservatism was never a significant predictor.

RESULTS

We conducted analyses at both the county level and the individual level to determine whether there was disparity in the imposition of economic sanctions. At both levels there was.

County-Level Analyses

Our first goal was to understand the imposition of economic sanctions at the county. These analyses focused on two questions: (1) whether there was variation between counties in the number of economic sanctions; and (2) whether there was variation between counties in the amount of costs/fees and fines.

Number of economic sanctions imposed. Across the 67 counties in Pennsylvania, the number of different economic sanctions imposed varied from 40 to 147 (Mean = 81; Median = 75). Using various county characteristics that we obtained from the census (e.g. urban/rural differences, federal expenditures per capita, crime rate), we conducted several county-level analyses to try to explain the variation in the number of different types of economic sanctions that counties impose. Increased average annual wages, more Hispanic residents, more total residents, and more urban residents in a county were associated with more types of economic sanctions, whereas more African American residents were associated with fewer types of economic sanctions. The size of the population and the average annual wage had a very small positive relationship with the number of different types of economic sanctions used.

Most of the variation between counties in the number of different economic sanctions imposed came from sanctions unique to each county. For example, one county has a "Cost in Lieu of Community Service" penalty, and another county has its own "Drug Investigation" fee. Of the 2,629 different economic sanctions used in the state, 2,371 are county costs/fees and 79 are county fines. About 44% of all economic sanctions imposed were county costs/fees and nearly 7% were county fines. Across the 67 counties in Pennsylvania, the percent of sanctions imposed that were county sanctions ranged from 10% to 70% (mean = 48%, mode = 41%).

Imposition of mandatory state fines. To understand how and whether mandatory economic sanctions are imposed across counties, we identified eight state-wide sanctions that should be applied to all adjudications.[1] Across counties, mandatory sanctions were imposed in about 55 to 58% of all offenses, and counties imposed an average of five mandatory sanctions per offense.

Besides county court costs, victim-related fines were among the most commonly imposed economic sanctions in the state. Victim impact/witness fees were imposed in 44% of the offenses and 90% of judicial proceedings, and the fine for the Crime Victims Compensation (CVC) Fund was imposed in 45% of the offenses and 93% of judicial proceedings.

Individual-Level Analyses

In addition to understanding how the imposition of economic sanctions varied across counties, we were also interested in how the imposition of economic sanctions varied across individuals, particularly on two legally-relevant variables, the type of offense the offender was convicted of and the offender's prior record. As shown in the table below, there were significant differences among offense types in the amount of economic sanctions imposed. Traffic offenses have the highest total economic sanctions probably because individuals need to drive and thus are willing to pay the fines and fees that the State has imposed on these offenders.

---

[1] Commonwealth Costs (Act 167 of 1992), State Court Costs (Act 204 of 1976), County Court Costs (Act 204 of 1976), Crime Victims Compensation (Act 96 of 1984), Firearm Education and Training Fund (Act 158 of 1994), Victim Witness Services (Act 111 of 1998), Judicial Computer Project Fund, and the Access to Justice Fee.

Mean Amount of Total Economic Sanctions Imposed by Type of Offense

Type of Offense	Mean Amount
Traffic Offense (DUI)	$1349
Drug Offense	$881
Person	$701
Property	$669
Other Type of Offense	$630
Public Order Offense	$624

We also computed the mean amount of economic sanctions by type of prior record. Those with no prior record had the highest average total economic sanctions, those with low prior records had the next highest, and those with the highest prior records had the lowest total economic sanctions. These differences still appeared even after controlling for other individual-level factors, including whether or not the offender received a sentence involving incarceration.

Mean Amount of Total Economic Sanctions Imposed by Prior Record

Prior Record	Mean Amount
No prior record	$862
Low prior record	$825
High prior record	$691

Mandatory fines. As at the county level, we were interested in what factors at the individual level were related to the imposition of mandatory fines related to Crime Victims Compensation (CVC) and all victim-related assessments. Referencing type of offense, the mean dollar amount of CVC for person offenses (e.g., assault) was three times the mean amount of CVC for property, drug, traffic, and public order offenses. For all victim-related economic sanctions, person offenses had the highest average dollar amount, followed closely by property offenses. The average dollar amount of victim-related economic sanctions for drug, traffic, and public order offenses was about half as much. As for prior record, offenses committed by persons with no prior record had the highest average amounts of CVC and total victim-related assessments.

Multivariate Analyses.

Using offense, case, and offender characteristics to predict the imposition of the total amount of economic sanctions for a given offense, we found that the type of offense, the offense gravity score, prior record, and age were the strongest predictors. Higher economic sanctions were imposed for traffic offenses and more severe offenses. In terms of individual characteristics, lower economic sanctions were imposed for individuals with longer records and for younger offenders.

SUMMARY OF THE FINDINGS

These results indicate that there are a large number of economic sanctions imposed in Pennsylvania (more than 2.5 million per year), and these sanctions are from more than 2,000 different categories. There is significant variation between counties in the number of different types of economic sanctions imposed and in the average and median amounts of economic sanctions imposed per case. In general, counties with larger populations and higher percentages of citizens in urban areas impose more economic sanctions and more different types of economic sanctions.

There are also significant differences between individuals based on prior criminal record, although the difference is not in the expected direction. That is, those who have the most serious criminal records are likely to have lower economic sanctions imposed. With regard to type of crime, DUI offenders have much higher economic sanctions imposed than drug, person, and property offenders. As might be expected, younger individuals, who are less likely to have jobs, were significantly less likely to receive economic sanctions.

There is also strong evidence that some mandatory economic sanctions are not imposed when they should be. We found that the average number of the eight mandatory fines imposed for offenses across counties ranged from a low of about one per offense to a high of about seven.

Together, these results indicate first that there is inconsistency in the imposition of economic sanctions between individuals and between counties. Counties vary in the number of economic sanctions used and in the amounts of economic sanctions imposed. Second, the results indicate that there is some uncertainty in the imposition of economic sanctions. In judicial proceedings (i.e., trials in which multiple offenses are handled), even when the economic sanctions are mandatory, an average of only about seven (of a possible eight) mandatory state fines are imposed. This finding is not surprising, given that judges typically order that all applicable economic sanctions be imposed. They do not list all 15 or 20 or 90 individual economic sanctions that are being imposed. Instead, they issue an order that all applicable fines, fees, and costs be imposed. Essentially, they are relying on a clerk, and in some counties, a computer program, to impose these economic sanctions.

Other research we have conducted suggests that the system of economic sanctions in Pennsylvania is too complex. Offenders do not know how much they owe, how much their monthly payments should be, and where the money they pay goes (Ruback, Hoskins, Cares & Feldmeyer, 2006). Conversations with court employees suggest that no one in the court system understands all of the economic sanctions or the order in which they are supposed to be paid, this despite a statute called "The Allocation of Monies in the Uniform Disbursement Schedule."

POLICY IMPLICATIONS

The clear implication of these findings showing that there is disparity in the imposition of economic sanctions between counties and between individuals is that this disparity should be reduced. It is unfair to offenders that whether sanctions are imposed, including mandatory sanctions, depends on the particular county in which the trial is held. Even when sanctions are imposed, there are differences between counties and between individuals in the amounts of the economic sanctions. The attempt to reduce disparity in the imposition of economic sanctions should be part of a larger process to increase fairness.

Until the 1970s, trial court judges had, with the exception of statutorily defined maximum penalties, almost unlimited discretion regarding the imposition of criminal sentences (Frankel, 1972). Beginning in the 1970s, there were calls for sentencing reform, driven in part by evidence of sentencing disparity from analyses of both actual decisions and simulations. In addition to disparity between judges, there were concerns that bias based on race and class produced unwarranted disparities in punishment and that one way to reduce these disparities was to limit judicial discretion. Disenchantment with rehabilitation, based on reports that "nothing works" in terms of rehabilitating offenders or reducing crime led many to oppose indeterminate sentences, which were premised on the ideal of rehabilitation.

Moreover, there was general concern that all legal processes should be made fairer by making the rules clear and predictable (Frankel, 1972) and by instituting review of decisions. To meet this concern, many states instituted sentencing guidelines, which, depending on the state, structure sentencing based on offense seriousness, criminal history, and system-related factors such as prison capacity and intermediate sanctions. There have also been arguments for guidelines governing intermediate sanctions (e.g., Tonry & Lynch, 1996). We believe that guidelines for the imposition of economic sanctions would provide clarity, predictability, certainty, and uniformity. And, based on our analyses of economic sanctions in the Pennsylvania over a two-year period, we believe that there is a need for an overall structure for economic sanctions that accomplishes three goals: (a) reduces the number of different types of economic sanctions, (b) reduces disparity between offenders and between locations, and (c) introduces rationality in the imposition of economic sanctions in terms of achieving deterrence, rehabilitation, and punishment.

REFERENCES

Frankel, M.E. (1972). Lawlessness in sentencing. *University of Cincinnati Law Review, 41,* 1-54.

Glaze, L.E. & Bonczar, T.P. (2007). *Probation and Parole in the United States, 2006.* Washington, DC: Bureau of Justice Statistics.

Gordon, M.A. & Glaser, D. (1991). The use and effects of financial penalties in municipal courts. *Criminology, 29,* 651-676.

Hillsman, S. (1990). Fines and day fines. In M. Tonry & N. Morris (Eds.), *Crime and Justice: A Review of Research, Volume 12* (pp. 49-98). Chicago, IL: University of Chicago Press.

Hillsman, S. & Greene, J.A. (1992). The use of fines as an intermediate sanction. In J. M. Byrne, A. J. Lurigio & J. Petersilia (Eds.), *Smart Sentencing:The Emergence of Intermediate Sanctions* (pp. 123-141). Newbury Park, CA: Sage.

Moxon, D., Sutton, M. & Hedderman, C. (1990). *Unit Fines: Experiments in Four Courts.* London, UK: Home Office.

Office for Victims of Crime. (1998). *New Directions from the Field: Victims' Rights and Services for the 21st Century.* Washington, DC: U.S. Department of Justice.

Olson, D.E. & Ramker, G.F. (2001). Crime does not pay, but criminals may: Factors influencing the imposition and collection of probation fees. *Justice System Journal, 22,* 29-46.

Ruback, R.B. & Bergstrom, M.H. (2006). Economic sanctions in criminal justice: Purposes, effects, and implications. *Criminal Justice and Behavior, 33,* 242-273.

Ruback, R.B., Hoskins, S.N., Cares, A.C. & Feldmeyer, B. (2006, December). Perception and payment of economic sanctions: A survey of offenders. *Federal Probation,* 26-31.

Ruback, R.B., Ruth, G.R. & Shaffer, J.N. (2005). Assessing the impact of statutory change: A statewide multilevel analysis of restitution orders in Pennsylvania. *Crime and Delinquency, 51,* 318-342.

Ruback, R.B. & Shaffer, J.N. (2005). The role of victim-related factors in victim restitution: A multi-method analysis of restitution in Pennsylvania. *Law and Human Behavior, 29,* 657-681.

Ruback, R.B., Shaffer, J.N. & Logue, M.A. (2004). The imposition and effects of restitution in Pennsylvania: Effects of size of county and specialized collections units. *Crime and Delinquency, 50,* 168-188.

Sabol, W.J., Couture, H. & Harrison, P.M. (2007). *Prisoners in 2006.* Washington, DC: Bureau of Justice Statistics.

Tonry, M. & Lynch, M. (1996). Intermediate sanctions. In M. Tonry (Ed.), *Crime and Justice:A Review of Research, Volume 20* (pp. 99-144). Chicago, IL: University of Chicago Press.

Weisburd, D., Einat, T. & Kowalski, M. (2008). The miracle of the cells: An experimental study of interventions to increase payment of court-ordered financial obligations. *Criminology & Public Policy, 7,* 9-36.

IF IT'S DISPARITY, SURE

CANDACE MCCOY

This very interesting paper from Ruback and Clark addresses an issue that they correctly note will become increasingly important in the next few years, primarily because intermediate sanctions in sentencing and decarceration will finally get the attention they deserve in sentencing policy and practice. As examples of intermediate punishments, financial sanctions need to be understood much more clearly. Ruback and Clark's research is exactly the sort of project that every sentencing and probation expert should be conjuring up right now.

This particular paper, however, is probably only the first step in an ongoing research agenda on the topic. Ruback and Clark use the rich data from the studios of the group of artists I call "The Pennsylvania School" of sentencing researchers (Kramer, Ulmer, Johnson, Steffensmeier, Demuth, Eisenstein, wow!). Big databases from the Pennsylvania Sentencing Commission, matched to other data from the state Administrative Office of Courts, continue to provide these able researchers with a wonderfully detailed yet extremely broad picture of how lower courts work in that state. The data have pitfalls, though. I surmise that Ruback and Clark might be caught in one of them right now, but with revision the research will right itself.

The authors set out to study sentencing disparity, and they find it along with highly unexpected explanations for it. The authors describe what they call disparity between counties and between individuals whose cases are adjudicated in those counties. Huge inconsistencies in how fines and court costs and victim compensation orders are imposed are described, and then the various "usual suspects" of independent variables are regressed on the dependent variable (which is amount of financial sanction imposed?) to explore what may account for the inconsistencies. Or, as the authors insist: the disparities.

Surely, if there is unwarranted disparity in the imposition of economic sanctions, it should be reduced. Notice two words in that previous sentence: "if" and "unwarranted." As it currently stands, I am unsure whether this research actually demonstrates that the wide variations the authors find describe are indeed as wide as claimed. As for whether the variations are illegal or even inadvisable and thus amount to sentencing disparity, there is room for debate.

Begin with the basics: what is sentencing disparity? This question has been a political battleground over the past three decades. Most academics (as opposed to policymakers) agree that disparity is "differences in sentences attributable to factors that are not legally relevant." The goal is to "treat like cases alike." Thus, there can be *warranted* disparity and *unwarranted* disparity. The former involves differences in sentences attributable to factors that the law defines as relevant and presumably are not a problem, since "the cases are not alike." The latter is differences attributable to factors that are not part of the law and thus should not influence punishments, but unfortunately do. An offense committed by a white person that is identical in its major attributes to that committed by a black person should receive identical punishment, but, as we know, often will not.

In the 1970s and 1980s, sentencing reformers on the left disingenuously thought everyone agreed that "sentencing disparity" meant unwarranted differences attributable to individual defendants' race, ethnicity, gender, age, and/or economic status. They were surprised when policymakers on the right, beginning about the time of the first Bush administration, defined "unwarranted disparity" as sentences attributable to "lenient" judges' unwillingness to regard crimes of medium severity as deserving of prison sentences (equally, in *any* cases) even though the law permitted incarceration, or to differences in sentencing outcomes among varied jurisdictions which are subject to identical laws. The right won the policy game, and sentencing among offenses became more uniform because it became equally more severe. As for differences in sentencing among jurisdictions, the experience in the federal system illustrates the policy game. Federal Attorneys General beginning with John Ashcroft have fumed about differences in sentencing outcomes among the many states. The Feeney Amendment, in its attack on the structure of judicial departures from sentencing guidelines' "scores," was an attempt to force U.S. Attorneys and judges in "lenient" states to match the punishments meted out in states where the going rate was harsher. Ashcroft's insistence that every federal murder case be reviewed for death penalty eligibility by staff in Washington, not local U.S. Attorneys, is another example.

These ideas apply to Ruback and Clark's paper because they raise questions about whether the variation described here can be called disparity. In the case of differences among counties, is variation such a bad thing? If the Pennsylvania law applies to all counties, just as the United States Code applies to all states, is there no room for legally warranted variation? Beaver Falls is not Philadelphia; Philadelphia is not Pittsburgh. Indiana is not California; California is not Texas. If judges have some discretion under the law – as we know from the sad history of mandatory sentencing that they must – it is legally warranted that they will apply the law so as to do justice in the particular context of the social conditions that the defendants and the courts find themselves in. Insofar as the Pennsylvania law on court costs, victim compensation, and some types of fines provides a wide variety of discretionary options that allow judges to tailor these intermediate sanctions to the norms and needs of the counties in which the judges preside, variation in outcomes might be warranted and, therefore, not sentencing disparity under its usual definition.

To expect that mandatory fines will always be imposed in all counties because the law says so is naïve. Further, as a matter of fairness but not as a matter of law, perhaps they *shouldn't* be. In general, a mandatory anything is a bad idea when it comes to criminal justice decision-making, a maxim whose wisdom has been ably demonstrated in sentencing research over the past three decades. Insofar as the Pennsylvania law described here contains provisions for mandatory fines, it seems that the policy prescription would be to formulate a "guided discretion" law to replace it and train judges in how to use it, just as has been done with the Pennsylvania Guidelines for incarcerative punishments.

Certainly, however, the variations among individuals (as opposed to counties) described here would be legally unwarranted and therefore constitute disparity. This is so, but I have some questions about whether this paper as it currently stands accurately describes that variation. Of course it is impossible for the authors to describe their data and methods of analysis adequately in the space given to them, so perhaps they will do so when we meet in Philadelphia to discuss this work. When we do, I want to hear about the database and what it covers.

From the get go, what does it mean to say there are 1½ million cases but only half a million guilty pleas and verdicts, and then 677,453 sentences and 5.6 million economic sanctions in the AOC data? (These would be the cases of least seriousness.) What is the unit of analysis? Cases or charges? The numbers may indicate that perhaps the analysis is on *charges*, i.e. each allegation the prosecutor made against each defendant. How else to explain 1½ million cases but only half a million convictions, absent the explanation that 2/3 of the cases were dismissed outright? (Were they?)

Of course, there can be one or several charges made simultaneously against a defendant. Together, these charges constitute a "case." As the case proceeds through the system, charges get dismissed depending on the outcome on other charges in the case. In other words, plea negotiation as well as judicial discretion in dismissing charges for which there is no probable cause produce a final group (or single) charge of conviction. The movement of these charges through the system is very important from the point of view of studying prosecution and plea bargaining, but less important for the study of sentencing. For sentencing, what we want to know is: what was the punishment the defendant got? That punishment is the total of sanctions meted out for the package of charges of conviction.

If there are 1½ million cases but only half a million guilty pleas and verdicts in this database, it seems to me that something is wacky. Might Ruback and Clark be studying 1½ million *charges,* many of which are dismissed by judges or, if the charges ended in conviction, they were part of a larger case in which some charges received particular punishments and other charges in the case received different ones? That would explain these odd numbers: 1½ million charges (not cases) result in half a million convictions because so many are dismissed or dropped as part of a guilty plea to other charges in the case. Perhaps there is some other explanation, and the authors will give it. Of course, that does not explain why there are 67,453 sentences attached to only half a million cases of conviction! Has it finally come to be in America that we punish people for charges that are dismissed? (That was a gratuitous slap at the original U.S. Sentencing Guidelines, which did indeed do so under its "real offense" provisions). If my musings are correct, and Ruback and Clark have fallen into the all-too-common pit that constantly bedevils sentencing researchers – i.e., using charge of conviction rather than case as the unit of analysis, due to the difficulty of aggregating criminal charges into cases brought against individual defendants and then determining the outcome of the cases as affected by what happened to each of the multiple charges – they will not be the first to have done so. Believe me, SPSS does not have an "aggregate" function capable of dealing with this adequately. The usual fix is to aggregate the counts by case, count the most serious charge as the offense type for purposes of categorizing the case, and determine the sentence as the sum total of punishment imposed for the aggregate of charges of conviction. This fix allows researchers to portray much more accurately what sentences imposed on each defendant were, but it is hard to do. Nevertheless, it is essential because, without it, a very inaccurate picture of case disposition and punishment is produced. That is because of the operation of plea bargaining.

Charges get dismissed or reduced in severity in plea negotiation. Also as part of plea bargaining, a punishment on one charge in a case is dependent on the punishment imposed for other charges. If a judge sentences a person to long jail time for the most serious charge contained in a case, the judge is much more likely to impose less serious sanctions on the lower charges. Conversely, if the judge gives probation instead of jail time, other sanctions contained in the case are likely to be the most severe, and these will likely be the in-community sanctions. Thus, if Ruback and Clark find an inverse relationship between offense severity and amount of economic sanctions, or between number of prior convictions and severity of financial sanctions, these odd results would not be quite as surprising if it is charges (as opposed to cases) that constitute the unit of analysis. Many charges may have extremely low financial sanctions imposed, but they are perhaps the charges embedded in a larger case which includes other charges on which a high sanction was imposed. If we analyze these data by charge, instead of by case, the effect of punishments meted out on one charge and how it affects the judge's decision about punishments for other charges in the case is impossible to determine. We might end up with odd results showing high punishments for low charges, and the reverse, because the judge sentenced the defendant holistically by case rather than charge-by-charge but we are seeing only average results for each charged offense category.

Another finding in this paper is that, oddly, traffic offenses produce higher economic sanctions than property or drug offenses. If the unit of analysis is "charges," this is to be expected. In a traffic case, there is usually only one charge and a set "going rate" for it. Property cases, by contrast, usually involve multiple charges in the "kitchen sink" approach to prosecution. A conviction based on a guilty plea in a theft case, for example, might involve a dismissed charge of "unlawful taking" but conviction on the charge of receiving stolen property, with the punishment of a moderate fine and a larger amount of victim compensation ordered depending on the value of the item stolen. If we look at the charges separately and regard them as "cases," the dismissed charge on the most serious offense will show up as "zero punishment" for theft, when in fact the case as a whole produced a fine and victim compensation order. If the unit of analysis is "charge," perversely the average punishment for the offense of receiving stolen goods will show up as having a higher sentencing severity than punishment for actual theft. And when these offense categories are compared to traffic cases, in which there is usually only one charge, the traffic cases will have an average higher sentence because judges do not sentence "holistically" in those cases: there is no related charge upon which a punishment is imposed.

In sum, the variation in both number and severity of economic sanctions can be described accurately only if the unit of analysis is the case, not charge. If indeed the unit here is case, i.e., the "basket" of many charges, and economic sanctions attached to the case as a whole, then Pennsylvania judges have a lot of explaining to do. If, however, the unit of analysis here is "charges," then we sentencing researchers will push forward and try to solve the next computer problem: how to aggregate these charges into cases so that a more accurate picture of sentencing disparity is produced.

At that point, we will be able to ask: is this really unwarranted disparity, and if so, what can and should we do about it? This will raise another debate, because what we have learned about sentencing disparity in the past thirty years is that it is attributable not only (and not even primarily) to judicial prejudice against defendants of certain colors or genders, but to laws which pander to public panics (see, for instance, the "disparity" between crack and powder cocaine, which is legally required and thus not disparity at all under the definition set out above.) We have come to see disparity as being rooted in deeper economic and situational conditions in which courts are one more coercive tool in controlling the urban underclass. We have come to see sentencing disparity as something that can be controlled to a degree but, considering that the majority of variation in sentencing is usually unexplained by the variables we have available, it is rooted in court practices and policies that are still poorly understood. Yet we must push forward, and research like Ruback and Clark's is a good start.

Use Information Technologies to Empower Communities & Drive Innovation in the Criminal Justice System

Tracy Siska

Citizen access to the criminal justice system has focused exclusively on the concept of making agents of the system more accessible to community input through initiatives like community policing. This essay proposes a policy shift to the use of information technologies to empower communities while simultaneously driving innovation within the criminal justice system. The current level of data restrictions within the criminal justice system do not serve to empower community members and community based organizations from having a great role in determining how the system will operate in their communities.

To leverage the power of information technologies policies and practices on how and what data is collected, stored, and released to the public need to be re-conceptualized. Standardization protocols need to be created so that criminal justice agencies collect data in a manner that will drive efficient tracking of data across agencies. It is not enough that single agencies within an urban criminal justice system have great procedures for data management. Each agency within that local system, i.e. police, prosecutors, court, corrections, must work collaboratively to ensure the integrity of the data and that each of their systems is collecting data harmoniously with the other agencies.

Efforts to drive the increased use of information technologies in the criminal justice system both on the state and national levels focus exclusively on information sharing between agencies (Assistance, 2005; System, 2009). These efforts do not address how information technologies can revolutionize a community's potential to participate in the system and how that participation occurs. The ability of any community to hold their public officials accountable flows directly from the community's ability to obtain information about the actions of their public officials. Nowhere is this accountability more important than within a system that has the legal authority to restrain a person's liberty or use deadly force.

When using the term data I refer to any piece of information collected by agents of the criminal justice system in processing of a case from complaint through disposal including demographic information about the suspect, victim, and the communities they come from. It is important that the information captured is both reflective of case processing from within the system and community based information. Only with a rich data set that includes information from within the system and the community will the benefits of information technologies be harnessed.

Current data management practices within the criminal justice system keeps information siloed within each individual agency; thus, attempts by community members to track data across agencies requires significant effort to obtain access from each independent agency and then another effort to put the information together in a usable format. With the creation and implementation of data standardization protocols the criminal justice system can release data in formats that would allow community members to efficiently track data across the breath of the system.

The public is too often shut out of meaningful discourse involving the patterns and practices of criminal justice agencies and the system as a whole because the public lack access to data that would empower them to participate in an fully informed manner. In Chicago's famed community policing program there are monthly meetings between police and community members. Officers discuss raw numbers of arrests in the community but the police turn down requests by residents to obtain copies of whatever documents the officer is reading the statistics from. The officers politely tell the residents they are not permitted to give them a copy or let them see the document (Siska, 2007).

This example displays the inability of the Chicago Police to meet the needs voiced by community members through their request to acquire on paper the numbers read aloud during the meeting. This is a limitation of the current data access policies in place within the Chicago Police Department. While this limitation is easily identified there is a greater limitation that the community fails to realize while the numbers of arrests are being read aloud to them. The numbers read aloud only detail the numbers of arrests and do not provide any insight into a more holistic view of the results of those arrests within a larger criminal justice system perspective. With the application of information technologies numbers that represent a more holistic view of the system could be presented to community members and thus empowering the audience members with information that would allow them to make an informed decision about the appropriateness of the system's activities.

A holistic view of the system would include information from every stage of the live course of a complaint / case within a local criminal justice system. This type of view of the system can provide communities with detailed information from every level of the system about a single complaint / case involving a community member or detailed information regarding how a single type of complaint, i.e., sexual assault, is investigated and processed through the entirety of the system. The holistic view would empower community members with knowledge of how every level of the system plays a role in how other levels operate and respond to community needs.

In a report titled "Taking Rape Seriously: Sexual Assault in Cook County" DePaul University Law School Senior Research Fellow Jody Raphael addresses the impact of a lack of information kept by the Chicago Police Department in reference to sexual assault. According to Raphael the Chicago Police Department has a system for not recording in official statistics allegations they believe to be false or unfounded, yet when requested to produce in writing the criteria for how an officer would determine if an allegation is false or unfounded they were unable to do so within six months of the request (Raphael, 2008). Raphael notes that the Chicago Police Department has reported that over the last decade the number of sexual assaults reported to the Chicago Police has dropped; however, without properly collected and maintained data on the number of allegations that have come to the Department and the number that have not been registered in official statistics the reliability of the down turn in sexual assaults in Chicago is less than credible (Raphael, 2008).

The practice of failing to account for a percentage of allegations without retaining overall numbers of complaints received results in an inability for the community or policy makers to determine to what degree the weeding out process is affecting the overall reported number of complaints. If the numbers were collected and maintained properly survivor advocates and researchers would get a much more complete picture of the number of overall incidents that are reported to authorities. There is significant community interest in being provided a more holistic picture of the crime of sexual assault in their community and how those complaints did or did not proceed through the system, and why.

The absence of valid and reliable data initiates a chain reaction of disempowerment. Community members are not able to question district level police officials about the number of complaints that were not registered in official statistics because they have no knowledge that this practice takes place nor the data to prove how much the practice is occurring in their community. Local level political leaders are not aware that the practice takes place nor that their constituents are concerned about the issue because the community has not come to them to make them aware of the issue. High level police officials are not aware of any problem with the practice because neither local political officials nor lower ranking local police officials have come to them to voice the concerns that were voiced to them, because none were. An additional limitation that the improper statistics on sexual assault create is that absent the correct data policy makers are left without evidence of a compelling need to tweak current or create new legislation to assist criminal justice agencies is their work of pursuing perpetrators of sexual assault. The chain effect of disempowerment is real and is a direct effect of improper data collecting priorities.

A true effort to apply information technologies by the criminal justice system will motivate the solution of one of the most pressing issues confronting the criminal justice system from the perspective of communities of color throughout American, consistency to racial and ethnic coding. This issue also falls into how empowering or disempowering the access to data can be for communities. In the fall of 2008 the Illinois Juvenile Justice Commission authored a booklet entitled "Instructions and Guidelines for Collecting and Recording Race and Ethnicity of Youths in Illinois Juvenile Justice System". This booklet is designed to push the criminal justice system into a standardized set of guidelines that will significantly reduce the inappropriate categorization of juveniles that enter the criminal justice system. Reliable and valid categorization of youth will allow policy makers to better address the needs of the communities these children come from in hopes of staving off future criminal acts by other youth from these communities (Commission, 2008).

Accountability within the system must start with an informed citizenry that possesses the ability to determine if the actions taken by their public officials fulfill their immediate needs while also achieving the long-term goals of a society. The National Criminal Justice Commission Act of 2009 introduced by Virginia Senator Jim Webb is an attempt through the creation of a national commission to determine to what degree local criminal justice policies are not serving neither our local nor national long-term interests.

The main purpose of the Commission is to explore answers to why "The United States has the highest reported incarceration rate in the world" (The Committee, 2009, Sec. 2). The Criminal Justice Commission Act of 2009 details that there is an understanding that the majority of policies driving our national incarceration rates are local policies and laws (The Committee, 2009). The current state of information technologies leave both criminal justice authorities in most large and small jurisdictions and the communities they serve powerless to answer any predicted inquiries form the Commission.

The reality is that underserved communities bare the brunt of both the majority of violent crime and misdeeds by criminal justice agencies in America's larger urban centers. Accountability in the criminal justice system has at least a dual meaning in underserved communities. When the system fails to appropriately deal with violent criminals the result is that community members in underserved communities are most often the victims of subsequent violent crime. Internal mechanisms looking to root out improper patterns and practices within criminal justice agencies often find that the victims of abusive patterns and practices of the system often reside in underserved communities (Conroy, 1990; Heinzmann, 2007). This dual victimization complicates how both community residents and accountability mechanisms within the system deal with the concept and reality of accountability from the perspective of underserved community residents.

Researchers, community members, policy makers, and authorities within the system are constantly confronted with a plethora of questions about the system and how it operates and we are almost always left with more questions that answer. Through the application of information technologies into the operations of the criminal justice system many of the questions about racial disparities and other discriminatory practices can be more closely examined. In the system's efforts to provide a holistic view of the system to community members many other audiences including the agencies themselves will be empowered.

As the criminal justice system applies information technologies to meet community access needs the system will simultaneously be building an infrastructure to greatly increase the efficiency with which the agencies operate and communicate with other criminal justice agencies. Efficiencies within the system translate into agents of the system being able to apply the freed up time to situations that were other wise underserved because of the mounting case loads.

Currently each independent criminal justice agency has separate systems for entering, maintaining, and using data. At a minimum this equates to a duplication of work at each entry point at each unique agency that with the application of information technologies could be reduced to a single entry point that applies across the breadth of the system. With cooperation among agencies each entry point could collect data needed data for the entire system thus removing duplication of efforts. Each agency can still collect unique data from individuals when needed to suit the agency's purposes.

As acceptance within the system grows additional benefits will be revealed. The move from paper records to all digital data input originating from data terminals in police cars and the various other entry points within the system will greatly increase efficiency at every level of the system. Expenses consumed with duplication of paper records and the eventual storage will be erased as digitalization of processes and digital storage of information continues to become increasingly less expensive.

Most importantly innovation in every aspect of the system will be driven by new ways of examining data that will inspire agents throughout the system. Oversight will need to be re-conceptualized as the holistic view of the system generated for community members is now also provided to supervisors throughout the criminal justice system. Traditional practices of police officials not having the ability to track if and how the arrests of their officers proceed throughout the criminal justice system will now be able to be completed in automated reports that take only an initial effort to set up but no effort by supervisors to pull data because the technology can do all the work. Automated reports will be generated for legislative oversight that can be tailored to either a holistic view of the entire system or a smaller more targeted report for local elected representatives on system activity with in their district.

Through the application of information technologies in the criminal justice system the possibilities for driving innovation within the system and for greatly expanded community participation and understanding of how the system in working in their communities are boundless. Data access will support the work of the dedicated agents within the system and motivate their ability to be creative in bringing forth solutions to the complex problems our criminal justice system faces. At first greater sunlight on the patterns and practices of the criminal justice agencies will be greeted with skepticism by distrustful agents of the system while underserved communities will second-guess the validity of the data being released. Over time as efficiencies are demonstrated to the agents of the system and communities realize they are being empowered by reliable and valid data distrust will be reduced on both sides.

With the current state of information technologies the ability to answer what criminologists, researchers, policy makers, and community members have traditionally believed to be unanswerable about how the system operates is upon us. While we will still not get at every level of the role discretion plays in our criminal justice system we will be much closer then we ever have been before. In the absence of publicly aired reliable data about how the system operates fears of racial disparities, many very valid, have plagued community / system relations. Through the application of information technologies to increase transparency and engage community participation with the system racial disparities will be either verified and dealt with or shown not to be valid. In either case community / system relations will be greatly advanced all the while innovation from within the system will be empowered to challenge old solutions to complex modern problems facing our criminal justice system.

References

Bureau of Justice Assistance (2005). *Building Exchange Content Using the Global Justice XML Data Model.* Washington, DC: Department of Justice.

Conroy, J. (1990) *House of Screams,* Chicago Reader.

Heinzmann, D., Lighty, T., & Coen, J. (2007, August 16). Feds join in probe of city's elite police. *Chicago Tribune.*

Illinois Juvenile Justice Commission (2008). *Guidelines for Collecting and Recording the Race and Ethnicity of Youth in Illinois' Juvenile Justice System.* Chicago: Illinois Juvenile Justice Commission.

Illinois Criminal Justice Information Authority (2009). *Annual Report 2009.* Chicago: Illinois Criminal Justice Information Authority.

Raphael, J. (2008). *Taking Rape Seriously: Sexual Assault in Cook County.* Chicago: DePaul University College of Law.

Siska, T. (2007). Field notes from Chicago Area Study of North Lawndale. Chicago: Unpublished field notes from CAPS meetings in North Lawndale community. University of Illinois at Chicago.

The National Criminal Justice Commission Act of 2009, (2009). Available online: http://webb.senate.gov/email/criminaljusticereform.html

RESPONSE TO SISKA

SUSAN TURNER

A central argument of Siska's piece is "that the public is too often shut out of meaningful discourse involving practices of criminal justice agencies and the system as a whole because the public lacks access to data that would empower them to participate in a fully informed manner." The author proposes a policy shift that would use information technologies to empower communities while simultaneously driving innovation within the criminal justice system. Siska would like the public to have access to any piece of information collected by agents of the criminal justice system in processing a case, plus information about the communities they come, derived from an automated system in which agencies work collaboratively to ensure integrity of the data and sharing of data among agencies. Such access will help answer questions about racial disparity and discretion within the system. Automation will also help the agencies become much more efficient.

While the goal of community access to information is a laudable one, Siska's solution raises a number of issues. This discussion piece will focuses on four areas raised by his piece: 1) motivation for the policy shift; 2) expectations for the overall policy shift; 3) key components of the policy shift; 4) potential unintended consequences of the policy shift. My discussion is informed by the recent Byrne and Rebovick (2007) edited collection, The New Technology of Crime, Law, and Social Control.

Motivation for Policy Shift

An underlying motivation for change appears to be a concern that the justice system is not being truthful or providing the public with data that could be used to hold criminal justice agencies accountable. Siska points to several examples where justice agencies have not provided statistics presented in community policing meetings, criteria for recording official sexual assault statistics, or appropriate categorization of juvenile offender race and ethnicity. At the same time, Siska feels such an information infrastructure will greatly increase the efficiency of the agencies. It seems as if the author is suggesting that the primarily reason for automation is for public accountability and the ability of the community to determine how "the system will operate in their communities," with an additional benefit to criminal justice agencies.

Research has shown differential treatment of members of minority groups (Hartney and Vuong 2009; Western, 2006) and the concern about a racist justice system is one of the most pressing issues in our society. Few would disagree that – in theory --making the workings of the criminal justice system more transparent and integrating disparate data systems holds promise in addressing inequities in our justice system, and potentially creating efficiencies within justice agencies.

EXPECTATIONS OF THE OVERALL POLICY SHIFT

In fact, efforts are already underway to make the system more transparent and integrate data systems across agencies. Performance-based outcomes, including the use of Compstat by police, are efforts to bring more accountability and transparency to criminal justice agencies. Data silos are breaking down . The events of September 11th have changed the attitude about data sharing significantly. As Corbett (2007, p. 218) notes, "turf wars have given way to a new universal call for interoperability and collaboration." The use of integrated criminal justice information systems in the form of data warehouses – a private sector idea – allows data collected from a variety of sources from arrest to release to be centralized and accessible to different criminal justice agencies (Corbett, 2007).

It is not clear, however, that community members and the general public at large necessarily have the expertise to determine how justice agencies should work or to develop strategies based on the access to data. Policy makers and researchers (in addition to the agency staff) may be better suited to these tasks. Siska should provide concrete examples of how community input has resulted in better data collection, operations and outcomes to strengthen his argument. The lack of access in the past does not necessarily mean access in the future will change things for the better.

The secondary benefit of technology to agencies, in terms of innovation and efficiency, as suggested by Siska, may be less than hoped. For example, as Harris (2007, p. 180-181) notes with respect to Information Technology (IT), "there is little evidence that IT has revolutionized policing when compared to the earlier eras of policing and the adoption of the telephone, two-way radio, and automobile." As Corbett (2007, p. 213) notes with respect to the courts and soft technology, "while the IT movement continues full throttle, it is hampered by a very checkered record of implementation so far." Many projects are cancelled before completion, cost much more and take longer to complete than expected. Courts still are still primarily paper driven, despite IT technologies available for their use.

Key Components of the Policy Shift

Siska is asking a lot of justice agencies, but the details of the request are broad and vague in places. My comments here center on access to information and the role of the community. It is a far leap from being provided information at a community policing meeting to requesting "any piece of information collected by agents of the criminal justice system in processing of a case from complaint through disposal, including demographic information about the suspect, victim, and the communities they come from." The author mentions community-based information a number of times. What is meant by this? Is it census-based information about the community, or other data that are gathered by agencies? How would community-based information be used? A clear mapping of 1) data/variables of interest to 2) problems that could be solved would provide a more solid argument for the importance of information being requested. How access is achieved has important ramifications for issues related to privacy (discussed below). Would identifiable data be available on line via the web, as for sex offender registries, or would community members need to be vetted in some manner to make sure they would properly handle private and sensitive information?

The role of the community is central to Siska's policy shift. Data will empower community members with knowledge to make changes. The author could help us understand better how this might work by talking about the mechanisms he envisions for working with justice agencies to bring about change. It is not likely that merely presenting information to agencies will create change; careful thought needs to be given to how the community will use information to bring about change, whether it is by court-action, participation on citizen boards, collaborating with academic researchers funded by the federal government, etc.

POTENTIAL UNINTENDED CONSEQUENCES OF THE POLICY SHIFT

Increased access to individual data by the public raises the question of the balance between the public's right to know and the privacy of the individual. Potent integrated data systems, linking together demographic and justice system data, may jeopardize privacy, particularly if the databases contain social security numbers, financial data, protected health information, including participation in drug and alcohol programs, etc. The availability of personal information from automated court records – motions, briefs, and affidavits – are more easily retrieved than in the past. As Corbett comments, "whether mild or severe, the 'data mining' that follows from newly available personal information is the dark side of court automation." (Corbett, 2007, p. 224).

Publically available databases can empower the public but can also have negative uses, particularly in the area of sex offender identify and location. Knowing where sex offenders live can help citizens protect their homes (target hardening) and monitor their children's activities in play and en route to school. However, as Harris and Lurigio (2007) point out, one of the unintended consequences of these registries is that community members have used violence or the threat of violence to remove sex offenders from their neighborhoods. Fear of this type of behavior may cause sex offenders not to register and report as required. As the authors note, "It is one of the paradoxes of sex offender registration and community notification that in order to prevent one form of victimization (by sex offenders who recidivate), we create the opportunity for another form of victimization (against sex offenders) (Harris and Lurigio, 2007, p. 110).

CONCLUSION

Siska has outlined a policy shift he suggests holds promise for empowering the public and creating efficiencies in data sharing among criminal justice agencies. His argument would be enhanced by providing more concrete details about components of the proposed shift. The criminal justice system is already making some progress in areas he proposes, however, users of integrated and publically available information must be aware that automation has limitations as well as unintended consequences.

REFERENCES

Corbett, R. O. (2007). The courts and soft technology. In J.M. Byrne and D.J. Rebovich (Eds.), *The New Technology of Crime, Law and Social Control.* New York: Criminal Justice Press.

Harris, A.J. (2007). The police and soft technology: How information technology contributes to police decision making." In J.M. Byrne and D.J. Rebovich (Eds.), *The New Technology of Crime, Law and Social Control.* New York: Criminal Justice Press.

Harris, A.J. and Lurigio, A.J. (2007). Crime prevention and soft technology: Risk assessment, threat assessment, and the prevention of violence. In J.M. Byrne and D.J. Rebovich (Eds.), *The New Technology of Crime, Law and Social Control.* New York: Criminal Justice Press.

Hartney, C. and Vuong, L. (2009). *Created Equal: Racial and Ethnic Disparities in the US Criminal Justice System.* San Francisco: National Council on Crime and Delinquency.

Western, B. (2006). *Punishment and Inequality in America.* New York: Russell-Sage.

LEAVE THE MINIMUM DRINKING AGE TO THE STATES

PHILIP J. COOK

For the first time in a generation there is real debate over the minimum drinking age. The Amethyst Initiative, signed by over 100 college presidents and chancellors, calls for a reconsideration of the federal law that resulted in adoption of 21 as the minimum drinking age in every state. The Vermont legislature is now considering a resolution to ask Congress to issue waivers to states that wish to lower the minimum age,[i] and advocates of liberalization, most prominently Choose Responsibility, are generating national attention. A common theme is that age-based prohibition has not "worked" any better than universal prohibition did in the 1920s. I support the call for a lower minimum drinking age. But unlike many who favor liberalization, I find that the MLDA actually does reduce alcohol abuse and saves lives. Indeed, Prohibition was also successful in that sense (Cook, 2007). With the minimum drinking age, as with so many other types of regulation of risky behavior, there is a tradeoff between life and liberty. In this instance, I submit that the claims of liberty have the upper hand over the claims of public health and safety. This judgment is informed by science and logic but ultimately rests on my personal weighting of valued outcomes. In the last section I suggest one approach that would preserve both life and liberty.

THE ASCENDANCE OF 21 AS THE MINIMUM AGE

Following the repeal of Prohibition in 1933, most states set the minimum age for legal purchase of alcohol at 21. New York and Louisiana were outliers, with a MLDA of 18, while a dozen other states had a split age, lower for beer than liquor. These age limits remained quite static through the 1960s, albeit with some changes in the scope and penalties associated with the prohibition (Mosher, 1980). But that was not to last. The coming of age of the Baby Boomers and the political pressures engendered by the Vietnam War led to adoption of the 26th Amendment in 1970, giving 18 year olds the right to vote. In the five years following, 29 states lowered their minimum age for drinking. By 1975 most states had established 18 or 19 as the minimum age for all beverages.

At the time, lawmakers' did not entirely ignore the possibility of an increase in youthful drinking as a result of the lowered minimum age, but that concern gave way to wartime rhetoric. As Michigan State Senator Daniel Cooper observed, "If he is responsible enough to serve as a platoon leader with eight or 10 men under him in a life or death combat situation, you can't tell him he's not responsible enough to drink."[ii] In any event, there was little systematic evidence on the effects of minimum age laws on public safety. What was obvious was that such laws were routinely violated by millions of youths. Few arrests and sanctions were made. The laws appeared to be merely a symbolic expression of official views regarding appropriate behavior (Bonnie, 1978).

But during the 1970s, evidence started accumulating that these laws had greater effects than previously believed or understood. States that lowered their minimum age limits experienced an increase in traffic fatalities resulting from drinking by young drivers. The evidence was sufficiently persuasive to reverse the political tide, by that time already weakened by the end of the Vietnam War. No states lowered their minimum age after 1976, and a number reversed previous reductions. In 1983, President Reagan's Commission on Drunk Driving recommended that Congress establish a national minimum age of 21, citing the evidence on the beneficial effects of raising the MLDA on traffic safety and the particular problems stemming from neighboring states with different MLDAs. Subsequent Congressional hearings made much of a study by the Insurance Institute for Highway Safety which estimated that a national minimum of 21 would save 730 lives per year (Williams et al., 1983; Males, 1986; Wagenaar, 1993).

Congress did not directly legislate national minimum age, but rather enacted a provision that pressured each state to adopt 21 as the minimum age by threatening to withhold some federal highway funds. The Supreme Court eventually ruled this law Constitutional, despite the 21st Amendment's stricture that the authority to regulate alcohol was a state prerogative.[iii] By 1988 the last state (Wyoming) had complied, and 21 was the minimum age of purchase and public possession everywhere in the United States.

PUBLIC SAFETY BENEFITS

The churning of state minimum age laws during the 1970s and 1980s created a natural experiment that provided considerable information on the effects of such laws. The "experimental" feature is important because without a valid control group it is difficult to isolate the effects of the law from other influences on drinking and traffic safety.

One review article summarized dozens of peer-reviewed studies (Wagenaar & Toomey, 2002). Most of the 79 high-quality studies of MLDA on traffic crashes found the expected result that a reduction in age was associated with an increase in the relevant fatality rate, or that an increase in age was associated with a reduction in the relevant rate; none of these studies found contrary conclusions.[iv] In addition, there were reputable studies demonstrating that a higher MLDA reduced other problems, such as suicide and crime. Various speculations about possible harmful effects of a high MLDA – that it might aggravate drinking problems later in life, or increase marijuana use – appear unfounded (Pacula, 1998; Wagenaar & Toomey, 2002). A variety of statistical methods have been used in these evaluation studies, some yielding more persuasive results than others.

George Tauchen and I introduced the so-called "difference-in-difference" quasi-experimental approach in our article assessing the effects of MLDA reductions (Cook & Tauchen, 1984); in a panel regression analysis of state data, we found that the traffic fatality rate for 16-20 year olds increased by about 7 percent as a result of a reduction in the MLDA from 21 to 18. This method has been utilized by a number of other scholars for various outcomes (and types of regulations) since then (Cook, 2007). For example, a study by Centers for Disease Control found that the effect of the MLDA reduced the incidence of gonorrhea by about 7 percent (Chesson, Harrison, & Kassler, 2000).

The qualitative conclusion is clear: If a state decided to reduce its MLDA this year and made no other changes in alcohol control, there would be some increase in alcohol abuse by teens, with consequences for public health and safety. Just how many lives are at stake is not known or even knowable, since the estimates are out of date. But it appears that the stakes are lower now than they were in 1984, when the National Minimum Drinking Age Act was enacted. Back when states were changing their MLDAs (and thus generating statistical evidence), the American public drank more and was more likely to drive after drinking.

The fact is, youthful drinking closely follows adult drinking (Cook and Moore, 2001). For the US population (age 14 and older) annual consumption of alcoholic beverages stood at 2.65 gallons of pure ethanol in 1984, near the peak level recorded in 1980-81. By 1998 it had dropped nearly 20 percent, and has stayed low (albeit with some upward creep) since then. Meanwhile, the 30-day prevalence of drinking by high school seniors (as estimated by the survey Monitoring the Future) fell from 67% in 1984 to about half in 1993, and has remained at about that level.

The figure below depicts the trends in the traffic death rate and in overall injury death rate (including homicide, suicide, and other injuries, as well as traffic). During the 1990s, the injury death rate for older teens declined from 70/100,000 to 50/100,000. For the 16-20 age group, the number of alcohol-related traffic fatalities nationwide declined by over half between the mid 1980s and 2002. The decline in alcohol-related fatalities outpaced the decline in traffic fatalities that did not involve alcohol for this group. This trend cannot be attributed to more stringent MLDA laws, since they did not change (Hingson and Winter, 2003).

Why are youths drinking less and generally safer now than in the 1980s? For traffic deaths in particular, there are three interacting trends – safer vehicles and highways, the general reduction in drinking, and the success in persuading both youths and adults to refrain from driving after drinking. For youths, the Zero Tolerance (ZT) laws have been particularly effective. After several states imposed ZT with good results (Hingson Heeren & Winter, 1994), Congress made them a requirement in 1995 for all states under threat of withdrawing highway funds. The federal law required that states extend DWI laws to include youths driving after just one or two drinks (a BAC of .02 percent or greater), rather than the normal standard for adults of .08 percent. These laws have had some influence in persuading youths to separate drinking and driving, but have also had the unexpected additional benefit of reducing youthful drinking (Carpenter, 2004).

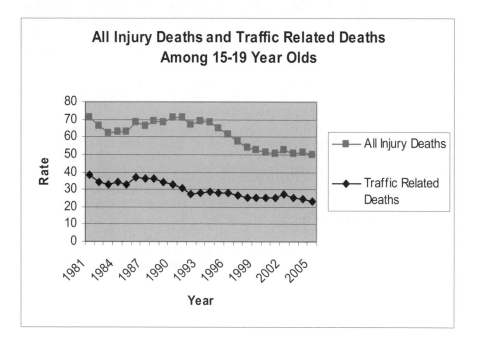

The longer-term developmental effects of youthful drinking are also noteworthy, albeit difficult to quantify. Ongoing research offers evidence that alcohol can do permanent damage to the development of the adolescent brain. While the brain achieves its full size well before adolescence, it continues to mature through age 20 or later (Zeigler et al., 2005). The prefrontal area of the brain becomes more efficient as it matures, and better able "to execute such tasks as planning, integrating information, abstract thinking, problem solving, judgment, and reasoning" (Zeigler et al. 2005, 26). The hippocampus and other limbic-system structures also develop during this period. From experiments on animals, and from brain scans and cognitive tests of human adolescents, it appears that drinking may interfere with the brain's development and cause impairment that continues into adulthood. The evidence of damage is particularly strong with respect to learning and memory (Zeigler et al., 2005). But it is not clear at this time what the "dose response" curve looks like, and in particular whether moderate drinking has deleterious effects. In any event, it appears that increases in the MLDA during the 1970s and 1980s had no effect on high school graduation or college matriculation rates (Dee and Evans, 2003).

LIBERTY AND ADULTHOOD

The bottom line is that the MLDA does reduce alcohol abuse and associated risky behavior by youths, although these benefits are likely smaller now than in 1984. If public safety were the only outcome that should be considered in formulating policy, then there would be no case for lowering the MLDA, and indeed, a real argument for raising it. After all, traffic fatality rates and alcohol abuse rates are even higher for those in their early 20s than those of college age.

The central dilemma here arises whenever freedom conflicts with safety. Classical liberals would make a distinction between self-hazardous behavior and the safety of others, and both dimensions are relevant here. John Stuart Mill's harm principle provides some guidance, stating that protection of the individual is never justification to use the coercive power of government to restrict his or her choices. But Mill did not apply this stricture to youths, who he thought must be protected from their actions {Zimring 1982, p.16}. (Mill leaves open the question of at what age or other indicator of adulthood government policy should become more concerned with protecting freedom when it comes to self-hazardous behavior). For adults, harm to others is the necessary but not sufficient condition for regulating behavior in Mill's doctrine. If it is deemed necessary to act, the question is what form that regulation should take, and that too hinges on the question of adult status. Since Repeal, risky behavior associated with alcohol abuse by "adults" has justified regulation and criminal penalties, but there is no public support for a return to national prohibition.

While specifying just what birthday defines the transition to adulthood is inevitably arbitrary, choose we must. The choices made in other arenas offer rather clear guidance. For a broad spectrum of rights and responsibilities, adult status is granted or imposed by age 18. At that age individuals can vote, serve on juries and hold most public offices, enlist in the military or work at any job without parental consent, undertake contractual obligations, marry, and buy lottery tickets, cigarettes and rifles. By age 18 or before (depending on the state) they have adult status in the criminal justice system, qualify for an unrestricted driver's license, and are no longer subject to protection from statutory rape laws. But in every state, the purchase of alcohol is restricted to those who have had their 21st birthday.

International comparisons reinforce the view that 21 is too old. Almost all European countries have adopted a minimum age for alcohol purchase of 18 or younger (Room 2004, p. 662). Canada's provinces have set theirs at 18 or 19, and Mexico at 18. Only in America can a 20-year-old soldier be arrested for celebrating her safe return from war by drinking with friends, or a 20-year-old bridegroom be required to toast his new wife with nothing stronger than grape juice.

Liberalization of the MLDA laws is a logical step in acknowledging the assessment of the 26th Amendment that 18 year olds are to be full partners in our political process. Why should we not also respect their judgment about whether to drink, subject to the same rules as for other adults? It is more than ironic that the millions of 18-20 year olds who choose to drink despite the prohibition are subject to adult criminal penalties for their choice.

REGULATION VS. PROHIBITION

While I favor a reduction in the MLDA, my enthusiasm for this project is muted by concern for the negative consequences. Ideally, any state that reduced its MLDA would take steps to curb the increase in youthful alcohol abuse through higher taxes and appropriate regulation.

The case for higher excise taxes on alcoholic beverages is strong and multifaceted. Higher tax rates are readily justified as a corrective to the high external costs of drinking – not just by youths, but by adults as well. The notion here is that individuals should be free to drink, but only if they are paying the full costs of their drinking. There is extensive evidence that higher taxes would reduce abuse and its consequences. A recent report of an expert panel of the National Academy of Sciences called for an increase in excise taxes as part of a portfolio of policies to combat underage drinking (Bonnie & O'Connell, 2004). Unfortunately, we've been going in the wrong direction: The real value of excise taxes (both state and federal) on beer and liquor have been eroded by general inflation (Cook, 2007). Restoring the value of excise taxes to the level of, say, 50 years ago, would go a long way to raising alcohol prices sufficiently to negate the effect of liberalizing the MLDA on consumption levels.

The end of state prohibition for college-aged youth would open the door for a more productive regulatory approach to alcohol in residential colleges, where now the administration has to give lip service to the legal ban while dealing with the reality that most students drink. For all youths of that age group, there is no logical reason that the Zero Tolerance laws could not be continued despite lower MLDAs; these laws could be re-branded to focus on inexperienced drivers rather than underage drivers.

One of the hidden costs of the national MLDA has been the loss of opportunity to experiment with alternative approaches. Fosdick and Scott's (1933) remarkable guide for creating alcohol-control systems following Repeal has this observation: "...the forty-eight states will constitute a social science laboratory in which different ideas and methods can be tested, and the exchange of experience will be infinitely valuable for the future" (p. 150). If that laboratory is allowed to function again, perhaps we will find a way around the bitter tradeoff between individual liberty and safety.

REFERENCES

Bonnie, R.J. (1978). Discouraging unhealthy personal choices: Reflections on new directions in substance abuse policy. *Journal of Drug Issues, 8*, 199-219.

Bonnie, R.J. & O'Connell, M.E. (2004). *Reducing Underage Drinking: A Collective Responsibility*, Washington DC, National Academies Press.

Carpenter, C. (2004). How do zero tolerance drunk driving laws work? *Journal of Health Economics, 23*(1), 61-83.

Chesson, H., Harrison, P, & Kassler, W. (2000). Sex under the influence: The effect of alcohol policy on sexually transmitted disease rates in the US. *Journal of Law and Economics, 43*, 215-238.

Cook, P.J. (2007) *Paying the Tab: The Economics of Alcohol Policy.* Princeton: Princeton University Press.

Cook, P.J. & Moore, M.J. (2001). Environment and persistence in youthful drinking patterns. In J. Gruber (Ed.), *Risky Behavior Among Youths: An Economic Analysis,* (pp. 375-437). Chicago: University of Chicago Press.

Cook, P.J. & Tauchen, G. (1984). The effect of minimum drinking age legislation on youthful auto fatalities, 1970-77. *Journal of Legal Studies 13* (January), 169-190.

Dee, T.S. & Evans, W. (2003). Teen drinking and educational attainment: Evidence from two-sample instrumental variables estimates. *Journal of Labor Economics 21*, 178-209.

Fosdick, R.B. & Scott, A.L. (1933). *Toward Liquor Control.* New York: Harper & Brothers.

Hingson, R., Heeren, T. & Winter, M. (1994). Lower blood alcohol limits for young drivers. *Public Health Reports, 109*(6), 738-44.

Hingson, R. & Winter, M. (2003). Epidemiology and consequences of drinking and driving. *Alcohol Research & Health, 27*, 63-78.

Males, M.A. (1986). The minimum purchase age for alcohol and young-driver fatal crashes: A long-term view. *Journal of Legal Studies, 15*, 181-217.

Miron, J.A. & Tetelbaum, E. (2009). Does the minimum legal drinking age save lives? *Economic Inquiry, 47*, 317-336.

Mosher, J.F. (1980). The history of youthful-drinking laws: Implications for current policy. In H. Wechsler (Ed.), *Minimum-Drinking-Age Laws: An Evaluation,* (pp. 11-38). Lexington, MA: Lexington Books.

Pacula, R.L. (1998). Can increasing the beer tax reduce marijuana consumption? *Journal of Health Economics, 17*, 557-86.

Room, R. (2004). Drinking and coming of age in cross-cultural perspective. In R.J. Bonnie & M.E. Çonnell (Eds.), *Reducing Underage Drinking: A Collective Responsibility* (pp. 654-77). Washington, DC: National Academies Press.

Wagenaar, A.C. (1993). Research affects public policy: The case of the legal drinking age in the United States. *Addiction, 88* (Suppl.), 75S-81S.

Wagenaar, A.C. & Toomey, T.L. (2002). Effects of minimum drinking age laws: Review and analysis of the literature from 1960 to 2000. *Journal of Studies on Alcohol,* (Suppl. 14), 206-25.

Williams, A.F., Zador, P.L., Harris, S.S., & Karpf, R.S. (1983). The effect of raising the legal minimum drinking age on involvement in fatal crashes. *Journal of Legal Studies,* 12, 169-79.

Zeigler, D.W., Wang, C.C., Yoast, R.A., Dickinson, B.D., McCaffree, M.A., Robinowitz, C.B. & Sterling, M.L. (2005). The neurocognitive effects of alcohol on adolescents and college students. *Preventive Medicine.* 40, 23-32.

Zimring, F.E. (1982). *The Changing Legal World of Adolescence.* New York: Free Press.

ENDNOTES

[i] www.leg.state.vt.us/docs/2010/resolutn/JRH021.pdf

[ii] New York Times July 24, 1971, p. 29 "Michigan to give 18-year-olds adults' legal rights and duties."

[iii] *South Dakota v. Doles,* 483 U.S. 203 (1987).

[iv] For a recent example of a null finding, see Miron and Tetelbaum (2009). But most recent articles continue to support the conclusion that the MLDA is effective.

The Minimum Legal Drinking Age: "Leaving it to the States" vs. Uniformity at a Lower Age

Mark A.R. Kleiman

The United States currently has a uniform Minimum Legal Drinking Age (MLDA) of 21, brought about by federal financial pressure on the states through the distribution of highway-construction funds. That represents a policy reversal from the Vietnam War-era trend toward 18 as the MLDA. The observation that reducing the MLDA correlated with high rates of automobile fatalities, not just for the 18-to-21 cohort but also for the 16-to-18 cohort (presumably due to "leakage" of alcohol from, e.g., 18-year-old high school seniors to 16-year-old high school sophomores) generated political pressure leading to the adoption of the new federal policy.

One result of the new policy has been massive, and largely unpunished, lawbreaking; when I ask students in my drug-policy classes how many of them know someone with a fake ID, about half the hands in the room go up. There are now calls, including one from a group of college and university presidents, to repeal the federal law and once again leave the MLDA to the states.

Philip Cook, in a typically acute, clear-headed and fair-minded analysis, endorses that call, pairing his endorsement with a suggestion that other offsetting policies, including higher alcohol taxes, be adopted at the same time to prevent an increase in automotive fatalities and other sequellae of youthful drinking, including risky sexual behavior and violence.

If in fact the combination of higher taxes and a lower drinking age could result at once in less drinking, less drinking-related damage, less lawbreaking, and more personal liberty, that would indeed represent a "free lunch."

However, there are two different questions here: the average MLDA, and the pattern of variation around that average. Cook demonstrates to my satisfaction that the reduction (combined with offsetting tax increases) would be good policy. And repealing the federal policy that virtually forces states to adopt a 21-year MLDA would lead to a reduction in the average MLDA. But (unless the states acted in lock-step) it would also increase the dispersion around that average. And the case for increasing the dispersion is not nearly as air-tight as the case for reducing the average.

Allowing state-to-state variation has its own advantages, of course. Cook mentions the gain to knowledge from allowing the states to serve as data-points in what are in effect ongoing policy quasi-experiments. It is also possible that the optimal drinking age varies from state to state. Moreover, a national MLDA is not fully consistent with the principles of federalism; it is clear that the Congress did not have the power to mandate it directly.

Even if the Supreme Court was correct in ruling that the work-around via the Highway Trust Fund was within the letter of the Constitution, it could be reasonably argued that nationalizing such questions is a bad idea as a matter of institutional design.

But there are important disadvantages to set against those advantages. Not only would re-opening the MLDA question, along with the alcohol-tax question, in every state generate efforts – legal, quasi-legal, or flatly illegal, but in any case undesirable – by the alcoholic beverage industries to convert money into political power, the patchwork of laws that would likely result would carry its own set of costs.

The most important disadvantage of state-to-state variation is the creation of border effects. These are already evident in alcohol taxation and sales regulation, with retailers in, for example, New Hampshire and New Jersey eagerly exploiting the willingness of residents of Massachusetts and Pennsylvania, respectively, to evade their home states' taxes and regulations. If one of two neighboring states maintains a 21-year MLDA while the other drops the age to 18, the state with the lower age will attract both bar and liquor-store traffic from residents of the higher-age state. This is precisely the sort of interstate-commerce question that the Constitution empowers the Congress to deal with, but it would be hard to invent any federal legislation or enforcement activity, other than the current virtual mandate for uniformity, that could effectively deal with the problem.

Border effects would effectively limit the capacity of any state to maintain a higher drinking age than any of its neighbors, at least with respect to the part of its population living near the relevant border. And given the economic benefits of having a lower drinking age than a neighboring state – especially for small states with large neighboring populations – we might expect to see some "race-to-the-bottom" effects, fueled both by state governments' need for revenue and political contributions from beer distributors.

Border effects are inseparable from any sort of decentralized system. But in the case of alcohol their impact may be even worse than merely diminishing the efficacy of restrictive policies. When Wisconsin had a lower drinking age than Illinois, under-21 Chicagoans used to drive to Kenosha to go to bars, get drunk, and drive back.

That the current policy is suboptimal seems hard to doubt; but the suboptimality comes not from its uniformity (which is in some ways an advantage) but from setting the uniform age too high and the tax rate too low. Thus where Cook offers a choice between two policies – a national 21-year MLDA and leaving it to the states – I would add a third option to the mix: an 18-year MLDA (I might want to make it even lower) combined, as Cook proposes, with higher taxes and also with a zero-BAC standard to define driving under the influence for under-21 motorists.

LEGAL REGULATION OF MARIJUANA: THE BETTER WAY

PATRICIA G. ERICKSON
ELAINE HYSHKA
ANDREW HATHAWAY

Marijuana is by far the most widely used illicit drug in the world. In Canada, as in other western nations, marijuana has become an embedded feature of the drug scene over the past 35 years. Findings from past studies (Erickson, 1989) as well as recent national drug surveys (Adlaf, Begin & Sawka, 2005a; Adlaf, Demers & Gliksman, 2005b) indicate its use is not confined to a 'deviant subculture' or the margins of Canadian society. Overall, 44.5% of Canadians report using marijuana at least once in their lifetime, and 14.1% reported use during the 12 months before the survey (Adlaf et al., 2005a). Younger people are more likely to have used it in their lifetime and are more likely to be recent users. Almost 70% of those 18 to 24 years old reported using the drug at least once. Nearly half of those 18 and 19 years old and 30% of 15-17 year olds report past-year marijuana use. Data from drug surveys in the 1990s and 2000s showed dramatic growth trends in most age categories, including the older cohort. Marijuana use among youth escalated in the 1990s, along with lowering perceived risk of associated harms (Adlaf, Ivis, Smart & Walsh, 1996; Poulin & Elliot, 1997). Also use by young adults, 18 to 29 years, more than doubled in Ontario from 1996 to 2005—from 18 to 38% (Adlaf, Ialomiteanu & Rehm, 2008).

Canadian marijuana use continues to increase in spite of federal criminal penalties for marijuana possession; these include fines, probation, discharge, diversion, and jail, with a maximum penalty of $1000 and 6 months imprisonment for a first offence (Erickson, 2005). While receiving a criminal record imposes a social burden on users who are caught, and a threat to the vast majority who are not, this punitive response ignores the potential adverse health and social consequences of different patterns of use (Erickson, 1980; Hathaway, 2003). Prevention continues to rely mainly on the ineffective legal deterrent, at the expense of harm reduction (Erickson, 1976; Hathaway, Macdonald & Erickson, 2008). In the early part of the present decade, despite special legislative committees, draft laws, and a proposal (before the previous Liberal government) to remove criminal records for possession of small amounts, no significant change in drug policy towards marijuana occurred (Hyshka, 2009; Senate Special Committee on Illegal Drugs, 2002). Indeed the current Conservative Prime Minister, Stephen Harper, has transformed Canada's drug strategy into an Anti- drug strategy, proposing increased enforcement and penalties, sending a clear message that marijuana use must and will remain illegal.

Indeed, as in past decades, marijuana arrests have continued at a high level, with nearly 60,000 recorded mainly for possession in 2005, and increasing in major cities by 20% to 50% in 2006 (Canadian Press, 2007; Erickson & Oscapella, 1999; Statistics Canada, 2006).

While public opinions surveys are not always consistent in the meanings attached to "decriminalization," support for policy reform appears to have been growing in Canada. In the 1980's endorsement of the elimination or reduction of penalties for marijuana use was held by a large minority, and this stance had become more robust by the 1990's (Savas, 2001). By the 2001-2006 period, a national survey indicated that about 2/3 of Canadians supported "a limited fine as a maximum penalty for marijuana possession (Fischer, Ala-Leppilampi, Single & Robbins, 2003: 277). A Toronto-based random household survey conducted in 2004 indicated that over half (54%) of adults 18+ agreed that marijuana should be legally available (Hathaway, Erickson & Lucas, 2007). Interestingly, since most large-scale surveys provide few demographic correlates, the supporters of legalization were significantly more likely to be white, male, Canadian-born, better educated and with a higher income than those who were not, but a majority of all age groups (56% of 18-34 year olds, 54% of those 35-45, and 51% of ages 55 and up) supported legal availability (Hathaway et al., 2007:48). In a measure that more closely approximates decriminalization, 69% of the Toronto respondents said that "private use by adults should not be liable to arrest and a criminal record" (Hathaway et al., 2007:50).

Hyshka (in press) has analyzed the Canadian socio-political context in a effort to shed light on the quandary of progressive, evidence-based initiatives dating back to the Le Dain Commission contrasted with the total legislative inertia that has marked the past 3 decades. In a comparative case study with Western Australia, where significant reform of marijuana policy has occurred, successfully decriminalizing possession and production for personal use (Lenton, 2004), Hyshka concludes that several favourable factors present in the Australian scenario were missing or less pronounced in the Canadian context. These included support by key interest groups including law enforcement (opposition from both RCMP and Association of Chiefs of Police), user/activist consensus on the proposals (Canadian reform advocates favoured legalization, not decriminalization), political survivability of the party proposing the change (Canada had a minority government by 2004), and built in proposals for evaluation and review of the new policy's impact, providing reassurance that revision can occur (never explicitly proposed in Canada's draft legislation). What both countries shared, in support of liberalization, were public opinion polls endorsing change and considerable research evidence on the harms of the existing laws (Fischer et al., 2003; Hathaway & Erickson, 2003; Lenton, Heale, Humeniuk & Christie, 2000). An additional factor noted by Hyshka (in press) that likely mitigated against successful reform in Canada was the federal framework for drug laws, that disallowed "experiments" at the provincial level, unlike the Australian states' criminal law powers. As well, the confusion and antipathy towards the often publicly interchangeable terminology of "decriminalization" and "legalization" were avoided in the Australian context by the use of the term "prohibition with civil penalties" to denote the continuation of penalties under their particular expression of decriminalization (Hyshka, in press).

THE NORMALIZATION OF MARIJUANA USE

In a way, the preceding social and political factors described are harbingers of the theoretical concept of normalization. Despite its illegal status, widespread use of marijuana is a reality, creating over half a million official criminals and upwards of 4 million undetected current users. The debate on drug policy reform in Canada often has seemed to be going in circles, reprising the issues first raised by the Le Dain Commission (1972) followed by recurring periods of initiatives and legislative inactivity (Erickson, 2005; Erickson, Hathaway & Urquhart, 2004; Fischer, 1997; Hyshka, 2009). When policy change towards marijuana has occurred in other countries, it seems to follow an opening of a political window of opportunity, with evidence-based arguments playing at least some role in this process (Lenton, 2004; MacCoun & Reuter, 2001). In Canada, the potential for reform may be facilitated not only by relevant new data but also by a new perspective or approach in which to frame the consideration of policy change. It is evident that the research efforts of past decades, couched in conventional terms of lack of deterrence and considerable individual and social costs, have not paved the way for significant reform (Erickson, 1980; 1998).

Fortunately, recent theoretical endeavors have emerged to explain the persistent spread of illicit drugs consumption by 'ordinary,' otherwise conventional young people in the context of contemporary lifestyles. In particular, Howard Parker's (2005) normalization thesis, has been influential. This perspective is concerned with 'recreational' drug use, understood as "the occasional use of certain substances in certain settings and in a controlled way" (Parker, 2005: 206). The pattern of infrequent and situation specific use is overwhelmingly what characterizes the majority of marijuana use (Adlaf et al., 2005a, 2005b; Hathaway, 2004a, 2004b; Shukla, 2005). Indeed, research in several countries has documented that marijuana has become part of mainstream culture for many youth and otherwise conforming adults who do not abandon its use when more mature roles and responsibilities are assumed (DeCorte, 2001; Duff, 2005; Hathaway, 1997, 2004a, 2004b; Osborne & Fogel, 2008; Pearson, 2001; Shiner & Newborn, 1997; Williams and Parker, 2001). A possible wave of long-term marijuana consumption in a significant proportion of Canadian young (and increasingly older) adults carries profound implications for a prohibitionist drug policy, and generates a reassessment of the challenges to law, criminal justice and public health (Hammersley, 2005).

The five dimensions of normalization outlined by Parker, Aldridge and Measham (1998) and Parker, Williams and Aldridge (2002) are (1) increasing access and availability of illicit drugs in the community; (2) increasing prevalence of this drug use; (3) increasingly tolerant attitudes towards drug use among both users and non-users; (4) future expectations about drug use among current users and abstainers; (5) the "cultural accommodation" of drug cultures in youth oriented film, TV and music; In Parker's most recent iteration (Parker, 2005) he added a sixth, more liberal policy-oriented shifts, in recognition of the gap in many countries between appropriate socio-legal response and the drug taking behavior of an increasing number of adolescents and young adults.

Indeed, evidence suggests that recreational marijuana use amongst young adults has become increasingly normalized in the last decade. In addition to increased use rates and recent efforts to liberalize Canadian marijuana laws, some research indicates that marijuana availability is increasing. Adlaf and Paglia (2003) report that since 1989, "the perceived availability of cannabis has increased to the point that more than half of secondary school students report the drug is 'easy' or 'very easy' to obtain" in Ontario. In addition, Hathaway (2004a) reports that the majority of marijuana users say supply-related problems have decreased over time. These trends coincide with a broader acceptance of marijuana in Canadian culture, including movies, TV, print and radio and other mainstream media outlets and have prompted some Canadian researchers to begin speaking of the "cultural normalization" of cannabis use (see Erickson, 2005; Hathaway, 2004b; Osborne & Fogel, 2008).

In addition to this contextual evidence, some qualitative research has explored the extent of marijuana normalization in Canada. Osborne and Fogel's (2007) qualitative study of 41 middle class marijuana users in Alberta indicates support for the normalization thesis in that the participants all reported being able to integrate their recreational marijuana use into their otherwise conventional and law-abiding lives and in a controlled way. That is, they used marijuana for pleasure and relaxation and set boundaries to keep their use in check and ensure that it did not interfere with other facets of their lives. Shukla (2005) indicates similar findings with a sample of adult marijuana users in Oklahoma. Moreover, research currently underway by the authors further supports these findings (Hyshka et al., forthcoming) In interviews with adult marijuana users aged 20-49 who had stable housing and employment in Toronto, Ontario, we found that the majority of participants reported that their peers and family members generally accepted their marijuana use. In particular, many of the younger respondents indicated that their parents were knowledgeable or accepting of their use. One participant summed it up succinctly:

Interviewer: How do [your parents] know?
Participant: I told them. I just don't, I don't know. I guess I feel like, my parents know that I drink alcohol, why shouldn't they know that I smoke pot too? [female, 25, graduate student]

Moreover, marijuana users in our study seemed more preoccupied with the health risks associated with marijuana—perceived variously to be ambiguous, not serious, or less dangerous than tobacco—than any risk of detection and arrest. Also they viewed marijuana use as more of a personal choice, rather than one associated with being a member of a particular social group or subculture. This reflects accurately the penetration of marijuana use into all strata of society, as evidenced in the epidemiological surveys (Adlaf et al., 2005a, 2005b). The disjunction between users' perceptions and experiences and the continued existence of punitive criminal sanctions is partially neutralized by their (mis)belief that the law is less severe than it is, or that they will not be caught. Thus, researchers and policymakers in Canada would be wise to consider the shifting social context of cannabis use, and the changing risks and costs associated with these patterns, as a template for the consideration of other drug policy options, including decriminalization and legal regulation.

CONCLUSION

Analysis of drug policy is generally undertaken in a quantitative way, examining statistics of enforcement, incarceration, prevalence rates, public opinion surveys, social costs, etc. (Fischer et al., 2003; MacCoun & Reuter, 2001). While these measures are undoubtedly important, it is also evident that amassing such data for over 35 years has not led to reform of Canadian law regarding marijuana (Erickson, 1998; Hyshka, 2009; Senate Special Committee on Illegal Drugs, 2002). The lived experience of marijuana users, reflected in qualitative interview data, can bring home a reality that is easily lost in a welter of statistics. What the emerging concept of normalization and related research have illustrated is that socially mainstream users are functioning well in society and essentially acting as if marijuana was already legal. They are not apologetic nor do they conceal this behavior from family and peers. They are concerned with responsible use, open to health concerns, and they have no intention of stopping. This evidence of normalization is at sharp odds with the legal reality of a punitive prohibition with potential for incarceration.

It can reasonably be asked, what would be accomplished by subjecting the marijuana users such as those in our and other studies of normalized users to arrest and criminal records? How much is a reasonable concern with long term health effects of marijuana use obscured by the legal threat attached to any and all use? Criminal law does not exist to extend a health message. The most suitable framework would be a public health approach of legal regulation that recognized individual rights to choose, within certain limits and with appropriate controls (Erickson & Ottaway, 1994). Even a modest measure of decriminalization of possession would be a more suitable match for the normalization of recreational marijuana use than a policy of punitive prohibition.

Although it is premature to speculate on what initiatives, if any, the new Obama administration might take in relation to national marijuana policy, there are some encouraging signs of a less war-like approach. Two examples are the appointment of a less militant drug czar and the backing away from prosecution of medicinal marijuana cases. These may be harbingers of some re-visiting of various empirical sources favoring the extension of decriminalization beyond the current states where it has existed since the 1970's (MacCoun & Reuter, 2001). While this government admittedly has many pressing issues to deal with, and might wish to avoid one that has been as politically divisive as drug policy reform, the financial costs of recent high levels of criminalization may also be a factor to consider. It would be ironic if, after the past (unwarranted) US criticism and pressures placed upon Canadian marijuana decriminalization proposals and other relatively minor harm reduction efforts (cf. opiate maintenance and safe injection sites), Canada had a model of liberalization to follow from its southern neighbor.

REFERENCES

Adlaf, E., Begin, P. & Sawka, E. (Eds.). (2005a). *Canadian Addiction Survey (CAS): A National Survey of Canadian's Use of Alcohol and Other Drugs: Prevalence of Use and Related Harms: Detailed Report.* Ottawa: Canadian Centre on Substance Abuse.

Adlaf, E., Demers, A. & Gliksman, L. (Eds.). (2005b). *The 2004 Canadian Campus Survey.* Toronto: Centre for Addiction & Mental Health.

Adlaf, E., Ialomiteanu, A. & Rehm, J. (2008). *CAMH Monitor eReport: Addiction and Mental Health Indicators Among Ontario Adults, 1977-2005.* Toronto: Centre for Addiction & Mental Health.

Adlaf, E., Ivis, F., Smart, R. & Walsh, G. (1996). Enduring resurgence or statistical blip? Recent trends from the Ontario Student Drug Use Survey, *Canadian Journal of Public Health, 87,* 189-192.

Adlaf, E. & Paglia, A. (2003). *Drug use among Ontario students, 1977-2003. Findings from the OSDUS.* Toronto: Centre for Addiction & Mental Health.

Canadian Press. (2007, July 9). Pot busts bound back.

DeCorte, T. (2001). Drug users' perceptions of 'controlled' and 'uncontrolled' use. *International Journal of Drug Policy, 12,* 297-320.

Duff, C. (2005). Party drugs and party people: examining the 'normalization' of recreational drug use in Melbourne, Australia. *International Journal of Drug Policy, 16*, 161-170.

Erickson, P. (1976). Deterrence and deviance: the example of cannabis prohibition. *Journal of Criminal Law & Criminology, 67*, 222-232.

Erickson, P. (1980). *Cannabis Criminals: The Social Effects of Punishment on Drug Users.* Toronto: ARF Books

Erickson, P. (1989). Living with prohibition: Regular cannabis users, legal sanctions and informal controls. *International Journal of the Addictions, 24*, 175-188.

Erickson, P. (1998). Neglected and rejected: a case study of the impact of social research on Canadian drug policy. *Canadian Journal of Sociology, 23*, 263-280.

Erickson, P. (2005). Alternative sanctions for cannabis use and possession. In P. Begin and J. Weekes (Eds.), *Substance Abuse in Canada: Current Challenges and Choices* (pp. 39-43). Ottawa: Canadian Centre on Substance Abuse.

Erickson, P., Hathaway, A. & Urquhart, C. (2004). Backing into cannabis reform: The CDSA (Controlled Drugs and Substances Act) and Toronto's diversion experiment. *Windsor Review of Legal and Social Issues, 17*, 9-27.

Erickson, P. & Oscapella, E. (1999). A persistent paradox: Drug law and policy in Canada. *Canadian Journal of Criminology, 41*, 275-284.

Erickson, P. & Ottaway, C. (1994). Policy –alcohol and other drugs. In P.E. Nathan, J.W. Langenbucher, B.S. McCrady and W. Frankenstein (Eds.), *Annual Review of Addictions Research and Treatment,* Volume 3 (pp. 331-341). New York: Elsevier.

Fischer, B. (1997). The battle for a new Canadian drug law: A legal basis for harm reduction or a new rhetoric for prohibition? In P. Erickson, D. Riley, Y. Cheung & P. O'Hare (Eds.), *Harm Reduction: A New Direction for Drug Policies and Programs* (pp. 47-68). Toronto: University of Toronto Press.

Fischer, B., Ala-Leppilampi, K., Single, E. & Robbins, A. (2003). Cannabis law reform in Canada: Is the 'saga of promise, hesitation and retreat' coming to an end? *Canadian Journal of Criminology and Criminal Justice, 45*, 265-297.

Hammersley, R. (2005). Theorizing normal drug use. *Addiction Research and Theory, 13*, 201-203.

Hathaway, A.D. (1997). Marijuana and lifestyle: Exploring tolerable deviance. *Deviant Behavior, 18*, 103-124.

Hathaway, A.D. (2003). Cannabis effects and dependency concerns in long-term frequent users: A missing piece of the public health puzzle. *Addiction Research & Theory, 11*, 441-458.

Hathaway, A.D. (2004a). Cannabis careers reconsidered: Transitions and trajectories of committed long-term users. *Contemporary Drug Problems, 31*, 401-423.

Hathaway, A.D. (2004b). Cannabis users' informal rules for managing stigma and risk. *Deviant Behavior, 25,* 559-577.

Hathaway, A.D. & Erickson, P.G. (2003). Drug reform principles and policy debates: Harm reduction prospects for cannabis in Canada. *Journal of Drug Issues, 33,* 467-496.

Hathaway, A.D., Erickson, P. & Lucas, P. (2007). Canadian public opinion on cannabis: How far out of step with it is the existing law? Canadian Review of Social Policy, 59, 44-55.

Hathaway, A.D., Macdonald, S. & Erickson, P. (2008). Reprioritizing dependence and abuse: A comparison of cannabis clients in treatment with a non-treatment sample of users. *Addiction Research & Theory, 16,* 495-502.

Hyshka, E. (2009). The saga continues: Canadian legislative attempts to reform cannabis law 2003-2008. *Canadian Journal of Criminology and Criminal Justice, 51,* 3-91.

Hyshka, E. In press. Turning failure into success: What does the case of Western Australia tell us about Canadian cannabis policymaking? *Policy Options* X.

Hyshka, E., Clark, C., Lambert, L. Plante, E. & Walker, A. Forthcoming. Hiding in plain sight: Trouble and triumph recruiting mainstream cannabis users in 4 Canadian cities. In G. Szarycz (Ed.), *In Troubled Waters: Navigating Through the Unexpected Challenges and Dilemmas of Social Research.* Amherst, NY: Cambria Press.

Le Dain Commission (The Commission of Inquiry into the Non-Medical Use of Drugs). (1972). *Cannabis.* Ottawa: Information Canada.

Lenton, S. (2004). Pot, politics and the press - reflections on cannabis law reform in Western Australia. *Drug and Alcohol Review, 23,* 223-233.

Lenton, S., Heale, P., Humeniuk, R. & Christie, P. (2000). Infringement versus conviction: The social impact of a minor cannabis offence in South Australia and Western Australia. *Drug and Alcohol Review, 19,* 257-264.

MacCoun, R. & Reuter, P. (2001). *Drug War Heresies: Learning from Other Vices, Times and Places.* Cambridge, UK: Cambridge University Press.

Osborne, G. & Fogel, C. (2007). The normalization of marijuana use by adult Canadian users. *International Journal of Crime, Criminal Justice and Law, 2,* 187-212.

Osborne, G. & Fogel, C. (2008). Understanding the motivations for recreational marijuana use among adult Canadians. *Substance Use & Misuse, 43,* 539-572.

Parker, H. (2005). Normalization as barometer: Recreational drug use and the consumption of leisure by young Britons. *Addiction Research and Theory, 13,* 205-215.

Parker, H., Aldridge, J. & Measham, F. (1998). *Illegal Leisure: The Normalization of Adolescent Drug Use.* London: Routledge.

Parker, H., Williams, L. & Aldridge, J. (2002) The normalization of sensible recreational drug use: More evidence from the North West England longitudinal study. *Sociology, 36,* 941-964.

Pearson, G. (2001). Normal drug use: Ethnographic fieldwork among an adult network of recreational drug users in inner London. *Substance Use and Misuse, 36,* 167-200.

Poulin, C. & Elliot, D. (1997). Alcohol, tobacco and cannabis use among Nova Scotia adolescents: Implications for prevention and harm reduction. *Canadian Medical Association Journal, 156,* 1387-1393.

Savas, D. (2001). Public opinion and illicit drugs: Canadian attitudes towards decriminalizing the use of marijuana. In P. Basham (Ed.), *Sensible Solutions to the Urban Drug Problem.* Vancouver: The Fraser Institute.

Senate Special Committee on Illegal Drugs. (2002). *Marijuana: Our Position for a Canadian Public Policy.* Ottawa: Information Canada.

Shiner, M. & Newburn, T. (1997). Definitely, maybe not? The normalization of recreational drug users in Edinburgh, Scotland. *Sociology, 31,* 1-19.

Shukla, R.K. (2005). Using marijuana in adulthood: The experience of a sample of users in Oklahoma City. *Journal of Ethnicity in Substance Abuse, 4,* 151-179.

Statistics Canada. (2006). *Juristat.*

Williams, L. & Parker, H. (2001) Alcohol, marijuana, ecstasy and cocaine: Drugs of reasoned choice amongst young adults in England. *International Journal of Drug Policy, 12,* 397-413.

Radical Drug Control

Hal Pepinsky

I thank the authors of this always timely plea to de-demonize cannabis. Cannabis has long been a drug of choice for millions. My attitude toward this or any drug use has nothing to do with my drug preferences.

In an article I wrote for Criminology editor Jim Inciardi's 1980 special issue on what has come to be called critical criminology, I explained how I had come to define myself instead as a radical criminologist. I explained then as I still believe that to me, being radical—reaching to the roots of one's very own understanding—entails having a uniquely individual understanding of any social issue rather than being reduced to taking sides in organized political debates.

I am pro-choice when it comes to who decides what is taken out of one's own body. I am equally pro-choice when it comes to what one ingests, inhales, injects or decides what feels right or wrong, good or bad. At root, I conclude that all attempts to decide what anyone puts into or takes out of her or his body only compounds any violence we suffer. Governments have perfectly legitimate roles in my view ensuring that when we go into the grocery store or the pharmacy, we know what's in what we are consuming, and in offering safe refuges for people to go ahead and drug themselves to death if that's their choice. Consider the savings in drug enforcement expenditure alone.

Spare me assessments of which drugs are worse or better than others. Doctors tell us too much salt can kill us. On the other hand, as Gandhi recognized, taking salt into our bodies is essential to every one of our lives. Opium appears to be so organically close to endorphins we produce internally, that opiates with remarkable potential to relieve pain are not toxic in themselves. Commentators on diets, like Michael Pollan, warn us to choose our drugs by roaming the walls of grocery stores rather than picking up processed foods in the middle. Yes, what we put into our bodies, including the air we breathe, is central to living. Here's to free exchange of information about how our various uses of drugs enrich or impoverish and reduce our lives...and leave it at that. Enough of drug regulation, period.

Regulation includes taxation. Just as sale of produce is for the most part exempt from sales tax, as Gandhi argued, things we consider vices should not be taxed. That only makes social welfare depend more heavily on a "vice." The idea of decriminalizing and taxing rather than just plain legalizing mary jane is especially ludicrous. I call marijuana the democratic drug. All you need is a closet and a light bulb, and voila, you too can become self-sustaining. Taxing marijuana is like patenting traditional medicines.

119

The more intimately you control people's bodies, the more totally you control their minds. The long line of devil drugs from alcohol continues to bedeviling a designer substitute for coca, the kola nut, and coffee: crystal meth, a concentrated smokeable upper. Ritalin is becoming another designer upper drug of choice, supplied inter alia by young people who are sick and tired of being zoned out at school on the prescriptions their doctors, guardians and teachers conspire to require them to take so that they sit still in their seats and master the correct answers on high-stakes tests to make teachers and parents proud. This isn't about, as Nancy Reagan put it, just saying no. It's about taking what doctors and pharmaceutical houses and other corporate advertisers tell you to put in your body instead of your having a chance to experiment and make your own decisions about how to live a mentally and physically cleaner life. It gets so absurd that like Roman circuses, we invest zillions in trying to prove that our athletes are engaging in "fair" competition, when the whole point of competition is winning by getting a physical and mental edge over others. Why do we care? On the whole, I try to avoid investing in competition (got out of the stock market in 1982); I trust decisions we make far more readily when people are deciding about their own lives than I trust any expert including my criminological self, to certify winners and losers.

Drug wars are competitions between rich who are becoming richer and better connected, and as Jeffrey Reiman put it, the young and poor and people of color who go to one form or another of detention. That isn't fair, but worse, I believe that drug wars press us into becoming political sheep, figuring out that our futures depend on whether we decide to drink Diet Pepsi or Coke and avoid coca leaves, focusing us narcissistically on cleaning up our personal selves rather than focusing on what our governments can do to make us safer in fact rather than by promoting utopian visions of a drug-free planet. Let's get real.

I am personally frustrated to see how fitfully marijuana decriminalization progresses. More fundamentally, I am frustrated by how close to the political surface discussion of the very idea of drug control remains.

International Cooperation, Not Unilateral Policies May Be The Best Counterterrorist Strategy[i]

Gary LaFree
Sue-Ming Yang
Martha Crenshaw

While researchers began to assemble open source terrorism event data bases in the late 1960s, until recently most of these data bases excluded domestic attacks. This could be a particularly misleading exclusion for the United States because the U.S. is often perceived to be a central target of transnational terrorism. We began the research on which this essay is based with 53 foreign terrorist groups that have been identified by U.S. State Department and other government sources as posing a special threat to the United States (LaFree, Yang & Crenshaw, 2009). Using newly available data from the Global Terrorism Database (GTD) that includes both domestic and transnational terrorist attacks, we examined 16,916 attacks attributed to these groups between 1970 and 2004. We found that just over three percent of attacks by these designated anti-U.S. groups were actually directed at the United States. Moreover, 99% of the attacks that targeted the United States did not occur on U.S. soil, but were aimed at U.S. targets in other countries (e.g., embassies or multilateral corporations). We also found that over 90% of the non-U.S. attacks were domestic (nationals from one country attacking targets of the same nationality in the same country).

We used group-based trajectory analysis (Nagin, 2005) to examine the different developmental trajectories of U.S. target and non-U.S. target terrorist strikes and concluded that four trajectories best capture attack patterns for both. These trajectories constitute three waves, occurring in the 1970s, 1980s and the early twenty-first century, as well as a trajectory that does not exhibit wave-like characteristics but instead is characterized by irregular and infrequent attacks.

Terrorism event data bases generally use the electronic and print media to collect detailed information on the characteristics of terrorist attacks. LaFree and Dugan (2007) describe eight of these event data bases, with varying coverage going back as far as 1968. In LaFree et al. (2009) we included both domestic and transnational terrorist events in an examination of the attack patterns of 53 foreign non-state organizations identified by the Department of State as posing the greatest threat to Americans. This strategy was animated by the overwhelming public and policy preoccupation with the questions of "why do they hate us" in the wake of the 9/11 attacks (Crenshaw, 2001). This frequently asked question led us to focus on foreign groups that target or have targeted the United States in order to put al Qaeda and the 9/11 attacks in perspective. In addition, most quantitative analysis of terrorism to this point has used terrorist attacks as the unit of analysis, often in relation to country-level data on economic, political and social indicators (e.g., Enders & Sandler, 2006; Li, 2005). We noted a near complete absence of analyses of the groups themselves and their targeting patterns. Thus, we linked attacks to the specific groups that the U.S. government itself deemed most threatening to U.S. interests.

ATTACK PATTERNS OF 53 ANTI-US FOREIGN TERRORIST GROUPS

Total attacks against the United States by these groups were considerably higher in the 1970s and 1980s and declined in the 1990s—a likely consequence of the decline of Marxist-Leninist oriented terrorist groups following the collapse of the Soviet Union and developments in the Middle East after the first Gulf War. After reaching a high point of 38 attacks in 1974, total attacks against the U.S. declined to a low of 5 attacks in 1980. They then increased steeply before reaching the series high point of 41 attacks in 1990 and then again declined steeply. From 1998 to the end of the series attacks on U.S. targets increased somewhat, but remained far below the totals found for much of the 1970s and 1980s.

As with total attacks, total fatal attacks against the United States during this period were relatively high in the 1970s and 1980s and then declined throughout the 1990s. However, the major difference in the two trend lines is that fatal attacks against the U.S. increased strongly in the late 1990s, reaching their highest level (9) in the last year of the series. Apart from the peak in 2004, there were seven years when there were six fatal attacks against the United States: 1973, 1979, 1985, 1988, 1990, 1991 and 2002.

In general, terrorist attacks against the United States from these groups have actually declined since 1990. In fact, they were at a 35-year low just before the 9/11 attacks. The two years in the series with the fewest anti-U.S. attacks were 1995 and 1997. Similarly, fatal attacks were generally more common in the 1970s and 1980s and reached a series low in the decade before 9/11. However, fatal attacks directed at the U.S. have increased since the end of the 1990s. While low in absolute terms, they reached their peak during 2004, the last year included in the analysis.

In our earlier paper we repeated the analysis for total and fatal attacks on non-U.S. targets by the same 53 groups. The most obvious difference between attacks on U.S. and non-U.S. targets was the magnitude of the scales—non-U.S. attacks by these groups were nearly 30 times more common than U.S. attacks. Thus, these groups that are perceived to be dangerous to the United States are in fact much more dangerous to citizens in other countries. In general, non-U.S. trends for total and fatal attacks by these groups resembled a boom and bust cycle with long and fairly steady increases beginning in the 1970s and reaching a peak in the late 1980s/early 1990s and then trailing off significantly until the end of the series. As the U.S. trends also showed, there was an increase in both total non-U.S. attacks and fatal attacks in the late 1990s, but this increase was much less pronounced for the non-U.S. attacks than it was for the U.S. attacks.

In general, total attacks and total fatal attacks against non-U.S. targets reached a peak in the early 1990s, and since then have remained far lower. Total attacks increased slightly in the last few years spanned by the data, but the total number of attacks in 2004 was still lower than it was from 1994 to 1997.

Because no previous data base could compare domestic and transnational terrorist attacks over several decades, we were especially interested in using the GTD to examine the proportion of attacks by these purportedly anti-U.S. groups that were actually directed against U.S. targets. We found that from 1970 to 2004, only 570 (3.4%) of all attacks of these nominally anti-U.S. groups were actually directed against the United States. And of the total anti-U.S. attacks, only 5 (less than one percent) actually occurred on U.S. soil. Major targets for anti-U.S. attacks in other countries included U.S. businesses (233), U.S. diplomats and embassies (106), and the U.S. military (96). The rest of the attacks are widely scattered in terms of target selection and include U.S. educational institutions, journalists, non-governmental organizations, and tourists.

The proportion of terrorist fatalities suffered by the U.S. was almost three times as high as the proportion of total attacks against the United States—although the total proportion of fatalities was still only 9.4 percent. Moreover, a very large proportion of these anti-U.S. fatalities (3,007 or 76.3%) were accounted for by the 9/11 attacks. In short, to a remarkable extent, these data show that over a 35-year period, the attacks of foreign groups identified as especially dangerous to the United States have not been aimed at the U.S. homeland or even at U.S. targets in other countries, but rather at non-U.S. targets. Attacks by these groups on the U.S. are exceptional.

We next explored the ratio of domestic to transnational attacks. Because of al Qaeda's international connection, any attacks by al Qaeda were classified as transnational. For all other groups, a transnational attack was one that occurred outside the boundaries of the countries of origin or against targets of a different nationality within the group's home country. Based on this classification, nearly 90% of the attacks and 84% of the fatalities in the data base were classified as domestic attacks. Of the transnational attacks, 4.9% were committed by al Qaeda and another 34.6% by five groups that had either two or three countries of origin (Black September Organization, the Abu Nidal Organization, al-Gama'at al-Islamiyya, the Eritrean Liberation Front, and the Popular Front for the Liberation of Palestine). In short, the vast majority of total non-U.S. attacks by the anti-U.S. terrorist groups we examined were against domestic targets at home. This finding underscores the fact that most terrorism—like most crime—is a local matter.

We next explored the extent to which these anti-U.S. groups changed their selection of targets over time. In general, the ratios of attacks and fatal attacks against the U.S. to non-U.S. attacks by these terrorist groups were much higher in the 1970s than in subsequent decades, which might explain why many of them were originally considered as "anti-U.S." groups. In fact, for one year in the analysis (1971) the absolute number of attacks against the U.S. actually exceeded the number of non-U.S. attacks. In short, the ratio of U.S. to non-U.S. attacks and fatal attacks has changed over time and in a way that some might find surprising. In general, the designated anti-U.S. groups attacked a much higher proportion of U.S. targets in the 1970s than in subsequent decades.

Rapoport (1992: 1064) has offered an influential argument that since the late nineteenth century, terrorist attacks can be divided into four "political turning-points," or waves. Following Rapoport, we asked whether the attacks of these 53 terrorist groups since 1970 could also be divided into distinct temporal patterns. For this part of the analysis we rely on group-based trajectory analysis (Nagin, 2005). Despite the fact that non-U.S. attacks outnumbered U.S. attacks by nearly thirty to one, the attack trajectories for the U.S. and non-U.S. attacks showed considerable similarity. In both cases, we found that four trajectories best explained the attack patterns from 1970 to 2004. We identified three "waves" of terrorist attacks with relatively sharp ascents and declines (waves in the 1970s, 1980s and early 21st century), and a fourth and largest trajectory of groups that struck for only a short period of time or infrequently. The three waves support the views of Rapoport (1992) and others. However, the activities of approximately half of the groups we analyzed did not fit neatly into one of the three waves.

As with the U.S. analysis, we found that about half the groups fit into a sporadic, low frequency trajectory. Likewise, we found some evidence for waves in the 1970s, and in the 21st century. Compared to the 70s wave for the U.S., the 70s wave for the non-U.S. attacks included about as many terrorist groups. By contrast, compared to the 21st century wave for the U.S., the 21st century wave for the non-U.S. attacks included about three times more terrorist groups. The most striking difference between U.S. and non-U.S. attacks was the huge importance of the 80s wave for the latter. While it included only 11 of the terrorist groups in the analysis, from the late 1970s until the early 1990s, it was responsible for the vast majority of all terrorist attacks by these groups against non-U.S. targets. Thus, while the 70s wave reached a smaller peak in 1978 and a higher peak in 1991, it was totally overshadowed by the rise of the 80s wave. Similarly, while the 21st century wave showed some increases after the mid-1990s, these increases were dwarfed by the 80s wave.

In short, our trajectory analysis revealed considerable similarities in the attack patterns of these groups against U.S. and non U.S. targets over the

35 years covered by the data. For both types of target, we found four distinct trajectories—three sequential waves and a fourth trajectory made up of groups that attack sporadically or were short lived. For both the U.S. and non-U.S. attacks, the sporadic trajectory accounted for nearly half of all the groups in the analysis. However, there was a substantial difference between the U.S. and non-U.S. trajectories for the 80s wave: while the 80s wave was responsible for over 85% of all non-U.S. attacks, it accounted for just over 56% of all U.S. attacks.

Policy Implications

Our findings point to several critical policy implications. First, they underscore the importance of proximity to terrorist targeting. Even though the groups identified here might have ample interest in striking the United States, actually doing so is not an easy task. Anti-American objectives are not sufficient. As Clarke and Newman (2006: 139) put it, "Proximity to the target is the most important target characteristic to terrorists." Mounting an attack against the United States from primary bases outside the United States is extremely challenging. Clarke and Newman (2006: 154) conclude that: "Terrorists are constrained by geography. Like criminals, they will choose targets that are close to their operational base."

Foreign attackers typically face an environment in which they have an imperfect understanding of local language, culture, and daily life. This impediment may explain why recent research (Smith & Damphousse, 2009) has shown that international terrorist attacks against the United States have a much longer planning time horizon than attacks by domestic groups. To overcome cultural and linguistic obstacles, foreign attackers will probably be more likely than domestic attackers to rely on immigrant communities or Diaspora within the target country. Similar reasoning leads Clarke and Newman (2006: 143) to conclude that "externally based terrorists will mount their attacks from locations that are as close as possible to the target." Put in another way, foreign terrorist groups need locals. Thus a recent report by the U.S. State Department (2008) stresses the importance to al Qaeda of local recruits, especially in the West. More generally, the results underscore both the uniqueness and the lethal ingenuity of the 9/11 attacks. Al Qaeda was able to engineer 9/11 without using locals, but instead relied on specially trained and highly qualified foreign operatives. The ability to commandeer such assets is undoubtedly rare.

Second, compared to the percentage of total attacks on U.S. targets, the total percentage of fatalities suffered by U.S. targets is nearly twice as high. This finding suggests that when foreign terrorists do succeed in striking outside their domestic base of operations, they aim to cause large numbers of casualties. As Clarke and Newman (2006: 154) observe, in situations where terrorists have but one opportunity to carry out an attack, they will probably seek to cause as much damage as possible. We could thus expect such attacks to be carefully planned over a long period of time. They will not be easily repeated.

Third, the attack trajectories of about half of the terrorist groups included in the analysis exhibit wave-like boom and bust cycles. This supports earlier research (e.g., Rapoport, 2001; Sedgwick, 2007) that suggests that the decision to resort to terrorism is to some extent contagious. Once an upward trajectory begins, it tends to follow an accelerating path for several years. The cycle hypothesis also underscores the need to improve our understanding of the processes that end a cycle of terrorist attacks (cf., Cronin, 2008; Jones & Libicki, 2008; LaFree & Miller, 2009). But it is also equally important to emphasize that nearly one-half of the groups we examined were responsible for infrequent or sporadic attacks and therefore did not fit this pattern. Hence, their attacks are likely to be the most unpredictable.

Finally, the fact that total attacks by this set of designated anti-U.S. organizations is so lopsidedly against non-U.S. targets is consistent with the proposition that the decision of anti-U.S. terrorist groups to attack the U.S. is often strategic. As Crenshaw (2001) suggests, the United States may become a preferred target if domestic challengers cannot succeed at home unless the scope of the conflict is expanded beyond local boundaries. Crenshaw points out that the U.S. is a useful target for pragmatic as well as ideological reasons: attacks on Americans are highly visible and both acts of terrorism and the American response may well arouse popular emotions in an audience of importance to the terrorist organization. Beyond these considerations, attacks on U.S. targets can be useful for directly influencing American policies—such as compelling the U.S. to withdraw from a military commitment that supports a local government. The bombing of the Marine Barracks in Lebanon in 1983 is a prominent example. Crenshaw also argues that terrorism directed at the U.S. may be a mechanism for drawing the U.S. into a local conflict, perhaps to pressure the government to make reforms or to undermine its legitimacy.

Regardless of the strategic intent behind attacks on the United States, or the virulence of anti-American ideology, our results show that the vast majority of terrorist attacks by foreign groups deemed dangerous to national security by the American government are in fact directed at non-U.S. targets. Local governments suffer the most. U.S. decision-makers might be well-advised to avoid parochialism and keep in mind the fact that even the most seriously threatening groups direct most of their activities elsewhere. This view of the issue suggests that international cooperation, not unilateral policies, may be the best counterterrorist strategy.

REFERENCES

Clarke, R.V. & Newman, G.R. (2006). *Outsmarting the Terrorists.* Westport, CT: Praeger.

Crenshaw, M. (2001). Why America? The globalization of civil war. *Current History, 100,* 425-32.

Cronin, A.K. (2008). *Ending Terrorism: Lessons for Defeating al-Qaeda.* Abingdon, Oxon: Routledge for the International Institute for Strategic Studies.

Enders, W. & Sandler, T. (2006). Distribution of transnational terrorism among countries by income class and geography after 9/11. *International Studies Quarterly, 50,* 367-93.

Jones, S.G. & Libicki, M.C. (2008). *How Terrorist Groups End: Lessons for Countering al Qaeda.* Santa Monica, CA: Rand Corporation.

LaFree, G. & Dugan, L. (2007). Introducing the global terrorism database. *Terrorism and Political Violence, 19,* 181-204.

LaFree, G., Dugan, L. & Korte, R. (2009). The impact of British counter terrorist strategies on political violence in Northern Ireland: Comparing deterrence and backlash models. *Criminology, 47,* 501-530.

LaFree, G. & Miller, E. (2009). Desistance from terrorism: What can we learn from criminology? *Asymmetric Conflict* (forthcoming).

LaFree, G., Yang, S.M. & Crenshaw, M. (2009). Trajectories of terrorism: Attack patterns of foreign groups that have targeted the United States, 1970 to 2004. *Criminology & Public Policy* (forthcoming).

Li, Q. (2005). Does democracy promote or reduce transnational terrorist incidents? *Journal of Conflict Resolution, 49,* 278-297.

Nagin, D.S. (2005). *Group-based Modeling of Development over the Life Course.* Cambridge, MA: Harvard University Press.

Rapoport, D.C. (1992). Terrorism. In M. Hawkesworth and M. Kogan (Eds.), *Encyclopedia of Government and Politics,* Volume II. New York: Routledge.

Rapoport, D.C. (2001). The four waves of modern terrorism. In A.K. Cronin and J.M. Ludes (Eds.), *Attacking Terrorism.* Washington, DC: Georgetown University Press.

Rapoport, D.C. (2005) Four waves of terrorism. In D.K. Gupta (Ed.), *Terrorism and Homeland Security.* Belmont, CA: Wadsworth.

Sedgwick, M. (2007). Inspiration and the origins of global waves of terrorism. *Studies in Conflict and Terrorism, 30,* 97-112.

Smith, B.L. & Damphousse, K.R. (2009). The life course of American eco-terrorists: Informal and formal organizations. *Criminology & Public Policy* (forthcoming).

United States Department of State. (2008). *Country Reports on Terrorism, 2007.* Washington, DC: Office of the Coordinator for Counterterrorism

ENDNOTES

[i] Direct correspondence to Gary LaFree (glafree@crim.umd.edu), Sue-Ming Yang (syang@gsu.edu) and Martha Crenshaw (crenshaw@stanford.edu). Support for this research was provided by the Department of Homeland Security (DHS) through the National Consortium for the Study of Terrorism and Responses to Terrorism (START), grant number N00140510629. Any opinions, findings, and conclusions or recommendations in this document are those of the authors and do not necessarily reflect views of DHS. The following reference contains much of the analysis upon which this essay is based: LaFree, Gary, Sue-Ming Yang and Martha Crenshaw. 2009. *Criminology & Public Policy* (forthcoming).

Applying Crime Theory to Terrorism Research

Leslie W. Kennedy

In the study of approximately 17,000 cases from the Global Terrorism Database, Lafree, Yeng and Crenshaw find that the majority of events involved attacks on local targets; this despite the fact that the groups involved espouse action against the United States as their main philosophical orientation. The conceptualization of terrorism based on these data appear to require a model that focuses less on the international components of terrorism and more on the steps that local authorities can take to prevent and to thwart these attacks. When we get past the "wow" factors of the results, offering the surprising findings that the United States has actually avoided any sustained terrorist action, we can examine these facts for what they mean for the theories that deal with the origination of terror and the responses needed in preparing for and preventing its occurrence. Through this analysis, we find that there are strong parallels to explanations based on criminological theory that can assist in developing a firmer basis for the conceptualization of terrorism, a subject already initially explored in LaFree and Duggan (2004).

In the literature, there has been an interest in what has been called the "crime terror nexus" that has been offered as a way of examining the extent to which criminal actions are connected to terrorism (Cornell, 2006). The suggestion that local law enforcement can assist in detecting and preventing terrorism through the identification of precursor crimes is one part of the nexus. There is, as well, a belief that parallel crimes occur in aid of terrorists, including the involvement of drug cartels in promoting terrorist actions; the forays of terror groups into common crimes, such as robbery, to support their activities; and the use of forgery and identity theft to facilitate terrorist activities.

LaFree et al. suggest another approach, both in their analytical framework and their conclusions: that is, that we view terrorism as we would crime. Using this approach, the behavior of terrorists is assumed to operate along the same principles that provide opportunities and pose constraints to criminals. In other words, the model pays more attention to terrorism in terms of its procedures and consequences and looks less at the motivations that govern it. This is not to say that we can completely understand terrorism without examining the ideological dimensions of these actions or the organizational dynamics of the terror groups in the ways in which they recruit and deploy members. But, if we are interested in discerning the patterns and consequences of terrorism, using techniques drawn from analysis of common crime provides a means by which we can make more sense of the way terrorism evolves.

From the analysis presented in this paper, we can draw four separate conclusions about the similarities of terrorism to crime. First, like crime, terrorism is local. Second, terrorism operates in waves, as does crime. Third, terrorism, like crime, can be prevented. Fourth, terrorism, similar to crime, has elements of risk that can be calculated and can influence whether or not incidents take place. So, let's take a look at each of these, in turn.

LaFree et al. suggest that the major finding of their paper is that terrorism is a local phenomenon. They find that most terrorist acts occur in close proximity to the territory in which the terrorists operate and it is in rare circumstances that these actions actually extend across borders or in distant locations. This is true, they say, because it is difficult to plan and mobilize resources far away from one's familiar territory. There are dangers involved in working in areas that are unknown and where terror members may be seen as strangers, provoking suspicion. In the parallel to crime, the literature on everything from burglary to serial killers suggests the importance of proximity in determining the likelihood that criminals will act (Rossmo, 2008). The police understand that the search radius for many offenders is likely to include areas that they regularly frequent and in which they can easily function without raising questions about their behavior. Even in the case of organized crime groups that may be involved in international transactions, the groups are divided into local segments that can operate in a known territory. To suggest that terrorism is local goes against the popular notion that these groups primarily pose an international threat. Yet, if we see that they are constrained in their actions in the same way that criminals are (restricted knowledge of territory, limited access to valid identities, limited resources, and so on), it is not surprising that if they do act, they will do so in their own country. This is what the Lafree et al. study suggests happens.

Second, Lafree et al. analyze their data over time for patterns of occurrence and find that there are distinct "waves" of terrorism. On the face of it, this appears to be a surprising finding, as each group functions separately and the targets and prevention strategies would seem to be independent of one another. But, like crime, there are patterns in the terrorism data that appear to be a function of the influence of outside factors and a connection to the overall raised level of activity. Obviously, political and economic factors influence these waves but so, too, do the reactions of counter-terror agents and local law enforcement. Again, these waves suggest a similar framework to what is seen with crime. There is also a reactive component to these waves, as with crime, where moral response become important in mobilizing a response to these outbreaks (Sacco, 2005).

Third, there is a strong emphasis in this paper on the role that prevention plays in reducing the likelihood of terrorism. Pushing against the view that terrorism is hard to control and even harder to prevent, LaFree et al. suggest that there are procedures that can work to prevent terror events, some of these borrowed from the ideas of situational crime prevention (Clarke and Newman, 2006) and others that expand beyond target reduction strategies to emphasize the importance of community resistance to terrorism (Hamm, 2007). Again, these approaches resonate with those that focus on more traditional crime prevention.

Fourth, the paper suggests that we might begin to understand the origins of terrorism if we are better able to understand the nature of the risks that we face. In this approach, terrorism is viewed not as a singular event but rather one that emerges out of an environment that spawns threats in a predictable way. This leads us to consider literature in criminology that sees crime and its prevention from the perspective of a risk society, where the use of intelligence and strategic resource allocation strategies prevail over more reactive tactics (Van Brunschot and Kennedy, 2008). The new developments in intelligence led policing (and related approaches connected together in terms of risk based policing) suggest models that emphasize the risk approach to crime may have real relevance in the efforts to counter terrorism.

So, this paper provides not only a surprising set of findings related to terrorism but demonstrates ways in which we can connect the fairly atheoretical perspectives of terrorism research to the more rigorous approaches already used in criminology. The emphasis on proximity, crime waves, prevention, and risk resonates in the work being done in crime analysis. The degree to which this analysis is supported by these approaches shows its usefulness and encourages us to think more broadly about the integration of terrorism research into criminology.

REFERENCES

Clarke, R.V. & Newman, G. (2006). *Outsmarting the Terrorists.* Westport, Conn.: Greenwood Press.

Cornell, S. (2006) The narcotics threat in greater central Asia: From crime-terror nexus to state infiltration? *China and Eurasia Forum Quarterly,* 4(1), 37-67.

Hamm, M. (2007). *Terrorism as Crime from Oklahoma City to Al-Qaeda and Beyond.* NY: NYU Press.

LaFree, G & Dugan, L. (2004). "How Does Studying Terrorism Compare to Studying Crime?" In Deflem, M. (Ed.), *Terrorism and Counter-terrorism: Criminological Perspectives.* pp. 53-74. New York: JAI Press.

Rossmo, D.K. (2008). Place, space, and police investigations. In D. Canter and D. Youngs (Eds.), *Principals of Geographic Offender Profiling,* pp. 149-164. Farnham, UK: Ashgate.

Sacco, V. (2005). *When Crime Waves.* Thousand Oaks, Ca: Sage.

Van Brunschot, E. & Kennedy, L.W. (2008). *Risk, Balance and Security.* Thousand Oaks, Ca.: Sage.

Theoretical and Methodological Innovations in Terrorism Research: A Response to LaFree, Yang and Crenshaw

Cynthia Lum

Large sample, empirical and quantitative research on terrorism often raises more questions than it answers regarding the nature of political violence. The reason for this is the relative newness of empirical quantitative analyses of terrorism and counterterrorism as compared to other topics in the social, political, and behavioral sciences. The growing pains of this research area reflect the sensitive nature of these issues and the difficulty of obtaining quality data. Our knowledge about multiple terrorism incidents, as LaFree, Yang and Crenshaw point out, comes primarily from newspaper or official accounts, data aggregated to large geographic units (such as countries) or from a few incident datasets (e.g., Mickolus et al.'s ITERATE dataset). As Lum et al. (2006) found, not only have the majority of studies published on terrorism occurred after 2000, but there exists only a minute fraction of peer-reviewed studies that are conducted on empirical, quantitative data; only seven of which have actually evaluated the effectiveness of counterterrorism interventions with moderate methodological rigor.

The Global Terrorism Database (GTD), a systematically collected large-scale dataset compiled by LaFree and colleagues, is a major step forward in improving our understanding of politically motivated criminality and opens a wide range of prospects for quantitative and comparative study. However, just as this database offers the potential for addressing current issues through empirical examination, the resulting analyses can also lead to further questions and hypotheses about the nature of terrorism and its prevention. LaFree, Yang and Crenshaw's essay is a compelling example, as their analysis evokes three new lines of inquiry worth pursuing:

1. The connection between theories and applications of criminology and criminal justice with terrorism and counterterrorism, respectively;
2. The use of group-based longitudinal methods (i.e., Nagin's trajectory approach) applied to non-person, and somewhat unstable, units of analysis; and,
3. The influence that macro sociological, historic, and political forces might have on patterns of the use of terrorism by micro units (individuals and groups).

CRIMINOLOGY, CRIME, AND TERRORISM

A number of criminologists have recently undertaken the task of drawing parallels between criminology, crime, and the study of terrorism (see for example, Forst et al., forthcoming; Weisburd et al., forthcoming). The reasons for this are logical; terrorism involves violence, fear, property destruction, and the state's response (or lack thereof) – issues which have been central to the study of criminology and criminal justice. Of course, whether existing criminological theories and prevention techniques can be validly applied to the field of terror studies must be assessed by empirical testing (Lum and Koper, forthcoming). LaFree, Yang and Crenshaw's analysis of GTD data is an example of this endeavor and further reinforces the possibility that parallels can be drawn.

In particular, Kennedy discusses four similarities between terrorism and crime that emerge from LaFree et al.'s analysis – that crime is local, that it operates in waves, that it can be prevented, and that it has elements of risk that can be calculated. In totality, these four characteristics are common propositions of criminological theories, such as rational choice, routine activities, and risk-based perspectives. Routine activities theory is especially interesting, given that LaFree et al. employ a group-based longitudinal analysis to compare trajectories of offending by groups committing domestic and international terrorism. This method of trajectory analysis, discussed further below, implies that global temporal trends can be connected to individual or group behavior over time, which in turn suggests that such global and macro social, political or historical forces may influence different trajectories of individual units. Routine activities theory, as it was initially envisioned by Cohen and Felson (1979), is a crime theory that connects broader social phenomenon with individual deviant behavior, and may be useful in pursuing this endeavor. Future studies that test criminological perspectives, especially those theories that connect global trends to individual behavior, may be fruitful in deepening our understanding of political violence.

In addition to the possible connection of criminological theories and crime prevention applications to the topic of terrorism and counterterrorism, an additional interesting interpretation of the authors' descriptive statistics shares similar themes with studies of criminology. As with "everyday" crime, it appears that perpetrators of terrorism and their crimes are seen as dangerous by those least likely to be affected by them. The authors' analysis shows that there appears to be a disconnect between groups identified as being of greatest concern for the U.S. and the actual risk such groups and their activities pose for U.S. citizens and residents both in the U.S. and abroad. Such a disconnect can lead to negative collateral consequences, especially in advanced democracies, stemming from policies that are developed to address such "moral panics". These might include supporting wars in the name of counterterrorism, fear, discrimination against Muslims and others appearing to be of Middle Eastern descent, or harsh or unreasonable immigration policies. LaFree, Yang and Crenshaw's statistics remind us that the same problems in legitimacy and governance that arise when the state deals with crime can also arise when the state deals with terrorism, again an important focus of future studies.

GROUP-BASED TRAJECTORY ANALYSIS

The second interesting line of inquiry evoked by this essay is methodological: Can longitudinal, group-based approaches used to understand trajectories of "everyday" offending of individuals be validly applied to discern trajectories of the frequency of activities of terroristic groups? If broader social or political phenomena are to be connected with the trends of individual terrorism-wielding groups, methods like trajectory analysis, hierarchical linear modeling, or structural equation modeling may be needed. At first glance, the use of the trajectory approach by the authors appears logical and effective in discerning patterns of terrorism across groups or within the specific types of terrorism (domestic versus international). The authors' use of trajectory analysis allows the 53 seemingly distinct individual time series of incidents attributed to organizations of special concern to the U.S. to be grouped into common temporal paths. Collapsing the trends of these individual groups into a few common temporal trends suggest that terrorism is indeed not random, and may be explained by broader global phenomena.

However, in the case of terrorism-wielding groups, trajectory analysis may be less effective than its current use in criminal justice. Trajectory analysis is most commonly used to examine the life courses of individuals as units of analysis (see Nagin, 1999, 2005). In Weisburd, Bushway, Lum and Yang (2004), trajectory analysis was extended to very small, micro geographic units (street blocks) to examine crime at these places over time. However, individuals, by definition, and even small micro places because of their size, are relatively stable units of analysis. In other words, individual behavior and psychology may change over time, but the crime that an individual commits can always be attributed to that individual (give or take attempts to change names or identities). Similarly, small micro places are relatively stable over time in physical make-up, social and economic conditions, and crime as Weisburd et al. discovered. However, when applied to terror groups, trajectory analysis may not be as meaningful if those groups are more unstable in both membership and ideology over time. Further, there can also be changes over time in how acts are attributed to these groups either by the suppliers of terrorism or by those who categorize and define it; these attributions may have little to do with the group's actual activity.

The consequences of using trajectory analysis on such an unstable unit of analysis could significantly affect conclusions made about the temporal patterns of group behavior. Due to the exploratory nature of trajectory analysis, it is already quite sensitive to both the units that are chosen for analysis, and how actions (for example, terrorism incidents or crimes) are attributed to those units. The more unstable the units are, the more questionable the allocation of incidents, which reduces the validity of the results. This may be the reason why LaFree et al. find half of the groups falling into a sporadic trajectory; the instability of the unit of analysis could reduce the strength of the trends that may have been found had a different allocation of incidents been carried out. The trajectories may be less indicative of actual patterns of behavior, and more reflective of sociological forces that influence why acts are attributed to these groups in the first place. Of course, this problem could also occur with everyday offending (laws change, the public's tolerance may shift, etc.). Terrorism may be much more prone to this sort of misattribution.

MACRO EXPLANATIONS FOR MICRO-LEVEL BEHAVIORS

Let us suppose, however, that the membership and meaning of terror groups was stable enough for trajectory analysis to be applied, and that the four-group solution found by LaFree et al. was valid enough for generalizations. With these assumptions, LaFree, Yang and Crenshaw's essay raises a third line of inquiry: What social and political forces are creating these boom and bust trends seen in the 1970s, 1980s, 1990s, and now? Such broader trends could include (globally or at the national or regional level) modernization, democratization, globalization, industrialization, economic trends, or even regional or country-level forces, such as unemployment or political transition. Determining these causes is important, especially since the authors' title suggests that alternative and international approaches may be more fruitful in reducing and preventing terrorism than those focused on a unilateral actions or bilateral agreements towards tracking and arresting the individuals or groups of greatest concern (e.g., capturing bin Laden or investigating hidden terrorist cells).

Hypothesizing about how broader social and political changes affect terrorism is certainly not new. However, the use of trajectory analysis may be theoretically beneficial, as it allows us to attribute particular trends to specific phenomena over time. In turn, such empirical analysis may provide a better evidence-base as to what might be useful in countering and preventing such trends. Future empirical testing about what contributes to these different trajectories of terrorism by these 53 groups compared to trajectories of the full sample may shed light on the nature of terrorism from a global perspective. For example, waves of terrorism have coincided with a number of mini-waves of democratization found in what is known more generally as the "third wave" of democratization (see Diamond, 1999; Huntington, 1993; Linz and Stepan, 1996). The 1970s began the third wave of democratization, followed by rashes of movements in Latin and South

America in the 1980s, and then Eastern Europe and Asia during the 1990s. The authors' finding of the large wave of non-US attacks in the 1980s , for example, could be the result of political transitions and major social movements in Latin and South America (or event towards the end of the decade, in Eastern Europe) during this time in which these same groups employed themselves (because the data was not shown here, this was uncertain). There may be differences in the relationship between U.S. and non-U.S.-threatening groups as to how trends in their activities relate to democratization, given that the U.S. is often associated with democratization (as with other global phenomena such as modernization, capitalization, or globalization).

If the forces of democratization, modernization and globalization are connected to political violence, then scholars and policy makers need to focus on thinking about what factors might mollify, prevent, or counteract this collateral consequences of these social and political changes. Indeed, international cooperation against terrorism may be one solution, but more needs to be understood about why such phenomena lead to violence, and subsequently, how to anticipate and prevent it.

REFERENCES

Cohen, L. E., & Felson, M. (1979). Social change and crime rate trends: A routine activity approach. *American Sociological Review, 44,* 588-608.

Diamond, L. (1999), *Developing Democracy: Toward Consolidation.* Baltimore, MD: The Johns Hopkins University Press.

Huntington, S. (1993), *The Third Wave: Democratization in the Late Twentieth Century.* Norman, OK: University of Oklahoma Press.

Linz, J. and Stepan, A. (1996), *Problems of Democratic Transition and Consolidation: Southern Europe, South America, and Post-Communist Europe.* Baltimore, MD: Johns Hopkins University Press.

Lum, C., Kennedy, L.W. & Sherley, A. (2006). Are Counter-Terrorism Strategies Effective?: The Results of the Campbell Systematic Review on Counter-Terrorism Evaluation Research. *Journal of Experimental Criminology 2(4).*

Lum, C., & Koper, C. (forthcoming). Is crime prevention relevant to counter-terrorism? In B. Forst, J. Greene, & J. Lynch (eds.), *Criminologists on Terrorism and Homeland Security.* New York: Cambridge University Press.

Mickolus, E., Sandler, T., Murdock, J. and Fleming, P. (1993). *International terrorism: Attributes of terrorist events 1988-91* (ITERATE 3). Dunn Loring: Vinyard Software.

Nagin, D.S. (1999). Analyzing developmental trajectories: A semiparametric group-based approach. *Psychological Methods, 4,* 139-157.

Nagin, D.S. (2005). *Group-Based Modeling of Development.* Cambridge, MA: Harvard University Press.

Weisburd D., Feucht, T., Hakimi, I., Mock, L. & Perry, S. (eds.). (forthcoming). *To Protect and to Serve: Police and Policing in an Age of Terrorism - and Beyond.* New York: Springer.

Weisburd, D., Bushway, S., Lum, C., & Yang, S.-M. (2004). Trajectories of crime at places: A longitudinal study of street segments in the city of Seattle. *Criminology, 42(2),* 283-321.

POLICYMAKERS AND LAW ENFORCEMENT MUST CONSIDER THE UNINTENDED CONSEQUENCES OF THEIR PROPOSED RESPONSES TO EXTREMIST AND TERRORIST GROUPS[i]

STEVEN M. CHERMAK
JOSHUA D. FREILICH
DAVID CASPI

The 9/11 attacks dramatically impacted American society. Greater numbers of scholars from a variety of disciplines began to engage terrorism research. Their goal was to increase understanding of a topic that pre-9/11 might have been viewed as a fringe research area. Lum, Kennedy and Sherley (2006) systematically reviewed over 14,000 studies that evaluated the effectiveness of counter terrorism measures, published since the early 1970s. They found that over 50% percent of the studies were published post 9/11 (p. 7). This conclusion is not surprising because such 'enormous' events help justify the need for changes to be implemented. Accordingly, there was an expectation that policy makers and law enforcement personnel would build upon these studies to develop effective and innovative tactics to combat terrorism.

This paper focuses on policy makers and law enforcement responses to terrorist acts and the threat posed by political extremists.[ii] A review of the accumulated empirical evidence demonstrates three important points. First, political extremists pose a threat to public safety. Second, these threats are dynamic and change over time. Third, policy interventions and strategic tactics often have unintended consequences. Sometimes these interventions have created backlash effects that led to greater numbers of crimes. Policy makers, law enforcement personnel and crime analysts must therefore carefully monitor political extremists and consider the unintended consequences of their proposed responses to extremist and terrorist groups.

We review these three points and then outline alternative policies that the authorities could implement in response to our findings.

1. Political extremists pose a threat to public safety

Political extremists pose a risk to the American community. Recently, attention has focused on Al Qaeda because of the devastating attacks it committed on September 11th and its desire to strike again within the United States. However, LaFree, Dugan, Fogg and Scott (2006) found that the United States also faces homegrown threats as domestic terrorism attacks generally outnumber international ones 7 to 1 in a typical year. Hewitt (2003; see also Smith, 1994) found that between 1954 and 2000 over 3,000 terrorist incidents were perpetrated in the United States, mostly by domestic extremists. These acts claimed over 700 lives, and caused hundreds of millions of dollars in damage.

Freilich and Chermak's (2009a) United States Extremist Crime Database (ECDB) study examines all crimes committed by far-right[iii] extremists in the United States since 1990. The ECDB includes federal and state crimes, offenses committed by groups and lone wolves, violent and nonviolent crimes, and ideological and non-ideological offenses. They have identified over 4,300 criminal events, including over 275 homicide incidents involving more than 530 homicide victims (and over 360 homicide victims excluding the Oklahoma City bombing). The victims included over 40 law-enforcement personnel killed in the line of duty.

Smith and Damphousse's (2009) American Terrorism Study (ATS) documents the tremendous property damage and financial losses that left-wing environmental and animal rights attacks have caused in the United States. Indeed, one group "The Family" committed twenty-one arson and "ecotage" incidents between 1995 and 2001. The group's most serious act was an arson attack at the Vail ski resort in the late 1990s that caused over $25 million dollars in damage.

2. Terrorist threats are dynamic and change over time

A review of the accumulated empirical evidence finds that terrorist threats are not static. Smith's (1994) study of terrorist strikes in the United States found far-left groups to be the most active in the 1970s. Carlson (1995) surveyed police chiefs in large-sized American cities (>100,000) in the early 1990s. He asked the chiefs to rank the top four groups that, in their opinion, were most likely to commit a terrorist act within the next two years. Despite the celebrated nature of the 1993 Trade Center bombing, police chiefs did not think that Middle-Eastern terrorists posed the greatest threat. Instead, anti-abortion perpetrators and white supremacists were rated the two greatest threats. Riley and Hoffman's (1995) RAND survey of state and local agencies over two years in the early 1990s similarly found that issue specific organizations (e.g., anti-abortion) and right-wing groups posed the greatest terrorist threat. Freilich, Chermak and Simone's (2009; see also Riley, Treverton, Wilson & Davis, 2005) more recent survey of state police agencies found that almost all respondents strongly agreed that Islamic Jihadists were the top national security threat and most strongly agreed or agreed that they were a significant threat to state security.

These results demonstrate that terrorism threats are dynamic and change over time.   Carlson's results from almost fifteen years ago placed anti-abortion activists as the greatest threat. Freilich, Chermak and Simone (2009) found that state police agencies, however, do not currently rate them as posing a great threat to either national or their state's security. The attacks of September 11th have clearly impacted concerns about the potential threat of Islamic extremists in the United States. While Smith's (1994) domestic terrorism study found far-left groups to be the most active in the 1970s, currently state police agencies do not rate them a major threat on either the national or state-level.

Similarly, current terrorism scholars rarely examine the militia movement. In the 1990s, however, this movement grew in response to concern about political issues like gun control and specific incidents (e.g., Ruby Ridge and Waco), of perceived government overreaching. The militia movement at that time garnered much attention and was viewed as a significant threat (Chermak, 2002).

Relatedly, the strength of individual groups, and the larger the movement they belong to, also evolve over time. Research by LaFree and Dugan (2007), Jones and Libicki (2008) and Rapaport (1992; see also Freilich, Chermak & Caspi, 2009) demonstrate that most terrorist and extremist groups last less than one year. For a legal group to exist and thrive, members must be creative in fundraising, recruitment, generating support, propagandizing, using technology and other types of expertise. For groups that choose to employ violence there are additional obstacles to overcome. Both extremist and terrorist groups and their external environment are dynamic. For example, research finds that the militia movement was impacted by the Oklahoma City bombing, forcing many individuals to leave the movement, others to join, and some to go underground or seek other extremist organizations in fear of government infiltration (Chermak, 2002). Extremist organizations and terrorist groups must adapt to changes occurring in their external environment. It is not surprising therefore that most terrorist and extremist groups are unable to so and fail in a relatively short time.

Empirical evidence also finds that the rise and fall of extremist organizations are linked to critical events and organizational level variables that enhance or disrupt the group. For example, Freilich, Chermak and Caspi (2009) identified factors that produced growth and decline within four far right extremist organizations (e.g., the National Alliance, the Aryan Brotherhood, Public Enemy Number 1, and the Oklahoma Constitutional Militia). The groups that grew did do because they (1) had able leadership that set forth a clear ideological message and goals, (2) undertook concrete actions to further their ideology and goals and had the finances necessary for this, (3) took advantage of political opportunities, and (4) were internally cohesive. The groups declined, however, because of organizational instability and/or responses by law enforcement and non-state-actors, such as watch-groups. The fall/decline of a particular group likely affects other groups in the same movement.

3. Policy makers must carefully monitor political extremists and consider the unintended consequences of their proposed interventions

These findings suggest that law enforcement intelligence and analysis have an important role to play in countering terrorism. Again, one obstacle is that understanding which threats should be prioritized is like hitting a moving target and analysts must engage in dynamic analyses (Freilich, Chermak & Simone, 2009; Sageman, 2008; Smith, 1994). Changes in contextual and organizational factors may cause a group to increase or decrease in strength and potential to commit violent acts. Paying attention to such changes will allow law enforcement to better assess a group's threat level as it changes, differentiate between truly dangerous groups and less dangerous groups, immediate versus potential future threats, and develop policies to best address these threats (Chermak, Freilich & Shemtob, 2009; Duffy & Brantley, 1997; McGarrell, Freilich & Chermak, 2007).

Presently, different types of counter terrorism strategies have been implemented to reduce the number of terrorism attacks in the United States and abroad. Most strategies are "hard control" measures, such as retaliatory attacks, increasing punishments, and using law enforcement measures to 'crack down' on certain active groups. Lum and colleagues' (2006: 22) systematic review, concludes that there are few positive results: "Many effects are close to, or cannot be statistically discerned from, a zero effect."

A review of recent empirical research produces two conclusions. First, previous studies have found that responses by both the state and non-state actors may contribute to the decline of specific terrorist or extremist groups. Jones and Libicki's (2008) study that examined 268 terrorist groups worldwide found that 40% of the organizations ended because local law enforcement and intelligence agencies arrested or eliminated key members. Smith (1994: 91; see also Hamm, 1993) concludes that skinhead groups declined in the United States in the 1980s because of a "double barreled blast of aggressive federal criminal prosecutions and private civil rights attorneys. Hamm (2007) reached similar conclusions about the demise of the Arizona Patriots (see also Crothers, 2003; Hewitt, 2003; Horschem, 1991; Kaplan, 1996; McAdam, 1999; Ruggiero, 2005).

Second, and importantly, such responses, although contributing to declines in these group, may also have unintended consequences. For example, counterterrorism strategies related to disrupting the funding of terrorist organizations, such as regulations in the banking sector and freezing funds from charities, "may have caused terrorist elements to utilize different techniques for fundraising and money laundering" (O' Neil 2007: 5). Hamm's (2007) important analysis examining terrorist involvement in traditional crime also supports this point. He discusses how terrorist groups seek standard or traditional means of funding until such funding is unavailable. Groups then adapt and seek other sources of revenue. Hamm examines the effects of a crackdown on the IRA's efforts to raise money. In the 1970s, law enforcement shut down the IRA's fund raising efforts in the United States, but this success increased the IRA's reliance on other sources of revenue. This shift may have also increased the harm caused by the organization as it moved to more traditional criminal and organized crime activities to finance operations, including bank robberies, smuggling goods and weapons, and extortion.

Lum and colleagues' (2006: 26) systematic review that evaluates several types of counter terrorism measures also found that such interventions often produce unintended and counterintuitive findings. For example, the implementation of metal detectors in airports were effective in decreasing airport hijackings, but caused displacement effects and increased the use of other types of terrorism, such as kidnappings, assassinations, and bombings.

Similarly, Freilich, Chermak and Caspi (2009) found that after the National Alliance and the Aryan Brotherhood imploded for various reasons after the deaths of their well known leaders, other groups, such as skinhead organizations, seemed to benefit. They concluded that groups within a larger movement are inter-related. Strategies that might mitigate activities against only one sector of a movement may result in unanticipated consequences to other sectors of that movement.

Relatedly, it seems obvious that successful law enforcement operations can eliminate a group or individuals that have engaged in crimes. This appears to bolster deterrence and incapacitation views that call for harsh responses to extremist groups. Many watch-groups call for firm government actions against extremist organizations (Chermak, 2002; Freilich, 2003).

A review of empirical research in this area again finds, however, that there may be unintended consequences to such responses. Perceived harsh government and police actions may lead to consciousness raising (Dobratz & Shanks-Meile, 1997; McAdam, 1982) that outrages the wider movement and cause a backlash. Other extremist groups and the movement at large may grow and individuals and groups may become further radicalized and turn to violence. A growing number of studies find that harsh government responses to terrorism often have no deterrent impact and sometimes lead to a backlash (Kaplan, 1996; Jones & Libicki, 2008; LaFree, Dugan & Korte, 2009; McCauley, 2006; Pridemore & Freilich, 2007; Sageman, 2008; Silke, 2005; 2008). For example, a systematic review of the impact of counterterrorism strategies concluded that retaliatory strikes after a terrorist incident (i.e., the United States attack on Libya in 1986 in response to a bombing in Berlin) actually led to additional attacks. In fact, Lum and colleagues (2006: 29) conclude, the attack on Libya resulted in a statistically significant increase in the number of terrorist attacks in the short run, with a weighted effect size of 15.33 events.

Similarly, Freilich, Chermak and Caspi (2009) found that the racist Aryan Nations group capitalized on the killings of Gordon Kahl and Robert Mathews by law-enforcement in the 1980s and the organization's popularity increased. In addition, Mathews partially created the notorious group "The Order"- the premiere domestic terrorist group in the 1980s (responsible for five murders and spectacular armored car robberies) because of anger over Kahl's death. The National Alliance, the militia movement and other far-right groups grew in reaction to the to the government's excesses at Waco and Ruby Ridge In the early 1990s.

ALTERNATIVE POLICIES

Based upon a review of the empirical findings in this area we conclude that the authorities must balance a carefully calibrated campaign that eliminates dangerous groups and stresses violence will not be tolerated, with responses that avoid outraging and possibly increasing crime from the larger movement. There are several options to consider. First, law enforcement should only use deadly or harsh responses as a last resort. For instance, harsh government actions at Waco and Ruby Ridge in the early 1990s that led to the death of cult members and far-rightists outraged the anti-government far-right. Most observers conclude that these harsh policies led to a backlash and fueled the growth of the paramilitary right (Chermak 2002; Freilich 2003, Wright, 2007). Conversely, the ADL (2003; see also Wright, 2007) explains that law enforcement's nuanced and patient response that allowed far-right extremists to save face led to a peaceful resolution of sieges in Montana in 1996 and in Texas in 1997.

The government should consider accompanying harsh law enforcement actions against violent groups with "outreach" programs to non-violent wings of extremist movements. These strategies should encourage members of the movement to forsake illegal behaviors in favor of participation in the political system or other legal activities. Jones and Libicki's (2008) study found that 43% of 268 terrorist groups worldwide- the largest category- ended because of a transition to the political process. Significantly, F.B.I. agents charged with monitoring domestic extremists have made similar arguments. Agents Duffy and Brantley (1997) created a typology of four categories of far-right militia groups that ranged from non-criminal to organizations that conducted serious- e.g., homicide, bombings- crimes. Duffy and Brantley (1997: 2) urged local police to open a dialogue with leaders from the two non-violent categories "so that the two sides can voice their concerns and discuss relevant issues in a non-confrontational way."

These strategies should be used today, especially when law-enforcement is involved in a crackdown on a specific movement. These outreach policies could build upon law-enforcement efforts to build bridges with immigrant communities that are suspicious of the government (Clarke & Newman, 2006; Freilich & Chermak, 2009b) with extremist movements that are also hostile to the government and the police. Newman and Clarke (2008) recently set forth steps that police agencies could take to reduce tension with migrant communities that have come under suspicion because a few terrorists, such as the 9/11 hijackers, used them to fit in. These steps included assigning community police agents to solely work with migrant communities, taking advantage of ethnic media outlets to communicate with the larger community, and clearly publicizing the police agency's mission and policies. Similar strategies could be taken with the "moderate" portion of extremist movements. In addition, to initiating dialogue with non-violent groups, agencies could assign officers to appear on extremist media outlets. Such campaigns should explain the government response, and note that it is only directed at those who commit crimes. Authorities should reassure non-criminal members of the movement that their rights will be protected and encourage them to focus on lawful activities while stressing that violence will not be tolerated.

While there are hard-core terrorists who have no interest in pursuing change through legitimate processes, it is also true that most extremist individuals and groups do not engage in violence or terrorism themselves. Further, some "terrorists" are reluctant participants and are not strongly committed to an extremist ideology. McGarrell and colleagues (2007) discuss how most (nearly 70 percent) of the individuals linked to a series of bombings and detained terrorists were not ideologically-committed.

Finally, backlash effects are usually found when a government takes action after a crime or terrorist act has been committed. Strategies that prevent- for e.g., by using situational crime prevention- the crimes these groups commit to raise funds and further their objectives (Clarke & Newman, 2006; Freilich & Newman, 2009; Hamm, 2007; Jones & Libicki, 2008; Newman & Clarke, 2008) may preempt the harsh police responses to these crimes and thus avoid backlash effects.

CONCLUSION

This paper focuses on policy makers and law enforcement responses to terrorist and extremist groups. A review of the accumulated empirical evidence found that extremists and terrorists pose a threat to public safety. In addition, these threats are not static but evolve over time. Third, and importantly, policy and law enforcement responses often have unintended consequences. Many harsh government responses are ineffective, lead to unexpected adaptations by groups and/or movements, do not deter and instead may lead to a backlash. We concluded the chapter by discussing other policies such as, restraint and outreach programs to extremist groups and situational crime prevention tactics that may yield more effective results.

Future research must pay more attention to evaluating responses to terrorism. While empirical research on terrorism has historically been lacking, in the last few years it has blossomed. Systematic examinations of counterterrorism policies, however, have lagged. Lum et al.'s review uncovered only seven studies with rigorous designs. As policy makers continue to experiment with new multidimensional strategies and other emerging tactics researchers should keep pace and systematically examine these responses.

REFERENCES

ADL (Anti-Defamation League). 2003. Deadly domains: Standoffs with extremists. Retrieved January 2, 2009 from www.adl.org/LEARN/ safety/deadly_domains.asp.

Barkun, M. (1989). Millennarian aspects of white supremacist movements. *Terrorism and Political Violence, 1,* 409- 434.

Berlet, C. & Lyons, M.N. (2000). *Right-wing Populism in America: Too Close for Comfort.* New York: The Guilford Press

Carlson, J.R. (1995). The future terrorists in America. *American Journal of Police, 14,* 71- 91.

Chermak, S.M. (2002). *Searching for a Demon: The Media Construction of the Militia Movement.* Boston: Northeastern University Press.

Chermak, S.M., Freilich, J.D. & Shemtob, Z. (2009). Law enforcement training and the domestic far-right. *Criminal Justice and Behavior.* Forthcoming.

Clarke, R.V. & Newman, G.R. (2006). *Outsmarting the Terrorists.* New York: Praeger Security International.

Coates, J. (1987). *Armed and Dangerous: The Rise of the Survivalist Right.* New York: Hill and Wang.

Crothers, L. (2003). *Rage on the Right: The American Militia Movement from Ruby Ridge to Homeland Security.* New York: Rowman & Littlefield Publishers.

Dobratz, B.A. & Shanks-Meile, S.L. (1997). *White Power, White Pride! The White Separatist Movement in the United States.* New York: Twayne Publishers.

Duffy, J.E. & Brantley, A.C. (1997). Militias: Initiating contact. Federal Bureau of Investigation Law Enforcement Bulletin. Available online: http://?www.fbi.gov/library/leb/1997/July975.htm.

Durham, M. (2003). The American far right and 9/11. *Terrorism and Political Violence, 15,* 96-111.

Freilich, J.D. (2003). *American Militias: State-level Variations in Militia Activities.* New York: LFB Scholarly LLC.

Freilich, J.D. & Chermak, S.M. (2009a). United States Extremist Crime Database (ECDB), 1990- 2008: Preliminary results. Presented at the Department of Homeland Security University Network Research and Education Summit, Washington D.C. (March).

Freilich, J.D. & Chermak, S.M. (2009b). Preventing deadly encounters between law enforcement and American far-rightists. In J.D. Freilich and G.R. Newman (Guest Eds.), *Crime Prevention Studies,* Vol. 26: Countering Terrorism Through Situational Crime Prevention. Monsey, NY: Criminal Justice Press. Forthcoming.

Freilich, J.D., Chermak, S.M. & Caspi, D. (2009). Critical events in the life trajectories of domestic extremist groups: A case study analysis of four violent white supremacist groups. *Criminology & Public Policy.* Forthcoming.

Freilich, J.D., Chermak, S.M. & Simone, J. (2009). Surveying American state police agencies about terrorism threats, terrorism sources, and terrorism definitions. *Terrorism and Political Violence.* Forthcoming.

Freilich, J.D. and Newman, G.R. (Guest Eds.). (2009). *Crime Prevention Studies, Volume 26: Countering Terrorism Through Situational Crime Prevention.* Monsey, NY: Criminal Justice Press. Forthcoming.

Gruenewald, J., Freilich, J.D. & Chermak, S.M. (2009). An overview of the domestic far-right and its criminal activities. In B. Perry and R. Blazak (Eds.), *Hate Crimes: Hate Crime Offenders* (pp. 1-21). Westport, CT: Praeger

Hamm, M.S. (1993). *American Skinheads: The Criminology and Control of Hate Crime.* Westport, CT: Praeger.

Hamm, M.S. (2007). *Terrorism as Crime: From Oklahoma City to Al Qaeda and Beyond.* New York City: New York University Press.

Hewitt, C. (2003). *Understanding Terrorism in America: From the Klan to Al Qaeda.* New York: Routledge

Horschem, H.J. (1991). The decline of the Red Army Faction. *Terrorism and Political Violence, 3,* 61-74.

Jones, S.M. & Libicki, M.C. (2008). *Why Terrorist Groups End: Lessons for Countering Al Qaida.* Santa Monica: Rand Corporation.

Kaplan, J. (1993). The context of American Millenarian revolutionary theology: The case of the 'Identity Christian' church of Israel. *Terrorism and Political Violence, 5,* 30-82.

Kaplan, J. (1995). Right wing violence in North America. *Terrorism and Political Violence, 7,* 44-95

Kaplan, J. (1996). Absolute rescue: Absolutism, defensive action and the resort to force. In M. Barkun (Ed.), *Millennialism and Violence* (pp. 128-163). London: Frank Cass & Co. Ltd.

LaFree, G. & Dugan, L. (2007). Introducing the Global Terrorism Database. *Terrorism and Political Violence, 19,* 181- 204.

LaFree, G., Dugan, L., Fogg, H. & Scott, J. (2006, May). Building a Global Terrorism Database. Final Report to the National Institute of Justice

LaFree, G., Dugan, L. & Korte, R. (2009). The impact of British counter terrorist strategies on political violence in Northern Ireland: Comparing deterrence and backlash models. *Criminology, 47,* 501-530.

Lum, C., Kennedy, L.W. & Sherley, A.J. (2006). The Effectiveness of Counter-Terrorism Strategies: A Campbell Systematic Review. Available online: http://db.c2admin.org/doc-pdf/Lum_Terrorism_Review.pdf

McAdam, D. (1982). *Political Process and the Development of Black Insurgency.* Chicago: University of Chicago Press.

McAdam, D. (1999). The decline of the civil rights movement. In J. Freeman and V. Johnson (Eds.), *Waves of Protest: Social Movements Since the Sixties* (pp. 325- 348). New York: Rowman & Littlefield.

McCauley, C. (2006). Jujitsu Politics: Terrorism and responses to terrorism. In P. Kimmel and C.E. Stout (Eds.), *Collateral Damage: The Psychological Consequences of America's War on Terrorism* (pp. 45-66). New York: Praeger

McGarrell, E. F., Freilich, J.D. & Chermak, S.M. (2007). Intelligence-led policing as a framework for responding to terrorism. *Journal of Contemporary Criminal Justice, 23,* 142 –158.

Mullins, W.C. (1988). *Terrorist Organizations in the United States.* Springfield, IL: Charles C. Thomas Books.

Newman, G.R. & Clarke, R.V. (2008). *Policing Terrorism: An Executive's Guide.* Washington, DC: Office of Community Oriented Policing Services.

O'Neil, S. (2007). *Terrorist Precursor Crimes: Issues and Options for Congress.* Washington, DC: Congressional Research Service.

Pridemore, W.A. & Freilich, J.D. (2007). The impact of state laws protecting abortion clinics and reproductive rights on crimes against abortion providers: Deterrence, backlash or neither? *Law and Human Behavior,* 31, 611- 627.

Rapoport, D. (1992). Terrorism. In M. Hawkesworth and M. Kogan (Eds.), *Encyclopedia of Government and Politics,* Volume II (pp. 1061-1072). New York: Routledge.

Riley, J.K. & Hoffman, B. (1995). *Domestic Terrorism: A National Assessment of State and Local Preparedness.* Santa Monica: Rand Corporation.

Riley, J.K., Treverton, G.F., Wilson, J.M. & Davis, L.M. (2005). *State and Local Intelligence in the War on Terrorism.* Santa Monica: RAND Corporation.

Ruggiero, V. (2005). Brigate Rosse: Political violence, criminology and social movement theory. *Crime Law and Social Change, 43,* 289- 307.

Sageman, M. (2008). *Leaderless Jihad: Terror Networks in the Twenty-first Century.* Philadelphia: University of Pennsylvania Press.

Silke, A. (2005). Fire of Iolus: The role of state countermeasures in causing terrorism and what needs to be done. In T. Bjorgo (Ed.), *Root Causes of Terrorism* (pp.241-255). Oxford: Routledge.

Silke, A. (2008). Holy warriors: Exploring the psychological processes of jihadi radicalization. *European Journal of Criminology, 5,* 99- 123.

Smith, B.L. (1994). *Terrorism in America: Pipe Bombs and Pipe Dreams.* Albany: State University of New York.

Smith, B.L. & Damphousse, K.R. (2009). The life course of American eco-terrorists: Informal and formal organizations. *Criminology & Public Policy.* Forthcoming.

Sprinzak, E. (1995). Right wing terrorism in a comparative perspective: The case of split delegitimization. *Terrorism and Political Violence, 7,* 17-43.

Weinberg, L. (1993). The American radical right: Exit, voice, and violence. In P. Merkl and L. Weinberg (Eds.), *Encounters with the Contemporary Radical Right* (pp. 185- 203). Boulder, CO: Westview.

Wright, S.A. (2007). *Patriots, Politics and the Oklahoma City Bombing.* Cambridge: Cambridge University Press.

ENDNOTES

[i] This chapter includes new material and also draws from materials published in two larger articles that appeared in the July 2009 issue of Terrorism and Political Violence (Freilich, Chermak & Simone (2009)) and the August 2009 issue of Criminology and Public Policy (Freilich, Chermak & Caspi (2009)). The research was supported by the United States Department of Homeland Security through the National Consortium for the Study of Terrorism and Responses to Terrorism (START), grant number N00140510629. However, any opinions, findings, and conclusions or recommendations in this document are those of the authors and do not necessarily reflect views of the U.S. Department of Homeland Security.

[ii] "Political extremists" are operationalized as individuals who (1) subscribe to a belief system that endorses a political, economic, religious, or social goal (LaFree and Dugan, 2007), and believe that (2) the American government and/or society is evil and corrupt, and poses a threat to their group and/or cause, and as a result (3) illegal behaviors including violence against the American government and/or society are necessary. The overwhelming majority of political extremists who killed, wounded, or targeted civilians or law enforcement personnel in the United States since 1990 were supporters of far-right, far-left, Islamic Jihadist, Black nationalist, Jewish extremist (e.g., JDL) Puerto Rican nationalist (e.g., FALN) beliefs or single issue (like anti-abortion, or pro-animal rights and environmental rights) causes. Although the ideologies of these movements diverge widely all meet the requirements above. All endorse worldviews that proclaim both a political, economic, religious or social goal as well as a hatred for the American government or society.

[iii] Defining the domestic far-right is not easy because there is no universally-accepted definition and prior research has not sufficiently addressed this issue. Drawing upon our systematic review of studies (Gruenewald, Freilich, and Chermak, 2009) published on far-right extremism in general and its association with political crimes in particular-- including important works that offered typologies, definitions and descriptions (see, for e.g., Barkun, 1989; Berlet & Lyons, 2000; Coates, 1987; Duffy & Brantley, 1997, Durham, 2003; Kaplan, 1993; 1995; Mullins, 1988; Smith, 1994; Sprinzak, 1995; see also Dobratz & Shanks-Meile, 1997; Weinberg, 1993), we rely upon the following description. The domestic far-right is composed of individuals or groups that subscribe to aspects of the following ideals: they are fiercely nationalistic (as opposed to universal and international in orientation), anti-global, suspicious of centralized federal authority, reverent of individual liberty (especially their right to own guns, be free of taxes), believe in conspiracy theories that involve a grave threat to national sovereignty and/or personal liberty and a belief that one's personal and/or national "way of life" is under attack and is either already lost or that the threat is imminent (sometimes such beliefs are amorphous and vague, but for some the threat is from a specific ethnic, racial, or

religious group), and a belief in the need to be prepared for an attack either by participating in paramilitary preparations and training and survivalism. It is important to note that mainstream conservative movements and the mainstream Christian right are not included.

RECOMMENDATIONS ABOUT RECOMMENDATIONS: REGARDING THE NEED FOR SUFFICIENT FUNDING, SOPHISTICATED DATA ANALYSIS, AND DISCIPLINE MATURITY

KELLY DAMPHOUSSE

I started studying terrorism in September 1994 when I became an assistant professor at the University of Alabama at Birmingham. My department chair, Brent Smith, had just published what has become the seminal book on American terrorism (Smith, 1994) and he was working on a paper that was eventually published in Criminology. A reviewer had suggested that he add structural equation modeling to his paper and Brent asked me for assistance. That anonymous reviewer's request was one of the luckiest breaks of my career.

At that time, most Americans knew very little about terrorism, except that it was something that happened in the Middle East. Even though terrorists had attempted to destroy the World Trade Center in 1993, terrorism was a niche topic even among criminologists (Damphousse, Lawson, and Smith, 2004). Indeed, in the immediate aftermath of the 1995 Oklahoma City bombing, the initial suspects were said to be Middle Eastern terrorists. Still, between 1995 and 2001, academic terrorism research suffered from a lack of federal attention and funding (apart from the short-lived research portfolio at the Memorial Institute for the Prevention of Terrorism). There were no terrorism-specific requests for proposals at the National Institute of Justice and NIJ funded few terrorism-related studies. Indeed, the bulk of NIJ's terrorism portfolio flowed through MIPT. In addition, no terrorism studies were funded by the National Science Foundation or the National Institute of Health during that time (Zahn and Strom, 2004). The result was that a criminological approach to terrorism suffered from the lack of quality data and a relatively narrow methodological and theoretical perspective. Most studies, especially those conducted by historians and political scientists, focused on small-sample case studies of imprisoned terrorists – not unlike criminological studies from the 1920s.

It has become passé to say so, but 9/11 changed all that. For the first time, criminologists noticed that terrorism was an important issue that was not going away, allowing it to become "mainstream." Either attracted by the anticipated huge increase in terrorism-related research requests for proposals or, more likely, by an appreciation for how terrorism fits into our discipline (LaFree and Dugan, 2004), research and expertise on terrorism blossomed in the first decade of the current century. Perhaps nothing shows how the federal government's approach to terrorism research changed post-9/11 better than the creation of no fewer than eleven centers of excellence at research universities across the nation – funded as part of the mandate that created the Department of Homeland Security. Criminologists have benefitted most greatly from the National Consortium for the Study of Terrorism and Responses to Terrorism (START) located at the University of Maryland.

Unfortunately, as more social scientists began terrorism research in order to make policy recommendations, it did not take long to discover that there was not much data available to actually study. There was no "National Longitudinal Terrorist Survey" or "Uniform Terrorism Report" (i.e., the "NLTS" or "UTR") to be downloaded from ICPSR. This is not surprising, given the relative rarity of terrorism attacks and the lack of federal funding available prior to 9/11. So, the short history of the criminological approach to terrorism has focused on (1) the analysis of the few available criminological datasets that pre-dated 9/11 (e.g., Smith and Damphousse's American Terrorism Study [Smith and Damphousse, 1996; 1998]), (2) the discovery and enhancement of historical incident-based terrorism datasets (e.g., Gary LaFree's heroic efforts to turn the Pinkerton Global Intelligence Service data into the Global Terrorism Database [LaFree, Dugan, Fogg, and Scott, 2006]), or (3) the creation of new terrorism databases from whole cloth designed to answer specific questions.

The recent work of Chermak and Freilich is among the best of this latter category – representing a new generation of terrorism researchers who, like Brent Smith thirty years earlier, have created a methodology that allows them to provide answers to important empirical questions about terrorism in America (Freilich and Chermak, 2009). For the past few years, Chermak and Freilich have been creating the United States Extremist Crime Database based on open-source records (primarily media reports). Their work on this important new database, along with their participation in the University of Maryland's START Center, makes them well-placed to begin making empirically informed policy recommendations about counter-terrorism efforts. Their essay (co-authored with David Caspi) is wisely based on three major findings from previous studies upon which policy makers should rely when setting policy.

First, despite limited public awareness about the history of American extremism, seasoned researchers and federal law enforcement know full well that political violence in America neither starts with 9/11 nor ends with Al Qaeda and other international terrorists. Indeed, perhaps the greatest threat to American security is terror from within (i.e., domestic terrorism). Frankly, this has most always been the case – terrorism only became "internationalized" in the 1970s, especially following the Black September attacks at the 1972 Olympic games in Munich (Hoffman, 2006). Most terrorism is domestic terrorism and that has been the American experience in the past half-century (with some obvious exceptions). With the rise of the violent left in the 1960s and 1970s, followed by the rise of the violent right in the 1980s and 1990s, and more recent increases in violence related to the anti-abortion movement and the earth/animal liberation movements, American terrorism scholars have long recognized the serious threats that exist within our own borders. Thus, while policy makers and law enforcement are correct to worry about terrorism from afar, they are also wise to not ignore the threat from the home front.

Second, terrorism is not static. While Chermak, et al. focus on the dynamic terrorism threat (suggesting that American law enforcement agencies will face a variety of terrorist threats over relatively short periods of time), it is also true that terrorist groups themselves change (or evolve) over time to survive. There is an interesting symbiotic relationship between terrorists and counter-terrorists. In this "evolution of revolution," we can observe counter-terrorist actors adapting to new trends by terrorist groups, who, in turn, adapt to their changing conditions in order to survive.

The best example of this evolutionary process may be the change in group structure that was observed among the violent right in the mid-1990s. When the Aryan Nations' World Congress declared war in 1983 - the so-called "War in 84" (de Armond, 2005), the federal government's response mirrored the successful counter-terrorism strategy employed by the Algerian government decades earlier (Morgan, 2007). The strategy included arresting lower-level participants, learning about the terrorist group leadership in exchange for a favorable plea bargain, and then "beheading" the terrorist groups by charging the leaders with seditious conspiracy (Damphousse and Shields, 2007). This shift in strategy by the federal government occurred only after the adoption of the new Attorney General Guidelines 1983 that were themselves a response to increased violence among the extreme left (Smith, 1994).

Even though many of the subsequent conspiracy trials resulted in acquittals, the leadership of the extreme right recognized the threat that their organizational structure posed. In 1992, therefore, Louis Beam introduced the concept of "leaderless resistance" in an effort to shield leaders of the violent right from being exposed to criminal prosecution (Beam, 1992). The result was a shift from large terrorism enterprises (the focus of the federal authorities) to the creation of the "lone wolf." Tim McVeigh's actions in Oklahoma City in 1995 may well have been one of the first examples of leaderless resistance. It is interesting to note that the FBI acknowledged this change in its 2004-2009 Strategic Plan, signalling a possible modification of future counter-terrorism strategy.

The most significant domestic terrorism threat over the next five years will be the lone actor, or "lone wolf" terrorist. They typically draw ideological inspiration from formal terrorist organizations, but operate on the fringes of those movements. (FBI, 2007: 15).

Thus, policy makers must understand that terrorism is not a monolith (e.g., environmental terrorists act differently from right wing terrorists). Extremist groups with different ideological orientations use different tactics, recruit different kinds of people, and pose threats to different kinds of targets (Damphousse, Smith, and Sellers, 2003). One size does not fit all.

Finally, Chermak et al. suggest that law enforcement has had relatively limited success eliminating "terrorism" in what has become known as the "war on terror" – more recently referred to as "man caused disasters" and the "global contingency operation" (Wilson and Kamen, 2009). For the most part, counter-terrorism tends to be reactive; waiting for terrorists to attack and then responding – first by mitigating the effects of the attack and then by investigating, arresting, trying, and punishing the attackers. The success rate of terrorism prosecutions by the federal government has been very solid since the mid-1980s (Damphousse and Smith, 2004) and Chermak, et al. acknowledge that individual terrorist groups have been eliminated through these strategies. The authors suggest, however, that these successes have resulted in unintended consequences, pointing to the growth industry of new illegal activities designed to prop up the group (e.g., bank robbery and money laundering). This reminds us of the "paradox of reform" described so eloquently in Crouch and Marquart's seminal book on the history of the Texas prison system (Crouch and Marquart, 1989), where the elimination of the building tender system created a power vacuum that resulted in increased violence.

What needs to be emphasized here is that counter-terrorists can eliminate specific terrorist actors but eliminating terrorism as a tactic is nearly impossible. Other terrorist groups spring up to replace those who are eliminated. In addition, the manner in which counter-terrorists combat terrorism can actually increase the efforts of their opposition – the martyrdom of Gordon Kahl, the deaths of innocents at Ruby Ridge and Waco, and the torture tactics by the Algerian government, are clear examples.

So, in light of these findings, what are counter-terrorists to do? First, we need to clarify what we mean by "counter-terrorists." We typically refer to the federal government when we ask such a question since the FBI has authority to investigate all terrorism activity in the United States. But, as the current work of Chermak and Freilich well demonstrate, terrorism is a local problem, where terrorists "think global but act local" (Smith, Cothren, Roberts, and Damphousse, 2008) and local law enforcment officers are most likely to be the first to encounter terrorists. So, the suggestions by Chermak, et al. need to apply to both federal and state/local justice agencies.

The authors make two policy recommendations. First, they suggest that counter-terrorism efforts should be "measured" – aggressive enough to end the potential for future attacks but not so aggressive that they spawn new and larger attacks. There is a too-often ignored corollary here as well – terrorist groups must be careful to not be so violent that their message gets lost in the rubble. The Oklahoma City bombing, for example, did not have the desired effect of stimulating a call to arms against the federal government. Instead, public opinion, largely stimulated by the media panic, turned largely against the right wing and especially the militia movement (Chermak, 2002).

Second, the authors point to a "softer" form of counter-terrorism – the outreach approach. This was actually used successfully in the years after the OKC bombing. The FBI adopted an informal "take your local militia leader out to lunch" program in an effort to explain the federal government's position on gun laws and to establish personal relationships with militia leaders (Hull, 1999). This recommendation is also similar to the community policing movement with which most criminologists are already familiar.

What is missing from these recommendations is the need for counter-terrorist agencies to engage in more direct human intelligence activities to stop terrorist acts before they start. There are at least two ways that terrorist attacks can be stopped before they occur - the number one priority of the FBI. First, aware citizens can bring suspicious activity to the attention of the police. In the wake of the 9/11 attacks, the New York City Metropolitan Transportation Authority engaged in a successful "See Something, Say Something" campaign that encouraged citizens to report suspicious behavior (Litman, 2005). Other governments have similarly followed suit – signs posted in Canadian international airports, for example, ask citizens to "Share the Responsibility" by providing a terrorism tip line (Ross, 2008). The best example of how this works may be the January 2006 case of an alert video store clerk in New Jersey who was asked by would be terrorists to transfer suspicious looking videotape to a DVD (Russakoff and Eggen, 2007). His notification of authorities foiled an alleged plot to attack Fort Dix. Counter-terrorists would be wise to expand these efforts to engage the advantage of eyes and ears "on the ground" in the form of the general public.

Second, law enforcement can increase the use of confidential informants or undercover agents who are inserted into extremist groups to learn about potential terrorist attacks. The use of paid confidential informants to combat terrorism is not new. Indeed, the 1984 Act to Combat International Terrorism and the 2001 USA PATRIOT Act both specify mechanisms for rewarding people who provide actionable information that result in the arrest of potential terrorists. What is less common, however, are efforts by law enforcement to infiltrate extremist groups. One interesting exception is the efforts by the federal government to deal with the Republic of Texas. This "independence" group commonly posted meeting times and locations on its website and federal agents were commonly in attendance at those public meetings (see also Southern Poverty Law Center, 2006).

An argument can be made, therefore, that counter-terrorists could be more proactive by infiltrating extremist groups. One area of that counter-terrorist agencies could find very fruitful would be analysis of websites that are maintained by extremist groups. Right wing extremists were early adopters of the Internet as a tool to communicate with its adherents and with its audience - the general public (Damphousse and Smith, 1996; Damphousse, 2009). The anti-abortion movement and the earth/animal liberation movements have also used the Internet extensively, suggesting a novel approach to leaderless resistance. Indeed, the Earth Liberation Front's website provides a "diary of actions" wherein "elves" can register ELF-related attacks on behalf of the environment. Counter-terrorist agencies would do well to monitor these websites for potential future problems.

The paper by Chermak, Freilich, and Caspi provides for us important first steps in moving from the findings based on academic research to empirically-based recommendations for counter-terrorism actions. They are wisely modest in their proposals, since terrorism research is still in its relative infancy, but their suggestions move us all closer to where our discipline needs to be – in a position to inform justice officials and policy makers about how best to keep us all safe while maintaining the freedoms that we treasure so much.

REFERENCES

Beam, L. (1992). Leaderless resistance. *The Seditionist, 12*, 12-13.

Chermak, S.M. (2002). *Searching for a Demon: The Media Construction of the Militia Movement.* Boston: Northeastern University Press.

Crouch, B. & Marquart, J. (1989). *An Appeal to Justice: Litigated Reform of Texas Prisons.* Austin: University of Texas Press.

Damphousse, K. (2009). The dark side of the web: Terrorists use of the internet. In F. Schmalleger & M. Pittaro (Eds.). *Crimes of the Internet* (pp. 573-592). Upper Saddle River, NJ: Prentice Hall.

Damphousse, K.R. & Smith, B.L. (1998). The internet: A terrorist medium for the 21st century. In H. Kushner (ed.) *The Future of Terrorism: A Reader for the 21st Century* (pp. 208-224). Thousand Oaks, Ca.: Sage.

Damphousse, K.R. & Smith, B.L. (2004). Terrorism and empirical testing: Using indictment data to assess changes in terrorist conduct. In Mathieu Deflem (ed.) *Terrorism and Counter-Terrorism: Criminological Perspectives,* (pp. 75-92). Philadelphia, PA: Elsevier Science.

Damphousse, K.R., Smith, B.L., & Sellers, A. (2003). The targets and intended victims of terrorist activities in the United States. In D. Das & P. Kratcoski (eds.). *Meeting the Challenges of Global Terrorism: Prevention, Control, and Recovery* (pp. 171-187). Lanham, MD: Lexington Books.

Damphousse, K.R., Lawson, J. & Smith, B.L. (2004). The forgotten attack: The 1993 World Trade Center trial. In F. Bailey & S. Chermak (eds.) *Famous Crimes and Trials, Volume 5* (pp. 229-248) Westport, CT: Praeger Publishing.

Damphousse, K.R. & Shields, C. (2007). The morning after: Assessing the effect of major terrorism events on prosecution strategies and outcomes. Journal of Contemporary Criminal Justice 23(2), 174-194.

de Ormond, P. (2005). *Racist Origins of Border Militias.* Bellingham, WA: Public Good Project.

FBI. (2007). *Strategic Plan: 2004-2009.* Washington, DC: United States Printing Office.

Freilich, J.D. & Chermak, S.M. (2009). United States Extremist Crime Database (ECDB), 1990- 2008: Preliminary results. Department of Homeland Security University Network Research and Education Summit. Washington, DC.

Hoffman, B. (2006). *Inside Terrorism.* New York, NY: Columbia University Press.

Hull, C.B. (1999, July 12) FBI Meets with Militia Groups: Program Is a Legacy of Oklahoma City Bombing. *Associated Press,* July 12, 1999.

LaFree, G. & Dugan, L. (2004) How does studying terrorism compare to studying crime? In M. Deflem (Ed.), *Sociology of Crime, Law and Deviance, Volume 5: Terrorism and Counter-Terrorism: Criminological Perspectives* (pp. 53- 74). Amsterdam: Elsevier.

LaFree, G., Dugan, L, Fogg, H. & Scott J. (2006). Building a Global Terrorism Database. Final Report to the National Institute of Justice, May 2006.

Litman, T. (2005). Terrorism, transit and public safety: Evaluating the risks. *Journal of Public Transit, 8(4),* 33-46.

Morgan, T. (2007). *My Battle of Algiers: A Memoir.* New York: Collins.

Smith, B.L. (1994). *Terrorism in America: Pipe Bombs and Pipe Dreams.* Albany: State University of New York.

Smith, B.L. & Damphousse, K.R. (1996). Punishing political offenders: The effect of political motive on federal sentencing decisions. *Criminology 34(3),* 289-322.

Smith, B.L. & Damphousse, K.R. (1998). Terrorism, politics, and punishment: A test of structural-contextual theory and the 'liberation hypothesis.' *Criminology, 36,* 67-92.

Smith, B.L. & Damphousse, K.R. (2009). The life course of American eco-terrorists: Informal and formal organizations. *Criminology & Public Policy.* Forthcoming.

Smith, B.L., Cothren, J., Roberts, P. & Damphousse, K. (2008). Final Technical Report: Geospatial Analysis of Terrorist Activities: The Identification of Spatial and Temporal Patterns of Preparatory Behavior of International and Environmental Terrorists. National Institute of Justice. Washington, DC: Office of Justice Programs.

Southern Poverty Law Center (2006). Going under cover: Former FBI agent Mike German spent years infiltrating violent groups on the radical right. SPLC Intelligence Report, Issue 121. Retrieved June 15, 2009 from http://www.splcenter.org/intel/intelreport/article.jsp?aid=616

Ross, C. (2008). The threat from within. *RCMP Gazette, 70(3),* 8-10.

Russakoff, D. & Eggen, D. (2007, May 9). Six Charged in Plot To Attack Fort Dix: 'Jihadists' Said to Have No Ties to Al-Qaeda. *Washington Post,* A1.

Wilson, S. & Kamen, A. (2009, March 25). 'Global War On Terror' is given new name. *Washington Post,* A1.

Zahn, M. & Strom, K. (2004) Terrorism and the federal social science research agenda. In M. Deflem (ed.), Terrorism and Counter-Terrorism, (pp. 111-128). St. Louis, MO: Elsevier.

ALLOW EXTREMIST PARTICIPATION IN THE POLICY-MAKING PROCESS

LAURA DUGAN
JOSEPH YOUNG

At 7:05 A.M. on Saturday, April 4, 2009 Pittsburgh police Officers Paul Sciullo II and Stephen Mayhle responded to a call on a domestic dispute between a woman and her son in Pittsburgh's Stanton Heights neighborhood. As the officers reached the doorway, Richard Poplawski shot each in the head; and a third officer was shot as he pulled up to the scene. This scene turned into a four hour standoff, with hundreds of rounds of ammunition exchanged between SWAT officers and Poplawski who, while wearing a bullet proof vest, was heavily armed with an AK-47 and several handguns. The standoff ended at 11:00 A.M. when Poplawski surrendered—not long after the utility crews cut off power to his house (Fuoco, 2009). While friends of Poplawski were shocked by these events, they also knew that he was upset over the election of Barack Obama and feared that his right to own weapons was going to be taken away (Fuoco, 2009). Later it was discovered that Poplawski was active on the white supremacist Web site, Stormfront, where he posted at length a prediction that the U.S. faces an economic collapse that is being engineered by a Jewish conspiracy (Roddy, 2009b). He was convinced this cabal will use the military to enslave U.S. citizens, eradicate free speech, and take away his firearms (Roddy, 2009a).

While this attack denotes only one incident of violence the Department of Homeland Security (DHS) recently released an unclassified report to law enforcement warning of more to come. It claims that the current economic and political climate is expanding the potential for rightwing extremists to recruit and radicalize others, setting the stage for increased violence (DHS, 2009). In essence the report explains that the conditions that led to the growth of rightwing terrorism in the 1990s are once again present today, but are much more pronounced, likely extending the pool of potential recruits even further. Economic conditions are worse today, and rightwing internet chatter is exploiting the loss of U.S. jobs and home foreclosures while attributing these losses to a conspiracy of Jewish elites to draw in recruits like Poplawski (DHS, 2009). Policies such as free trade and a perceived tolerance of illegal immigration—both contributing to the loss of jobs for U.S. workers—are being used to rally the disgruntled into action. Also, with the election of Barack Obama, the political climate has shifted to the left, raising the concern that gun control legislation will become more restrictive. In fact, reports show an increased hording of weapons and ammunition stockpiles as well as paramilitary training by rightwing extremists (DHS, 2009). The election also fueled recruitment for the extreme rightwing who have exploited racial prejudices and galvanizing fear over electing an African American President. In fact, authorities have uncovered at least two plots to kill then Senator Obama in August and October of 2008 (Healy, 2008; Lichtblau, 2008). The two men arrested in October also planned to kill black children at school while claiming allegiance to Aryan ideology (Lichtblau, 2008).

The DHS report raises other concerns that the dangerous extreme rightwing paranoia of the 1990s that interpreted the dissolution of the Soviet Union as a threat to the United States' global position might be reawakened today by the rise in power of China, India, and Russia (DHS, 2009). Furthermore, extremists in the 1990s were able to recruit or influence a small percentage of well trained military veterans returning from Operation Desert Shield, including Timothy McVeigh, to exploit their skills and combat experience to further their cause. Evidence not only shows that this pattern continues today as military veterans return from Iraq, but a large number of rightwing extremists have joined the U.S. military and are returning home trained in the art of warfare (DHS, 2009). In fact, Richard Poplawski was trained by the Marines before being discharged for assaulting his superior (Roddy, 2009a).

A final concern raised in the report is that since the 1990s internet technologies have significantly advanced, giving extremists greater access to information on weapons, training, tactics, and targets (DHS, 2009). Groups now openly exploit the Internet to raise funds, recruit members, disseminate ideological messages, plan attacks, and publicize the results of these attacks (Weimann, 2006). Further, with ongoing advances in technology, terrorist capabilities continue to expand. For example, a report by the Army's 304 Military Intelligence Battalion Open Source Intelligence Team (2008) describes how mobile technology and the social networking site Twitter can be used strategically with Google Maps by terrorists for counter-surveillance, command, and control of tactical operations.

In sum, the DHS report demonstrates our vulnerability to terrorist violence when the economic and political climate is perceived as contributing to the grievances of the disenfranchised. This group of disenfranchised individuals is being targeted by extremist organizations to participate in their violent agenda. We propose targeting the same group of disenfranchised persons to engage in the policy process, making them active stakeholders and reducing their vulnerability to radical rhetoric. We expect that by allowing those who are directly affected by policy—such as the economically disenfranchised, returning veterans, and single-issue constituencies—to be represented in the policy process, the option to violently express grievances become less appealing. Research evidence described below suggests that countries with policy processes that are more amenable to a broad range of perspectives experience less terrorism. By considering this evidence and the need for terrorist organizations to effectively recruit and maintain a loyal constituency, we confidently conclude that those nations that allow extremists to participate in their policy-making process will experience less terrorist violence.

REDUCING THE WILLINGNESS TO PARTICIPATE IN VIOLENCE

In this essay, we consider the role that strain plays in increasing a country's vulnerability to terrorist violence. Strain can be thought of as the pressure felt by disadvantaged members of the community due to actual or perceived barriers to success imposed by the actions or policies of others. Without legitimate options, strained individuals experience negative affect (e.g., become angry and sanctimonious), pressuring them to resort to illegal alternatives such as criminal violence or terrorism (Agnew, 1992). LaFree and Dugan (2009) show that a broad range of well-documented theoretical concepts link strain to political violence including relative deprivation (Gurr, 1970), social disorganization (Davies, 1962), breakdown (Tilly, Tilly & Tilly, 1975); tension (Lodhi & Tilly, 1973), and anomie (Merton, 1938; Rosenfeld, 2004). Following LaFree and Dugan (2009), we consider all of these concepts as a form of grievance, which is defined by Gurr and Moore (1997, p. 1081) as "widely shared dissatisfaction among group members about their cultural, political and/or economic standing vis-a-vis dominant groups." Most importantly, this sort of strain incentivizes individuals to organize outside of institutional politics and to develop social movements to address these grievances (Weinberg, Pedahzur & Perlinger, 2008).

While the DHS report describes a large set of political and economic conditions in the U.S. that are instrumental to producing grievance, we must recognize that these conditions are global, and likely producing strain for individuals throughout the world—many of whom are vulnerable to recruitment by violent social movements such as terrorist organizations. Research by Cioffi-Revilla and Starr (1995) explains that one of the necessary conditions for political violence is a set of actors who are willing to use this tactic (see also Starr, 1978). While there are likely aggrieved people in all societies, opportunity is also necessary for producing political violence. Democracies often provide opportunity by allowing freedom of speech, movement, and association (see Eubank & Weinberg 1994, 1998, 2001). In contrast, democracies damper violence, especially terrorist attacks, by allowing participation and access to the policy making process (Li, 2005, Young & Dugan, 2008). While reducing opportunities for violence is one strategy for eliminating terrorism, the cost is often civil liberties and citizen rights. Another option is to try and reduce willingness to join violent groups. Crenshaw (2001) explains that terrorist organizations must maintain a strong membership to survive. Thus without a viable recruitment pool terrorist violence will likely weaken.

Furthermore, terrorist organizations generally cannot remain active without the support of their surrounding populations or sympathetic constituencies (Cronin, 2006). Some terrorists feel that it is their duty to take up arms to defend their people; and indeed, members of the community often join the terrorist organization (Horgan, 2005). This dynamic is especially relevant for terrorist organizations that have explicitly sought independent states for their constituencies, such as Basque Fatherland and Freedom (ETA) for the Basques, Kurdistan Workers' Party (PKK) for the Kurds, the Irish Republican Army (IRA) for the people of Northern Ireland, and Hamas for the Palestinians. Group dependence on the community is also more apparent when you consider groups such as the IRA who have multiple generations of the same family as members. Consider also the case of the West Bank and Gaza strip where many terrorist organizations are held in high social regard and involvement can bring respect to families (Berko & Erez, 2005).

This evidence demonstrates how strong ties to a constituency would increase the terrorist threat. However, in all of the above examples, the terrorist organization openly contributes to the well-being of the constituency, remaining in its favor. For example, even before its members were elected into office, Hamas ran networks of hospitals, schools, and other charitable organizations (Mitnick, 2006). Yet, evidence also demonstrates that, in some cases, when the constituency withdrew its popular support from the organization, its strength declined (Cronin, 2006; Dugan, Huang, McCauley & LaFree, 2009; United States Institute for Peace, 1999). In fact, some in the Basque region have been trying to separate themselves from ETA, strongly disagreeing with the need to use violence to address political problems (Funes, 1998). After the 1983 bombing of Orly Airport that killed many innocent civilians, the Armenian Diaspora withdrew public support from the Armenian Secret Army for the Liberation of Armenia (ASALA), possibly leading to its dissolution (Dugan et al., 2009). After the Real Irish Republican Army (RIRA) committed a series of attacks in 1998 that resulted in civilian casualties, the Northern Irish community responded with outrage, leading the group to declare a cease-fire (Cronin, 2006). Ross and Gurr (1989) explain that one of the leading reasons that the terrorist organization Front de Libération du Québec (FLQ) lost political strength was because a similar, yet non-violent political party gained electoral power, providing an alternative to the violence for the constituency. Taken together, these cases strongly suggest that terrorist organizations that lose the support of their constituency might substantially weaken, highlighting the importance of encouraging these constituencies to participate in legitimate policy dialog.

Terrorists are well-aware of the importance of maintaining constituency support. One strategy they use to preserve the loyalty of their constituency and to expand their pool of recruits is to sabotage the legitimacy of the target that they are opposing (LaFree & Dugan, 2009). Hence, much of the terrorist strategy is to manipulate perceptions by undermining the government's legitimacy resulting in increased popular support for their cause. One of the worst situations for governments opposing terrorism is to face multiple groups that are competing for the loyalty of a sympathetic population. As Bloom (2005) shows, this can result in a ratcheting up of violence and lead to such tactics as suicide bombing. The increasing popularity of ASALA to the Armenian Diaspora likely led to the formation of a second terrorist organization, Justice Commandos of the Armenian Genocide (JCAG), as a strategy to draw that support back to the Armenian Revolutionary Federation (ARF), a non-violent political organization (Dugan et. al., 2009).

While governments might also be well aware of the need to preserve legitimacy, this is often overlooked in the aftermath of terrorist violence. Taking advantage of this, terrorists often rely on the overly repressive responses to terrorism by government to win the sympathies of would-be supporters (Crenshaw, 1983; Higson-Smith, 2002; Lake, 2002). It appears that a partial motivation for the September 11th attacks in the U.S. was to elicit a harsh response from the administration of George W. Bush according to a November 2004 videotape by bin Laden who bragged that al-Qaeda found it "easy for us to provoke the administration" (Kydd & Walter, 2006, p. 71). Consequently, aggressive counterterrorism strategies can sometimes do more to increase terrorism rather than end it (LaFree & Dugan, 2009). While these actions may reduce the opportunities for violence, they likely stoke the willingness of others to participate. In fact, research that models the effects of interventions by the British government attempting to reduce republican terrorist violence in the U.K. suggests that most efforts led to more terrorism, not less (LaFree, Dugan & Korte, 2009). Once again, these findings highlight the importance of engaging at-risk constituencies in the policy process. Their participation can help preserve government legitimacy, directly weakening the terrorists' case for violence.

EMPIRICAL FINDINGS

In this section, we provide an overview of empirical support suggesting that the more amenable the government's policy process is to accommodating a broad range of perspectives, the less terrorism that nation will experience. The initial empirical evidence gathered by Eubank and Weinberg (1994, 1998, 2001) finds that democracies tend to promote terrorism. Research by Eyerman (1998), which uses more sophisticated quantitative methods, however, shows that compared to autocracies, democracies experience less terrorism. Eyermen (1998) does find that new democracies are especially prone to terrorist violence.

Li (2005) acknowledges these contradictory findings and argues that different aspects of democracy have competing effects. Similar to the above claims about opportunity and willingness, Li (2005) finds that participation in institutional politics, or a reduction in willingness, tends to reduce terrorism. Executive constraints or an increase in opportunity leads to more terrorism. While Li (2005) is by far the most sophisticated study theoretically and methodologically, there are still some problems with the conclusions. First, Li uses data on transnational terrorism while the argument seems related to all types of terrorism and especially domestic terrorism. Next, few states in his data exhibit less terrorism after a reduction in executive constraints. In fact, reductions in executive constraints seem to correlate with increases in terrorism suggesting that states with fewer executive constraints may be the targets of terror but reducing them further does not have the desired effect.

Like Li (2005), Young and Dugan (2008) look at different aspects of political regimes to help explain the resort to terrorist violence. Young and Dugan (2008) argue that the more veto players, or the number of actors who can block policy change, present in a political system, the more likely the system is to experience deadlock. Given the inability of societal actors to change policies through nonviolent and institutional participation, these regimes will have a greater likelihood of experiencing terror events. They improve on Li (2005)'s study by modeling international and domestic terrorist violence world-wide from 1970 to 1997 using data from the Global Terrorism Database (GTD) and, indeed, find that countries with more veto players are more likely to experience terrorism. These countries are also more likely to experience a higher number of attacks compared to those with less restrictions in the policy process. This again suggests that states that increase opportunities for meaningful political participation can reduce terrorist violence without unintentionally creating more willing violent actors. Ongoing research re-estimates and extends the Young and Dugan (2008) model up to 2008 removing all known attacks by foreign perpetrators.

CONCLUSIONS

Opportunity for violence combined with the willingness of individuals to partake in these activities is the volatile mix that can produce terrorism in any society. Theories of terrorism expect that states that allow participation of individuals and groups in formal politics will reduce grievances or strain and thus willingness to use terrorism as a political tactic. While the empirical evidence also suggests involving extremists in the policymaking process to reduce terrorism, how can this be accomplished?

Irvin (1999) argues that terrorist groups who lay down their weapons and participate in institutional politics are explicitly acknowledging the legitimacy of the institutions. As Weinberg and colleagues (2008, 142) claim "a group's willingness to...participate in the electoral process represents a significant concession." Unless this group can gain something in the policy making process, a return to violence is always possible.

In the US context, the new administration has been making efforts to engage a diverse range of perspectives in the relevant policy processes. One improvement over past administrations is the redesigning of the whitehouse.gov website to encourage all to participate in the dialog on important issues. For example, in March 2009, whitehouse.gov hosted an online town hall inviting questions for the president. More than 92,000 participants submitted over 100,000 questions, which received more than 3.5 million votes. President Obama answered those questions that received the most votes including one that asked about legalizing marijuana (Vargas, 2009). In addition to keeping readers informed on legislative progress and the White House's stance on important issues, the website includes a blog that posts videos and reports on the status of White House initiatives. In fact, the blog sometimes streams live video of working groups, encouraging listeners to post suggestions. Finally, the White House does not rely exclusively on those who directly access their website. President Obama now has a presence on the social networking sites of Facebook, MySpace, and Twitter, soliciting feedback from a broader audience.[i]

Another strategy by the new administration is to focus more on common ground when addressing controversial topics. For example, when President Obama was asked about signing the Freedom of Choice Act after delivering his First 100 Days speech, he explained that he wants to reduce the number of unwanted pregnancies, a goal that is widely agreed upon by all parties. To do this he has established a task force within the Domestic Policy Council of the West Wing that is working with pro-choice and pro-life groups to arrive at a consensus (Obama, 2009). This task force is only one of many efforts to engage key, yet divergent, stakeholders in regional forums to address important issues. Perhaps the most prominent at this time is the series of White House Forums on Health Reform which bring together republicans, democrats, members of the community and key stakeholders such as businesses, hospitals, insurance companies, pharmaceutical companies, patient advocates, and others.[ii] Throughout March 2009 the forums were held in Washington, DC, California, North Carolina, Iowa, Vermont, and Michigan. On May 13, 2009 President Obama reported the progress of healthcare reform to more than 13 million email addresses, making this the first time that the White House has used email for mass correspondence.

The efforts by the current administration to transparently engage representatives from all viewpoints to shape policy appears especially groundbreaking after the six years of failed efforts to uncover a list of participants from the previous administration's task force to develop a national energy policy. Spokesperson, Lea Anne McBride explained that the "vice president has respectfully but resolutely maintained the importance of protecting the ability of the president and vice president to receive candid advice on important national policy matters in confidence, a principle affirmed by the Supreme Court," (Abramowitz & Mufson, 2007, p. A01). Unsurprisingly, once released, the task force documents reveal that most of the advisors were representatives from energy-producing industries such as the American Petroleum Institute and Exxon Mobil. In fact, environmental groups were brought in only after an initial draft of the report was complete and President Bush had been briefed on its progress

(Abramowitz & Mufson, 2007). Lawsuits filed by the liberal Sierra Club and the conservative Judicial Watch to release the names and roles of the participants of the task force demonstrate that the White House's attempt to appease broad-ranged viewpoints failed (Greenhouse, 2004). We expect that it is this type of failure that heightens strain on disadvantaged individuals potentially pushing them toward extremist viewpoints and possible action.

In sum, we recommend that to avoid increased strain on extremists, the current administration should attempt to bring those representing the groups' views into the policymaking process. Gun rights issues should be addressed by incorporating both advocates for gun control as well as strict adherents of the second amendment. The extreme left also has several groups who use terrorism including the Earth Liberation Front (ELF) and the Animal Liberation Front (ALF). Since these groups operate using a "leaderless resistance" strategy, using force, or reducing opportunity for violence, to stop them is likely to be ineffectual. Instead, reducing the willingness of participants to use terrorism is likely the only means to completely stamp out this so-called eco-terrorism.

REFERENCES

Abramowitz, M. & Mufson, S. (2007, July 18). Papers detail industry's role in Cheney's energy report. *The Washington Post,* A01.

Agnew, R. (1992). Foundation for a General Strain Theory of crime and delinquency. *Criminology, 30,* 47-87.

Army's 304 Military Intelligence Battalion Open Source Intelligence Team. (2008). Sample Overview: al Qaeda-Like Mobile Discussions and Potential Creative Uses. Available online:
http://www.fas.org/irp/eprint/mobile.pdf

Berko, A. & Erez, E. (2005). 'Ordinary people' and 'death work': Palestinian suicide bombers as victimizers and victims. *Violence and Victims, 20,* 603-623.

Bloom, M. (2005). *Dying to Kill: The Allure of Suicide Terror.* New York: Columbia University Press.

Cioffi-Revilla, C. & Starr, H. (1995). Opportunity, willingness, and political uncertainty: Theoretical foundations of politics. In G. Goertz and H. Starr (Eds.), *Necessary Conditions, Theory, Methodology, and Applications* (pp. 225-248). Lanham, MD: Rowman and Littlefield Publishing Group.

Crenshaw, M. (1983). *Terrorism, Legitimacy, and Power.* Middleton, CT: Wesleyan University Press.

Crenshaw, M. (2001). Theories of terrorism: Instrumental and organizational approaches. In D.C. Rapoport (Ed.), *Inside Terrorism Organizations* (pp. 13-29). London: Frank Cass.

Cronin, A.K. (2006). How al-Qaida ends. *International Security, 31,* 7-48.

Davies, J.C. (1962). Toward a theory of revolution. *American Sociological Review, 27,* 5-19.

Department of Homeland Security (DHS). (2009). *Rightwing Extremism: Current Economic and Political Climate Fueling Resurgence in Radicalization and Recruitment.* Washington, DC: Office of Intelligence and Analysis Assessment.

Dugan, L., Huang, J., LaFree, G. & McCauley, C. (2009). The Armenian Secret Army for the Liberation of Armenia and the Justice Commandos of the Armenian Genocide. *Asymmetric Conflict,* (forthcoming).

Eubank, W. & Weinberg, L. (1994). Does democracy encourage terrorism. *Terrorism and Political Violence, 6,* 417-435.

Eubank, W. & Weinberg, L. (1998). Terrorism and democracy: What recent events disclose. *Terrorism and Political Violence, 10,* 108-118.

Eubank, W. & Weinberg, L. (2001). Terrorism and democracy. *Terrorism and Political Violence, 13,* 155-164.

Eyerman, J. (1998). Terrorism and democratic systems: Soft targets or accessible systems. *International Interactions, 24,* 151-170.

Funes, M.J. (1998). Social responses to the political violence in the Basque country: Peace movements and their audience. *Journal of Conflict Resolution, 42,* 493-510.

Fuoco, M.A. (2009, April 5). Deadly ambush in Stanton Heights claims the lives of 3 police officers. *Pittsburgh Post Gazette.* Available online: http://www.post-gazette.com/pg/09095/960749-53.stm

Greenhouse, L. (2004, April 28). Justices hear arguments in energy task force case. *The New York Times.* Available online: http://www.nytimes.com/2004/04/28/politics/28SCOT.html

Gurr, T.R. (1970). *Why Men Rebel.* Princeton, NJ: Princeton University Press.

Gurr, T.R. & Moore, W.H. (1997). Ethnopolitical rebellion: A cross-sectional analysis of the 1980s with risk assessments for the 1990s. *American Journal of Political Science, 41,* 1079-1103.

Healy, P. (2008, August 28). A possible plot against Obama. *The New York Times.*

Higson-Smith, C. (2002). A community psychology perspective on terrorism: Lessons from South Africa. In E. Stout (Ed.), *The Psychology of Terrorism,* (pp. 3-22). Westport, CT: Praeger.

Horgan, J. (2005). *The Psychology of Terrorism.* New York: Routledge.

Irvin, C. (1999). *Militant Nationalism.* Minneapolis, MI: University of Minnesota Press.

Kydd, A.H. & Walter, B.F. (2006). The strategies of terrorism. International *Security, 31,* 49-80.

LaFree, G. & Dugan, L. (2009). Research on terrorism and countering terrorism. In M. Tonry (Ed.), *Crime and Justice, Volume 38.* Chicago, IL: The University of Chicago Press. Forthcoming.

LaFree, G., Dugan, L. & Korte, R. (2009). The impact of British counterterrorist strategies on political violence in northern Ireland: comparing deterrence and backlash models. *Criminology, 47,* 17-45.

Lake, David. 2002. Rational extremism: Understanding terrorism in the 21st century. *Dialogue-IO, 1(1),* 15-29.

Li, Q. (2005). Does democracy promote or reduce transnational terrorist incidents. *Journal of Conflict Resolution, 49,* 278-297.

Lichtblau, E. (2008, October 28). Arrests in plan to kill Obama and black schoolchildren. *The New York Times,* A14.

Lodhi, A.Q. & Tilly, C. (1973). Urbanization, crime and collective violence in nineteenth century France. *American Journal of Sociology, 79,* 296-318.

Merton, R. (1938). Social structure and anomie. *American Sociological Review, 3,* 672-82.

Mitnick, J. (2006, October 20). Hamas charities thrive despite U.S.-led fund freeze. *The Washington Times.*

Obama, B. (2009, April 29). First 100 Days. Speech and Press Conference, Washington, DC.

Roddy, D.R. (2009a, April 5). Suspect in officers' shooting was into conspiracy theories. *Pittsburgh Post Gazette.* Available online: http://www.post-gazette.com/pg/09095/960750-53.stm

Roddy, D.R. (2009b, April 7). Poplawski's web postings warned of 'enemies.' *Pittsburgh Post Gazette.* Available online: http://www.post-gazette.com/pg/09097/961072-53.stm

Rosenfeld, R. (2004). Terrorism and criminology. In M. Deflem (Ed.), *Terrorism and Counter-Terrorism: Criminological Perspectives* (pp.19-32). Amsterdam: Elsevier.

Ross, J.I. & Gurr, T.R. (1989). Why terrorism subsides: A comparative study of Canada and the United States. *Comparative Politics, 21,* 405-426.

Starr, H. (1978). `Opportunity' and `willingness' as ordering concepts in the study of war. *International Interactions, 4,* 363-387.

Tilly, C., Tilly, L. & Tilly, R. (1975). *The Rebellious Century.* Cambridge, MA: Harvard University Press.

United States Institute of Peace. (1999). *How Terrorism Ends.* Special Report, No. 48. Washington, DC: United States Institute for Peace.

Vargas, J.A. (2009, May 11). Grading WhiteHouse.gov, round two. *The Washington Post.*

Weimann, G. (2006). *Terror on the Internet.* Washington, DC: United States Institute for Peace.

Weinberg, L., Pedahzur, A. & Perliger, A. (2008). *Political Parties and Terrorist Groups* (2nd Ed.). New York: Routledge.

Young, J. & Dugan, L. (2008). Terrorism and veto players. Paper presented at the annual meeting of the International Studies Association, San Francisco, CA.

ENDNOTES

[i] http://www.facebook.com/barackobama; http://www.myspace.com/barackobama; http://twitter.com/BarackObama
[ii] http://www.healthreform.gov/forums/whitehouseforums.html

INCLUDING EXTREMISTS IN THE POLITICAL PROCESS: "IRRECONCILABLES," CONSTRAINTS ON VIOLENCE, AND THE SOCIAL SCIENTIFIC ANALYSIS OF TERRORISM

BRIAN NUSSBAUM

This essay is designed to respond to Laura Dugan and Joe Young's excellent policy piece "Allow Extremist Participation in the Policy Process." It attempts to do so on two levels, both a direct look at where this inclusive approach may be useful and where it may fail, but also at a somewhat broader philosophical level about why the empirical, and largely quantitative, studies they use for support may be problematic in examining the phenomena of terrorism.

Increasing the political participation of "extremists" and allowing them access to the political process is indeed both a noble and practical way to address some of the dynamics that can underpin terrorism. It is an important tool in countering terrorism that has both pragmatic and idealistic advantages. It will likely offer an alternative pathway to political activism for some, decrease the alienation and discouragement that can lead to radicalization for others, and it fits well with our conception of democratic and pluralistic values. In all these ways, political inclusion serves to help deal with the problem of terrorism.

That said, it is not a panacea, and it is important to understand and acknowledge its limitations. In some cases it will likely not produce meaningful effects, at least on certain varieties of terrorism or with certain kinds of terrorists. Rather, inclusion of extremists must be part of a larger "tool kit" for countering terrorism, including some tools which are equally pragmatic, but perhaps slightly less idealistic.

Inclusion will likely have minimal impacts on some important groups that pursue terrorism, and particularly on groups that may pursue particular kinds of terrorism. The scale and scope of goals pursued by terrorists will do much to determine the utility of political inclusion, as will the extent to which the organization is beholden to the people it claims to represent.

GOALS: SCOPE, SCALE AND THE PROBLEM OF "COSMIC" ACTIVISTS

Groups that have well-defined, discrete, and "worldly" political goals are far more likely to be dealt with effectively through political inclusion strategies, than those with broad, vague, cosmic or even apocalyptic goals. Many commentators have made the case that those who adopt terrorism as a tactic in what they proclaim to be a cosmic battle between good and evil

169

are not people who can be negotiated with or compromised with in a meaningful way. (Benjamin & Simon, 2002; Bale, 2007; Juergensmeyer, 2003) While some ethno-separatists, right or left wing terrorists, single-issue militants, and even religious terrorists may indeed have political agendas that can be satisfied through debate, compromise and political inclusion, others simply may not. This may be particularly true of groups whose ideologies envision the wholesale revolution of society (whether economic, social or religious in nature) or those who fundamentally reject the humanity of some other group of participants in society. Certain committed revolutionaries, be they Marxist, Jihadist, or otherwise ideologically inspired, may reject working within existing political frameworks wholesale (see Maqdisi's arguments regarding Democracy as an alternative "religion").

This dynamic of those with cosmic or sacred goals, rather than worldly goals is well encapsulated by former CIA Director James Woolsey:

> *It wasn't too long ago that terrorists wanted to principally have a place at the table. Take ETA, the Basque terrorists in Spain, for example. Yes, they blow things up, they kill people and they're a terrible terrorist organization, but they are after something specific. Whereas, some of the religiously motivated terrorists from the Middle East or a group like Aum Shinrikyo from Japan and some of our home grown people here, such as the Identity Movement ... they rather want to kill everyone who's sitting at the table and maybe blow the table up and that's a different kind of thing.*

CONSTITUENCIES: POPULAR SUPPORT, VANGUARD ORGANIZATIONS AND A SACRED AUDIENCE

In a similar vein, terrorist groups that rely on popular support for maintaining their continued viability will of course also be more likely to fall victim to political inclusion strategies than those who envision themselves as a vanguard organization acting on behalf of either "sleeping" masses or a sacred (rather than popular) constituency. There are indeed examples of terrorist groups experiencing serious decline after excesses committed on behalf of some constituency, like the Armenian Secret Army for the Liberations of Armenia (ASALA)'s loss of support following its attack on Orly Airport (Huang et al., 2009).

There are however also clear cases of "vanguard" groups claiming to work on behalf of both local and sacred constituencies, and engaging in horrendous slaughter long after public support had faded away (the Armed Islamic Group in Algeria was a prime example) (Hafez, 2003). In this case, political inclusion may indeed address some of the underlying conditions that foster radicalization and allow terrorist groups to recruit, however in many causes there will remain "irreconcilables" capable of causing huge damage long after popular support evaporates (Bale, 2007).

Cosmic Goals and Un-Constrained Organizations

Unfortunately, some have made a compelling case that those groups who fall into these areas of not being affected by the political inclusion techniques along these same dichotomies (hardliner/cosmically-motivated and vanguard or less accountable), are the same groups that are most likely to pursue weapons of mass destruction and catastrophic mass casualty terrorism. Some research has shown that those groups with "cosmic" audiences are in fact significantly more likely to kill more people than those groups with worldly audiences. (Asal & Rethemeyer, 2008) In fact this dynamic constitutes much of the rhetoric about "the New Terrorism." While some have indeed argued compelling cases that the most mass casualty terrorism does not involve the notorious "weapons of mass destruction" (Asal & Blum, 2005), others have argued with strong evidence that those kinds of attacks are increasingly likely (Mohtadhi & Murshid, 2006), not as hard to perpetrate as we might expect (Allison, 2005; Carlson, 2003), and that they are the most likely to have broad civilizational impacts (particularly catastrophic nuclear or biological terrorism).

Terrorism, Data and the Problem of the Social Scientific Study of Terrorism

Terrorism is a tactic and is used by many disparate groups pursuing innumerable goals; as such it can be hugely problematic to study terrorism as a single phenomenon. It may be the case that many studies proclaiming to examine one phenomenon: terrorism, are in fact conflating numerous phenomena with wildly different causal stories, outcomes, and meanings.

Even those scholars that narrow the phenomenon greatly by looking at particular types of terrorist attack - like suicide terrorism (Pape, 2005; Atran, 2006) - may be capturing two or more separate phenomena. In this case Pape's causal story of suicide bombing (Pape, 2005) appears to fit very well with the bulk of those attacks between 1979 and 2001, but then appears to be missing out on some key developments later on (Atran, 2006). There is a serious danger in relying too heavily or uncritically on quantitative social science to study terrorism. (See Bale, 2009 for supporting discussion)

Most terrorism data-sets (GTD, MIPT, and ITERATE being amongst the most commonly used) address terrorism at the incident level, however there are some important reasons to believe that terrorist attacks don't make good data points. The most important is that *not all terrorist attacks are created equal.* These attacks and incidents vary so greatly in their scale (injuries/fatalities), goals (motivation) and symbolic or geo-political importance, that comparing them may not be useful for the kinds of probabilistic mathematical study that the scholars cited by Dugan and Young conduct.

Particular attacks, like those on September 11th, 2001 in the United States (which killed 2,974 people) or the bombing of the Al Askari or "Golden" Mosque in Samarra, Iraq in 2006 (an attack that killed no one, but sparked sectarian slaughter), have had such massive societal impacts, that comparing them to "similar" events may not be meaningful. The foiled 1984 plot by "Jewish Underground" terrorists to bomb the Dome of the Rock Mosque in Palestine could well have led to a regional war because of the symbolism of the building; even if, like in Samarra, no one was killed. Terrorism is interestingly an area of study in which the outliers are often as important (or more so) than the trends or probabilities.

Consider this thought exercise: Would most American security officials have preferred to have overseen a 50% drop in terrorist incidents between 1995 and 2005, or alternatively to have seen no change in those statistics but to have prevented the attacks of September 11th?

It is hard to imagine that many officials would choose a 50% drop in terrorist incidents, which would doubtless save some lives, but arguably have less impact on society than preventing one attack in which 19 young men devastated an entire society in September of 2001. This exercise encapsulates the insufficiency of data-based empirical models to deal with some of the realities of terrorism. While the exercise is obviously fictional and a false dichotomy, it points out the problematic nature of using terrorist attacks as data points.

This same problem of vastly differing impacts of terror attacks has been recognized in another field that relies on the quantitative analysis of terrorism: Insurance. Terrorism insurance has presented a huge problem because of the fact that terrorism does not lend itself to traditional statistical or actuarial analysis. The losses (impact) vary so greatly, and have such catastrophic outliers, that even "good" data about frequency is not meaningful. Michelle Boardman described the problem accurately "In the pragmatic mathematical realm of the actuary, both war and terrorism now represent incalculable risks capable of rendering key elements of the insurance industry insolvent" (Boardman, 2005). Boardman (2005) argues compellingly that because of data problems, the fact that major attacks are uncommon, and that the impacts vary so greatly (including the closely correlated property damage, loss of life, and business continuity issues) that terrorism risk is currently un-insurable. These fundamental problems in analyzing terrorism risk quantitatively are the reason that the Terrorism Risk Insurance Act has been continually re-authorized to support the potentially major losses of this incalculable risk.

All that said, this line of argument is not intended to dismiss empirical quantitative models for studying terrorism, but rather to put them in their proper perspective. As statistician George Box said "Remember that all models are wrong, but some are useful" (Box, 1979). These models are indeed useful for studying various aspects and dynamics of terrorism, but to present them as providing empirical evidence for policy choices on such a complex issue should only be done with the utmost care.

REFERENCES

Allison, G. (2004) *Nuclear Terrorism: The Ultimate Preventable Catastrophe.* New York: Times Books.

Asal, V. and Blum, A. (2005) Holy Terror and Mass Killings? Reexamining the Motivations and Methods of Mass Casualty Terrorists. *International Studies Review, 7,* 1.

Asal, V. and Rethemeyer K. The nature of the beast: Organizational structures and the lethality of terrorist attacks. *Journal of Politics, 70.*

Atran, S. (2006) The moral logic and growth of suicide terrorism. *The Washington Quarterly. 29* (2)

Bale, J. (2007) Social and Economic Solutions. Talk to Asilomar Conference. Available online:
http://fora.tv/2007/05/05/Social_And_Economic_Solutions

Bale, J. (2009) Jihadist Cells and "IED" capabilities in Europe: Assessing the present and future threat to the west. Unpublished working paper.

Benjamin, D. and Simon, S (2002). *The Age of Sacred Terrorism.* Random House. New York.

Boardman, M. (2005) Known unknowns: The illusion of terrorism insurance. *The Georgetown Law Journal.* Vol 93.

Box, G. (1979) Robustness in the strategy of scientific model building. In R.L. Launer & G.N. Wilkinson (Ed.), *Robustness in Statistics,* Academic Press.

Carlson, R. (2003) The Pace and Proliferation of Biological Technologies. *In Biosecurity and Bioterrorism: Biodefense Strategy, Practice and Science.* Vol 1. No. 3.

Dugan, L. Huang, J. LaFree, G. and McCauley, C. (2008) Sudden desistance from terrorism: The Armenian Secret Army for the Liberation of Armenia and the Justice Commandos of the Armenian Genocide. *Dynamics of Asymmetric Conflict. 1(3).*

Hafez, M. (2003). From marginalization to massacre: A political process explanation of GIA violence in Algeria. In Wiktorowicz, Q. (Ed.) *Islamic Activism: A Social Movement Theory Approach.* Indiana University Press.

Juergensmeyer, M. (2003). *Terror in the Mind of God: The Global Rise of Religious Violence.* Berkeley, CA: University of California Press.

Maqdisi, A. Al-Deemoqratiyya Deen (Democracy is a Religion). --- Numerous translations are available on Jihadist chatrooms and web forums. See discussion in Brandon, J. (2008) Jordan's Jihad Scholar al-Maqdisi is Freed from Prison. *Jamestown Terrorism Monitor.* Available online: http://www.jamestown.org/single/?no_cache=1&tx_ttnews[tt_news]= 4828

Mohtadhi, M. & Murshid, A.P. (2006). Is the tail wagging the dog? What is the risk of catastrohpic terrorism? Available online: http://papers.ssrn.com/sol3/papers.cfm?abstract_id=893149

Pape, R. (2005) *Dying to Win: The Strategic Logic of Suicide Terrorism.* New
    York: Random House.
Woolsey, J. (n.d.) Interview with the Public Broadcasting System. Available
    online: http://www.pbs.org/wgbh/pages/frontline/shows/plague/
    interviews/woolsey.html

Preventing Firearms Use By Terrorists In The U.S. Through Enhanced Law Enforcement And Intelligence Cooperation[i]

Richard L. Legault
James C. Hendrickson

In recent years, terrorism has been a named cause of significant procedural changes in the U.S. criminal justice system.[ii] Many of these changes have led to policy debates that are neither informed by empirical evidence nor based on well founded or tested hypotheses. Furthermore, many of these policies have been criticized for their infringement of privacy rights, especially by law enforcement and intelligence services (Beeson & Jaffer, 2003), for expanding the definition of terrorism to be overly vague (Martin, 2002), and removing legal standards for constitutional protections (Podesta, 2002). The end objective of these policies lies in the hope of preventing individuals who may be inclined to commit acts of terrorism from carrying out attacks or limiting their ability to cause damage. However, we argue that this can be better accomplished by developing an understanding of the criminal behaviors of terrorists to allow more measured policy responses that take civil liberties protections and other key considerations into account.

One of the recent policy debates surrounding the terrorism-crime nexus that is well suited to criminal justice perspectives is firearm use by terrorists in the United States. A number of policy proposals have been advanced. For example, recent news reports have raised alarm that terrorist suspects may obtain firearms legally (Lichtblau, 2005) and have publicized government attempts to integrate firearms purchase regulations with anti-terrorism efforts (Luo, 2007) via existing firearms background checks (Krouse, 2005). Along these lines, at least one bill being considered by Congress aims to ban firearms purchases by those who may be linked to terrorist activities.[iii] On the other hand, terrorism and participation in terrorism is extremely rare, and the individual rights of gun owners have been at the forefront of national debates in the wake of *District of Columbia v. Heller.* Balancing these two valid interests is valuable if not challenging.

Three policy options may address the acquisition of firearms by terrorists in the United States. First, increased monitoring of secondary firearm markets may decrease the ability of all classes of criminals to obtain firearms from otherwise legal sellers, including terrorists. Second, changing current laws to ban ownership of firearms for individuals who are named in Federal watch lists such as the Violent Gang Terrorist Organization File (VGTOF) may deny firearms to individuals involved in terrorism. Third, enhancing law enforcement and intelligence abilities to communicate and monitor the activity of terrorist groups may also prevent use and acquisition of firearms for terror. Each of these options has significant advantages, disadvantages, and inherent obstacles, and each of these will be described in turn.

Ultimately, the utility of any academically generated policy recommendation is uncertain; however a reasonable set of criteria for evaluating these policy recommendations would include effectiveness, political feasibility and compatibility with American civil freedoms. A review of criminological research can provide a body of facts relevant to drawing an effective policy regarding terrorism and firearms.[iv] For instance, the use of firearms by American "street" criminals has been well established, and a similar examination of the dynamics of firearm involvement among terrorists has the potential to shed light on these activities. Past gun policy has been based on this knowledge. Controlled market access and supply side restrictions of firearm possession is fairly well understood and has motivated many of the firearms policies and enforcement activities at State and Federal levels in the United States aimed at reducing criminal firearm violence (Cook & Braga, 2001; Cook et al., 1995). A similar understanding of terrorist participation in firearms crime has yielded similar, policy relevant recommendations (Legault & Hendrickson, 2009).

Terrorism, Crime, and Guns

Policy relevant research on counter-terrorism using advanced statistical methods is almost totally lacking in the social science literature. For example, in a recent Campbell Collaboration systematic review, Lum and colleagues (2006) examined 6,041 peer reviewed publications and found only 7 that used statistical tests sufficiently robust for effective evaluation of counter-terrorism policies. Further, while a great deal is known about criminals who use firearms, little empirically based knowledge is available regarding terrorism and crime or terrorist use of firearms in the U.S. In order to address some of these shortcomings it is useful to discuss the studies that have used quantitative methodology to explore the intersection of crime and terrorism as well as past research that has informed our understanding of firearms crimes among criminals who are not terrorists.

Terrorism and Crime
Dugan, LaFree, and Piquero (2005) used data from the Federal Aviation Administration and the RAND Corporation to examine 828 air hijackings occurring before 1986. They found that an overall increase of perceived costs of hijacking via metal detectors, and increased law enforcement at passenger checkpoints was effective in reducing non-terrorist hijacking, but

that terrorist hijackings were largely unaffected, leading to the conclusion the rational choice perspective was in need of further examination and that the level of motivation, goals, and perception of risk differs between terrorist and non-terrorist hijackers. This work echoes previous studies (Enders & Sandler, 2006) examining the effects of policy interventions such as airport security increases, international conventions and countries' counterterrorism policies on international terrorism incidents by utilizing a number of econometric techniques including intervention analysis (Box-Jenkins models) and game theoretical models (Enders & Sandler, 2006).

Although quantitative methods have only recently been applied to data about individuals who participate in terrorist activities, as opposed to events (Legault & Hendrickson, Forthcoming), qualitative work addressing individual characteristics of terrorists is available from a criminological perspective. Working primarily from court transcripts, supplemented with personal interviews, Hamm (2005; 2007) outlined the process of terrorist group formation, commission of attacks, and group dissolution as well as the role of individuals in these processes using routine activities and social learning perspectives.

In particular, Hamm argues that use of firearms use by terrorists can be intimately associated with a routine activities perspective. For example, in Hamm's discussion of the ultra-right wing Aryan Republican Army, the success of the ARA in bank robbery was dependent partially[v] on Cohen's notion of "capable guardians" such as bank security measures or police surveillance (2005), but also that the ability of the ARA to engage in bank robbery was greatly facilitated by their use of all types of firearms (2002).

Felons and Firearms

To further the discussion of research relevant to policy considerations for the terrorism crime nexus, it is important to be acquainted with the results of research on firearms use by felons. An understanding of the character and nature of criminals who use firearms is usually derived from surveys of incarcerated felons who have used guns in the past or are serving a sentence for firearms crimes as part of their most recent conviction and usually, but not always, focus on State prisoners (Scalia, 2000; Wright & Rossi, 1994). Self report surveys of arrestees and delinquents are also common (Bjerregaard & Lizotte, 1995; Decker, Pennell & Caldwell, 1997; Lizotte & Sheppard, 2001). These studies reveal patterns of illegal gun use and details about where criminals obtain guns, criminals' preference for certain types of firearms, reasons for carrying or using firearms, and, in some cases, demographic details and criminal history.

Criminals tend to obtain firearms through illegal means. For instance, a vast majority of both State and Federal inmates report that they obtained their last gun through illegal sources (33% and 39.2% respectively) or it was "borrowed" from a friend or family member (39.6% and 35.4%) (Scalia, 2000; Wolf Harlow, 2001). A minority of gun criminals purchase firearms, and even fewer purchase them from a legal source. Only about

22% of Federal gun criminals obtained their firearms at retail outlets, pawnshops, flea-markets, or gun shows, and only about 14% of State inmates purchased their guns legally.

The types of firearms that tend to be preferred by both State and Federal inmates are similar. Most gun offenders reported carrying a gun during their most recent offence, 83% of State inmates and 87% of federal inmates reported carrying a handgun (Wolf Harlow, 2001). This agrees with other, similar studies and demonstrates that most criminals prefer small, easily concealed weapons for criminal activities when they are available.[vi] It is important to note, though, that in Federal Courts firearms possession charges are much more common than use charges. Over 70% of the illegal firearms possession charges between 1992 and 1998 included no other substantive charge (Scalia, 2000).

Among those criminals who carry firearms, the most often self-reported reason for doing so is self-protection (Bjerregaard & Lizotte, 1995; Decker et al., 1997; Lizotte & Sheppard, 2001; Wolf Harlow, 2001; Wright & Rossi, 1994). When inmates who had used a gun in the commission of a crime were asked information on the extent of their firearm use they often reported that they brandished the weapon to, "scare someone" or "get away" (Wolf Harlow, 2001). These findings indicate that a complex set of relationships motivate firearms offending and that theoretical explanations for firearm use have important implications for enforcement policy. These relationships are yet more complex among terrorists (Hamm, 2007).

Terrorism and Weapon Choice

Addressing the complex relationship between terrorism and gun use requires an organizing viewpoint. The routine activities perspective provides a framework with which to make sense of the situations in which crimes occur within the limits of the systemic activities of daily life (Felson, 1994). In this case terrorism is the crime of interest. Implicit in this perspective is the means to develop policies, strategies, and tactics that take advantage of these systemic necessities or habituations of criminals to develop plans of situational crime prevention (Felson, 1994). Clarke and Newman (2006) utilize this perspective to develop a situational terrorism prevention model that relies on weapon choice as one of the four pillars of terrorist opportunity.[vii] They further outline the expected attributes of weapons that terrorists would prefer as, "multipurpose, undetectable, removable, destructive, enjoyable, reliable, obtainable, uncomplicated and safe" (p.108). Guns fit each of these attributes very well, especially in the U.S., because they are widely available. Also, while they may lack some of the shock value of explosives,[viii] their availability, lethality, relative safety, and ease of use make guns popular among terrorists historically. For instance, according to data available in the Global Terrorism Database version 1.1, about 41% of all terrorist incidents for which weapon type is known between 1970 and 1997 (LaFree & Dugan, 2008) were perpetrated with firearms (Authors' calculation of GTD1.1 data).

Accounts of terrorist activity suggest that terrorists differ from other types of criminals in several key respects that are pertinent to weapon acquisition behavior. First, a core, perhaps defining, activity of terrorism is the commission of violent, purposive illegal acts of a political nature (Schmid & Jongman, 1988). In contrast, criminal acts are widely recognized to be committed in a haphazard fashion generally lacking in foresight (Gottfredson & Hirschi, 1990). Second, the types of crimes committed by terrorists appear different from those of "street" criminals. Terrorists disproportionately engage in acts such as kidnapping, assassinations, mass assaults, etc, as well as a variety of organizational maintenance crimes such as identity fraud, bank robbery or RICO violations (Hamm, 2007). In contrast to terrorists, felons in general tend to be less involved with rare crimes like assassination, kidnapping, or mass murder. Felons also tend to be less involved with group offending – at least during later stages of the life course (Piquero, Farrington & Blumstein, 2007). Thus, one might hypothesize that terrorists have substantively different motivations and engage in different patterns of behavior than other types of criminals.

These differences appear to impact patterns of firearms offending. Distinct from terrorists, criminals are likely to see firearms as a secondary tool that allows for commission of a crime to be easier, escape to be possible, and victim compliance to be greater thus reducing the chance that victims will be hurt (Wright & Rossi, 1994). In such cases, criminals who wish to commit a crime with a firearm yet are unable to obtain one, often report that they would forgo the gun and still perpetrate the original criminal act (Wright & Rossi, 1994).[ix] This suggests that firearms are not instrumental to the criminal act in most cases.

In contrast, terrorist crime appears more strongly linked to firearms involvement. The research in this area is primary anecdotal but it is voluminous, so we illustrate just a few examples here. Post, Sprinzak, and Denny (2003) outline the role of motivation and values in 35 interviews with incarcerated Middle Eastern terrorists. They note that psychological constructions of value and meaning are intimately associated with armed attacks and are often carried out using commonly available Kalashnikovs and pistols (Post, et al., 2003). Regarding patterning of offenses Hamm (2007) writes that involvement with firearms played a prominent role in bank, armored car, and interpersonal robberies committed by white supremacist terrorists in the 1980s and 1990s, and was an integral part of planning for acts of violence against the Federal government in several instances (Hamm, 2002; 2005). Research on Irish political assassinations indicates that nearly 81% of political murders were committed with a firearm as opposed to only 24% of non-political murders (Lyons & Harbinson, 1986). Finally, Legault and Hendrickson (2009) noted that terrorists are much more likely to be charged with firearms crimes then other felons in the U.S. In short, evidence suggests that terrorists are much more likely than other types of criminals to be involved with firearms due to both motivational differences and patterns of offending.

THE IMPORTANCE OF ACCESS TO FIREARMS MARKETS

Firearms are prominent part of American trade. Estimates indicate that between 190 and 290 million firearms are privately owned in the U.S. with four to six million being added every year (Legault, 2008). Generally speaking, firearms are not easily homemade and must be obtained from manufacturers via primary or secondary markets (Cook et al., 1995).

Access to firearms is an important theoretical and policy issue. Aside from the aforementioned motivational and behavioral differences between terrorists and other felons with regards to seeking out and use of guns, firearms may also be more available to terrorists because they may have overall greater access to firearms markets in the U.S. As noted earlier, firearms may be obtained in primary (legal), secondary legal, and secondary illegal firearms markets (Cook et al., 1995). Primary markets include federally licensed firearms dealers (FFLs) and are usually retail points of sale. The noteworthy difference between primary and other markets is that primary markets require a firearm purchaser to produce identification, require the seller to record the details of the sale for review by the Bureau of Alcohol Tobacco Firearms and Explosives (BATFE), and require a National Instant Check System (NICS) background check before the firearm can be transferred to the purchaser (Gun Control Act of 1968, 2006). These markets require actions that result in exposure of the purchaser to Federal law enforcement authorities at some point in the sale. Secondary firearms markets have no such requirements regardless of the type of transaction and include both legal sales by private parties and sales or trade through illegal sources (Cook et al., 1995). Obtaining firearms through legal sources may expose terrorists to law enforcement scrutiny because they would need to participate in a legal transaction to obtain the gun. Furthermore, if there is a long planning period for terrorist acts, the purchase may precede the crime by weeks or months if not longer (Cothren et al., 2008). If terrorists have a less serious criminal history than other felons, as some have shown (Legault & Hendrickson, 2009) and others have speculated (Meissner, 2004; Sageman, 2006) there would be greater opportunity for terrorists to legally obtain firearms via primary markets and greater access to secondary markets.

Legault and Hendrickson (2009) have offered one comparison of firearm use between a sample of federal felons and all federal felons involved in terrorism as identified by the American Terrorism Study (Smith & Damphousse, 2006). Findings suggest that those felons who were involved in terrorism had a much less pronounced criminal history than other types of felons, and that terrorists had almost an *8 fold* greater odds of participating in all types of firearms crime and a *5 fold* increase in the odds of having a firearm crime as a primary offense. This indicates that terrorists have a greater predilection to both possessing and using firearms. Accordingly the greater access to primary firearms markets is a matter of no small policy concern.

POLICY OPTIONS & CONCLUSION

The three policy options presented earlier all carry significant advantages and disadvantages. We address each in turn: secondary market monitoring with Brady background checks, restrictions on VGOTF listees and enhanced cooperation of law enforcement and intelligence agencies. Considering all of the evidence presented here it is probably more important to implement greater law enforcement oversight and involvement rather than try to impose and enforce additional purchasing restrictions. The criteria are described below.

Secondary Market Monitoring

Monitoring secondary firearms markets is often discussed by policymakers as an option to block criminal access to guns. In regard to terrorism prevention, this approach has three distinct failings. First, illegal secondary markets (theft, trade, illegal street purchase) cannot be monitored with background checks, and this is where a majority of criminals obtain firearms (Wright & Rossi, 1994). Current Federal restrictions on firearms purchases forbid the sale or transfer of firearms to those persons who are: indicted or convicted of felonies, fugitives from justice, addicted to or use controlled substances, adjudicated as a mentally defective, illegal aliens, discharged from the armed forces under dishonorable conditions, those who have renounced U.S. citizenship, subject to a court protective order restraining contact with an intimate partner, or convicted of a misdemeanor of domestic violence (Gun Control Act of 1968, 2006). There are currently no provisions that prevent individuals named in the VGOTF from purchasing weapons unless they are otherwise ineligible (Krouse, 2005). While evidence regarding terrorist access to firearms is still anecdotal, some research suggests terrorist offenders can make use of illegal secondary markets (Hamm, 2007). Second, including secondary market monitoring alone would not increase the effectiveness of the current background checks because terrorist have less of a criminal history then other types of offenders (Legault & Hendrickson, 2009). In other words, transaction checks would pose no more of a challenge to terrorists without a criminal background than the current monitoring of primary markets – they simply will not get "picked up" by the background check system. Finally, imposing Brady checks on legal, private sales would be difficult if not impossible to enforce. While some research indicates that terrorist or individuals affiliated with terrorist groups have purchased long guns legally on secondary markets (Hamm, 2007), using the Brady system would be unlikely to prevent these sorts of private but legal purchases if non-compliance rates prove to be high. Considering that there are as many as 290 million firearms[x] in private hands in the U.S. (Legault, 2008), the size of the inventory makes the volume of potential transfers expensive if not nearly impossible to track successfully. In sum, a number of reasons suggest secondary market monitoring suffers from feasibility and effectiveness problems and is thus not an optimal policy solution.

Executive Discretion over VGTOF Listees' Gun Purchases

The second policy option is executive discretion over VGTOP listees. This typically takes the form of something similar to proposed legislation before congress allowing the Attorney General's the discretion to restrict the sale and possession of firearms to those named in the VGTOF (U.S. Congress, 2007; U.S. Congress, 2009). This approach has its own set of serious civil liberties, legal feasibility and effectiveness challenges. First, the proposed house bill allows the Attorney General to withhold information regarding a denial of firearm purchase if the information is considered a matter of national security, although we are not sure how this might be germane to domestic terrorism, this would justifiably draw the ire of civil rights groups as well as gun owners' rights activists. Considering that the VGTOF lists over 1 million names, and is intended to list persons of interest who have not necessarily been convicted of a crime, legal challenges to the constitutionality of such a law are inevitable. Second, the legal feasibility of such a policy is questionable. In light of recent Supreme Court decisions (*District of Columbia v. Heller,* 2008; *Nordyke v. King,* 2009) firearms restrictions based on executive decree would likely face legal challenges under the 2nd and 14th Amendments. Increased backlash from innocent citizens who may be wrongly included in the VGTOF combined with the action of grass roots firearms rights groups would make the policy difficult to pass into law or to implement. In short, the ongoing controversy and changing legal climate regarding firearms laws would likely make VGOTF restrictions legally problematic.

Third, the ability to deny the right to purchase a gun based on VGTOF membership would appear to be ineffective in preventing terrorist acquisition of firearms given the large number of "false positives" in the VGTOF. The efficacy of this type of monitoring was recently examined by the Government Accountability Office (GAO). During the 5 months of the GAO study, NICS recorded about 650 hits on terrorist lists during firearm background checks, of which only 44 were valid. Of the 44 valid alerts, 35 were ultimately allowed to proceed for lack of cause for denial, 1 was not resolved, and 2 were listed as "unknown status". Six transactions (0.9%) were ultimate denied for cause (GAO, 2005). In the end, the VGTOF was publically criticized for generating hundreds of false positives where innocent citizens are identified as potential terrorists (GAO, 2006). The very low number of true VGTOF hits (.9%) indicates that it is a very imprecise tool for preventing terrorist firearms access. Thus, the incompatibility with civil liberties, lack of feasible implementation due to inevitable legal challenges and questionable effectiveness as indicated by a high number of false positives suggests that alternatives other than executive discretion should be considered.

Increased Law Enforcement and Intelligence Scrutiny of VGTOF

A third option available to policymakers is increased scrutiny of persons in the VGTOF. We argue this policy approach has several advantages not present in the alternatives above. First, identification of terrorists who are not already felons but who are listed in the VGTOF could be an important law enforcement tool. It could allow law enforcement (LE) officials to begin gathering information for intelligence and investigations without necessarily violating constitutional protections, alerting terrorist to the attention that they are receiving from LE officials, or changing any current laws. Further, the Government Accountability Office has reported that Federal law enforcement / counter-terrorism authorities have, "not routinely monitored States' handling of NICS transactions involving terrorist records in the VGOTF" (2005: 21). We recommend that integration of the VGOTF with NICS checks be continued with additional FBI counter-terrorism oversight and coordination.

Second, a potential added benefit of such a policy includes the ability to update the VGTOF based on information gained in intelligence and investigatory actions that would reduce the number of false positives in the VGTOF, and hence the accuracy of the list. This would improve other areas where this information is used. Additionally, the infrastructure to utilize this information already exists.

Third, unlike relying on executive discretion, greater scrutiny is politically and legally feasible. Although State Fusion Centers have recently come under fire in the media for alleged violations of civil liberties (Sizemore, 2009) they are already politically accepted, funded, and provide an open method for the coordination necessary for this information to be shared and used properly, although we note that lack of information sharing has been an obstacle in the past (GAO, 2005; Kean & Hamilton, 2004). As terrorists have less criminal history, on average, they may find it easier to obtain firearms legally through available, primary market retail sources and pass Brady background checks. This suggests that policymakers should continue including the Violent Gang and Terrorist Organization File (VGOTF) as part of the National Instant Check System (NICS) criteria. More importantly, however, procedural changes regarding how that information is communicated to Federal and State law enforcement agencies should be improved in light of the proclivity of terrorists to participate in firearm crimes (Legault & Hendrickson, Forthcoming), a lack of coordination on this subject between State and Federal agencies, and a history of allowing these purchases to be completed (GAO, 2005).

In conclusion, a general lack of sound social scientific knowledge regarding appropriate counter terrorism policy has often led to ill informed efforts that may, in fact, be counterproductive. However, a careful review of literature on criminals' firearm offending patterns as well as recent research on individual terrorists' gun use suggests that policy considerations should be sensitive to the dynamics of gun policy and the complex legal and social landscape surrounding their use in the United States. Finally, when weighed against the criteria of feasibility, effectiveness, and compatibility with American civil traditions we argue that policymakers should enhance law enforcement investigative abilities and intelligence based responses to prevent the use and acquisition of firearms by terrorists and improve the accuracy of the VGTOF.

REFERENCES

Beeson, A. & Jaffer, J. (2003). Unpatriotic acts: The FBI's power to rifle through you records and personal belongings without telling you. American Civil Liberties Union Publication. Retrieved January 10 2009 from http://www.aclu.org/ FilesPDFs/spies_report.pdf

Bjerregaard, B. & Lizotte, A.J. (1995). Gun ownership and gang membership. Journal of Criminal Law and Criminology, 86, 37-58.

Clarke, R. & Newman, G.R. (2006). Outsmarting the Terrorists. Westport, CN: Praeger Security International.

Cook, P.J. & Braga, A.A. (2001). Comprehensive firearms tracing: Strategic and investigative uses of new data on firearms markets. Arizona Law Review, 43, 277-309.

Cook, P.J., Ludwig, J., Venkatesh, S. & Braga, A.A. (2007). Underground gun markets. The Economic Journal, 117, F558-F588.

Cook, P.J., Molliconi, S. & Cole, T.B. (1995). Regulating gun markets. The Journal of Criminal Law and Criminology, 86, 1, 59-92.

Cothren, J. Smith, B., Roberts, P. & Damphousse, K.R. (2008). Geospatial and temporal patterns of preparatory conduct among American terrorists. International Journal of Comparative and Applied Criminal Justice, 32, 23 -41.

Decker, S.H.. Pennell, S. & Caldwell, A. (1997). Illegal Firearms: Access and Use by Arrestees. Washington, DC: U.S. Department of Justice.

District of Columbia v. Heller. (2008). 478 F. 3d 370.

Dugan, L., LaFree, G. & Piquero, A. (2005). Testing a rational choice model of airline hijackings. Criminology, 43, 1031-1065.

Enders, W. & Sandler, T. (2006). The Political Economy of Terrorism. New York, NY: Cambridge University Press.

Felson, M. (1994). Crime in Everyday Life. Thousand Oaks, CA: Pine Forge Press.

Gottfredson, M. & Hirschi, T. (1990). A General Theory of Crime. Stanford, CA: Stanford University Press.

Gun Control Act of 1968. (2006). 18 U.S.C. § 944.

Hamm, M. (2002). In Bad Company: Americas Terrorist Underground. Dexter, MI: Northeastern University Press.

Hamm, M. (2005). Crimes Committed by Terrorist Groups: Theory, Research and Prevention. Retrieved March 28, 2008 from http://www.ncjrs.gov/pdffiles1/nij/grants/211203.pdf.

Hamm, M. (2007). Terrorism as Crime: From Oklahoma City to Al-Qaeda and Beyond. New York, NY: New York University Press.

Hoffman, B. (2006). Inside Terrorism. New York, NY: Columbia University Press.

Kean, T.H. & Hamilton, L.H. (2004). The 9/11 Commission Report: The Final Report of the National Commission on Terrorist Attacks Upon the United States. New York, NY: Norton.

Krouse, W.J. (2005). Terrorist screening and Brady background checks for firearms. CRS Report for Congress. Retrieved June 21, 2007 from: http://www.fas.org/sgp/crs/terror/ RL33011.pdf.

Meissner, D. (2004). Statement to the Seventh Public Hearing of the National Commission on Terrorist Attacks Upon the United States, January 26, 2004. Retrieved July 1, 2008 from http://govinfo.library.unt.edu/911/hearings/hearing7/witness/meissner.htm.

LaFree, G. & Dugan, L. (2008). Global Terrorism Database 1.1, 1970-1997 [Computer file]. ICPSR22541-v1. College Park, MD: University of Maryland [producer], 2008. Ann Arbor, MI: Inter-university Consortium for Political and Social Research [distributor].

Legault, R.J. (2008). Reporting error in household gun ownership in the 2000 General Social Survey. Crime and Delinquency Online. Available online: http://cad.sagepub.com/cgi/rapidpdf/0011128707308216v1

Legault, R.L. & Hendrickson, J.C. (2009) Weapon choice and American political violence: A comparison of terrorists in federal custody to other felons. *Criminology & Public Policy*, forthcoming.

Lichtblau, E. (2005, March 9). Dozens of terror suspects buy guns legally in U.S., congressional study finds. The New York Times, pp. 4A.

Lizotte, A.J. & Sheppard, D. (2001). Gun Use by Male Juveniles: Research and Prevention. Washington, DC: U.S. Department of Justice.

Lum, C., Kennedy, L.W. & Sherley, A.J. (2006). The Effectiveness of Counter-Terrorism Strategies. Retrieved January 30 2007 from http://www.campbellcollaboration.org/doc-pdf/Lum_Terrorism_Review.pdf.

Luo, M. (2007, April 27). U.S. proposal could block gun buyers tied to terror. The New York Times, pp. A18.

Lyons, H.A. & Harbinson, H.J. (1986). A comparison of political and non-political murders in Northern Ireland, 1974-84. Medicine, Science and the Law. 26, 193-198.

Martin, K. (2002). Intelligence, terrorism, and civil liberties. Human Rights, 29, 5-7.

Nordyke v. King. (2009). 3d. F. Supp. 4465.

Piquero, A., Farrington, D. & Blumstein, A. (2007). Key Issues in Criminal Career Research: New Analysis of the Cambridge Study in Delinquent Development. Cambridge: Cambridge University Press.

Podesta, J. (2002). USA Patriot Act: The good, the bad, and the sunset. Human Rights, 29, 3-4,7.

Post, J.M., Sprinzak, E. & Denny, L.M. (2003). Terrorists in their own words: Interviews with 35 incarcerated Middle Eastern terrorists. Terrorism and Political Violence, 15, 171-184.

Sageman, M. (2006, August). Common myths about Al-Qaida terrorism. E-Journal USA. Available online: usinfo.state.gov/journals/itps/0806/ijpe/sageman.htm.

Scalia, J. (2000). Federal firearms offenders, 1992-98. Washington, DC: Bureau of Justice Statistics.Schmid, A.P. & Jongman, A.J. (1988). Political Terrorism: A New Guide to Actors, Authors, Concepts, Data Bases, Theories and Literature. New Brunswick, NJ: Transaction Books.

Sizemore, B. (2009, April 26). Report: Region may be a hotbed for terrorist recruiting. The Virginia-Pilot. Available online: http://hamptonroads.com/node/507190

Smith, B.L. & Damphousse, K.R. (2006). The American Terrorism Study Database: 1980-2002 [Computer file]. ICPSR04639-v1. Fayetteville, AR: Brent L. Smith, University of Arkansas/Norman, OK: Kelly R. Damphousse, University of Oklahoma [producers], 2007. Ann Arbor, MI: Inter-university Consortium for Political and Social Research [distributor].

United States Census. (2009). Annual Estimates of the Resident Population by Sex and Five-Year Age Groups for the United States: April 1, 2000 to July 1, 2008. Retrieved May 26, 2009 from http://www.census.gov/popest/national/asrh/NC-EST2008-sa.html

United States Congress. (2007). Denying Firearms and Explosives to Dangerous Terrorists Act of 2007, S. 1237, 110th Congress. Available online: http://thomas.loc.gov/cgi-bin/query/z?c110:S.1237:

United States Congress. (2009). Denying Firearms and Explosives to Dangerous Terrorists Act of 2009, H.R. 2159, 111th Congress. Available online: http://thomas.loc.gov/cgi-bin/query/z?c111:h2159:

United States Department of Justice. (2007). Letter to the President of the U.S. Senate regarding "Denying Firearms and Explosives to Dangerous Terrorists Act of 2007" Available online: http://lautenberg.senate.gov/assets/terrorgap/Cheney_DOJ_Drafted_Bill_Re_Dangerous_Terrorists_Act_2007.pdf

United States Government Accountability Office. (2005). Gun Control and Terrorism: FBI Could Better Manage Firearm- Related Background Checks Involving Terrorist Watch List Records. Washington, DC: United States Government Accountability Office.

United States Government Accountability Office. (2006). Terrorist Watch List Screening: Efforts to Help Reduce Adverse Effects on the Public. Washington, DC: United States Government Accountability Office.

Wolf Harlow, C. (2001). Firearm Use by Offenders: 1997 Survey of Inmates in State and Federal Correctional Facilities. Washington, DC: Bureau of Justice Statistics.

Wright, J.D. & Rossi, P.H. (1994). Armed and Considered Dangerous: A Survey of Felons and Their Firearms. Hawthorne, NY: Aldine Publishing.

ENDNOTES

[i] This research was supported in part by an appointment to the U.S. Department of Homeland Security Research Opportunity Program administered by the Oak Ridge Institute for Science and Education (ORISE) through a cooperative agreement between the U.S. Department of Energy and the U.S. Department of Homeland Security. ORISE is managed by Oak Ridge Associated Universities (ORAU) under the DOE contract number DE-AC05-06OR23100. All opinions expressed in this paper are the author's and do not necessarily reflect the policies and views of DHS, DOE, or ORAU/ORISE.

[ii] Terrorism in this study is defined as participation in alleged criminal activities that warranted counter-terrorism investigation by the FBI and led to Federal indictment. For an introduction to the vigorous debate regarding a functional definition of what types of behavior do or do not constitute terrorism *see* Hoffman (2006) or Schmid and Jongman (1988).

[iii] Senate Bill 1237, the "Denying Firearms and Explosives to Dangerous Terrorists Act of 2007" is currently under consideration and was drawn from a Department of Justice recommendation to provide the Attorney General with the discretion to deny firearms transfers to those who may intend to use the firearms for terrorist purposes as well as revoke Federal Firearms Licenses. This includes a provision for the Attorney to keep secret the reasons for denial or revocation if she or he considers those reasons to be important to National Security by the Attorney General (USDOJ Letter, 2007; S. 1237, 2007; HR 2159, 2009).

[iv] We do not imply that terrorists are essentially criminals, nor do we imply that they are not. This debate is beyond the scope of this paper. We simply wish to note that the perspective of criminology and the more general study of deviance is useful to shed light on activities that are defined as terrorism.

[v] Routine Activities makes up only part of Hamm's argument, as he observes that there is a pronounced social learning component to terrorist behavior in the learned tradecraft of terrorism.

[vi] Significantly fewer inmates reported carrying much more lethal types of firearms such as rifles (7% State, 9% Federal) or shotguns (13% State, 14% Federal).

[vii] The four pillars of terrorist opportunity are targets, weapons, tools, and facilitating conditions (Clarke & Newman, 2006).

[viii] This too is arguable when considering the U.S. perspective. While bombs are certain to make headlines, mass shootings, such as those that have occurred in high schools and universities in the U.S., have garnered immense public attention and reaction.

[ix] When asked what they would do if they were unable to obtain a handgun to commit a crime, 37% of State inmates reported that they would go unarmed, 24% stated that they would carry a knife or club, and 40% said that they would

carry a long gun that had been sawed-off to make it concealable (Wright & Rossi, 1994: 217).

[x] To illustrate the sheer number of guns available in the private gun stock in the U.S. we note that if there are about 290 million guns in private hands, this would equate to about 1.3 guns per person over the age of 20 in the U.S. (U.S. Census, 2009).

COMMENT ON LEGAULT AND HENDRICKSON

Alan J. Lizotte

In part I like Legault and Hendrickson's essay because it begins to think about firearms policy directed at terrorists by employing what we actually know about both issues. Because the area is so new and under researched it really requires building a knowledge base about terrorists and their use of firearms and then comparing them to other legal and illegal gun owners. In some ways this requires thinking outside the box. However, we could model building that knowledge base on what we did for informing policy on illegal gun use thirty years ago.

We know relatively little about terrorists' use of firearms and what we do know stems from research done by only a few authors (c.f. Hamm, 2002, 2005; Post, Sprinzak and Denny, 2003; Legault and Hendrickson, Forthcoming). Knowledge of just how firearms acquisition and use work for terrorists is, of course, critical for making policy. Policy should not be faith based -- essentially being directed by myth or political beliefs about how the world works. Rather, it should be reality based directed by the facts of the matter. The state of our knowledge of terrorists' use of weapons is reminiscent of the days thirty years ago or so when we knew almost nothing about legal and illegal use of guns. At that time it was common to hear such policy gems at "guns cause crime" and because handguns were the weapon of choice in homicides the thought was that banning them would certainly reduce the homicide rate. Policy makers and even researchers would say these things with a straight face even though they had no knowledge of how many handguns there were, who owned them, how difficult it would be to collect them up, whether bad guys would substitute other possibly more deadly weapons for them and so on.

Fact and knowledge can get in the way of ideology and politics when pursuing policy. In the 1970's David Bordua and I submitted a paper to a scholarly journal using county level data showing no relationship between men's rates of legal Firearms Owners Identification Card (FOIC) ownership and gun crime rates in Illinois counties (Bordua & Lizotte, 1979). The paper was initially rejected when the editor reasoned that everyone knows that guns cause crime so there had to be something wrong with the analysis. It had not occurred to very many people, other than legal gun owners, that there might be two somewhat distinct worlds of gun ownership and use, one legal and one illegal. Few had bothered to talk to the gun owners, whether legal or illegal, about there ownership. At least this was true until Tonso (1982), Kennet and Anderson (1975), Wright and Rossi (1986), Sheley and Wright (1995) and many others, myself included (Lizotte & Bordua, 1980a; Lizotte, Bordua & White 1981; and Lizotte & Bordua,

1980b) bothered to interview both legal and illegal gun owners about their ownership and use. Two worlds of gun owners emerged and the results informed policy on guns and gun control. The issue quickly became much more complicated.

Ignorance is bliss as the saying goes, but if you actually want the policy to work it is important to know something about the phenomenon that policy is to impact. While policy initiatives sometimes have intended benefits they frequently have associated costs, they can fail and they have unintended negative consequences (Wright, 1995 and Toch & Lizotte, 1992). Bummer, these types of outcomes, unfortunately, often result from policies that are uninformed by empirical evidence and scientific inquiry. Legault and Hendrickson use some morsels of insight to nurture their policy suggestions. This is a nice start, and a demonstration of both how knowledge in a new field should be built and how criminology con contribute valuable information to the study of terrorism. While I am not competent to comment on it, they also use what they know about terrorism to inform their policy.

WHAT HAPPENED AND WHAT'S NEXT

How the research on legal and illegal gun ownership proceeded in those early days may provide a road map for how research on terrorists' use of firearms should proceed. Wright, Rossi and Dailey (1983) summarized the state of knowledge on guns at that time. Then Wright and Rossi (1986) and Sheley and Wright (1995) surveyed felons about their gun use. O'Connor and Lizotte (1978), Lizotte and Bordua (1980a), and Lizotte, Bordua and White (1981) discovered cultural markers of legal gun ownership and use in a sample of legal sport and protection owners. Later investigation revealed that these characteristics of gun owners have remained unchanged over a long period of time (Legault, 2008). This suggested that controlling legal gun owners might not be so easy. I also contributed to a string of papers on adolescents legal and illegal gun use (Bjerregaard & Lizotte, 1995; Lizotte, Bonsell, McDowall, Krohn and Thornberry, 2002; Lizotte, Chu & Krohn, (2009); Lizotte, Howard, Krohn & Thornberry, 1997; Lizotte, Krohn, Howell, Tobin & Howard, 2000; Lizotte, McDowall & Schmidt, 2009; Lizotte and Sheppard, 2001; Lizotte, Tesoriero, Thornberry & Krohn, 1994; and Thornberry, Krohn, Lizotte, Smith & Tobin, 2003). These papers described the characteristics of adolescent illegal gun use and the intricacies of moving in and out of it. All of this enlightened how policy might directly impact illegal users without angering legal gun owners. Many other researchers contributed to our knowledge on all aspects of the legal and illegal gun worlds. Legault and Hendrickson learned this lesson well. They cite their work comparing imprisoned terrorists and plain vanilla felons' use of guns. Then they logically work through these differences to comment on the likely policy implications.

The point is that the one needs to know how the world works before attempting to impact it and this knowledge needs to be built from the ground up. Basing policy on guess work is wasteful and dangerous. Legault and Hendrickson use their knowledge of terrorists and other felons'gun use to inform their policy. More power to them.

REFERENCES

Bjerregaard, B. & Lizotte, A.J. (1995). Gun ownership and gang membership. *Journal of Criminal Law and Criminology, 86,* 37-58.

Bordua, D. J. & Lizotte, A. J. (1979). Patterns of legal firearms ownership: A cultural and situational analysis of Illinois counties. *Law and Policy Quarterly, 1,* 147-175.

Hamm, M. (2002). *In Bad Company: Americas Terrorist Underground.* Dexter MI: Northeastern University Press.

Hamm, M. (2005). *Crimes committed by Terrorist Groups: Theory, Research and Prevention.* Retrieved on 28 March, 2008. From http://www.ncjrs.gov/pdffiles1/ nij/grants/211203.pdf.

Kennett, L. & Anderson, J. L. (1975). *The Gun in America: The Origins of a National Dilemma.* Westport, CT: Greenwood Press.

Legault, R. L. (2008) *Trends in American Gun Ownership.* New York: LFB Scholarly Publishing.

Legault, R. L. & Hendrickson J. C. (2009). Weapon choice and American political violence: A comparison of terrorists in federal custody to other felons. *Criminology & Public Policy,* forthcoming.

Lizotte, A. J., Bonsell, T., McDowall, D., Krohn, M. D., & Thornberry, T. P. (2002). Carrying guns and involvement in crime. In R. A. Silverman, T. P. Thornberry, B. Cohen and B. Krisberg (Eds.), *Crime and Justice at the Millennium: Essays by and in Honor of Marvin E. Wolfgang.* (pp. 145-158). Boston: Kluwer Academic Publishers.

Lizotte, A. J. & Bordua, D. J. (1980a). Firearms ownership for sport and protection: Two divergent models. *American Sociological Review, 45,* 229-244.

Lizotte, A. J. & Bordua, D. J. (1980b). Military socialization, childhood socialization, and current situations: Veterans' firearms ownership. *Journal of Political and Military Sociology, 8,* 243-256.

Lizotte, A. J., Bordua, D. J. & White, C. S. (1981). Firearms for sport and protection: Two not so divergent models. *American Sociological Review, 46,* 499-503.

Lizotte, A. J., Chu, R., & Krohn, M.D. (2009). The impact of adolescent gun carrying on adult gun carrying. Manuscript in preparation.

Lizotte, A. J., Howard, G. J., Krohn, M. D., & Thornberry, T. P. (1997). Patterns of illegal gun carrying among young urban males. *Valparaiso University Law Review, 31,* 375-393.

Lizotte, A. J., Krohn, M. D., Howell, J. C., Tobin, K., & Howard, G. J. (2000). Factors influencing gun carrying among urban males over the adolescent-young adult life course. *Criminology, 38,* 811-834.

Lizotte, A. J., McDowall, D., & Schmidt, N. M. (2009). Longitudinal data and their uses. In M. D. Krohn, A. J. Lizotte & G. P. Hall (Eds.). *Handbook on Crime and Deviance.* New York: Springer Science+Business Media.

Lizotte, A. J. & Sheppard, D. (2001). *Gun use by male juveniles: Research and prevention.* U.S. Department of Justice, Office of Justice Programs, Office of Juvenile Justice and Delinquency Prevention.

Lizotte, A. J., Tesoriero, J. M., Thornberry, T. P., & Krohn, M. D. (1994). Patterns of adolescent firearms ownership and use. *Justice Quarterly, 11,* 51-73.

O'Connor, J. F., & Lizotte, A. J. (1978). The 'Southern subculture of violence' thesis and patterns of gun ownership. *Social Problems, 25(4),* 420-429.

Post, J. M., Sprinzak E. & Denny L. M. (2003). Terrorists in their own words: Interviews with 35 incarcerated Middle Eastern terrorists. *Terrorism and Political Violence 15(1),* 171-184.

Sheley, J. F. & Wright, J. D. (1995). *In the Line of Fire: Youth, Guns and Violence in Urban America.* New York: Aldine.

Thornberry, T. P., Krohn, M. D., Lizotte, A. J., Smith, C. A., & Tobin, K. (2003). *Gangs and Delinquency in Developmental Perspective.* New York: Cambridge University Press.

Toch H. & Lizotte A. J. (1992). Research and policy: The case of gun control. In P. Suedfeld and P. Tetlock (eds.), *Psychology and Social Policy* (pp. 223-240). New York: Hemisphere Publishing Co.

Tonso, W. R. (1982). *Gun and Society: The Social and Existential Roots of the American Attachment to Firearms.* Lanham, MD: University Press of America.

Wright, J. D. (1995). Ten essential observations on guns in America. *Society, 32,* 63-68.

Wright. J. D. & Rossi, R. H. (1986). *Armed and Considered Dangerous: A Survey of Felons and their Firearms.* New York: Aldine.

Wright, J. D., Rossi, P. H., & Daly, K. (1983). *Under the gun: Weapons, Crime, and Violence in America.* New York: Aldine.

REDUCE USING IMMIGRATION STATUS TO ADDRESS CRIME

RAMIRO MARTINEZ, JR.

In this policy proposal I will focus on the relationship between immigration and urban violence. Based on said summary of work, I will then discuss the policy implications of this literature. In particular, I will argue for 1) lessened restrictions on immigration to the United States and 2) for the need to deemphasize the (at least current) draconian policy direction encouraging local police to engage in federal activities including ascertaining immigration status or profiling Latinos, and 3) singling out Latino communities especially those on the U.S.\Mexico border for law enforcement activities that could result in family disruption, decreased trust in and willingness to report crime to the police. In this paper I will focus on point 3 and direct attention to the state of Texas since the state and federal government advocates building more walls on the Rio Grande as a mechanism to deter local crime. I will however discuss in more detail policy issues 1 and 2 in subsequent versions of the paper. I contend that federal and state authorities should refrain from using immigration status to address crime problems.

As someone who has carried out a great deal of research on immigration and violence, and as someone who understands and appreciates the latest public concern about immigrants and homicide, I am profoundly aware of the stereotypes that engulf this linkage. For example, politicians have claimed that "25 homicides a day are committed by people who are illegally in the country"[i] and self-styled political commentators report that "95 percent of all outstanding warrants for homicide targeted illegal aliens."[ii] Yet, such claims are at odds with official police data and elude replication by researchers in this field. These publicly aired and manufactured "findings" are also at odds with both old and nascent bodies of criminological research (Martinez & Lee, 2000; Moehling & Piehl, 2007; Sampson & Bean, 2006). Relative to sound bites in the media, the bulk of findings in the literature reflect the careful and scientific study of the immigration and homicide relationship and these offer little support for the positive link between immigration and crime erroneously promoted by politicians and the media.

Indeed, the study of immigration, crime, and justice broadly involves research on the effects of immigration on crime and on the extent of criminal involvement between the foreign-born and the native-born. Criminologists tend to favor examining the macro level impact of immigration or percent foreign-born, net of other social and economic factors, on violent crime rates including homicide at the community or city level, though some have also looked at individual level differences in involvement between immigrants and native-born individuals. Much of the current scholarship in this area is quantitative in nature. The results of these studies indicates, almost unanimously, that percentage foreign born is not positively associated with homicide and other violent crime rates; indeed, the relationship is either null (Butcher & Piehl, 2008; Lee, Martinez & Rosenfeld, 2001; Martinez & Lee, 2000) or negatively related to violence rates (Hagan & Palloni, 1999; Peterson & Krivo, 2005; Stowell, 2007). At the micro level, immigrants are not over-involved in crime relative to the native born; instead, they either are less involved or they do not differ in their levels of criminal involvement from native born Americans (see Butcher & Piehl 2008). Based on the results at both the macro and micro levels showing that immigration and immigrant status are not related to higher crime, the question asked is whether immigration leads to more violent crime, and if not, is singling out immigrant communities for harsher enforcement to prevent crime justified?

Clearly the immigration and crime literature does not stand alone. Research on immigration and incarceration has grown over the past decade and some social scientists also examine the effects of immigration on justice or public safety by using measures of incarceration as a proxy for criminal involvement. This entails consideration of all types of institutionalization including prisons, jails and half way houses. One of the first studies in this area is by Butcher and Piehl (1998); one of the most recent and comprehensive studies on immigration and corrections is also by Butcher and Piehl (2008). Hickman and Suttorp (2008) add to the debate over immigration deportation while Philips and colleagues (2002; 2006) contribute to the literature on the consequences of deportation. Rowland (2002) reminds us of the obstacles faced by the foreign and native-born in attempting rehabilitation. Rumbaut and Ewing (2007) survey the literature and report that immigrants in general and immigrant groups in particular are incarcerated at lower levels than other racial\ethnic groups. However one chooses to examine immigration and crime, the findings rarely support a positive relationship between immigration and incarceration.

Based on these data, it goes without saying that urban communities with growing levels of immigrants or percent foreign-born are not usually places that have high levels of crime and violence. Equally important is that these communities, including border communities, should not be singled out for public safety concerns about fighting crime on the border or targeting places presumed to have high levels of homicide, including gang-related killings. Even qualitative research supports this notion. In a forthcoming article Valdez, Cepeda, and Kaplan (2009) examine the complexity of street gang homicides within disadvantaged minority communities in San Antonio, Texas. This paper is unique in part because the analysis is based on homicides involving Mexican American gang members, a hard to find and difficult to interview group. In addition, the Valdez et al. study did not include any immigrant gang members involved in homicide, a finding that complements the quantitative results in this research area.

It should go without saying that I am not suggesting that borders should be opened without restrictions, that immigration decreased all types of violent crime across all communities in the United States, or that neighborhoods are not strong candidates for policy interventions to reduce violence. However, I note that the body of research reviewed generally concludes that neighborhood conditions and social processes are much more important predictors of violence beyond the percentage foreign born in the community or of the nativity attributes of individual residents themselves. The findings suggest that policy makers and politician should refrain from targeting immigrants or heavily immigrant communities in their efforts to prevent local crime as doing so is contrary to a growing and consistent body of empirical literature concerning the relationships between immigration and crime. Moreover, such enforcement efforts have a host of other implications. These include, but are not limited to, law enforcement activities resulting in family disruption (greater levels of which are a predictor of higher violence rates) when immigrants are targeted and deported, as well as decreased trust in and willingness to report crime to the police. In the latter case, the greater levels of reluctance to report crime and heightened cynicism toward the police are themselves problematic and may have implications for subsequent crime and violence rates in Latino and immigrant communities (Anderson, 1999; Sampson & Bartusch, 1998).

THE TEXAS CASE: THE MISMATCH BETWEEN BORDER CRIME AND BORDER CRIME CONTROL AND PREVENTION POLICIES

I use the state of Texas as one case study of immigration and crime. First, geographically it shares the longest portion of the southwest border with Mexico. Second, over the past decade, the size of the foreign-born population in Texas increased by 46%, and now approximately one in every six state residents has been born abroad. Texas now has the second largest Latino population in the nation (behind California), and this segment of the population is growing rapidly. Based on these trends, it is clear that the issue of immigration will play a prominent role in current policy debates and will inform resulting funding decisions for the foreseeable future. Last, it is also a location where state and federal government encourages the building of walls along the Rio Grande in an effort to prevent terrorism and local violence.

Although there are some minor differences in magnitude, the compositional and crime changes experienced in Texas over the past decade mirror the broad national trends. As mentioned above, the sharp increase in the size of the Latino population was driven largely by an influx of immigrants (increase of 46%). It is interesting to note that the size of the recent immigrant population (those who have been in the United States for 10 years or less) also grew substantially, increasing by nearly 37% in Texas. This latter point is important, as this subsection of the immigrant population, which includes individuals of mixed legal status, is often portrayed as a particularly crime-prone group (see Lee & Martinez, 2009; Martinez, 2002). Figure 1 presents the overall changes in the Latino, foreign-born and recent immigrant populations between 1994 and 2004.

Figure 1. Changes in Levels of Lethal Violence and Demographic Composition, Texas 1994-2004.

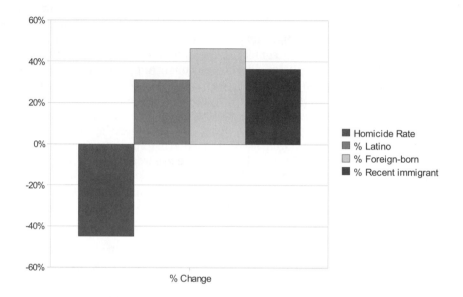

Source: IPUMS Current Population Survey (http://cps.ipums.org/cps) and Uniform Crime Reports (http://www.fbi.gov/ucr/ucr.htm)

In Figure 1, consistent with national trends, levels of lethal violence in Texas plummeted as immigration into the state flourished. Specifically, since 1994 the state's homicide rate declined by approximately 45%. There are two additional points worth noting regarding the dramatic reductions in violence. First, non-lethal violence has also declined dramatically. For example robbery rates fell by nearly 25%. Second, the observed reductions were not the artifact of exponentially large changes over a very short period, but instead reflect sustained changes over the entire time period.

Based solely on the trend data for Texas, the patterns do not support the belief that immigration, and particularly Latino immigration, has promoted a surge in levels of lethal or non-lethal violence, as conventional wisdom, the media, and politicians would have predicted. Instead, the descriptive findings are more consistent with the existing research literature. The temporal patterns suggest that the sizable changes in both the size and nativity composition of the Latino population may be associated with reductions in levels of violent criminal conduct.

To this point the discussion has concentrated on state-level trends. Although this represents an important starting point, focusing only on the state of Texas would not permit addressing many relevant questions; namely, an examination of levels of violence in areas situated on and along the US/Mexico border.[iii] The communities adjacent to the border are often a focal concern of policy makers because they are thought to be exceptionally violent and affected most directly by the negative consequences of illegal immigration. As such, scholars have observed that it is not uncommon for state and local governments to push for more stringent border security as a means of reducing local crime (see Martinez, Stowell & Cancino, 2008; Nevins, 2002). Despite the strong public concern regarding crime and undocumented immigrants, the evidence is again at odds with the perceptions. In both individual-level and macro-level studies, researchers fail to find support for the notion that undocumented migrants "pose a unique threat to public safety" (Hickman & Suttrop, 2008: 77; see also Hagan & Palloni, 1999). While these findings may be suggestive, it is not yet clear whether levels of violence are noticeably higher among the border areas within the state of Texas.

As an initial effort to address this question, in Figure 2 we compare county-level overall and Latino-specific homicide victimization rates disaggregated by proximity to the US/Mexico border. In this figure, it is clear that Latino homicide rates are higher than the state as a whole. Also observe that the overall homicide rates are nearly identical in the border and non-border counties. In fact, total victimization rates are slightly lower among the areas located on or near the border, suggesting that it is inappropriate to characterize border areas as inordinately violent locations.

Figure 2. Overall and Latino Homicide Victimization Rates by Border Proximity, Texas 2000.

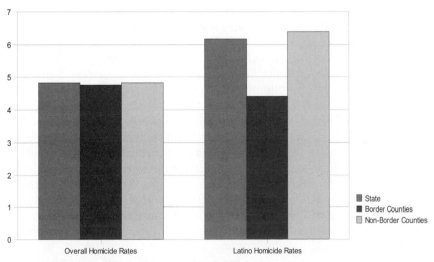

Source: Centers for Disease Control (CDC).

The differences in levels of homicide victimization are more pronounced for Latino-specific rates. Interestingly, we see that Latinos have a substantially lower homicide risk in the border counties as compared to the rest of the state. To place the differences in perspective, the homicide rate for Latinos in Texas was 6.2 per 100,000 persons, compared to 4.4 per 100,000 for Latinos residing in border counties. Moreover, the victimization rate for Latinos in the border counties, those with the largest foreign-born populations, is also lower than the overall state average.

From this simple comparison, I am unable to identify the specific factors that contribute to the observed differences. However, I do not believe that the lower homicide risks are largely reflective only of the increased enforcement efforts implemented around this time, as the temporal trends indicate that homicides were steadily declining prior to their enactment (see Nevins, 2002). The findings also raise questions concerning the mechanisms operating to lower levels of lethal violence. The descriptive results do hint at the possibility that immigration may be one of the causal factors suppressing crime, a premise supported by previous academic research (see Martinez, 2002, 2006; Martinez & Lee, 2000; Martinez et al., 2008).

To assess whether immigration is systematically associated with levels of lethal violence, we ran a series of multivariate regression analyses. Before discussing the results from these analyses, we will briefly describe the data and estimation techniques utilized. The homicide information was drawn from the county-level data compiled by the Centers for Disease Control (CDC). To ensure the stability of our estimates, the homicide data were pooled for the five-year period from 1997-2001 (see Lee et al., 2001; Martinez et al., 2008). In addition, because of the highly skewed nature of the homicide distributions, we estimated the regression models using Poisson-based negative binomial regression techniques (see Osgood, 2000). Demographic and social structural information for the independent variables was drawn from Census 2000 files and include an established array of indicators used in previous research on this topic (for a broader discussion of variable definitions see Lee, 2003; Martinez et al., 2008; Stowell, 2007).

Table 1 includes the results from the analyses predicting total homicide victims. In this table, note that social structural factors are associated with levels of lethal violence. Specifically, areas characterized with higher levels of disadvantage, racial/ethnic heterogeneity, and residential instability also tend to have higher levels of lethal violence. These patterns are entirely consistent with previous studies. These results confirm that homicide levels are significantly lower in the border counties, controlling for other potentially confounding factors. The analyses also reveal an inverse association between lethal violence and immigrant concentration. In other words, areas with larger foreign-born populations have lower levels of lethal violence. In subsequent analyses (available upon request), we find that immigrant concentration is also associated with fewer Latino, non-Latino white, and non-black homicide victims. Taken together, the multivariate analyses provide no compelling support for the conventional claims that 1) immigration facilitates criminal violence; and 2) that areas located near the border are likely to be more violent due primarily to undocumented immigration. In point of fact, the empirical evidence raises doubts about each of these hypotheses.

Table 1. Negative Binomial Regression Results for Total Homicide Victims, Texas 2000.

	B	s.e.
Disadvantage Index	0.075	0.035 *
Instability Index	0.112	0.056 *
Heterogeneity	2.100	0.460 ***
% Professional Employed	-0.034	0.010 **
Border	-2.578	1.014 *
Urban/Rural Index	-0.027	0.020
% Males 18-34	0.012	0.014
Immigrant Concentration	-0.013	0.003 ***
Intercept	-9.623	0.349 ***
N		254

*p<.05, **p<.01, ***P<.001
note: logged total population included as offset

CURRENT POLICY ENVIRONMENT

The policy position regarding immigration and crime in Texas also mirrors national sentiment. Indeed, the need to combat the increasingly high levels of violence tied to immigration, and especially border security, is listed as a key policy concern of the governor. The following statement clearly summarizes the state's position on this matter:

> *Citizens who live along the border suffer the daily consequences of border-related violent crime. The Governor recognizes that initiatives developed and executed by local law enforcement leaders are the most effective way to stop the criminal organizations deeply rooted in local areas along the border. To reduce violent crime, the Governor will directly fund and support the multi-agency investigative initiatives of local law enforcement agencies.[iv]*

In the above comment, both the crime producing impact of "criminal aliens" and the unduly violent border communities are presented as fact. More importantly, this statement shows that the governor is committed to allocating state resources to combat this perceived problem, in the absence of clear information supporting these claims. However, the findings from the above analyses underscore, if nothing else, the fact that additional research on this topic should predate the commitment of valuable assets.

More broadly, border security in Texas is framed as an issue of national security, as indicated in the following claims made by the current governor:

> *Al-Qaeda leadership plans to use criminal alien smuggling organizations to bring terrorist operatives across the border into the U.S. A vulnerable border also gives terrorists opportunities to smuggle weapons of mass destruction into the U.S. undetected. There can be no homeland security in Texas without border security.*

The manner in which the governor's office was made aware of the plans of an international terrorist organization, or the validity of such claims, were not made clear. The US/Mexico border has been discussed as a likely entry point for terrorists, in the years following the attacks of 9/11, although no large-scale smuggling operations have been identified. According to published newspaper accounts, state law enforcement officials claim that there have been many arrests made of individuals with suspected links to terrorist organizations. However, the details regarding these seizures are unclear, even to the national border patrol offices. In a recent newspaper report, one immigration officer indicated that she was unaware of any "border arrests of anyone with terrorist ties" (Carlton, 2007). One point can be safely drawn from this discrepancy: there is a general lack of clear and convincing evidence that a wave of terrorist operatives are entering the United States through Mexico, at least not of the magnitude portrayed by state and local officials.

Nevertheless, the governor has remained committed to a strategy of strengthening the border as a means of reducing crime in Texas. Furthermore, the governor has outlined a series of border security initiatives and provided estimates for how much financial and other material support will be required for their implementation. An overview of these programs, which include a mix of both state funded and collaborations with the federal government, will be summarized below.

BORDER SECURITY INITIATIVES

Many of the state of Texas programs center on increasing the number of law enforcement officers for a stronger presence on the border. These include allocating $3.7 million in Criminal Justice Grant funds to support local, multi-agency law enforcement initiatives, providing an additional $3 million in Criminal Justice grants to fund local officer overtime, establishing four rapid deployment teams and permanently assigning 54 criminal investigators to the border in support of local law enforcement agencies. Overall, these objectives, and especially the two which advocate for the permanent addition of hundreds of line staff, are founded on the premise that levels of violence in the areas along the border are greater than those in the other areas in the state. Again, it merits mention that this notion is at odds with the results discussed above.

Along the same lines, the governor has also identified a number of border security programs that involve a combination of state and federal law enforcement personnel. Estimates of the proportion of the funding for such programs that will be provided by the state were not disclosed, but they are likely to be substantial. The governor identified three key aspects of the state-federal partnerships, including hiring 10,000 more border and custom patrol agents, substantially expanding immigration detention facilities, and establishing a volunteer program within U.S. Customs and Border Patrol. Conservatively, the costs associated with the additional personnel and infrastructure desired to combat illicit immigration and, by consequence, to lower levels of crime in Texas, will run into the tens of millions of dollars annually. Based on the evidence, this planned exponential growth, both in terms of the number of law enforcement personnel and the resources earmarked for border security, does not seem proportionate to the need.

Clearly there are concerns about the discrepancies between empirical observations and proposed policy initiatives, not because I do not support or see the critical need for plans to reduce and/or prevent crime. Both the importance and the necessity of reducing crime for the public well-being are obvious. Nor do I believe that the Texas, other state governments, or the federal government should adopt an altogether stagnant approach to public safety. Rather, I draw attention to the fact that the extreme concentration of resources to this issue is misguided and will do little more than single out immigrants and immigrant communities in an attempt to deter crime in places with relatively lower levels of serious crime such as homicide. The inordinate amount of resources devoted to fighting crime on the border may be out of step with the actual needs of many of these communities, including education and public health.

CONCLUSION

In this paper, I have argued that policies designed to restrict immigration will not reduce crime. It is, of course, important for policy makers to base their decisions on detailed appraisals of a given issue. Arriving at a balanced policy platform is made even more difficult without the benefit of empirical evidence. Moreover, the absence of objective information can lead to the over-commitment of resources or to the implementation ineffective programs. As but one example, the strong push for increased border security in Texas, partially in response to deter immigration and decrease crime, provides a clear illustration of how an imbalance exists between perceived and actual needs. Recall, that our findings indicate that homicide rates in border counties (those portrayed as extremely violent) are slightly lower than they are in the rest of the state. We also find the lowest levels of lethal violence for Latinos in these same areas. Similarly, the results from our regression analyses reveal an inverse association between immigration and overall levels of homicide. And yet, the state maintains that there is an increasing need for resources and personnel to combat the excessive levels of violence in these areas and that need means closing the immigration flow into the area.

It is worth noting how the concentration of resources may contribute, though indirectly, to the disadvantages experienced by many Latinos along the border. In particular, Latinos in the state lag behind non-Latinos in both access to healthcare and in levels of educational attainment. These domains of public health and education have clear ties to policy and improvement in these areas can help minimize historic racial/ethnic inequalities. Such emphasis on the "dangerous" border areas and on their Latino and immigrant inhabitants, also serve to reinforce and perpetuate erroneous stereotypes concerning the criminal immigrant and high crime immigrant communities. More central to this paper, social policies designed to narrow the disparities across racial and ethnic groups will also help to foster stronger, and safer, communities. Such considerations are relevant because they illustrate the fact that the concentration of enhancing border security is not the only means by which to realize the broad goal of reducing violence. Indeed, such a narrow perspective overlooks other potentially important factors known to be associated with levels of crime, such as those related to economic disadvantage and extreme inequality, not one that targets border communities for tactics or strategies that other areas in the state and nation do not endure.

REFERENCES

Anderson, E.. (1999). *Code of the Street: Decency, Violence and the Moral Life of the Inner City.* New York: W.W. Norton & Company.

Butcher, K.F. & Piehl, A.M. (1998). Cross-city evidence on the relationship between immigration and crime. *Journal of Policy Analysis and Management, 17,* 457-493.

Butcher, K.F. & Piehl, A.M. (2008). Crime, corrections, and California: What does immigration have to do with it? *California Counts.* San Francisco: Public Policy Institute of California.

Carlton, J. (2007, September 13). Terrorism arrests made on Texas border: Insurgents connected to Hezbollah, Hamas, and Al-Qaida detained. *The Daily Texan.*

Hagan, J. & Palloni, A. (1999). Sociological criminology and the myth of Hispanic immigration and crime. *Social Problems, 46,* 617-632.

Hickman, L.J. & Suttorp, M.J. (2008). Are deportable aliens a unique threat to public safety? Comparing the recidivism of deportable and nondeportable aliens. *Criminology & Public Policy, 7,* 59-82.

Lee, M.T. (2003). *Crime on the Border: Immigration and Homicide in Urban Communities.* New York: LFB Scholarly Publishing.

Lee, M.T. & Martinez, R. Jr. (2009). Immigration reduces crime: An emerging scholarly consensus. In W. McDonald (Ed.), *Sociology of Crime, Law and Deviance, Volume 13: Immigration, Crime and Justice* (pp. 3-16). Bingley, UK: Emerald Group Publishing.

Lee, M.T., Martinez, R. Jr. & Rosenfeld, R. (2001). Does immigration increase homicide? Negative evidence from three border cities. *The Sociological Quarterly, 42,* 559-580.

MacDonald, H. (2005). Testimony at the Manhattan Institute for Policy Research. Available online:
http://www.manhattan-institute.org/html/mac_donald04-13-05.htm

Martinez, R. Jr. (2002). *Latino Homicide: Immigration, Violence, and Community.* New York: Routledge Press.

Martinez, R. Jr. (2006). Coming to America: The impact of the new immigration on crime. In R. Martinez, Jr. and A. Valenzuela (Eds.), *Immigration and Crime: Race, Ethnicity, and Violence,* (pp. 1-19). New York: New York University Press.

Martinez, R. Jr. & Lee, M.R. (2000). On immigration and crime." In G. LaFree and R. Bursik (Eds.), *Criminal Justice 2000, Volume I: The Nature of Crime: Continuity and Change* (pp. 485-524). Washington, DC: National Institute of Justice.

Martinez, R. Jr., Stowell, J.I. & Cancino, J.M. (2008).A tale of two border cities: Community context, ethnicity, and homicide. *Social Science Quarterly, 89,* 1-16.

Moehling, C. & Piehl, A.M. (2007). Immigration and crime in early 20th century America. National Bureau of Economic Research. Available online: http://www.nber.org/papers/w13576

Nevins, J. (2002). *Operation Gatekeeper: The Rise of the 'Illegal Alien' and the Remaking of the U.S.-Mexico Boundary.* New York: Routledge.

Osgood, W.D. (2000). Poisson-based regression analysis of aggregate crime rates. *Journal of Quantitative Criminology, 16,* 21-43.

Peterson, R.D. & Krivo, L. (2005). Macrostructural analyses of race, ethnicity, and violent crime: Recent lessons and new directions for future research. *Annual Review of Sociology, 31,* 331-356.

Phillips, S., Rodriguez, N. & Hagan, J. (2002). Brutality at the border? Use of force in the arrest of immigrants in the United States. *International Journal of Sociology of Law, 30,* 285-306.

Phillips, S., Hagan, J. & Rodriguez, N. (2006). Brutal borders? Examining the treatment of deportees during arrest and detention. *Social Forces, 85,* 93-110.

Rowland, M.G. (2002). Probation supervision of legal and illegal aliens: A study. *Federal Sentencing Reporter, 14,* 276-278.

Rumbaut, R. & Ewing, W. (2007). The myth of immigrant criminality and the paradox of assimilation. Immigration Policy Center. Available online: http://www.immigrationpolicy.org

Sampson, R.J. & Bartusch, D.J. (1998). Legal cynicism and (subcultural?) tolerance of deviance: The neighborhood context of racial differences. *Law and Society Review, 32,* 777-804.

Sampson, R.J. & Bean, L. (2006). Cultural mechanisms and killing fields: A revised theory of community-level racial inequality. In R. Peterson, L. Krivo and J. Hagan (Eds.), *The Many Colors of Crime: Inequalities of Race, Ethnicity and Crime in America* (pp. 8-37). New York: New York University Press.

Stowell, J.I. (2007). *Immigration and Crime: Considering the Direct and Indirect Effects of Immigration on Violent Criminal Behavior.* New York: LFB Scholarly Press.

Valdez, A., Cepeda A. & Kaplan, C. (2009). Homicidal Events among Mexican American Street Gangs: A Situational Analysis. *Homicide Studies, 13(3),* Forthcoming.

ENDNOTES

[i] A "fact" on immigrant homicides portrayed by Congressional representative Ted Poe. See www.chron.com/disp/story.mpl/metropolitan/casey/4217353.html. The FBI's 2005 Uniform Crime Reports (UCR) notes 10,083 persons (or 26.6 per day) were charged with a homicide. The UCR also reports that 49.1% of homicide arrestees were white and 48.5% were black. Data reported by thousands of police departments across the country counter the Ted Poe depiction.

[ii] For example, the testimony of Heather MacDonald at the Manhattan Institute for Policy Research (2005). In 2004, the LA Police Department reported 515 homicides and 474 homicides arrests. That same year the LA Sheriff's Department reported 338 homicides and 228 homicide arrests. Most homicides in LA were cleared with an arrest. Thus, it is not clear why a warrant was issued, for whom, or even how the number of "1,200 to 1,500" warrants was generated. Moreover, "legality" status for any crime was not available from either police department. The reported police data stand at complete odds with the unsubstantiated "claims" by MacDonald.

[iii] Rates based on pooled data over a five-year period (1997-2001).

[iv] http://www.governor.state.tx.us/priorities/other/border/border_security/view

RESPONDING TO IMMIGRATION AND IMMIGRATION "TALK"

SCOTT H. DECKER

In his thoughtful analysis of the relationship between immigration status and crime, Ramiro Martinez addresses a number of key questions. Martinez raises questions about the appropriate unit of analysis, the historical relationship between immigration and crime, and appropriate policy responses to immigration. He observes that crime rates – particularly violent crime rates – declined as immigration increased. This trend was observed at a national level, state level (Texas), and at the county level. Most specifically, Martinez's analysis showed that border communities have lower rates of crime than non-border communities. These relationships hold when relevant controls are introduced into multivariate models. As Martinez notes, these results stand in stark contrast to media images and resulting public perceptions of immigration fueling crime, and immigrants being heavily involved in crime. He then goes on to question the policy response of Texas, a response quite inconsistent with his findings.

Martinez' analysis raises a number of important questions that merit further scrutiny. The relationship between immigration and crime (among many other social ills) is one of the key issues of our time. Immigration, and immigrants, have been implicated in a number of contemporary maladies. These maladies include – but aren't limited to – H1N1 virus ("swine flu"), avian flu ("bird flu"), human trafficking, drug trafficking, prostitution, strains on schools and emergency rooms, and a decline in wages. Lacking in the public discussion about the relationship between immigration and social behavior is a well-defined set of questions, data to address those questions, and a rational discussion about the relationship between facts and policies. Unless and until questions are defined, measurement is established, and a sharper policy focus is established, we shouldn't expect much progress on this front. Perhaps even then a rational discussion may be too much to ask.

In this response I want to raise four sets of questions, each stimulated by Martinez' analysis. First, how do we reconcile the nearly unequivocal findings that in the 21st century, immigration and immigrants are related to lower rates of crime, while a century earlier immigrants and immigration were related to higher rates of crime.

Second, how do we assess the denominator issues in establishing the number of immigrants, and more relevant to the debate, undocumented immigrants. Criminology has been plagued by questions about the "dark figure of crime" which has typically been the numerator. In the case of assessing the relationship between immigration and crime, both the numerator and the denominator are difficult to establish.

Third, what are the manifest and latent consequences of criminalizing immigration status, particular by the law enforcement community? While the tendency of the criminal justice system is to expand and enhance the reach of the criminal law, it appears that in the case of immigration, there is a considerable risk of creating negative circumstances. That is, by targeting immigration status local law enforcement may discourage cooperation, reporting and civic participation among new American citizens.

Fourth, in the face of an economic crisis of considerable proportions and in the midst of two international conflicts that drag on, why does the immigration issue continue to receive the kind of attention that it has. In this discussion, I depend heavily on Cohen's (1985) analysis.

Martinez reports new findings about the relationship between crime and immigrants. These findings are consistent with the results of nearly all research in the last two decades that has examined this issue. New immigrants to the United States are less involved in crime than are Americans of longer tenure within the country. This is particularly true for crimes of violence, the crime type that has been examined most frequently, and has been reported by a number of analysts (Martinez and Lee, 2000; Sampson and Bean, 2006; Butcher and Piehl, 1998). Immigrants get arrested and imprisoned at lower rates than do Americans with documented citizenship. (In addition, there is evidence (Passell, 2009) that immigrants as a whole are also more likely to form families, hold jobs and complete high school than average American citizens). These are all desirable characteristics for new immigrant groups. A number of explanations may be offered for this finding: most new immigrants come from countries with lower crime rates than in the United States, new immigrants may be hesitant to draw attention to themselves by offending, new immigrant groups may escape the attention of authorities, new immigrant groups haven't learned to offend at the levels that native Americans do. Whatever the reasons, as Martinez notes, there is a substantial body of research that documents the fact that new immigrants – documented or not – offend at substantially lower rates than do native groups.

What makes this observation remarkable is the contrast between this finding, and research from a century earlier. Crime rates among new immigrant groups in the late 19th and early 20th century were substantially higher than those of their more established American counterparts. Criminological theory would predict that communities characterized by social disorganization, lacking in social capital, with high rates of poverty, and low school achievement would offend at higher levels. Yet, despite these 'apparent' deficits, new immigrant groups have lower levels of offending. Several explanations may account for this conundrum. First, the ability of American society to integrate and absorb new immigrants groups may be stronger now than it was a century earlier. If this assertion is true, it means that new immigrant groups are better able to integrate themselves into relationships and activities that provide some buffer against involvement in crime at the same time that groups with longstanding tenure in the US are not able to do so. Perhaps a more reasonable explanation is that the recent wave of immigration has yet to produce a second and third generation in large numbers, the generations in which their children will learn more about life in America, where crime rates are high, particularly among juveniles.

The second issue raised in this response concerns the denominator in immigrant rates of crime. Criminology is plagued with dilemmas about the denominator; the problem is worse for immigration, particularly undocumented immigrants. Quite simply, we don't know how many undocumented immigrants are in the United States, a specific state, a county or a census tract (Mears, 2001). Local estimates, more useful for purposes of social policy are seldom available. In addition, with the 2010 census approaching, many communities are concerned about undercounts of recent immigrant groups that may affect their ability to leverage an appropriate share of federal funding. As a consequence, any effort to construct a crime rate will be affected by the inability to construct a realistic denominator. There is a cycle to the attention to immigration of the sort that Martinez identifies in Texas: the more the public debate is based on media images with little foundation in reality, the less likely it is that new immigrants will be counted in population estimates. Undercounts are likely to deflate denominators and make rates appear higher than they are, thus there is a latent consequence to the public and political hue and cry over immigration.

The third question raised by Martinez' analysis is a concern about effective policy responses to immigration. If we don't fully understand immigration pressures and consequences, we can't respond to them effectively. That much is clear. But in the case of undocumented immigration, what is an understanding of the problem? Clearly this is an important issue for local law enforcement. Many new immigrant groups come from countries where trust in the government – particularly law enforcement – is low. Municipal police are faced with the task of responding the victimization of these groups, their reticence in reporting crime and lack of trust in agencies of government. These concerns are shared by local agencies as well as many citizens. There is concern among police leaders (IACP, 2007; Decker, Lewis, Provine and Varsanyi, 2009) that trust in law enforcement among new immigrant groups is low, that such groups are victimized at high levels and that they are reluctant to contact the police. Ironically, there is a cleavage between local police, and politicians and the public about the most appropriate course of action. Many police have eschewed the use of 287(g) the federal statute that allows local police to be trained by Immigration and Customs Enforcement (ICE) in enforcement of federal immigration statutes. This course of action reflects both the need for local police to remain integrated with their communities as well as the lack of resources to deal effectively with crime problems. Martinez describes the rather draconian approach proposed in Texas. The Arizona legislature has proposed legislation that would mandate asking immigration status by local police in a wide variety of circumstances. The legislature has taken this approach over concern that some municipalities had become "sanctuary" cities or endorsed a policy for their officers that only allowed them to ask immigration status subsequent to arrest. Both the 287(g) initiative and the approaches proposed in Texas and Arizona suggest a considerable shift away from local autonomy for law enforcement, usurping local and community level strategies in favor of state or federal priorities.

How do we reconcile the public perceptions of the immigration issues? A majority of police chiefs (Decker et al, 2009) find themselves at odds with public perceptions and political actions designed to respond to the presence of new immigrant groups. The constructions of problems in the media, by the public, and in political circles often bear little relationship to a more sober analysis. Instead, there is a large volume of immigration "talk", the reification of isolated incidents, incomplete data and pandering to public fears. The criminal law has been described as a "blunt instrument", incapable of dealing with many problems in the surgical manner they require. Immigration is clearly such a problem; police forces already stretched thin, concerned about jeopardizing already problematic relationships, are reluctant to take the lead on the response to a problem that requires broader solutions in the areas of employment, education, housing, and normalization of status. The attempt to use the criminal law to address such problems, well beyond the scope of the law, is likely to produce inequities and negative consequences in the implementation of the criminal law. But the inability of politicians and the public to move beyond immigration "talk" means that not only will the real issues not be dealt with, they will likely be made worse. Historically, immigration has been met with racism and xenophobia in the United States as well as Western Europe. We should not be surprised to see such a response at this historical juncture.

REFERENCES

Butcher, K.F. & Piehl, A.M. (1998). Recent Immigrants: Unexpected Implications for Crime and Incapacitation. *Industrial and Labor Relations Review, 51,* 4, 654-679.

Cohen, S. (1985). Visions of Social Control: Crime, Punishment, and Classification. Cambridge, MA: Polity Press.

Decker, S.H., Lewis, P., Provine, M. & Varsanyi, M. (2009). Local Responses to Immigration. In *Striking A Balance, the Role of Local Law Enforcement in Immigration.* Washington, D.C.: Police Foundation.

International Association of Chiefs of Police (2007). *A Police Chief's Guide to Immigration Issues.* Washington, D.C: International Association of Chiefs of Police.

Martinez, R. & Lee, M.T. (2000). On immigration and crime. In G. LaFree & R.J. Bursik (Eds.), *Criminal Justice 2000: The Changing Nature of Crime. Volume I.* (pp. 1-19). Washington, DC: National Institute of Justice.

Mears, D.P. (2001). The Immigration-Crime Nexus: Toward An Analytic Framework for Assessing and Guiding Theory, Research and Policy. *Sociological Perspectives, 44,* 1:1-19.

Passell, J. (2009). Unauthorized Immigrants, Trends, Characteristics, and Surprises. In Police Foundation, *Striking a Balance: The Role of Local Law Enforcement in Immigration.*

Sampson, R.J. & Bean, L. (2006). Cultural mechanisms and killing fields: A revised theory of community-level racial inequality. In R. Peterson, L, Krivo and J. Hagan (Editors), *The Many Colors of Crime: Inequalities of Race, Ethnicity, and Crime in America.* New York, NY: New York University Press.

Towards a Smarter and More Just Fortress Europe. Combining Temporary Labor Migration and Effective Policies of Return

Godfried Engbersen

Arjen Leerkes

The EU's restrictive migration regime is reaching the limits of its effectiveness. After two decades in which an impressive array of instruments to control migration has been developed, irregular migration remains a persistent problem. The European Commission estimated that at the beginning of the twenty-first century, between 4.5 and 8 million foreign nationals were illegally residing in EU territory. A lower figure for the year 2005 was provided by the Clandestino research team (2009), which estimated that the range was more likely to be between 2.8 and 6 million. This lower figure is a consequence of the enlargement of the European Union to include eight more countries (including Poland) in 2004, and another two (Bulgaria and Romania) in 2007. As a result, many migrants residing illegally in Western Europe were legalized overnight (Ruhs, 2007). In view of demographic developments – falling fertility rates and a declining working-age population – the need for low-skilled non-EU labor migrants is likely to continue (Organization for Economic Co-operation and Development (OECD), 2008). In combination with a restrictive EU immigration regime, this creates new groups of illegal migrants. In addition, the strict asylum procedures in place in the EU are generating a permanent contingent of failed asylum seekers who become illegal if they stay in the country. A Europe without illegal residence is inconceivable, though the size of that residence will fluctuate.

Governments may respond in several ways to the presence of illegal migrants. One strategy is to accept and tolerate them for economic and humanitarian reasons. This policy was characteristic of most West European countries in the period 1970-1990 (Cornelius, Martin & Hollifield, 1994). A second strategy, pursued mostly by South-European countries, is to legalize these groups through regularization programs (Levinson, 2005). A third strategy is to combat illegality. This Fortress Europe-strategy has been the principal strategy in most continental European welfare states since the early 1990s (Engbersen & Van der Leun, 2001). It is currently also becoming dominant in other European countries and has risen to the top of the European public agenda. It also is becoming more dominant in the Unites States (Jencks, 2007; National Conference of State Legislatures, 2009).

In this policy proposal we focus on this third strategy. We will show that the construction of Fortress Europe has led to various social problems in the terrain of criminal justice. Our argument is that these problems can be solved, at least in part, by admitting a larger number of temporary labor migrants from outside the EU, particularly if temporary labor programs are designed with an eye to source country development. Interestingly, research suggests that more space for legal labor migration does not necessarily obstruct restrictive aspects of immigration policy. On the contrary, there is good reason to believe that restrictive aspects can be carried out more effectively if more temporary labor migration is allowed for.

The defining characteristic features of 'Fortress Europe' are the following.

1.   Growing militarisation of the EU's external borders, especially at strategic places such as the 8.3 kilometer border separating Morocco and the Spanish enclave of Ceuta. However, EU enlargements in 2004 and 2007 created 4,787 kilometers of new eastern borders (Jesien, 2003). Such a long border makes hermetic border controls impossible.

2.   A greater focus on 'remote control' and 'internal' border controls given the porous nature of external borders. Migration control is expanding towards the 'outside' as well as the 'inside'. The shift to the outside is marked by the desire to prevent unwanted migrants and asylum seekers from reaching EU territory. This is done by means of carrier sanctions, but also by pressing source and transit countries to stop illegal migrants from entering the EU. As a consequence of this externalization of border control the de facto EU border has increasingly shifted to third countries (Lavenex, 2006). The shift to the 'inside' includes, among other things, various measures that exclude illegal migrants from the formal labor market and public provisions. This emphasis on internal border controls has led to increasing involvement on the part of employers and public housing corporations, welfare agencies, schools and healthcare bodies in those controls (Van der Leun, 2003). Such internal border control provides an interesting case of what Garland (2001: 124) has called 'responsibilization strategies', in which state agencies prompt action by non-state or semi-public organizations. Furthermore, employer sanctions, particularly in the Nordic and continental welfare states are enforced more strictly (Broeders 2009; Carrera & Guild 2007).

The shift to the inside also entails the tracing, identification and detention of unwanted migrants who reside in the territory in spite of external border control, as well as their exclusion from the formal labor market and the welfare state. In the past years states have obtained much more legal and technical possibilities to check identities. Large EU databases, such as SIS/SIS-II, VIS and Eurodac, have been developed to enable states to identify migrants' movements. These databases are storing a massive amount of data on migrants, including biometric markers. The idea is to register as many migrants as possible from 'suspect' legal categories (asylum seekers are registered in Eurodac) and 'suspect' countries of origin (visa-applicants will be registered in the VIS), in order to identify migrants who may cross the line into illegal residence at a later stage (Broeders, 2007).

3. An increase in detention capacity to facilitate the identification and expulsion of apprehended illegal migrants. There are now more than two hundred detention centers in the EU, both at traditional prisons and on islands, at airports and in large cities (Jesuit Refugee Service Europe, 2005). In 2007 13% of the penitentiary capacity in the Netherlands was intended for the administrative detention of illegal migrants (Van Kalmthout, 2007:103).

One can defend the position that the number of unwanted migrants has remained limited because of Fortress Europe's deterring effects (see also Jandl, 2007; Torpy, 2000). Still, Fortress Europe is unable to combat irregular migration effectively. In some countries large numbers of illegal migrants work in jobs that are hard to fill otherwise. Furthermore, in many countries the expulsion of illegal migrants remains problematic. In the Netherlands, for instance, less than half of the detained illegal migrants are effectively expelled from the country. Contrary to political rhetoric, that number has decreased in recent years (Van Kalmthout, 2007). This goes for other EU countries too. Fortress Europe has led to substantial human costs and social problems confronting the criminal justice system. We outline four of these below.

1. The increased difficulty of crossing the border legally has led to professional human smuggling (Jandl 2007; Kyle & Koslowski 2001). Stricter controls have made illegal crossing more risky, increasing migrants' dependence on human smuggling organizations. As Jandl (2007: 311) notes "(...) there is ample evidence for an increasing role of human smugglers in facilitating irregular migration".

2. There is a link between increased fatalities and intensified border controls (cf. Castles, 2006; Cornelius, 2001). Intensified controls have led to longer journeys under more dangerous circumstances. Although data are scarce and contested, the number of people that do not survive their journeys has increased. The number of annual fatalities reported by the NGO United varied between 770 and 1,300 in the 2002-2006 period. The total number of documented deaths between 1993 and 2006 is 7,200 (Spijkerboer, 2007).

3. A vulnerable undocumented outsider class is emerging throughout Europe (Engbersen, 1999). This is a heterogeneous category of migrants who, if they opt for illegal residence, are predestined to have an inferior social status, because they lack access to most social and political rights. Their presence has led to the return of pre-welfare state phenomena of exploitation, direct dependence on employers, illegal labor sub-contractors and family (Engbersen, 1999). For two reasons, criminal victimization rates are likely to be high among illegal migrants. They risk detention and expulsion if they call in help of the authorities (Goodey, 2003), and their

housing opportunities are spatially concentrated in high crime areas (Leerkes, 2009).

4. Detention and expulsion risks dampen crime rates; this is an important reason why crime among legal migrants tends to be limited. Yet there is evidence that illegal residence status may incite crime involvement, particularly in the context of a policy of internal border control. It appears that the increased need to identification has led to a major increase in 'residence crime', i.e., the use of false, borrowed or bought ID's. The case of Amsterdam provides an indication of the extent to which residence crime may occur. In this city of about 750,000 legal inhabitants, 92,500 ID's were reported lost over the last five years and only one fifth of these have been found. Furthermore, it appears that the institutional exclusion of illegal migrants from the formal labor market and public provisions generates forms of subsistence crime in relation to marginalization and extreme poverty (Engbersen, Van der Leun & De Boom, 2007; Leerkes, 2009). Illegal residence may also become a risk factor for problematic drug use, particularly in case of homelessness, which is often coupled with involvement in crimes to finance it. So far, this problem of marginalization and crime has been particularly documented for the Netherlands. More recently, similar observations have been reported on Belgium (Van Meeteren, Van San & Engbersen, 2008).

Restrictive immigration policy is in our opinion largely inevitable. In the more comprehensive welfare states, the paradox of solidarity and exclusion plays a key role (Freeman, 1995). Maintenance of national, comprehensive forms of internal solidarity (in the fields of health care, social security, education, public housing) for the benefit of native citizens and denizens implies the exclusion of unwanted outsiders from the welfare state's social entitlements (no external solidarity). If too many immigrants gain access too easily to welfare entitlements and don't pay taxes to support these, their continuation and legitimacy might be endangered. Aside from this, it is often felt that restrictive policies benefit the integration of those migrants who have arrived in previous immigration flows (Bade, 2004).

Yet the social problems created by Fortress Europe give rise to the question whether a more rational and just migration policy can be conceived. In our view the challenge will be to find the right balance between a closed and an open border, which will above all require a combination of a strategy of increased labor migration and a strategy of increased return migration. There should be more openings for legal labor migration in order to meet the very real demands in various sectors of the European labor market, now and in the future. The enlargement of the EU resulted in increased potential sources of labour, particularly from Eastern Europe, that can meet shortfalls (Black, Engbersen, Okólski & Panţîru, 2009). Over the last decade, third-country nationals have increasingly been replaced by workers from within the EU. It is nevertheless to be expected that in the longer term – after the end of the current economic crisis - wages within the EU will show fewer disparities, leading to reductions in internal

EU migration. This means that labour will ultimately have to come from non-EU countries.

Labour migration will counter the rise of human smuggling organizations and the occurrence of residence and subsistence crime. It will also reduce the number of 'bogus' asylum seekers because there is a legal labor channel they can use to find employment in Europe (Crisp, 2007). At the same time, it is essential that illegal migrants can be returned to their country of origin. This is crucial for the legitimacy of the European migration policy, but it will also ensure that problems of exploitation, victimization and of residence and subsistence crime can be reduced and will remain temporary, i.e., before repatriation takes place. Below, we will explain why both strategies can go together very well.

TEMPORARY MIGRATION

It is important to consider new systems of temporary migration. Considerable experience has been gained in Europe in recent years with temporary migrant worker programmes (TMP), covering working holidays, seasonal agricultural work, sector-based schemes, overseas students, intra-corporate transferees, etc. (OECD, 2008). But these programmes are limited and do not meet the demand for low-skilled workers in agriculture, construction, trades, hospitality and domestic work. Apart from the requirement of equal treatment on the labor market in terms of rewards and labor conditions, additional experiments should be based on two principles:

1. The temporariness of labor migration is central.
2. Labor migration programs will meet the demand for labor but are also designed to contribute to development objectives in the countries of origin.

Several pleas have already been made to realize such smart TMP's programs. Crucial elements are: (1) a clear delineation of the length of the contract (not exceeding five years); (2) employers initiate specific TMPs, but governments must create and control the conditions governing the arrival and return of temporary labor migrants (3) use is made of substantial return premiums, which could consist of social security savings, pensions savings, or a share of developmental aid money (4) there are schemes for facilitating the productive investment of return premiums (Crisp 2007; Global Commission on International Migration, 2005; Van Os van den Abeelen, 2007), such as reserving part of the return premiums for scholarship funds for the benefit of the migrants' children. In other words, TMP's should be designed and framed in ways that do justice to the interests of all parties involved (employers, governments, workers) in the countries of destination and origin. Because the effects of such programs will have to prove themselves in practice, it is recommendable to increase the number of serious experiments (Castles 2006; OECD 2008). Furthermore, we like to emphasize that temporary labor migration programs are not a replacement for regular labor migration programs and official developmental assistance (ODA). They are also not a form of 'total justice'. These programs will be highly selective just as the current irregular flows of labor migration. Very poor people without skills and economic and social capital do not migrate.

WHY TEMPORARY LABOR MIGRATION MAY ASSIST MIGRATION CONTROL

The effective exclusion of illegal migrants requires the co-operation of countries of origin and transit. That is increasingly acknowledged with respect to the initial phase of migration as we have described with the move towards the externalization of control. But it is also true for the final phase of return. Return may fail if illegal migrants conceal their identity and nationality, but also if source countries are reluctant to take migrants back. Dutch research, which was carried out in two big centers for Alien Detention, confirms that international relations influence expulsion rates. It turns out that illegal migrants who are in a political sense from 'near' countries – countries that are aspiring EU membership and the former Dutch colony Surinam – are more likely to be expelled than illegal migrants from other source countries, quite independent of differences in willingness to return on the part of illegal migrants (table 1).

Table 1. Expulsion chances of detained illegal migrants according to country of origin and willingness to return on the part the migrant.

	Released	Expulsed	Total
Countries aspiring EU membership[a] / Surinam:			
Wants to return	1 (9%)	10 (91%)	11 (100%)
Does not want to return	4 (19%)	17 (81%)	21 (100%)
Total	5 (16%)	27 (84%)	32 (100%)
Other countries:			
Wants to return	18 (32%)	38 (68%)	56 (100%)
Does not want to return	96 (50%)	97 (50%)	193 (100%)
Total	114 (46%)	135 (54%)	249 (100%)

Source: Secondary analyses of data (examination of dossiers and in-depth interviews) that was gathered in 2003 by Van Kalmthout, Graft, Hansen & Hadrouk (2004a; 2004b).
Notes: [a] This category includes all countries that have been admitted to the EU after Van Kalmthout's study had been completed (Czech Republic, Estonia, Hungary, Latvia, Lithuania, Poland, Slovakia, Slovenia, Malta, Cyprus, Romania and Bulgaria)

as well as all countries that are still, at the time of writing, candidates for EU membership (Croatia, Macedonia, Turkey).

Therefore, reluctant source countries will, of course, be more likely to cooperate with return migration if they gain by doing so. Indeed, a number of countries already demand concessions for their involvement in external border control (Lavenex, 2006). While such concessions do not necessarily have to lie on the terrain of migration policy – there is some evidence that the weapons ban on Libya was lifted in return for external border control (Human Rights Watch, 2006) – more space for legal labor migration is high on the political agenda of many source countries that have an interest to send unemployed workers abroad hoping that these will send remittances to the source country. In the present conditions, source countries risk losing a remitter if they cooperate with expulsion procedures, while it is uncertain whether other nationals will make it to the EU to replace the migrant. If there would be more space for TMP's, the 'replacement' of remitters would be less problematic. Furthermore, there is some evidence that an increase in the number of temporary migrants will result in a higher volume of remittances to source countries, even if this would presuppose a reduction in the number of nationals who settle more permanently. This is because there appears to be an inverted "U" time pattern in migrant remittances, where remittances tend to increase in the first five to eight years after migration, but eventually decrease with time spent in the country of destination (Amuedo-Dorants & Pozo, 2006).

Finally, more space for temporary legal labor migration may also contribute to a greater perceived fairness of the international migration regime. Sociology of law teaches that rules are more likely to be followed without formalized social control if these are perceived as legitimate by the actors involved. Although we lack systematic information on the perceived legitimacy of migration rules and its importance for migration behavior, it can be hypothesized that more space for labor migration will increase the willingness on the part of source countries and migrants to co-operate with migration control. That would constitute another reason to adopt the pragmatic idealism we have propagated in this policy proposal.

REFERENCES

Amuedo-Dorantes, C. & Pozo, S. (2006). The time pattern of remittances: Evidence from Mexican migrants. *Well-being and Social Policy, 2,* 49-66.

Bade, J. (2004). Legal and illegal immigration into Europe: Experiences and challenges. *European Review, 12,* 339-375.

Black, R., Engbersen, G., Okólski, M. & Panţîru, C. (Eds.). (2009). *A Continent Moving West? EU Enlargement and Labour Migration from Central and Eastern Europe.* Amsterdam: Amsterdam University Press.

Broeders, D. (2007). The new digital borders of Europe: EU databases and the surveillance of irregular migrants. *International Sociology, 22,* 71-92.

Broeders, D. (2009). *Breaking Down Anonymity. (Digital) Surveillance on Irregular Migrants in Germany and the Netherlands.* Amsterdam: Amsterdam University Press.

Carrera, S. & Guild, E. (2007, August). An EU framework on sanctions against employers of irregular migrants: Some reflections on the scope, features & added value. CEPS Policy Brief, 140. Brussels: Centre for European Policy Studies.

Castles, S. (2006). Guest workers in Europe: A Resurrection? *International Migration Review, 40,* 741-766.

CLANDESTINO. (2009). Irregular Migration: Counting the Uncountable, Data and Trends Across Europe. Available online: http:// clandestino.eliamep.gr and http://irregular-migration.hwwi.net (database)

Cornelius, W. (2001). Death at the border: Efficacy and unintended consequences of US immigration control policy. *Population and Development Review, 27,* 661–685.

Cornelius, W., Martin, P. & Hollifield, J. (Eds.). (1994). *Controlling Immigration: A Global Perspective.* Stanford: Stanford University Press.

Crisp, J. (2007). Temporary migration programmes: Potential, problems and prerequisites. In M. Jandl (Ed.), *Innovative Concepts for Alternative Migration Policies. Ten Innovative Approaches to the Challenges of Migration in the 21st Century* (pp. 19-28). Amsterdam: Amsterdam University Press.

Engbersen, G. (1999). The undocumented outsider class. In T. Boje, B. Van Steenbergen & S. Walby (Eds.), *European Societies: Fusion or Fission?* (pp. 88-102). London: Routledge.

Engbersen, G. & Van der Leun, J. (2001). The social construction of illegality and criminality. *European Journal on Criminal Policy and Research, 9,* 51-70.

Engbersen, G., Van der Leun, J. & de Boom, J. (2007). The fragmentation of migration and crime in the Netherlands. In M. Tonry & C. Bijleveld (Eds.), *Crime and Justice: A Review of Research, Volume 35* (pp. 389-452). Chicago: Chicago University Press.

Freeman, G. (1995). Modes of immigration politics in liberal Democratic states. *International Migration Review, 29,* 881-902.

Garland, D. (2001). *The Culture of Control: Crime and Social Order in Contemporary Society.* Oxford: Oxford University Press.

Global Commission on International Migration. (2005*). Migration in an Interconnected World: New Directions for Action: Report of the Global Commission on International Migration.* Cambridge: Cambridge University Press.

Goodey, J. (2003). Migration, crime and victimhood: Responses to sex trafficking in the EU. *Punishment & Society, 5,* 415-431.

Human Rights Watch. (2006). *Stemming the Flow. Abuses Against Migrants, Asylum Seekers and Refugees.* London: Human Rights Watch.

Jandl, M. (Ed.). (2007). *Innovative Concepts for Alternative Migration Policies. Ten Innovative Approaches to the Challenges of Migration in the 21st Century.* Amsterdam: Amsterdam University Press.

Jencks, C. (2007). The immigration charade. *The New York Review of Books,* 54, 49-52.

Jesien, L. (2003). Is the European Union changing its nature? The 2003 Blue Paper, Polish Forum of Lisbon Strategy, Gdańsk/Warszawa (in Polish)

Jesien, L. (2003). The open method of coordination: Its European context and meaning. The 2003 White Paper, Polish Forum of Lisbon Strategy, Gdańsk/Warszawa (in Polish).

Jesuit Refugee Service Europe. (2005). *Detention in Europe. Administrative Detention of Asylum-seekers and Irregular Migrants.* Available online: www.detention-in-europe.org

Kyle, D. & Kslowski, R. (Eds.). (2001). *Global Human Smuggling: Comparative Perspectives.* Baltimore and London: The John Hopkins University Press.

Lavenex, S. (2006). Shifting up and out: The foreign policy of European immigration control. *West European Politics, 29,* 329 – 350.

Leerkes, A. (2009). Illegal Residence and Public Safety in The Netherlands. Amsterdam: Amsterdam University Press.

Levinson, A. (2005). *The Regularization of Unauthorized Migrants: Literature Survey and Country Case Studies.* Oxford: Centre on Migration, Policy and Society, University of Oxford

National Conference of State Legislatures. (2009). *State Laws Related to Immigrants and Immigration in 2008.* Washington, DC: National Conference of State Legislatures.

Organization for Economic Co-operation and Development. (2008). *International Migration Outlook, Annual Report 2008 Edition.* Paris: Organization for Economic Co-operation and Development.

Ruhs, M. (2007). Changing status, changing fortunes? The impact of acquiring EU status on the earnings of East European migrants in the UK. Oxford: COMPAS.

Spijkerboer, T. (2007). The human costs of border control. European *Journal of Migration and Law, 9,* 147-161

Torpey, J. (2000). States and the regulation of migration in the twentieth-century North Atlantic World. In P. Andreas and T. Snyder (Eds.), *The Wall Around the West: State Borders and Immigration Controls in North America and Europe* (pp. 31-54). Lanham: Rowman and Littlefield.

Van der Leun, J. (2003). *Looking for Loopholes. Processes of Incorporation of Illegal Immigrants in the Netherlands.* Amsterdam: Amsterdam University Press.

Van Kalmthout, A. (2007). Foreigners. In M. Boone and M. Moerings (Eds.). *Dutch Prisons: Still Front Runner in Penal Policy?* (pp. 101-127). The Hague: Bju Legal Publishers.

Van Kalmthout, A., Graft, A., Hansen, L. & Hadrouk M. (2004a). *Terugkeermogelijkheden van vreemdelingen in de vreemdelingenbewaring. Deel 1 Het Dossieronderzoek. [Return Possibilities of Aliens in Aliens Custody. Part 1 Examination of Dossiers]*. Nijmegen: Wolf Legal.

Van Kalmthout, A., Graft, A., Hansen, L. & Hadrouk M. (2004b). *Terugkeermogelijkheden van vreemdelingen in de vreemdelingenbewaring. Deel 2 Evaluatie terugkeerprojecten [Return Possibilities of Aliens in Aliens Custody. Part 2 Assessment of Return Projects]* Nijmegen: Wolf Legal.

Van Os van den Abeelen, T. (2007). A new European employment migration policy. In M. Jandl (Ed.), *Innovative Concepts for Alternative Migration Policies. Ten Innovative Approaches to the Challenges of Migration in the 21st Century* (pp. 29-36). Amsterdam: Amsterdam University Press

Van Meeteren, M., Van San, M. & Engbersen, G. (2008). *Zonder papieren: Over de positie van irreguliere migranten en de rol van het vreemdelingenbeleid in België. [Without Papers: On the Position of Irregular Migrants and the Role of the Aliens Policy in Belgium].* Leuven: Acco.

The Criminalization of Migrants in Europe: A Comment on Engbersen and Leerkes

Dario Melossi

When, in 1977, I first left Italy for a long stint in the United States, I left a country where the strength of the working-class was remarkable. It was a situation that could have reminded one of the United States exactly 40 years earlier, when the sit-down strike at the General Motors plant in Flint, Michigan, contributed to give a firm class imprint to FDR's "New Deal". I went back to Italy in the mid-1990s, to a situation altogether different. If the "Reagan revolution" had not yet reached Italy – we are in the midst of it right now with our usual couple of decades of delay! – certainly, capitalists had won the class war hands down and there was no clearer indication of such a victory than the dominant presence in Italian public discourse of the preoccupation with "immigration" – an object which was totally inexistent when I had left in the late 1970s.

What had happened in those 16 years? Well, usually the story is told that around the early 1970s – 1973 is the usual culprit – an "oil crisis" developed which had a number of consequences, among which was the "stop" given to welcoming immigration policies in Central and Northern European countries and the beginning of a trickling down of migration flows toward Southern European countries – such as Greece, Italy, Portugal and Spain (Calavita 2005). Besides, in those central and northern countries, a process of slow substitution of "asylum-seekers" for the previous "economic migrants" also started to unfold. At the same time, and probably even more important, the "oil crisis" turned out to be also what certain authors have termed the beginning of a "post-Fordist" age, characterized by a reduction in industrial work and its technological transformation, the giant development of a "tertiary" sector, the start of what would be later called "information technology", without even mentioning, of course, the various "financial bubbles", the explosion of the last of which we have celebrated only very recently. What it is still lacking in this picture however is the realization that this new set-up, that started in the 1970s, was also a way, by the capitalists, to react against the enormous power that the working-class had assembled between the 1960s and the 1970s. At that time, in fact, a special historical conjunction of high wages and high union memberships, postcolonial uprisings, baby boom, and student and antiwar movements, had scared the hell out of conservatives (who have been very busy, since then and at the very least until the victory of Obama one year ago, to find ways of reacting against what was, for them, a terrible decade!)

In Europe, one of the very important aspects of such overall reaction has certainly been the huge immigration flow. It is clear in fact, why immigration is one of the weapons at capital's disposal. Similarly to technological investment or political repression, it is one of the ways in which capitalists manage to replace whole strata of the working class which have shown to be quite hard to manage with what it is (at first) a more amenable, divided, less determined, working class. This new working class, in the case of a country like Italy for instance, has come from Asia (the Mid-East as well as the Far-East), Africa (especially in its Northern and Central parts), Eastern Europe, and Latin America. It is a flow of defeated peoples, by and large, that the West has first subjugated by using the power of money and/or the power of weapons and from which has then extracted cheap labor power in ways not very dissimilar from what the old Roman Empire used to do when it conquered a new land and made its inhabitants the slaves of Rome (later on however the Romans granted Roman citizenship to all the inhabitants of the Empire – that is a level of political civilization that we have yet to achieve!). So, we find, among the people in the streets of Italy today, Moroccans and Tunisians, and Somalis and Ethiopians and Palestinians and Iraqis and Afghans, and those who used to live in the part of Europe called Socialist, and again people from the Indian subcontinent and China. Their ruin more or less corresponded – another uncanny coincidence! – to a period of remarkable economic development all throughout the West, in the 1990s. However, we did not want to part ourselves from this newly arrived wealth too hastily, and hoped, for some strange fantasy, that the lack of reproductive activity would let us enjoy our wealth a little bit longer. Maybe this was one of the reasons why we increasingly experienced, at the same time, the lowest birth rate in the world – in "Catholic" countries like Italy or Spain!

So, something strange started to happen. We were becoming older and older and we sorely needed people in our countries who would engage in occupations that were increasingly more disdainful to us, and yet we did not want to admit that such was the case and we kept our borders basically closed, at least in theory. At least since the 1970s oil crisis, the general European attitude toward immigration has been one based on limitation, discouragement and control much more than affirmative policies . The result has been that in very different ways in the various countries, migrants have been coming in anyway under the guise of "asylum seekers" or "clandestines" or more often "overstayers". Especially in Southern Europe their position has later been "regularized" because workers are anyway always inferior to need (at least until the current crisis), so their "illegal" migration has turned out to be perhaps illegal but certainly rational, making up, in a sense, for the irrationality of the political and legal decisions of European countries. A supreme case of hypocrisy, of course: we cannot politically accept that they may come in legally, but let them in anyway and, later on, let us make their position ok. As Kitty Calavita (2005) has well argued, this system has meant a hefty contribution to the segmentation of the labor market that is so functional to the new post-Fordist times. The only difference is how functional and to what kind of development: quite obviously there's a difference between the "normal" advantage that comes to (normal) capitalists from a well ordered, "regular", immigrant work-force and the "super-exploitation" that is made possible for (backward) capitalists by the "irregular" character of the same work-force.

The "criminalization" of the latter is but a corollary of the overall situation and goes together with its "inferiorization" and "racialization" (Calavita 2005). In fact, once the situation, as Thomas used to say, has been defined also legally in the way we just illustrated, the definition will be much more likely to stick. If one cannot apply for a legitimate job, because one does not have a permit to stay, it will be much more likely that will do something illegal. First of all he or she will do something illegal to the end of becoming legal: crimes of falsity will skyrocket, as Engbersen and Leerkes rightly notice (for Italy, see Ferraris 2009). And one will do illegal things in order to work: all kinds of transgressions of employment and fiscal laws will follow, both by workers and those who employ them. One will maybe sell counterfeit goods. And finally, if nothing else will avail, one will get into the other two huge underground markets that couple so nicely with the underground labor market: illegal drugs and sex for hire will become the favorite areas of employment for some of these migrants. However, as criminologists know very well, these are not areas where conflicts can be resolved peacefully. No lawyers here, at least no civil lawyers. So organized crime and violence will ensue. And if for very many this will mean prison and deportation, for a few it will mean the creation of a criminally based power, the recruitment of new levers of migrant crime and so on, and even if they become regular, at that point, will be very hard to exit a series of choices and a lifestyle that have both become a habit and a necessity in a sense. So, the circle will be perfect and the prediction of migrant crime will have become a sad and gritty reality of the new Europe.

And in fact, in Table 1, you can see what I would call the overrepresentation of foreigners in European prisons, limiting ourselves to the 15-country EU of before the latest enlargements. In this table, I have calculated (see column at the right end), for each country member of the EU, the ratio of the percent of foreign inmates to the percent of resident foreigners. We may notice an overrepresentation of foreigners that goes from a minimum of 1.74 for Luxemburg to about 7 times for Italy and the Netherlands.

A major difference may be made of course between old-immigration Central and Northern countries and recent immigration Southern European countries, for which the comparison with countries, which have a colonial past, may be unfair. In former colonial countries, such as France or the United Kingdom, there may be naturalized citizens, often of color, who are in prison because of social mechanisms not unlike those that preside to foreigners' imprisonment but obviously they do not show up in foreigners' statistics. In other words, what in other countries are the two separate issues of migration and ethnicity, in Southern Europe the two by and large still overlap. What is specific to Southern European countries is their high level of undocumented migrants, caused by the almost impossible task of immigrating legally, especially for reasons of work.

Table 1. Foreign Population in European Penal Institutions Ratio of Overrepresentation

	Percent of Foreign Inmates	Percent of Foreign Residents	Ratio of Over-representation
Austria	42.9	9.9	4.33
Belgium	41.6	8.7	4.78
Denmark	18.9	5.1	3.70
Finland	8.1	2.3	3.52
France	19.8	5.7	3.47
Germany	26.9	8.8	3.05
Greece	41.6	7.9	5.26
Ireland	12.6	10.2	1.23
Italy	32.3	4.9	6.59
Luxemburg	71.4	41	1.74
Netherlands	32.7	4.2	7.78
Portugal	18.5	4.1	4.51
United Kingdom (England & Wales)	14.0	6.0	2.33
Spain	31.2	10.2	3.05
Sweden	21.4	5.4	3.96
European Union (27 countries)		6.0	

Of course, as criminologists, we know very well that an imprisonment rate means very little, it does not mean, anyway, a measure of criminality, at most it may mean a measure of criminality times a measure of formal and informal social control by many actors. This table is therefore at most only suggestive. The social mechanisms that may produce such data are the most various, from the high visibility of migrants' crime vis à vis the low visibility of other kinds of crime ('crime in the street' vs. 'crime in the suites', as it is often said), to the specific crimes that only migrants can commit, from the public and legislative sensitivity against migrants to the discriminatory behavior of many public institutions, from the migrants' deprivation of the fundamental right to have an efficient defense to the impossibility of applying to migrants a host of pre- and after-trial benefits that keep natives out of prison but that railroad foreigners into detention. And of course this does not even touch on the basic issue of the social, economic, cultural and legal condition of disadvantage that many migrants start from!

Would the proposal by Godfried Engbersen and Arjen Leerkes to introduce a regime of less restrictive but temporary labor migration and "effective" policies of return – a sort of guest worker program – help to redress this overall sad state of affairs, sad for both the migrants and the host societies? I really doubt it. Engbersen and Leerkes state that "EU's restrictive migration regime has reached the limits of its effectiveness" but, it is appropriate to ask, has ever been "effective"? And effective to what end? Why does irregular migration (and, in certain countries, asylum-seekers) remain a persistent problem, which is estimated, they report, between a minimum of 2-4 and a maximum of 6-8 millions of people? They claim that in Europe three policies by and large have been followed, 1) to accept and tolerate irregular migration, 2) legalize it, and 3) contrast it. I think they intend these three policies to have been alternative to one another. However, as we have seen, these three policies have actually been going on at the same time and have actually implied each other. The "toleration" of irregular migration may only take place because irregular migration is supposedly "contrasted", at least on the book – even if, cyclically, in certain countries at least, waves of undocumented migration are "legalized" in order to fill the need for labor-power. I wonder whether a similar policy may not have turned around the expansion of the asylum-seeking category in other countries, such as Germany or the UK. In still other countries, a more rational and open adoption of the ius soli principle, as in France, may have "legalized" not the migrants but their children.

Engbersen and Leerkes point out the consequence of intensification of controls outside and inside. This is certainly the case. Control is externalized, that is passed on to "buffer countries" at the borders of the EU (one of the most shameful and egregious cases is that of the prisons and camps in Libya, well documented in the Italian film Come un uomo sulla terra). But at the same time it is intensified internally. So we have the paradox that while European citizens and their faraway descendents (such as Ukrainian Germans – so called Aussiedler – or many Latin Americans) are allowed to roam freely from Helsinki to Lisbon without having ever to show an id card, if you are the son of a Turk in Germany or a Moroccan in Italy, born and grown up in Germany or in Italy, when you turn 18 you may happen to be "sent back" to a country a culture and a language you have no idea of, for "administrative" reasons! To this end, a true network of "administrative detention" centers has been set up all throughout Europe (Giorgio Agamben has correctly pointed out, in his Homo Sacer (1995) that it was a system of "administrative detention" that constituted the seedling of the Nazi system of concentration camps in late 1930s Germany and indeed, if one wished to take seriously the law just passed in Italy exactly when I am writing these notes, according to which the lack of proper documentation is now a crime, and one should try to stop and arrest all the "clandestine" migrants in Italy – the number of which is roughly equal to 15 times the total number of inmates in already overcrowded prisons – one would have to set up a system much akin, at least in scope, to the one set up in Nazi Germany!). It is also certainly true that this whole system has caused, as Engbersen and Leerkes state, more smuggling of human beings and under much more dangerous conditions. The number of fatalities in the Mediterranean since the 1990s has certainly surpassed that on the very treacherous border between Mexico and the United States.

But, would a new guest worker system be the answer? Why should a "restrictive immigration policy" be "inevitable"? And why shouldn't migrants pay taxes, once they become "documented"? Engbersen and Leerkes refer to a "temporal character" of their proposal, of five years. But have they an idea of how many things may happen to a human being in 5 years? (After all, I met my future and current wife only about a month after I had debarked from the plane in San Francisco!) In my personal case the situation could be remedied by changing the ground for the residency permit (which is not always so easy!) but beyond personal issues, the point is the concept of work, and work force, that is revealed by such a plan. It is a concept of work that clashes head-on not only with the most elementary rights – among which the right to self-determine the trajectory of one's own life – but also with the idea of a work-force that we want to be able to reshape itself continuously, adapt to new circumstances, pursue education while working, in one word, be "flexible"! It is quite clear that this particular work-force is one that is pursued at first because of, and not notwithstanding, its unskilled character. But why should things stay that way? A work-force which is obliged for five years to do always the same kind of thing and at the end has to go back home comes very close to an idea of work-force as a at least temporary slave-force! All of this it is tightly linked with the notion of repatriation that is implied in Engbersen and Leerkes's scheme. Is the repatriation that they have in mind compulsory at the end of the 5 years? The fact that they mention the importance of the collaboration of countries which are supposed to "welcome back" the expelled migrants makes one think that is compulsory repatriation they have in mind. No objection could of course be made to incentives for voluntary repatriation, which is what happened in fact in Europe in the early 1970s. But if it is compulsory repatriation that we are talking about – a deportation without having committed any (real) crime – we should remember that a typical consequence of all temporary and restrictive policies is that of creating an increasingly broader area of illegalism in the country and an increasing recourse to family reunification, because migrants are afraid of not being allowed back into the country!

It seems to me that a possible alternative policy could be first of all that countries members of the European Union should take seriously the "communitarization" of migration policies agreed upon between the Amsterdam and the Tampere treaties, and should therefore decide together what ought to happen! This is an absolute necessity because migrants very often land on Italian coasts (for instance) not because they are particularly interested in Italy but because they want to go to the United Kingdom, or Germany, or France. Furthermore, we should devise a system that allows migrants to get visa in order to come and look for what they are looking for, that is work, and it is only those who commit serious crimes who should be sent back against their will. In between, specific schemes may be devised in order to encourage voluntary repatriation.

REFERENCES

Agamben, G. (1995) *Homo Sacer: Sovereign Power and Bare Life.* Stanford: Stanford University Press, 1998.

Calavita, K. (2005) *Immigrants at the Margins: Law, Race, and Exclusion in Southern Europe.* New York: Cambridge University Press.

Ferraris, V. (2009) Migrant's offside trap: A strategy for dealing with misleading rules and a hostile playing field. In J. Shapland and P. Ponsaers (Eds.), *The Informal Economy and Connections with Organized Crime: The Impact of National Social and Economic Policies.* Amsterdam: Boom Publishers.

Is There a More Just "Fortress Europe"? A Review of Engbersen & Leerkes

Nora V. Demleitner

In their article Towards a Smarter and More Just Fortress Europe: Combining Temporary Labor Migration and Effective Policies of Return, Godfried Engbersen and Arjen Leerkes outline a new migration policy which, in their view, would provide a "smarter and more just" approach to undocumented migration into the European Union (EU). The EU's immigration control regime has proven insufficient, as reflected in the growing number of irregular, or as they are called in the United States, illegal or undocumented migrants.[i] Intra-EU demand for low-skilled labor allows migrants to find employment, which remains a strong draw. Restrictive immigration policies, however, condemn a large group of non-EU citizens to illegality.

Earlier EU attempts at ignoring or legalizing the undocumented have given way to a fortress approach to immigration. The EU has increasingly militarized its external borders and ever more deputized third-country states to act as forward guards, preventing non-EU citizens from entering. Its domestic policies have been designed to preclude non-EU citizens from access to the labor market and to social services, the cherished and most protected characteristic of the European welfare states. With governments collecting ever more data on immigrants, they have deputized employers and state agencies as enforcement agents, with the goal of controlling, excluding, and removing those who are without stay rights. Therefore, as Engbersen and Leerkes describe it, the external border has been ever further pushed out while the internal border has been fortified.

These developments have led to the criminalization, or the criminal-like treatment of non-EU citizens. Parallel to the developments in the United States, the EU has witnessed a dramatic expansion in detention spaces, but appears to have been less successful in deporting those detained than the United States.[ii] Despite all of these efforts at deterrence, the number of the undocumented continues to climb, so the authors assert, with their attempts at reaching the EU becoming ever more dramatic and leading to increased human sacrifice. Human smuggling, and not mentioned by Engbersen and Leerkes, human trafficking, continue to increase as entry becomes more difficult. This is a development that has occurred on both sides of the Atlantic Ever greater difficulties in entry, will likely lead to more dangerous attempts and heightened abuse of the migrants by the smugglers. Heightened entry hurdles will also increase the price demanded of migrants, and therefore facilitate the building of criminal cartels whose division of labor is a shrewd business response to increased border controls.

Engbersen and Leerkes note, in passing, how a large number of irregular migrants suddenly became regularized as their countries of citizenship became EU members. This comment indicates how artificially constructed notions of irregularity – and attendant criminalization – can be. The criminal migrant may be the ultimate socially constructed offender.

As irregular migrants settle in EU countries, Engbersen and Leerkes find their livelihood will remain precarious. These migrants will be relegated to the poorest and most crime-ridden residential districts, and will likely end up working under abusive conditions. They are often crime victims; they may fall prey to alcohol and illegal drugs, and ultimately become law-breakers themselves. In addition, subsistence crime as well as involvement in identity theft, necessary to procure employment and other services, will increase. The authors reference the increase in document fraud which is a crime that flows directly from the criminalization of illegality and the need for documentation as internal borders and controls become more effective. Document fraud has become rampant in the United States where increasing enforcement of immigration laws in the workplace has not decreased the number of undocumented but instead created a flourishing identity theft and identity forgery business, which provides employers with plausible excuses for hiring the needed and/or desired undocumented workforce.

Engbersen and Leerkes conclude that in European welfare states, restrictive immigration policies will continue to dominate as extensive welfare for citizens makes the exclusion of non-citizens from such services virtually mandatory. Interestingly, these welfare policies are increasingly used to argue that the exclusion of the undocumented, or as the authors call them "unwanted outsiders," is crucial to provide such services not only to citizens but to "wanted immigrants," those who came earlier, and I would add, those who have been permitted to come more recently, which includes not only citizens of newly admitted EU countries but also, in many EU countries, the highly skilled. Only if those who have not contributed are excluded from services, can the services of the others be protected.

This argument may, however, be overly broad. First, if the "unwanted" were in fact regularized, as they are needed on the labor market, they could contribute to the social services fund by paying taxes. The United States, in its 1996 legislation, has excluded almost all immigrants from the receipt of social services, unless they have worked (and paid taxes) for a certain amount of time. While this may not constitute a "more just" approach, it could present another viable model. More extensive welfare states, however, may reject such a model, as it allows for the suffering of some within its borders, and re-writes the solidarity agreement. In addition, this model is based on a more extensive belief in the integrating function of the labor market, and market participation as an indicator of full participatory status than might be the case in Europe.

To solve the criminal justice issues resulting from the criminalization of a large group of migrants, Engbersen and Leerkes suggest a temporary migration policy. They view low-skilled immigration as necessary for European economies and inevitable. Some have disputed, however, the need for additional low-skilled labor, as it may be possible to fulfill any such demands from within the already settled domestic migrant population, at least in some EU member states, such as France which has a very high unemployment rate among its young immigrant population.

The article may also paint criminalization, on the one hand, and labor needs and labor-market responses, on the other hand, with too broad a brush. Despite EU-wide policies, responses to migrants often remain localized or at least nationally bounded, as exemplified by ongoing grants of amnesty, especially in more Southern European countries. One is left wondering whether an EU approach to short-term labor migration is achievable, and even desirable in light of nationally varying needs. However, without such a policy, further criminalization of all migrants is likely to occur in countries that are less immigrant-accepting.

In light of their assumptions, the authors argue that the existing temporary migration policies – and here they lump short-term low-skilled programs together with programs facilitating the stay of the highly skilled – have provided experience, and apparently counsel toward a much more broadly based low-skilled immigration scheme. Equal treatment in the labor market should be combined with a temporal limitation on the stay and a development policy for the sending countries. The authors set out the elements of such a stay policy: limited to a maximum stay of five years, but always clearly indicating the length of the stay; employer-demand driven, with government oversight; substantial return premium, combined with schemes to facilitate its productive investment. Such a design, the authors argue would "do justice to the interests of all parties involved (employers, government, workers) in the countries of destination and origin." They suggest that "the number of serious experiments" be increased. Nevertheless, the authors appear to have some concerns about their proposal. The time limitation, they argue, will guarantee that exploitation and any crime migrants may commit, will at least be temporally limited. Source countries must ultimately benefit from such an immigration scheme to guarantee the return of their citizens. Return should also be easier, the authors postulate, if all players consider the rules legitimate and fair.

Based on past experiments with time-limited labor migration, I have serious concerns about the re-invigoration of these proposals. While the proposal may increase the gains for both sending and receiving countries, it is doubtful that they provide the same benefit to the migrant.

People become increasingly the pawns of their governments. The Philippines, for example, train a substantial portion of their population essentially to be exported. The advantage for these immigrants, consists in gaining an education and human capital. It is imaginable that at least some sending governments may want to assure literacy and language skills of the receiving country for prospective migrants. Such language skills – though this would require bilateral, rather than regional, agreements between individual countries – would have the added benefit of preventing the most egregious abuses.

Presumably such short-term immigration programs would be limited to a relatively small number of sending countries to assure the long-term positive economic impact on such countries from this type of migration. If that were to occur, however, there could be a substantially negative impact on the economy and social capital of the sending country, as most of the migrants will presumably be younger and better educated. They may also leave behind families, and possibly young children, for extended periods of time. Family unification is obviously not a goal of such a migration program, especially as it would create ties to the receiving country which the authors do not seem to envision. While low-skilled migrants may have no other opportunity, the German "green card" design made it clear that without family unification rights, high-skilled immigrants have better options they can pursue.

Without family unification, one can imagine one of two scenarios arising: First, a relatively large number of young migrant men is being sent to the receiving countries. While they will have a strong incentive not to become involved in a crime, their likelihood of involvement remains high as they will lack legitimate forms of diversion, such as a family. Therefore, socially less attractive behavior may flourish, including prostitution. Alternatively, countries may send young women as migrants, with the attendant social consequence of their absence from the home, which can have a dramatic impact on family and social structure in a community. Sending countries may, in fact, prefer women for many of the positions envisioned by the authors, such as those in "hospitality and domestic work." Receiving countries may prefer women since they present less of a social threat and are generally perceived as more docile and compliant.

How attractive such temporary schemes are, and how persuasive they are to the local population, will also depend on whether avenues remain for migrants to stay. While it is attractive to envision that no migrant has such rights, what about migrants in whose home country conditions deteriorate so dramatically that an asylum claim becomes viable? How should such migrants be treated if they marry an EU citizen? Other conditions remain questionable: May migrants attend school during their stay, to enhance their skills? May an employer petition for them to stay, perhaps in a supervisory or management capacity? These are the question that, in commenting on immigration to his home country, led Swiss writer Max Frisch conclude, "we called for labor, but people came instead."[iii]

Many of the problems with such temporary work programs arise in conjunction with details of setting up such a regime, so-called institutional design questions. Often flaws in the design of such a short-term labor migration regime lead to enhanced enforcement and ultimately further criminalization of non-citizens. Are the employees tied to the employer who initially called them? May immigrants return for more than one stint in the EU country? May they travel within the receiving country and within other EU countries? What will happen to abusive employers? Will they be punished, and their workforce returned home? If the latter does not occur, what will happen to those migrants? While victim protection programs exist for human trafficking victims, for example, they have been designed only for a small number of victims, and have frequently missed their mark. How can migrants be protected from home country abuses, if they return with relatively large amounts of money?

Result-oriented questions also need to be raised. Will such short-term labor policies change European policies toward migrants? Are they supposed to do so? In light of the authors' focus on crime, one wonders whether a decline in perceived or real offenses committed by immigrants may lead to greater acceptance of immigrants within the EU, and whether that is or should be a goal of such a policy. On the other hand, the short-term nature of the engagements may lead to greater toleration but no real acceptance.

Who are we trying to protect? This proposed policy is clearly designed to give the EU countries almost everything they desire: The low-skilled labor necessary to continue production; a decrease in the expenses for external and internal controls; a better image abroad; and a population that can believe again in the power of the state to prevent the entry of the unwanted and control crime. Sending countries may benefit from a relief in population pressure and the direct and indirect developmental gains, which they may or may not be able to invest wisely. What does the migrant gain? In the best of circumstances, work experience, and perhaps useful training, and monetary remuneration, which s/he is hopefully able to use productively and with gain at home. The advantages of this proposal seems to rest clearly with the EU countries. The panacea of temporary labor migration appears to be heralded regularly. While it was initially merely designed to respond to labor shortages, Engbersen and Leerkes here use it to respond to concerns about undocumented migration, caused in large parts by such labor shortages. However, as attempts to fill labor needs with such migrants have run awry in the past, a short-term low-skilled migration problem cannot solve criminal justice concerns. What it will do is create further categories of criminalized migrants – those who have fallen out of, or do not quite fit into the new category. To sum up, the authors present interesting, thought-provoking ideas but not a solution to the criminalization of irregular migrants.

ENDNOTES

[i] In the academic community at least, the word choice depends on one's stance toward immigration and toward immigrants in general.

[ii] According to the Department of Homeland Security, in 2007 over 1.2 million people were removed from the United States or otherwise returned to their home country. Department of Homeland Security, Yearbook of Immigration Statistics 2007, Tbl. 36 (Dec. 31, 2008).

[iii] "Man hat Arbeitskraefte gerufen, und es kommen Menschen."

FOSTERING ACADEMIC OPPORTUNITIES TO COUNTERACT SOCIAL EXCLUSION

SANDRA M. BUCERIUS

Immigration and crime are inextricably linked not only in the public mind, but also among policymakers and even academics (see also Butcher & Piehl 1998; Chapin, 1997; Hagan & Palloni, 1998, 1999; Martinez & Lee, 2000; Mears, 2001; Schuck, 1996; Tonry, 1997). Concerns about immigration and crime are expressed across many countries, especially Western societies. These concerns are often sparked by rising crime rates, or arise in times of an immigration influx or after exceptional circumstances like 9/11. In fact, data collected for the recent General Social Survey indicate that almost three quarters of Americans believe that an increase in immigrants causes higher crime rates (cited in Rumbaut & Ewing, 2007).

Though at various points in time the majority of Americans favored immigration before 9/11, surveys have shown that this positive attitude towards immigrants has changed drastically after 9/11 (Kohut, Keeter, Doherty & Suro, 2006). Particularly in the context of the 9/11 terrorist attacks, there has been an automatic association of the word "immigration" with "terrorism" (Portes, 2003). Suddenly, immigrants are seen in a more negative light – despite the fact that none of the terrorists involved in the 9/11 attacks were, in fact, recent immigrants to the United States. In particular, several studies have shown, the public perception of *Muslim* immigrants changed dramatically (Gerstle, 2003; Hernandez, 2007; Naber, 2006; Wray-Lake, Syvertsen & Flanagan, 2008).

In light of these changes in the public perception of immigrants in general and Muslim immigrants in particular, studies have also shown that immigrants tend to face an emerging securitization in their everyday life (Rodriguez, 2008). Fueled by proliferating fears of terrorism that permeate through the general public and everyday life, surveillance practices towards immigrants are increasingly performed by non-state actors such as neighbors, public transport workers, co-workers, teachers, and classmates. Through these forms of everyday surveillance, the social marginalization of immigrants and their exclusion from mainstream U.S. society has also increased rapidly (Rodriguez, 2008).

These forms of marginalization, discrimination, and social exclusion become important because the quality of the reception of immigrants in the host country is one of the main indicators for successful integration into mainstream society (Peek, 2005; Portes & Fernandez-Kelly, 2008; Reitz, 2003; Reitz, Banerjee, Phan & Thompson, 2008). Hence, associating immigrants with high crime rates or terrorism and, thus, viewing them with suspicion may, in fact, contribute to weak social integration.[i]

MYTHS AND THE SECOND GENERATION

A number of recent studies have demonstrated that the ordinary public (and sometimes even criminological) view of immigrants as a cause of increasing crime rates is incorrect. As such, the increase in anti-immigrant sentiments in the United States and the frequent association of immigrants with terrorism seem quite ironic. Just as Sutherland (1924) assumed 85 years ago, Sampson (2006), Hagan and Palloni (1998), and Martinez and Lee (2000), among others, show that the first generation of immigrants in the United States is significantly less involved in criminal activity compared to the native-born population.[ii] Similar findings have been reported for first generation immigrants in England (Smith, 2005). Crime rates, however, increase for second generation immigrants, showing almost the same-level as their national counterparts. Although – on average – the second generation in the United States continues to commit crimes at a lower level than native-born youths (Hagan, Levi & Dinovitzer, 2008), they are significantly more likely to engage in risk behaviors such as delinquency, violence, and substance abuse than their parent generation (Bui & Thingniramol, 2005; Harris, 1999). According to official crime statistics and self-report studies, the crime rates of second generation youths in other Western countries, like Germany, even exceed those of their native-born counterparts (Goldberg, 2006; Pfeiffer, Kleimann, Schott & Petersen, 2005; Walter & Tautmann, 2003; Wetzels et al., 2001).

Looking at the increase of crime rates of the second generation may suggest that assimilation can enhance criminal involvement. Another way to explain the increase of crime rates among some groups of second generation immigrants is the group's lack of an actively chosen and consciously decided immigration experience. Thus, the first generation may interpret experiences of "othering" and exclusion in the host country as individual actions of a few rude people and not as systematic discrimination (Viruell-Fuentes, 2007). In sharp contrast, second generation immigrants are more affected by these systematic "othering" experiences and are less likely to interpret them as isolated incidents. Instead, they tend to rather view them as processes of discrimination, marginalization, disempowerment, and social exclusion (Bucerius, 2008; Viruell-Fuentes, 2007; Waldinger & Feliciano, 2004). Obviously, for second generation immigrants, the process of becoming American entails contending with and adapting to the country's racial stratification. The result is that they are relegated to a disadvantaged minority status.

Given the likelihood of increases in perceived social exclusion and the higher crime rates among second generation immigrants, it is clear that a main focus of policies regarding immigration and crime should be on this population. Consistent with the results of other studies, my ethnographic research with a group of drug-dealing second generation immigrants in Germany demonstrates that a significant number of second generation immigrants feel a strong sense of social, political, and economical exclusion that often translates into involvement in informal markets (Bucerius, 2009). As mentioned above, an increase in such exclusion tendencies has also been reported in the United States (especially following 9/11). Keeping in mind that first generation immigrants are considerably less involved in crime than their children (and native-born counterparts), it can be hypothesized that promoting social integration thereby counteracting increasing tendencies of "othering" and exclusion represents an effective means to prevent criminal involvement of second generation immigrants.

REDUCING SOCIAL EXCLUSION – TACKLING THE ACADEMIC GAP

Since the increase in crime rates in subsequent generations can be understood in the context of their perceived exclusion, I would suggest that policies that would have promise would be those that focus on reducing social exclusion and discrimination of second (and subsequent) generation immigrants. Numerous studies have shown that one key area in which second generation immigrants experience disadvantages and exclusion is the educational system. Although the majority of second generation immigrant youth make educational and occupational progress, a significant minority is left behind (Farley & Alba, 2002; Kasinitz, Mollenkopf, Waters & Holdaway, 2008; Portes & Fernandez-Kelly, 2008; Portes & Rumbaut, 2001; Rumbaut, 2008; Zhou, Vallejo, Tafoya-Estrada & Xiong, 2008). Those left behind are not randomly distributed across nationalities, but disproportionately originate from Mexico, Latin American and Caribbean countries, including El Salvador, Guatemala, Haiti, the Dominican Republic, and the West Indies (Farley & Alba, 2002; Kasinitz et al., 2008; Portes & Fernandez-Kelly, 2008; Portes & Rumbaut, 2001; Rumbaut, 2008; Telles & Oritz, 2008; Zhou et al., 2008). It is this minority that needs to be the focus of settlement policies. As Telles and Oritz (2008) have demonstrated in great detail, Mexican immigrants have been systematically excluded for multiple generations, thus suggesting that their situation in the United States deserves particular attention.[iii]

Consistent with reports on Mexican immigrants in the United States, the subjects of my five year ethnographic study performed poorly in the German educational system. In addition to being in the lower stream track of the educational system, they consistently felt discriminated by teachers and excluded from the opportunity of receiving a good education. The feelings of "othering" combined with a lack of community resources and social networks translated into failing in the school system and dropping out of school early in life. Based on their experience in the school system and their interactions with Germans in every-day life, their chances of being successful in the informal economy - specifically the drug market - seemed more realistic to most of my subjects than establishing their future within the formal economy.

Well, in elementary school I had lots of A's. I wanted to go to the highest stream, like everyone else did who had these grades. But the teacher told my mom that I should better go to the middle or low stream because school will get more difficult and my parents won't be able to help. She also said that the German will get more and more difficult. But I had an A in German. It's the only language I speak! What kind of an argument is that? I was so mad...I just did not understand why I would even try to get A's? So I went to the lowest stream and boy – I was really, really bored. Basically, it was party every day – the teacher just could not handle us at all. She was just...you could tell she could not care less about teaching us...Anyhow: I started selling in the streets...and at some point I realized that I will always make more money here. So I just stopped going.

(Ilber, 25 years, Turkish descent)[iv]

FOSTERING A STRONG LIASON BETWEEN PARENTS, COMMUNITY, AND SCHOOL

Based on my five year ethnographic research, I would suggest that the severity and continuity of the academic gap need to be addressed through the provision of community resources that increase the likelihood of academic success of students from disadvantaged backgrounds. Giving disadvantaged immigrants a realistic chance to succeed in mainstream society (e.g., in the school and educational system), is likely to have a significant influence on their life-decisions and their path into the formal economy. As studies have shown, targeted programs within the community and the assistance of "significant others" (like parents) are likely to affect the academic performance of youths and may also provide immigrant parents with poor socioeconomic backgrounds with the ability "to translate their immigrant drive into their children's scholastic achievement" (Harris, Jamison & Trujillo, 2008, 111; see also Portes & Fernandez-Kelly, 2008). I would suggest that the frustrating experiences of second generation immigrants in the educational system need to be counteracted with closer connections among the schools, parents, and the local community. Hence, investments in community resources would appear to be necessary to tackle the disadvantageous position of some immigrant groups in the United States.

The national 'No Child Left Behind' Act (NCLB), which is supposed to counteract racial differences in educational achievement, relies heavily on parental involvement as one way of improving the academic situation of disadvantaged students. However, it is not clear how parents should respond to poor or misjudged academic performance and what kind of impact adequate responses would have on the academic career of the children (see also Harris et al., 2008). My ethnographic research in Germany and other studies suggest that parents need to collaborate with schools and the wider community in order to meet the educational challenges facing their children (see Harris et al., 2008; Henderson & Mapp, 2002; Portes & Fernandez-Kelly, 2008). Since many disadvantaged immigrant families have limited knowledge and are suspicious of the school system, it is often difficult for school personnel to engage parents in the education of their children.

> *My parents just had no clue. I mean that they did not go to school here...they just had no fucking clue about anything here. They want you to do well and stuff, but they have no idea about anything. They did not even understand that they sent me to the worst school ever. Just because all the other Turks sent their kids there, too. For some reason, they were glad that I did not get into the Gymnasium* (highest of three possible school forms in Germany) *because they thought it would be strange if the kids of their friends would all go to a different school.*
>
> (Akin, 21 Years, Turkish descent)

Residents of the same local community in which immigrant families live often have the advantage of belonging to the same ethnic social network as parents and are in a significantly better position to convince parents to be involved with their child's academic development. Hence, community centers in disadvantaged immigrant neighborhoods need to offer targeted programs for the community's second generation. These programs not only have to involve the "significant others" (parents/partners) of the youths, but they also need to enhance the development and maintenance of a strong social network among their participants.

Several studies have shown that strong networks within ethnic groups and the quality of reception provided by the host country can make all the difference for second generation immigrants as they can determine whether one successfully assimilates into mainstream society (Portes & Fernandez-Kelly, 2008; Reitz, 2003; Reitz et al, 2008; Zhou et al., 2008). Moreover, social networks within ethnic groups have been identified as means to assist in translating the skills, credentials, and human capital of the first generation into educational and occupation achievement of the second generation (Portes & Fernandez-Kelly, 2008). On one hand, success significantly depends on family and ethnic community networks and resources, even for groups with high socioeconomic status (Zhou & Xiong, 2005). On the other hand, a hostile reception by the government and the public, coupled with weak or nonexistent social networks within ethnic groups, can hinder the achievement of second generation immigrants in securing commensurate occupations or educational opportunities (Portes & Fernandez-Kelly, 2008; Reitz 2003, Reitz et al., 2008; Zhou et al., 2008).

TARGETED PROGRAMS FOR DISADVANTAGED IMMIGRANTS

Given the research findings that family and ethnic social networks play a significant role in educational attainment, the importance of the triangle involving parents, schools, and community centers in disadvantaged neighborhoods seems to be a logical consequence. The subjects of my ethnographic research continuously addressed ways in which educational attainment could be significantly enhanced. In collaboration with the local community centre and local school, some of them eventually developed a program for subsequent generations of their community (Bucerius, 2009). This program is based on a strong liaison between parents, school, and community centre.

> *It's like nobody really knows shit about the other. Parents have no clue about school and don't trust the German teachers anyway. And the youth centers were just great places to hang out but nobody cared about homework or anything. It's like they don't talk to each other. My parents also hated the youth center. They never wanted me to hang out there because the social workers were German. So now, people talk to each other. If my brother doesn't show at the youth center, the social workers call the teachers and the parents and they make sure to find out where he is. People care. With us, we could just disappear. Nobody knew anything because nobody cared to talk to each other.*
>
> (Aissa, 24 years, Moroccan descent)

As described by Aissa, academic success can be significantly enhanced if school, community, and significant others (parents/partners) act in concert. Individual attempts by one (or two) of the three actors tended to fail in the past in large part because of a lack of communication among these three key social groups. Hence, a program that embraces all three actors seems to have more potential.

Parents are drawn into the program through social workers at the community centre, which is run by members with the same ethnic background. Social workers from the same ethnic community not only can engage parents more easily and develop an understanding for the educational possibilities of their children in the host country, but they can also serve as ethnic role-models to immigrant students (see also Anderson, 2000). The parents are responsible for enrolling their children in the program, which significantly helps to keep parents involved (Bucerius, 2009; Harris et al., 2008; Henderson & Mapp, 2002). The community centre provides the means to strengthen within ethnic group social networks by offering a structured afternoon program for students after school, including support with homework, language training, and leisure activities. Hence, students are not only able to receive help when needed, but also have a safe space to meet throughout the entire day (without having the same negative association for students that a school would have), which significantly reduces the possibility of spending time on the streets.

> *I mean, honestly, I just never knew what else to do. I mean, you go to school, or you just don't go to school. Nobody cares anyway. My parents never knew what I was up to. It's not that they did not care, they just did not have any time to worry about me. So you just start spending all your time hanging out. There is nothing else to do, really. And then you automatically get into trouble. That's just given if you grow up in this neighborhood. It's just bad when you spend your time in the streets. But this is just what happens.*
>
> (Mesut, 26 years, Turkish descent)

In order to create effective programs for disadvantaged immigrants in the United States that are accepted by the ethnic communities, the programs first need to be active in connecting parents, the school, and the community centers. In Germany, it appears that policies are needed to ensure the development and wider distribution of such successful programs. Further, there is a need to facilitate not only the allocation of necessary financial and human resources, but also the acceptance of the target programs within the ordinary public by communicating their necessity and purpose. It should be emphasized that the development of the target programs by way of explicit public policy should be seen as being realistic and economically feasible as the benefits of the programs should soon outweigh the associated financial cost to society of their development. Bringing parents, schools, and communities together can be an effective means of counteracting social exclusion by enhancing family and co-ethnic social networks and thus, fostering academic success.

The first necessary step, however, is to realize that the connection of 'immigration' to 'crime' is largely a function of the exclusion of second generation immigrants from the communities in which they were born.

REFERENCES

Anderson, E. (2000). *Code of the Street*. New York: W. W. Norton & Company.

Bucerius, S. (2008). Drug dealers between Islamic values, everyday life in Germany and criminal activity. *Zeitschrift für Soziologie, 3,* 246-265.

Bucerius, S. (2009). *Migration, soziale Exklusion und informelle Ökonomie.* Dissertation, Universität Frankfurt.

Bui, H.N. & Thingniramol, O. (2005). Immigration and self-reported delinquency: The interplay of immigrant generations, gender, race, and ethnicity. *Journal of Crime and Justice, 28,* 79–100.

Butcher, K. & Piehl, A.M. (1998). Cross-city evidence on the relationship between immigration and crime. *Journal of Policy Analysis and Management, 17,* 457-493.

Chapin, W. (1997). Auslander raus? The empirical relationship between immigration and crime in Germany. *Social Science Quarterly, 78,* 543-558.

Farley, R. & Alba, R. (2002). The new second generation in the United States. *International Migration Review, 36,* 669-701.

Gartner, R. (1990). The victims of homicide: A temporal and cross-national comparison. *American Sociological Review, 55,* 92-106.

Gerstle, G. (2003). Pluralism and the war on terror. *Dissent, 50,* 31-38.

Goldberg, B. (2006). Freizeit und kriminalität bei achtklässlern mit und ohne migrationshintergrund. In T. Feltes, C. Pfeiffer and G. Steinhilper (Eds.), *Kriminalpolitik und ihre wissenschaftliche Grundlagen* (pp. 861-892). Heidelberg: Müller Verlag.

Hagan, J., Levi, R. & Dinovitzer, R. (2008). The symbolic violence of the crime-immigration nexus: Migrant mythologies in the Americas. *Criminology & Public Policy, 7,* 95-112.

Hagan, J. & Palloni, A. (1998). Immigration and crime in the United States. In J.P. Smith & B. Edmonston (Eds.), *The Immigration Debate: Studies on the Economic, Demographic, and Fiscal Effects of Immigration* (pp. 367-387). Washington, DC: National Academies Press.

Hagan, J. & Palloni, A. (1999). Sociological criminology and the mythology of Hispanic immigration and crime. *Social Problems, 46,* 617-632.

Harris, A.L., Jamison, K.M. & Trujillo, M.H. (2008). Disparities in the educational success of immigrants: An assessment of the immigrant effect for Asians and Latinos. *The Annals of the American Academy of Political and Social Science, 620,* 90-114.

Harris, D. (1997). Driving while black and all other traffic offences: The Supreme Court and pretextual traffic stops. *The Journal of Criminal Law and Criminology, 87,* 544-582.

Harris, K.M. (1999). The health status and risk behavior of adolescents in immigrant families. In D.J. Hernandez (Ed.), *Children of Immigrants: Health, Adjustment, and Public Assistance* (pp. 286-347). Washington, DC: National Academy of Sciences Press.

Henderson, A. & Mapp, K. (2002). *A New Wave of Evidence: The Impact of School, Parent and Community Connections on Student Achievement.* Austin, TX: Southwest Educational Development Laboratory.

Hernandez, D.M. (2007). Undue process: Racial genealogies of immigrant detention. In C.B. Brettell (Ed.), *Constructing Borders/Crossing Boundaries: Race, Ethnicity, and Immigration* (pp. 59-86). Lanham, MD: Lexington Books.

Howell, S., Perry, H. & Vile, M. (2004). Black cities/white cities: Evaluating the police. *Political Behavior, 26,* 45-68.

Junger-Tas, J. (2001). Ethnic minorities, social integration and crime. *European Journal on Criminal Policy and Research, 9,* 5-29.

Kasinitz, P., Mollenkopf, J.H., Waters, M.C. & Holdaway, J. (2008). *Inheriting the City: The Children of Immigrants Come of Age.* Cambridge, MA: Harvard University Press.

Kohut, A., Keeter, S., Doherty, C. & Suro, R. (2006). *America's Immigration Quandary.* Washington, DC: Pew Research for the People and the Press & Pew Hispanic Center.

Martinez, R. Jr. & Lee, M.R. (2000). On immigration and crime." In G. LaFree and R. Bursik (Eds.), *Criminal Justice 2000, Volume I: The Nature of Crime: Continuity and Change* (pp. 485-524). Washington, DC: National Institute of Justice.

Mears, D. (2001). The immigration-crime nexus: Toward an analytic framework for assessing and guiding theory, research, and policy. *Sociological Perspectives, 44,* 1-19.

Naber, N. (2006). The rules of forced engagement: Race, gender, and the culture of fear among Arab immigrants in San Francisco post-9/11. *Cultural Dynamics, 18,* 235-267.

Organization for Economic Co-operation and Development (OECD). (2006). *Where Immigrant Students Succeed.* Paris: OECD Publications.

Peek, L. (2005). Becoming Muslim: The development of a religious identity. *Sociology of Religion, 66,* 215-242.

Pfeiffer, C. & Kleimann, M. & Petersen, S. (2005). *Migration und Kriminulität. Ein Gutachten für den Zuwanderungsbeirat der Bundesregierung.* Baden-Baden: Nomos.

Portes, A. (2003). Ethnicities: Children of immigrants in America. *Development* 46: 42-52.

Portes, A. & Fernandez-Kelly, P. (2008). No margin for error: Educational and occupational achievement among disadvantaged children of immigrants. *The Annals of the American Academy of Political and Social Science, 620,* 12-36.

Portes, A. & Rumbaut, R. (2001). *Legacies: The Story of the Immigrant Second Generation.* Berkeley, CA: University of California Press.

Reitz, J. (Ed.). (2003). *Host Societies and the Reception of Immigrants.* San Diego, CA: University of California, Center for Comparative Immigration Studies.

Reitz, J., Banerjee, R., Phan, M. & Thompson, J. (2008). Race, Religion, and the Social Integration of New Immigrant Minorities in Canada. Available online: http://www.utoronto.ca/ethnicstudies/RaceReligion.pdf

Rodriguez, R.M. (2008). (Dis)unity and diversity in Post 9/11 America. *Sociological Forum, 23,* 379-389.

Rumbaut, R.G. (2008). The coming of the second generation: Immigration and ethnic mobility in Southern California. *The Annals of the American Academy of Political and Social Science, 620,* 196-236.

Rumbaut, R.G. & Ewing, W.A. (2007). The Myth of Immigrant Criminality. Available online: *http://borderbattles.ssrc.org/Rumbault_Ewing/index.html.*

Sampson, R. (2006, March 11). Open doors don't invite criminals: Is increased immigration behind the drop in crime? *The New York Times,* A27.

Schuck, P. (1996). Alien rumination. *Yale Law Journal, 105,* 1963-2012.

Smith, David J. (2005). Ethnic Differences in Intergenerational Crime Patterns. In Tonry, Michael (ed.) *Crime and Justice: A Review of Research,* Volume 32. University of Chicago Press.

Sutherland, E.H. (1924). *Criminology.* Philadelphia, PA: Lippincott.

Telles, E.E. & Oritz, V. (2008). *Generations of Exclusion.* New York: Russell Sage Foundation.

Tonry, M. (1997). Ethnicity, crime and immigration. *Crime and Justice, 21,* 1.

Viruell-Fuentes, E.A. (2007). Beyond acculturation: Immigration, discrimination, and health research among Mexicans in the United States. *Social Science and Medicine, 65,* 1524-1535.

Wacquant, L. (2005). 'Enemies of the wholesome part of the nation': Postcolonial migrants in the prisons of Europe. *Sociologie, 1,* 31–51.

Waldinger, R. & Feliciano, C. (2004). Will the new second generation experience 'downward assimilation'? Segmented assimilation re-assessed. *Ethnic and Racial Studies, 27,* 376-402.

Walter, M. & Trautmann, S. (2003). Kriminalität junger Migranten – Strafrecht und gesellschaftliche (Des)-Integration. In J. Raithel and J.Mansel (Eds.), *Kriminalität und Gewalt im Jugendalter. Hell- und Dunkelfeldberichte im Vergleich* (pp.). Weinheim: Juventa: 64-86.

Wetzels, P., Enzmann, D., Mecklenburg, E. & Pfeiffer, C. (2001). *Jugendliche und Gewalt – eine repräsentative Dunkelfeldanalyse in München und acht anderen deutschen Städten.* Baden-Baden: Nomos.

Wortley, S. & Tanner, J. 2008. Respect, Friendship, and Racial Injustice, in: Frank van Gemert, Dana Peterson, Inger-Lise Lien. *Street Gangs, Migration and Ethnicity.* Devon: Willan Publishing: 192-208.

Wortley, S. & Tanner, J. (2004). Racial profiling in Canada: Survey evidence from Toronto. *The Canadian Review of Policing Research, 1,* 24-36.

Wray-Lake, L., Syvertsen, A.K. & Flanagan, C.A. (2008). Contested citizenship and social exclusion: Adolescent Arab American immigrants' views of the social contract. *Applied Developmental Science, 12,* 84-92.

Zhou, M. & Xiong, Y.S. (2005). The multifaceted American experiences of the children of Asian immigrants: Lessons for segmented assimilation. *Ethnic and Racial Studies, 28,* 1087-1118.

Zhou, M., Lee, J., Vallejo, J.A., Tafoya-Estrada, R. & Xiong, Y.S. (2008). Success attained, deterred, and denied: Divergent pathways to social mobility in Los Angeles's new second generation. *The Annals of the American Academy of Political and Social Science, 620,* 37-61.

ENDNOTES

[i] This seems particularly important because weak social integration may represent a risk factor for criminal activities (Gartner, 1990; Junger-Tas, 2001).

[ii] Considering that immigrants may receive harsher treatments in the criminal justice system and, thus, are likely to be overrepresented in crime and incarceration statistics (see Harris, 1997; Howell, Perry & Vile, 2004; Wortley and Tanner, 2008; and Wortley & Tanner, 2004), the true difference between immigrants and native counterparts may even be larger (Wacquant, 2005).

[iii] Similar to these experiences in the United States, which are mostly documented for Mexican immigrants (Kasinitz et al., 2008; Portes & Rumbaut, 2001; Telles & Oritz, 2008), Germany's Turkish immigrants perform significantly worse in the school system than native-born children and youths. In fact, in comparative Organization for Economic Co-operation and Development (OECD) studies, Germany continuously proves to be the country with the largest disparity between second-generation students and their native-born peers. Second generation immigrants of Turkish descent tend to be two school years behind their German counterparts, which is particularly disconcerting considering that these students have spent their entire life and school career in Germany (OECD, 2006).

[iv] All names have been changed.

DELINQUENCY, OPPORTUNITY AND THE SECOND GENERATION IMMIGRANT PUZZLE

FRANKLIN E. ZIMRING

In one encouraging sense, the puzzle of increasing crime and drug use in the second generation after immigration is the exact opposite of the usual contrast between knowledge and policy discussions of social status and criminality. Usually, we are confident we know why disadvantaged groups and neighborhoods have high rates of crime and disorder, but we are uncertain about whether and how to improve matters. Shaw and McKay documented the impact of social disorganization on crime in urban areas by 1931, but many of those same areas persist as engines of dysfunction in the 21st century (compare Laub 2002 at 187-88 with Testa and Furstenberg 2002 at 237-263). By contrast, we do not have a good theoretical account of what Sandra Bucerius regards as the paradoxical fact that second generations after immigration produce higher levels of crime involvement and substance abuse than their parents, but we do have a clear path to policies that aim to reduce the risks for the sons and daughters of immigrants all over the developed world. Dr. Bucerius is surely correct that enhancing school performance and economic development is the key strategy for youth development for immigrant families, as it is also for all other youth populations. The particular strategies of family and community involvement may differ for immigrant families with language and cultural distinctions, and may also be different for different types of immigrant cultures, but mainstreaming educational opportunity for immigrant populations is a social policy "no-brainer." So we know what goals to pursue, and there is reason to be optimistic that many immigrant family cultural systems are hospitable to policies that enhance educational opportunities for their children.

Then why do second generation kids have higher rates of crime and drug abuse than their parents? I think that one helpful method of addressing this question is to ask which element of the generational contrast is the larger social science puzzle - is it the low rate in the first generation or the higher rate for their children? From the standpoint of classical criminological theories like the Chicago area school, it is the low immigrant crime levels that are a surprise given their residence in highly disorganized zones and their marginal economic and social status. New arrivals are low risks.

Yet it turns out there are good reasons to expect that the first generation off the boat will have low crime rates. These are a self selected group who wanted to come to their new place of residence and who have succeeded in accomplishing this often difficult task. The immigrants who have children also have succeeded in staying long enough to be counted in a new nation's social statistics. The newly arrived immigrant is for that reason both happier to be here and possessed of survival skills that not all his countrymen share. It should be no surprise that his criminality and drug taking are lower than those of his non-immigrant neighbors.

The children of immigrants did not self-select in the same way, and may not have all the survival skills that helped their parents. This is why cultural difference, marginal social status, and lower economic status may injure or alienate them more than it did their parents. But just because the second generation of immigrants have higher rates of offending than their parents does <u>not</u> mean that they have higher rates of crime and drug use than the young people who live next door to them with similar economic status but with no recent family immigration history. So even if there were a universal crime increase in the second generation after immigration (and the data are far short of establishing this), it would not mean that rates of crime are higher for this group than for other young persons. The low rates exhibited by their parents may almost guarantee some increase in the next generation. The second generation rates might just be regression to typical levels expected from a normal population in that social and geographic situation.

There are, of course, some groups of new arrivals where second generation rates of crime rise to problematic levels. But there are also second and third generations with modest increases in crime to population rates no higher than in the general population and, for some groups, lower than average. The range of variation in second and third generations is probably quite high and the predictors of low rates are most likely family strength and educational progress.

This is an opportune era to study the determinants of educational progress and low levels of problematic behavior. Our experience with study of Hispanic, Asian and Pacific Islander patterns suggests both a wide range of second generation levels of crime and drug use and close links between school success and low levels of crime and deviance. The extent to which educational attainment is a cause of conformity rather than simply a powerful indication of those cultural values and adaptive skills that produce success in both the schools and the community is often difficult to determine, but I suspect that the link between school success and community conformity is as high in most of the diversity of recent immigrant communities as in the general society.

And while the cultural contexts of immigrant experience will differ, the theoretical framework for comprehending the socialization and delinquency outcomes of second generation immigrant cohorts is fundamentally similar to the theories we have developed for earlier generations of urban youth. The approach Dr. Bucerius recommends is in the tradition based on Robert Merton's insights as applied by Cloward and Ohlin in *Delinquency and Opportunity* (Cloward and Ohlin 1960). For it was Merton in Social Structure and Anomie who clearly showed that the roots of delinquent behavior are just as firmly rooted in socialization to American urban life as is conformity (Merton 1938). To the extent that socialization into mainstream values may become an engine of delinquent motivation, there is nothing mysterious about the generation that is more thoroughly socialized having the higher rates of illegal behavior.

REFERENCES

Cloward, R.A. & Ohlin, L.E. (1960). *Delinquency and Opportunity: A Theory of Delinquent Gangs.* New York: Free Press.

Laub, J.H. (2002). A century of delinquency research and delinquency theory. In M.K. Rosenheim, F.E. Zimring, D.S. Tanenhaus, and B. Dohrn (Eds.), *A Century of Juvenile Justice*, pages 179-205. Chicago: University of Chicago Press.

Merton, R.K. (1938). Social structure and anomie. *American Sociological Review* 3, 672-682.

Testa, M.F. & Furstenberg, F.F. (2002). The social ecology of child endangerment. In M.K. Rosenheim, F.E. Zimring, D.S. Tanenhaus, and B. Dohrn (Eds.), *A Century of Juvenile Justice*, pages 237-263. Chicago: University of Chicago Press.

Rethinking Policing: The Policy Implications of Hot Spots of Crime

Stephen D. Mastrofski
David Weisburd
Anthony A. Braga

What has come to be known as "hot spots" or "place-based" policing is a very promising approach for police to reduce crime and disorder in urban neighborhoods (Braga & Weisburd, unpublished manuscript; Weisburd & Eck, 2004). We argue that the available scientific evidence is sufficiently strong and supportive to justify the initiation of a major program of development and evaluation. This program would determine how and how much American police organizations should undertake major structural changes to implement this approach. We anticipate that its adoption would fundamentally restructure urban policing. We outline the changes that will support implementation of hot spots policing, and we suggest that the U.S. Department of Justice should promote these changes by awarding grants on a competitive basis to develop and rigorously evaluate hot spots policing.

The Evidence on Hot Spots and Hot Spots Policing

Hot spots policing means focusing policing activities on specific places where crime or other problems for police are highly concentrated. "Places" are much smaller than the typical police administrative unit, such as a precinct patrol beat, or census tract. They are addresses, buildings, block faces, street segments, or clusters of addresses (Eck & Weisburd, 1995). There is considerable variation *within* the larger geographic spaces that police now use in organizing their activities. Sensitivity to such micro-variation will yield substantial gains in the effectiveness and efficiency of the police response. What may be an attractive location to a robber at one part of a block may be unattractive just a few doors down the street or on the next block.

In fact, research has consistently shown that urban crime and disorder are not evenly dispersed within precincts and neighborhoods of urban jurisdictions, but rather they are highly concentrated in relatively few places occupying just a small part of those larger areas. The pioneering study of Minneapolis hot spots showed that about 50 percent of crime calls were generated by only 3.5 percent of the city's addresses (Sherman, Gartin & Berger, 1989), a finding replicated by a series of studies, some finding crime concentrated to an even greater extent (Brantingham & Brantingham, 1999; Crow & Bull, 1975; Pierce, Spaar & Briggs, 1988; Roncek, 2000; Sherman et al., 1989; Weisburd, Bushway, Lum & Yang, 2004; Weisburd &

Green 1994; Weisburd, Maher & Sherman, 1992; Weisburd, Morris & Groff, forthcoming).

Crime is concentrated at places more than it is concentrated among offenders. A Seattle study found that about 1,500 street segments accounted for 50 percent of the crime occurring each year in that city between 1989 and 2002, while during that same period 6,108 offenders accounted for 50 percent of the crime (Weisburd, 2008). Seattle police would need to track four times as many offenders as they would places to target the same amount of crime. This study also showed that such concentrations are stable over fourteen years (Weisburd et al., 2004). Hot spots tend to remain hot spots. This contrasts with the well-established finding that offending is highly unstable across the offender's life course, or even shorter time periods (Blumstein, Cohen, Roth & Visher, 1986; Gottfredson & Hirschi, 1990; Laub & Sampson, 2003; Wolfgang, Thornberry & Figlio, 1987). Whereas "natural" desistance is a frequent phenomenon in the experiences of offenders, the "cooling" of hot spots is not. And, unlike offenders and the population in general, hot spots do not move, so they are readily located by law enforcement. Finally, hot spots are not merely smaller pieces of a larger trend occurring at neighborhood or community levels. "Safe" parts of town can include some places where crime is highly concentrated, and "unsafe" areas typically have many street segments that are low crime or virtually crime free (Groff, Weisburd & Morris, 2009; Groff, Weisburg & Yang, unpublished manuscript).

This evidence means that it is easier for police to be efficient in concentrating on places than on people, because it is easier to predict *where* crime will occur than *who* will commit it (Weisburd, 2008). But can this knowledge be used in ways that actually reduce the risk of crime and disorder? The resounding answer is, "Yes!" Nine studies in six cities, five of which were randomized experiments, have examined police efforts to capitalize on the crime hot spots phenomenon, and they show with high consistency that concentrating police efforts on hot spots produces crime prevention effects (Braga, 2001). All but one study showed significant crime prevention benefits for hot spots policing. None produced evidence of displacement of crime to other places, and four of the five studies addressing the issue found diffusion of crime control *benefits* (Clarke & Weisburd, 1994). That is, areas proximate to the sites receiving the treatment experienced crime prevention improvements even though they were not targeted for intervention by the police. Crime is not easily displaced because offenders regard some areas as more opportunity-rich than others. The attractive features depend upon the type of crime, but typical offender concerns are knowledge of the people in the area and not intruding on other offenders' turf (Weisburd et al., 2006). The National Research Council committee found that place-based policing enjoys the strongest supportive evidence produced in testing police crime prevention approaches (Skogan & Frydl, 2004: 250).

HOT SPOTS POLICING: STATE OF THE ART

Hot spots policing has been around in one form or another for a long time, but its diffusion appears to be closely associated with the growth of computerized crime mapping (Weisburd & Lum, 2005). A 1999 national survey of municipal departments with 100 or more officers found that 88 percent of those engaged in Compstat reported doing hot spots mapping, while 65 percent of the non-Compstat departments reported the same (Weisburd et al., 2003: 442). Another survey of departments in this size category found that 62 percent were doing computerized crime mapping; 80 percent of those were conducting hot spots analysis, and two-thirds used hot spots policing as a patrol strategy (Weisburd & Lum, 2005).

Of course, there is a great deal more to hot spots policing than computerized crime mapping, and it is not yet clear just what the character, scope, and dosage of hot spots policing are as actually practiced in agencies across the United States. We think it likely that a random sample of departments would reveal considerable variation in the character, extensiveness, and intensiveness of hot spots policing implementation – just as studies of Compstat and community policing have shown (Mastrofski, 2006; Weisburd et al., 2003). Although interest and involvement in something resembling hot spots policing is fairly widespread among American agencies, the actual implementation probably falls short of some advocates' ideas of how it should be conducted, particularly according to the principles of problem-oriented policing (Eck, 2006).

What problem-oriented policing adds to hot spots policing is more thoughtfulness, evidence gathering, analysis, creativity, and critical assessment before, during, and after a hot spot is targeted for intervention (Braga & Weisburd, in progress). Yet a variety of national surveys and on-site case studies have indicated that the diagnosis of hot spot problems is typically perfunctory or rudimentary, if it occurs at all (Braga & Weisburd, 2006; Cordner & Biebel, 2005; Greenspan et al., 2003; O'Shea & Nicholls, 2003; Rosenbaum, 2006; Willis, Matrofski & Weisburd, 2007). The search for hot spot interventions typically employs "standard" law enforcement interventions, such as directed patrol, crackdowns, *Terry* searches, and more often than not relies on the agency's impressions of previous success with the approach rather than scientific evidence (Weisburd et al., 2003: 443). Remarkably, some evidence shows that even this "shallow" problem solving yields crime control benefits, albeit at levels lower than might be possible with more intensive problem-solving efforts (Braga & Weisburd, 2006:146). The National Research Council report on police practices judged the evidence to be strong supporting the crime reduction effects of hot spot policing guided by problem solving, and moderately strong evidence supporting similar effects when non-law enforcement tactics are employed in a problem-oriented framework (Skogan & Frydl, 2004: 249-251). And some evidence suggests that when hot spots interventions involve a more profound problem-oriented policing effort, the results can be quite impressive (Braga & Weisburd, in progress).

Thus, there is widespread interest in and adoption of at least some elements of hot spots policing around the nation, but as with other popular reforms, the implementation is spotty and rarely approaches the ideals of problem-oriented policing. Knowledge about the benefits of community policing and Compstat has developed fitfully because of the absence of a well-designed effort to identify and evaluate the core elements of these reforms and submit them to rigorous empirical testing (Eck & Maguire, 2000; Skogan & Frydl, 2004: 232). Unless such a program is launched, hot spot policing will also likely develop as a reform to which much lip service is paid, but about which relatively little is known – perpetually underdeveloped and under-deployed, remaining in the domain of an institutionally-, not technically-driven innovation (Mastrofski & Uchida, 1993; Weisburd & Braga, 2006: 225).

ORGANIZING FOR HOT SPOTS POLICING

A great deal must change to accommodate a serious police agency commitment to hot spots policing. Here we offer our perspective on the key organizational elements required for hot spots policing. Where possible we try to draw on evidence, but for the most part, the particulars are based on our observations of police organizations and speculation as to what is needed. Our recommendations cover systems to promote knowledge about hot spots, resource reallocation, and implications for preserving the integrity of the place-based model. In addition, we comment on some important issues for top police and government leadership to address.

Hot spots policing is information-driven, so police organizations need to develop systems for gathering that information. Because hot spots policing requires timely, accurate, and relevant empirical analysis, a top priority is gathering data that can accommodate the needs of place-based crime and problem analysis. Despite the growing popularity of crime mapping, the reports and data systems that dominate American police departments are offender-focused. To harness the rapidly developing geographic information system technology, police agencies must develop data structures that uniquely identify places (Weisburd, 2008:10).

Police agencies also need to gather place-based information that is at least as rich and complex as those now developed for tracking offenders (Weisburd, 2008). Such data systems need to track not only how much crime and disorder occur at places, but information about victims, offenders under community supervision, land use, and so on (Block & Green, 1994). Other types of problems that contribute to the police workload should be tracked, such as complaints *against* the police (Kane, 2002). But beyond that, police need to gather information on the things that might make a place "hotter" or "cooler." The choices are potentially limitless, so the use of scarce resources should be driven by theory and evidence. This means that police need to consult experts on theory and research most relevant to the spatial analysis of crime in place. Arguably the most appropriate theory currently available, at least regarding crime, is routine activities theory, which predicts its occurrence based on the convergence of suitable targets, the absence of capable guardians, and the presence of persons motivated to offend (Cohen & Felson, 1979; Felson, 1994). Ultimately, these innovations should strengthen the capacity of police organizations to predict the location of future crimes and the migration of crimes across hot spots (Braga & Weisburd, in progress; Johnson & Bowers, 2004).

One obvious deficiency in current police records systems is that agencies know much more about what offenders do than what their own officers do! Evidence indicates that the police, the "guardians" of interest, can have a preventive effect on crime simply by being present at a hot spot with sufficient frequency and duration. So police departments need a way to track where the police are spending their time, something enabled by contemporary electronic tracking devices that are more precise and less error-prone than old systems relying on officer self-reports (Amendola et al., 2006). And just as offender-based criminology has been vastly enriched by studying the life course of offenders, so too will place-based criminology (and its practical sibling, crime analysis) become more powerful as police gather data on the life course of hot spots. This is in sharp contrast to the current "whack-a-mole" approach to responding to short-term crime spikes appearing on maps circulated at Compstat meetings (Willis et al., 2007:174). There is nothing inherent in place-based policing that requires it to have a short-term focus or avoid considering the many forces at work that elevate a place to the level of hot spot (cf. Rosenbaum, 2006: 246). Indeed, we anticipate that because of the stability of hot spots over long time periods, place-based policing will facilitate dealing with chronic problem areas across the city's landscape.

The preferred evidence-based approach for hot spots is akin to maintaining comprehensive medical records on patients (Sherman, 1998: 12), but in this instance the "patient" is the hot spot. It facilitates the consideration of both short- and long-term intervention strategies. And making these data available to criminologists should enable them to advance general knowledge about the impact of natural forces and social control contrivances, knowledge that may be applied to the selection and fabrication of hot spot intervention strategies.

Evidence indicates that hot spot interventions can have heightened effectiveness if they are customized to the situation, and the success of the customization depends upon the consideration of evidence available, not only about the hot spot(s) in question, but about available treatments. Problem-oriented policing is designed to do this, and so we recommend that it become an integral part of hot spots policing (Braga & Weisburd, unpublished manuscript). A particular weakness of police problem-solving as practiced is the under-use of scientific evidence to diagnose and prescribe treatments effectively. This calls not only for beefing up the capacity of police organizations to locate such evidence, but for those who generate it to make it more readily accessible to practitioners (Sherman, 1998). Recognizing the many challenges of doing all this well (Braga & Weisburd, 2006), we still anticipate that even diluted versions of problem-oriented policing will have the salutary effect of reducing reliance on expensive, reactive law enforcement strategies (arrest and prosecution) to preventive strategies that reduce opportunities for crime and mischief at place. It also means that police officers and squads will have their performance evaluated on whether *places* become safer or more pleasant, rather than whether *offenders* are caught and convicted. Applying a Compstat-like accountability system in this fashion, and doing it down the chain of command to its lowest level, could do a great deal to institutionalize the hot spots approach (Braga & Bond, 2008; Braga & Weisburd, in progress; Willis, Mastrofski & Kochel, in progress).

Analytic activities for hot spots policing require profound changes in the staffing, hiring, and training of personnel who analyze hot spot data and prepare it for operational applications. First, assuming a jurisdiction-wide implementation of hot spots policing, most municipal departments will need to augment crime analysis units, adding persons with a variety of skills, including mapping and other forms of spatial analysis. Second, police agencies need to employ an applied criminologist who can bridge the worlds of science and police strategic decision making (Sherman, 1998: 13). That person's function is to see that the diagnosis of hot spot problems is done competently and that the best available evidence is considered when devising hot spot intervention strategies. Such a person must serve as a highly accessible resource to operational decision makers, becoming adept at communicating the key elements of theory and evidence that should, along with the "practical wisdom" of police practitioners (Moore, 2006: 336), shape strategic and tactical decisions. Third, American police departments tend to keep crime analysis and intelligence units separated, which impedes the integration of detailed intelligence information to the context of statistical patterns that crime analysts can provide. A less "stove-piped" analysis of information will facilitate sound problem diagnoses and treatment. One option is to integrate intelligence and crime analysis in the same unit, the "intelligence-led" approach popular in the United Kingdom (Ratcliffe, 2008).

Hot spots policing requires reconsidering how police resources are allocated and deployed (Weisburd, 2008). The creation of patrol beats has long served American police as a method for equalizing workload among officers and to establish a framework for accountability and service delivery. The team policing and community policing movements have reinforced the importance of maintaining the integrity of officers working in their assigned beats to strengthen police-community bonds (Skogan, 2006). Yet most departments struggle mightily to maintain that integrity while trying to sustain an acceptable degree of responsiveness to the calls-for-service workload. Officers are frequently dispatched outside their assigned beats to provide for a timely response to workload in other areas. Some community policing departments have achieved a degree of beat integrity by splitting the patrol force into officers who only respond to calls – and for whom beat boundaries are essentially meaningless – and officers who are expected to maintain beat integrity so that they can specialize in community problem-solving in their assigned beat (Skogan, 2006). This arrangement is readily adaptable to the requirements of hot spots policing, only instead of having officers specialize in entire beats, they focus their efforts on hot spots. Rather than spending their time in general community engagement work throughout a beat, they would focus their efforts entirely on hot spots.[i] In some parts of the city, a single officer's hot spot responsibilities might easily span more than one beat, while in other parts there might be a sufficient number of hot spots to justify several hot spot specialists working within one beat.[ii] As the need arises, the efforts of hot spot specialists would be supplemented by other officers, including investigators, traffic, special operations, and so on.

To the extent that hot spots, rather than beats, become the geographic work unit, departments will reallocate resources, and this will be consequential. One possible outcome is that significant patrol resources will be shifted from the traditional calls-for-service response and now popular community policing activities to hot spot-focused activities. Such a shift need not be so profound, if departments are willing to invest in tighter management of patrol officers' time. Research shows that on average, 50-80 percent of patrol officers' work time is spent on preventive patrol and other undirected activities, rather than responding to calls for service (Famega, 2009; Mastrofski & Parks, 2003). This undirected time is an untapped resource that could be harnessed to hot spots policing. In addition, hot spots policing affords opportunities to find more fruitful place-based work for criminal investigators, rather than traditional case-based modes of investigation, which declining clearance rates suggest are unproductive. Finally, hot spots policing calls for greater organizational flexibility than many, especially the largest, departments currently manifest. Managers need the capacity to move personnel across large geographic units and across work shifts, if new hot spots arise or become hyperactive.

The reallocation of resources to hot spots will be consequential for the community as well. The American public has become accustomed to having beat officers assigned to their neighborhoods, and most residents regard the presence of visible officers patrolling as an indicator of security and service. A shift to hot spots policing will undoubtedly reduce levels of this undirected activity, especially in areas where there are few or no hot spots (Rosenbaum, 2006: 256). Maintaining the political viability of a hot spots resource allocation system will require careful explanation to the public, a task that top police leaders and other government officials must vigorously and artfully undertake. Resisting countervailing pressures to deploy resources to areas that are not "hot" will require that police provide convincing and ongoing evidence of the success of hot spot interventions, and especially, where relevant, the diffusion of benefits to adjacent areas and the absence of adverse effects in areas receiving reduced police attention. Public education and accountability are key to the viability of hot spots policing undertaken on a large scale.

A number of other issues arise for top police leadership. Of central importance will be establishing thresholds for hot spot intervention. Do different thresholds of crime and disorder apply in different parts of the city, or should one standard apply to all? Should other indicators also be used to identify hot spots, such as the level of fear of crime in an area, the public's priorities (which often focus on quality-of-life neighborhood problems), or public hostility toward the police (Rosenbaum, 2006: 247)? How much control over the "certification" of hot spots should fall to headquarters, and how much should be delegated to precinct commanders? What public consultation obligations do police departments have in identifying hot spots and devising interventions? These are all important questions, but we do not presume to know at this stage how they should be answered. The answers require public debate and a transparent political process, although the implications can be examined objectively.

Place-based policing could lead to under-policing of calmer areas and overly aggressive policing of troubled or racial minority areas. These possibilities are matters of concern, but they are not insurmountable problems. First, a city might opt for a system that tracks a wide range of "problems" to identify hot spots, so that the most problematic areas of relatively un-afflicted neighborhoods could still receive some hot spot attention, attention that would be more effectively employed because it is both focused and customized to the situation. Second, hot spot policing need not resort solely to aggressive tactics. The principles of hot spot policing guided by a problem-oriented approach call for a broader search for effective interventions than just the usual aggressive enforcement methods. And finally, even when the police decide on forceful law enforcement interventions, there is nothing in the requirements of hot spots policing to preclude community consultation and involvement in the targeting of places for intervention, an approach used successfully in pulling-levers policing (Braga & Winship, 2006; Kennedy, 2006). Indeed, a serious commitment to hot spots policing requires an equally serious commitment to finding ways to strengthen and sustain the legitimacy of police in a system that will in all likelihood make highly visible the more selective application of police energies to particular areas within the city. Hot spots policing should not become a license to ignore community input, but rather must become part of a larger framework for incorporating community co-production in the policing process (Braga & Weisburd, in progress: Chapter 6; Taylor, 2006).

MOVING FORWARD: A NATIONAL HOT SPOTS POLICING POLICY

The time is ripe to launch a national program that supports the development and testing of hot spots policing. Scientific evidence indicates a strong likelihood of beneficial payoffs. With adequate funding the COPS Office could sponsor a competitive grant program for police departments to field well-planned, place-based programs of implementation, and NIJ could oversee rigorous evaluation of these efforts. We recommend a model that integrates the development and evaluation functions by requiring that applicant departments form a partnership with qualified researchers, such as NIJ fielded with the Spouse Abuse Replication Project and the Drug Market Analysis Project. These multi-site projects used similar measures and methods, permitting comparison of results across sites, while still allowing for variation in the intervention.

We think it is also time to launch evaluations at a national level allowing researchers, police, and the public to assess the overall impacts of hot spots policing on crime. We already know that police directed at hot spots can affect crime at those places. But the proven effectiveness of hot spots policing in reducing crime at place raises a broader question about the potential crime prevention benefits of reallocating police resources as we have suggested. A national program of support for creating hot spots policing departments would allow for the development of a large, multi-center trial (Weisburd & Taxman, 2000) for assessing the crime prevention and control impacts of hot spots policing. For example, the government could choose to launch such an effort sequentially, randomly allocating a set group of departments for hot spots policing implementation before a second set.

We also envision a number of focused multi-site efforts. One set could emphasize developing a better understanding of the effects of promising tactical interventions for selected hot spot problems. It would be valuable to examine different types of hot spot problems and to test the effectiveness of a variety of interventions at each – for example, ensuring that aggressive enforcement tactics were compared to other non-traditional preventive approaches. A variation on this would be studies that examine the effects of different intensity and timing dosage protocols in the tactical interventions – to establish what level of resource commitment yields the best "bang for the buck." Another set of projects might focus on rigorously testing the effects of varying the intensiveness of *problem-solving* methods in developing and implementing the hot spot intervention. Yet another set of studies could evaluate the impact of varying the department's overall resource commitment to hot spots policing. Such evaluations would focus not only on what happens to hot spots, but how different segments of the entire jurisdiction respond to this new approach, hence addressing concerns about community tolerance for a high dosage of place-based policing. All evaluations should carefully monitor the resource commitment to hot spots policing so that accurate measures of its efficiency can be obtained and compared to alternative strategic approaches to policing.

A key issue in hot spots policing is the impact of directed and focused police activities on citizens who live in or near the areas affected. We have strong evidence of the effectiveness of hot spots policing in reducing crime at specific places, but we do not have strong research on how such programs affect citizen fear, attitudes toward the police, and police legitimacy. Legitimacy has become a focus of police and scholarly interest, since it is assumed to influence, not only attitudes toward the police, but also the citizens' future behavior (Skogan & Frydl, 2004: Chapter 8). What impact does hot spots policing have on police legitimacy in the areas that it is implemented? Can hot spots policing increase legitimacy while preventing crime?

Regardless of the results of a rigorous program of evaluation, we do not envision that hot spots policing would or should entirely supplant other strategic approaches. Not all crime concentrates geographically (e.g., cybercrime, white collar crime, and various forms of organized crime) (Rosenbaum, 2006: 247), but even these forms of crime may submit to more effective crime reduction if place-based analysis is taken into account, such as linking network analyses of gang structure and the location of gang activity. And of course, we do not advocate the elimination of what has long been the core technology of policing: the calls-for-service-response system. That system is, after all, an essential source of data on where the problems are that the public wants the police to handle. But we do anticipate that there is room for more than one core technology in policing, and it appears that hot spots policing may offer an impressive addition. Stimulated by a federally sponsored, well-planned program of development and testing, we expect that American police agencies will respond in ways that allow the emergence of a science-based strategy into an industry that has traditionally been more influenced by employing poorly tested methods for making our communities safer and nicer places to live.

REFERENCES

Amendola, K.L., Weisburd, D., Groff, E.R., Ryan, M.J. &Wyckoff, L.A. (2006). *Where Are the Police and How Does Their Presence Impact Crime? Evaluating the Use of Automated Vehicle Locator Technologies in Policing.* A proposal submitted to the National Institute of Justice. Washington, DC: Police Foundation.

Block, C. & Green, L. (1994). *The GeoArchive Handbook: A Guide for Developing a Geographic Database as an Information Foundation for Community Policing.* Chicago, IL: Illinois Criminal Justice Information Authority.

Blumstein, A., Cohen, J., Roth, J. & Visher, C. (Eds.). (1986). *Criminal Careers and "Career Criminals."* Washington, DC: National Academies Press.

Braga, A.A. (2001). The effects of hot spots policing on crime. *Annals of the American Academy, 578,* 104-125.

Braga, A.A. & Bond, B.J. (2008). Policing crime and disorder hot spots: A randomized controlled trial. *Criminology, 46,* 577-608.

Braga, A.A. & Weisburd, D. (2006). Problem-oriented policing: The disconnect between principles and practice. In D. Weisburd and A.A. Braga (Eds.), *Police Innovation: Contrasting Perspectives* (pp. 133-154). Cambridge, UK: Cambridge University Press.

Braga, A.A. & Weisburd, D. In progress. *Policing Problem Places: Crime Hot Spots and Effective Prevention.* Manuscript submitted to Oxford University Press.

Braga, A.A. & Winship, C. (2006). Partnership, accountability, and innovation: Clarifying Boston's experience with pulling levers. In D. Weisburd and A.A. Braga (Eds.), *Police Innovation: Contrasting Perspectives* (pp. 171-187). Cambridge, UK: Cambridge University Press.

Brantingham, P.L. & Brantingham, P.J. (1999). A theoretical model of crime hot spot generation. *Studies on Crime and Crime Prevention, 8,* 7-26.

Clarke, R.V. & Weisburd, D. (1994). Diffusion of crime control benefits: Observations on the reverse of displacement. In R.V. Clarke (Ed.), *Crime Prevention Studies, Volume 2* (pp. 165-183). Monsey, NY: Criminal Justice Press.

Cohen, L.E. & Felson, M. (1979). Social change and crime rate trends: A routine activity approach. *American Sociological Review, 44,* 588-608.

Cordner, G. & Biebel, E.P. (2005). Problem-oriented policing in practice. *Criminology & Public Policy, 4,* 155-180.

Crow, W. & Bull, J. (1975). *Robbery Deterrence: An Applied Behavioral Science Demonstration, Final Report.* La Jolla, CA: Western Behavioral Science Institute.

Eck, J.E. (2006). Science, values, and problem-oriented policing: Why problem-oriented policing? In D. Weisburd and A.A. Braga (Eds.), *Police Innovation: Contrasting Perspectives* (pp. 117-152). Cambridge, UK: Cambridge University Press.

Eck, J.E. & Maguire, E. (2000). Have changes in policing reduced violent crime? An assessment of the evidence. In A. Blumstein and J. Wallman (Eds.), *The Crime Drop in America* (pp. 207-265). New York: Cambridge University Press.

Eck, J.E. & Weisburd, D. (1995). Crime places in crime theory. In J.E. Eck and D. Weisburd (Eds.), *Crime and Place* (pp. 1-34). Monsey, NY: Criminal Justice Press.

Famega, C.N. (2009). Proactive policing by post and community officers. *Crime and Delinquency, 55,* 78-104.

Felson, M. (1994). *Crime and Everyday Life: Implications and Insights for Society.* Thousand Oaks, CA: Pine Forge Press.

Gottfredson, M. & Hirschi, T. (1990). *A General Theory of Crime.* Stanford, CA: Stanford University Press.

Greenspan, R., Mastrofski, S.D., Weisburd, D., McNally, A.M. & Lane, E. (2003). *Compstat and Organizational Change: Short Site Visit Report.* Washington, DC: Police Foundation.

Groff, E., Weisburd, D. & Morris, N. (2009). Where the action is at places: Examining spatio-temporal patterns of juvenile crime at places using trajectory analysis and GIS. In D. Weisurd, G. Bruinsma and W. Bernasco (Eds.), *Putting Crime in Its Place: Units of Analysis in Spatial Crime Research* (pp. 61-86). New York: Springer Verlag.

Groff, E., Weisburd, D. & Yang, S.Y. (n.d.) Unpublished manuscript. Submitted to Journal of Quantitative Criminology.

Johnson, S. & Bowers, K. (2004). The burglary as clue to the future: The beginnings of prospective hot-spotting. *European Journal of Criminology, 1,* 237-255.

Kane, R.J. (2002). The social ecology of police misconduct. *Criminology, 40,* 867-896.

Kennedy, D.M. (2006). Old wine in new bottles: Policing and the lessons of pulling levers. In D. Weisburd and A.A. Braga (Eds.), *Police Innovation: Contrasting Perspectives* (pp. 155-170). Cambridge, UK: Cambridge University Press.

Laub, J.H. & Sampson, R.J. (2003). *Shared Beginnings, Divergent Lives: Delinquent Boys to Age 70.* Cambridge, MA: Harvard University Press.

Mastrofski, S.D. (2006). Community policing: A skeptical view. In D. Weisburd and A.A. Braga (Eds.), *Police Innovation: Contrasting Perspectives* (pp. 44-73). Cambridge, UK: Cambridge University Press.

Mastrofski, S.D. & Parks, R.B. (2003). *Beyond the Tyranny of 911 and the Myth of Reactive Policing.* Paper presented at the 13th World Congress of Criminology, International Society of Criminology, Rio de Janeiro, Brazil.

Mastrofski, S.D. & Uchida, C.D. (1993). Transforming the police. *Journal of Research in Crime and Delinquency, 30,* 330-358.

Moore, M.H. (2006). Improving police through expertise, experience, and experiments. In D. Weisburd and A.A. Braga (Eds.), *Police Innovation: Contrasting Perspectives* (pp. 322-338. Cambridge, UK: Cambridge University Press.

O' Shea, T. & Nicholls, K. (2003). *Crime Analysis in America: Findings and Recommendations.* Washington, DC: Office of Community Oriented Police Services.

Pierce, G.L., Spaar, S. & Briggs, L.R. (1988). *The Character of Police Work: Strategic and Tactical Implications.* Boston, MA: Center for Applied Social Research, Northeastern University.

Ratcliffe, J.H. (2008). *Intelligence-Led Policing.* Devon, UK: Willan Publishing.

Roncek, D.W. (2000). Schools and crime. In V. Goldsmith, P. McGuire, J.H. Molenkopf and T.A. Ross (Eds.), *Analyzing Crime Patterns: Frontiers of Practice* (pp. 153-165). Thousand Oaks, CA: Sage.

Rosenbaum, D.P. (2006). The limits of hot spots policing. In D. Weisburd and A.A. Braga (Eds.), *Police Innovation: Contrasting Perspectives* (pp. 245-263). Cambridge, UK: Cambridge University Press.

Sherman, L.W. (1998). *Evidence-Based Policing.* Ideas in American Policing series. Washington, DC: Police Foundation.

Sherman, L.W., Gartin, P.R. & Berger, M.E. (1989). Hot spots of predatory crime: Routine activities and the criminology of place. *Criminology, 27,* 27-55.

Skogan, W. (2006). *Police and Community in Chicago: A Tale of Three Cities.* New York: Oxford University Press.

Skogan, W. & Frydl, K. (Eds.). (2004). *Fairness and Effectiveness in Policing: The Evidence.* Washington, DC: National Academies Press.

Taylor, R.B. (2006). Incivilities reduction policing, zero tolerance, and the retreat from coproduction. In D. Weisburd and A.A. Braga (Eds.), *Police Innovation: Contrasting Perspectives* (pp. 98-114). Cambridge, UK: Cambridge University Press.

Weisburd, D. (2008). *Place-based Policing.* Ideas in American Policing series. Washington, DC: Police Foundation.

Weisburd, D. & Braga, A.A. (Eds.). (2006). *Police Innovation: Contrasting Perspectives.* Cambridge, UK: Cambridge University Press.

Weisburd, D., Bushway, S., Lum, C. & Yang, S.M. (2004). Crime trajectories at places: A longitudinal study of street segments in the city of Seattle. *Criminology, 42,* 283-322.

Weisburd, D. & Eck, J. (2004). What can police do to reduce crime, disorder and fear? *The Annals of the American Academy of Political and Social Science, 593,* 42-65.

Weisburd, D. & Green, L. (1994). Defining the drug market: The case of the Jersey City DMA System. In D.L. MacKenzie and C.D. Uchida (Eds.), *Drugs and Crime: Evaluating Public Policy Initiatives* (pp. 61-76). Newbury Park, CA: Sage.

Weisburd, D. & Lum, C. (2005). The diffusion of computerized crime mapping in policing: Linking research and practice. *Police Practice and Research, 6,* 419-434.

Weisburd, D., Maher, L. & Sherman, L. (1992). Contrasting crime general and crime specific theory: The case of hot spots of crime. *Advances in Criminological Theory, 4,* 45-69.

Weisburd, D., Mastrofski, S.D., McNally, A.M., Greenspan, R. & Willis, J. (2003). Reforming to preserve: Compstat and strategic problem solving in American policing. *Criminology and Public Policy, 2,* 421-455.

Weisburd, D., Morris, N. & Groff, E. Forthcoming. *Hot spots of juvenile crime: A longitudinal study of arrest incidents at street segments in Seattle, Washington.* Journal of Quantitative Criminology.

Weisburd, D. & Taxman, F. (2000). Developing a multi-center randomized trial in criminology: The case of HIDTA. *Journal of Quantitative Criminology, 16,* 315-339.

Weisburd, D., Wyckoff, L.A., Ready, J., Eck, J.E., Hinkle, J.C. & Gajewski, F. (2006). Does crime just move around the corner? A controlled study of spatial displacement and diffusion of crime control benefits. *Criminology, 44,* 549-592.

Willis, J., Mastrofski, S. & Kochel, T. In progress. *Maximizing the Benefits of Reform: Recommendations for Integrating COMPSTAT and Community Policing in America.* Report to the Office of Community-Oriented Policing. Manassas, VA: Center for Justice Leadership and Management, George Mason University.

Willis, J., Mastrofski, S. & Weisburd, D. (2007). Making sense of Compstat: A theory-based analysis of organizational change in three police departments. *Law & Society Review, 41,* 147-188.

Wolfgang, M., Thornberry, T.P. & Figlio, R.M. (1987). *From Boy to Man, From Delinquency to Crime.* Chicago, IL: University of Chicago Press.

ENDNOTES

[i] Their hot spots interventions would still require community engagement, but engagement that focuses on mobilizing community efforts to deal with hot spots.

[ii] Taken to an extreme, hot spot policing could result in the elimination of beats as a way for organizing patrol. At least two departments (Overland Park, Kansas, and Redlands, California) have adopted that approach, assigning officers to hot spot problem-solving tasks rather than patrolling beats.

TAKING IMPLEMENTATION SERIOUSLY: A RESPONSE TO MASTROFSKI, WEISBURD, AND BRAGA

EDWARD R. MAGUIRE

Mastrofski, Weisburd, and Braga (hereafter "the authors") propose an ambitious plan for the adoption and evaluation of hot spots policing in American police agencies. Their proposal is logical, rooted firmly in scientific evidence, and well-argued. I agree for the most part with its fundamental premise. At the same time I share some of the concerns raised about hot-spots policing in a recent critique by Dennis Rosenbaum (2006). Given page limits, I don't present a comprehensive critique, nor do I repeat most of the concerns already raised by Rosenbaum. Instead I focus on just one issue: the capacity of police agencies to implement and sustain the proposed reforms with the intended fidelity and dosage. Paying more serious attention to implementation issues will strengthen an otherwise sound proposal.

The study of innovation in organizations provides some useful insights for evaluating the authors' proposal. Innovation theorists have found it necessary to draw a distinction between different classes or categories of innovations. For example, more than three decades ago, Downs and Mohr (1976:701), in seeking to explain a pattern of disparate findings in innovation research, concluded that: "the most straightforward way of accounting for this empirical instability and theoretical confusion is to reject the notion that a unitary theory of innovation exists and postulate the existence of distinct types of innovations whose adoption can best be explained by a number of correspondingly distinct theories." Consistent with innovation research more generally, research on police innovation has drawn distinctions between different categories of innovations. For instance, Moore, Sparrow and Spelman (1997), drawing on Damanpour (1991), classified innovations in policing into four categories: strategic, administrative, technological, and programmatic. King (2000) used a similar scheme containing five categories: radical, management technical, line technical, administrative, and programmatic.[i]

Regardless of the specific typology used, thinking of different categories of innovation is vital for at least two reasons. First, some innovations are easier to adopt than others. Those that can be purchased or implemented in a canned way are more "adoptable" than those that lack specificity or require significant adaptation or tailoring to local circumstances. For example, getting agencies to purchase a new type of firearm or software is likely to be easier than implementing a strategic or radical innovation like hot spots policing whose adoption would "fundamentally restructure urban policing" (to use the authors' words).[ii] Second, understanding the differences between types of innovation focuses us more sharply on the explanatory variables most likely to influence the adoption of those innovations. The authors have clearly proposed a "radical" (King, 2000) or "strategic" (Moore, Sparrow, and Spelman, 1997) innovation – one that would significantly alter the way police work is carried out, managed, and structured. Given the ambitious and far reaching nature of the proposal, there are reasons to question whether the proposed innovation can (or will) be adopted with the prescribed levels of fidelity and dosage. It would be useful to test hypotheses about which social forces or explanatory variables regulate the nature and extent with which strategic innovations get adopted. The proposal pays short shrift to adoptability concerns.

We don't need to look back very far into the history of policing to find another radical or strategic reform movement – problem-oriented policing – with far reaching implications for how police work is done. In fact, the authors of this proposal have all contributed key insights to the literature on problem-oriented policing (POP). Several recent studies have cast doubt on the extent to which problem-oriented policing has been implemented in ways consistent with Goldstein's (1990) early reform prescriptions. For instance, Cordner and Biebel's (2005:155) research in the San Diego Police Department, an agency widely acclaimed as a worldwide leader in the implementation of problem-oriented policing, found that non-specialist officers only "tended to engage in small-scale problem-solving with little formal analysis or assessment." Cordner and Biebel (2005) concluded that it is time to draw a distinction between the everyday "problem-solving" carried out by officers, and the more intensive forms of "problem-oriented policing" envisioned by reformers. Bichler and Gaines (2005) examined the extent to which officers are effective in identifying the problems in their assigned geographic areas. They found "little consistency between focus groups of officers working in the same district" in a medium-sized southern police department (Bichler and Gaines, 2005:68). Taken together, this recent wave of research paints a glum picture of a reform movement in which the reality of what is practiced on the streets looks very different from what the original architects of the reform envisioned. While problem-oriented policing is practiced with fidelity by some officers and some specialized units some of the time, to our knowledge it is not practiced routinely by generalist police officers in any agency.

A recent reflection on the current state of problem-oriented policing by two of the proposal's authors concluded that shallow problem-solving efforts with "weak analyses, mostly traditional responses, and limited assessments" are the norm (Braga and Weisburd, 2006:149). Yet, they also concluded optimistically that even shallow implementation of problem-oriented policing still produces crime prevention benefits. They urge problem-oriented policing reformers to abandon their quest for the ideal and "embrace the reality of...ad hoc shallow problem-solving efforts" (Braga and Weisburd, 2006:149). It is not difficult to imagine researchers reaching a similar conclusion about hot spots policing a decade or two from now.

Radical or strategic reform efforts in policing, including team policing, community policing, and problem-oriented policing, all seem to have encountered a seemingly insurmountable set of constraints in their quest to alter the core technologies of policing. The current proposal pays insufficient attention to these constraints. Some of the "usual suspects" among these constraints include culture, structure, environment, history and tradition. Strategic reform efforts in policing often seem to clash with widely held beliefs among both officers and key stakeholders about how the job of policing should be done. The history of police reform is littered with well-intentioned and potentially effective reforms that paid insufficient attention to implementation constraints.

THE ROLE OF IMPLEMENTATION IN EVIDENCE-BASED CRIMINOLOGY

All three of the proposal's authors are affiliated with the Center for Evidence Based Crime Policy at George Mason University and their proposal is consistent with the emerging evidence-based criminology (EBC) movement. EBC holds significant promise for expanding the policy reach and the relevance of criminology. Evidence-based criminology tends to treat criminal justice organizations as a black-box. The implicit assumption seems to be that if there is sufficient evidence that a program or policy "works," organizations will embrace it, support it, and implement it. This viewpoint is consistent with a rational choice model of innovation adoption in organizations. However, four decades of research in the organizational sciences (including public administration) fail to find strong support for rational choice theories of organizational behavior. Since the late 1960s, organizational scholars have invested substantial effort in specifying and testing theories that seek to explain the seemingly irrational behaviors of organizations. Irrationality is a particular concern among public sector organizations, which are often able to persist in spite of compelling evidence of their ineffectiveness and inefficiency (Meyer and Zucker, 1989). The unfortunate reality is that evidence about what works is an insufficient motivator to compel people and organizations to do things differently. Implementation is currently the Achilles heel of the evidence-based criminology movement. Consider evidence-based medicine (EBM), an older and more mature evidence-based policy movement than EBC. In spite of all the progress made by EBM, many physicians continue to prescribe treatments that have been shown to harm (and sometimes kill) their patients. One study concluded that "there is sufficient evidence to suggest that most clinicians' practices do not reflect the principles of evidence-based medicine but rather are based upon tradition, their most recent experience, what they learned years ago in medical school or what they have heard from their friends. The average physician is said to read scientific journals approximately two hours a week and most are likely overwhelmed by the volume of material confronting them" (Eisenberg, 2000). Another study noted that the "lag between the discovery of more efficacious forms of treatment and their incorporation into routine patient care is unnecessarily long, in the range of about 15 to 20 years. Even then, adherence of clinical practice to the evidence is highly uneven" (Institute of Medicine, 2001). Although evidence-based medicine has attended to implementation issues much more seriously than evidence-based criminology, the medical field continues to evidence a substantial gap between knowledge and practice.

CONCLUSION

The authors articulate a clear argument for launching a national effort to support the adoption and evaluation of hot spots policing in American police agencies. The argument is based firmly in the evidence-based criminology tradition with its reliance on randomized trials "to assess the overall impacts of hot spots policing on crime." Although five randomized trials have already evaluated the effectiveness of hot spots policing, little (if any) scientific progress has been made in illuminating implementation issues. The current proposal would add to the existing collection of effectiveness studies but there is no indication that it would focus any systematic attention on implementation issues.

Organizations vary widely in their capacity to adopt innovation, and innovations vary widely in the extent to which they are easily adoptable by organizations. The authors propose the adoption of a particularly complex strategic innovation – one that will fundamentally alter the way police agencies do their work. While accumulating further research evidence on the effectiveness of the proposed innovation is certainly sensible, the time has come for evidence-based criminology to pay more attention to implementation issues. Evidence-based medicine researchers have discovered a lengthy "implementation gap" – the period of time between which scientific evidence becomes available and clinical practice begins to change in response to that evidence (Dopson, et al., 2003; Institute of Medicine, 2001). Evidence-based criminology has focused so intently on accumulating high-quality research evidence on the effectiveness of interventions that insufficient attention has been paid to understanding the agencies charged with implementing those interventions. As a result, little is known about the implementation gap in criminal justice.

The authors can improve the relevance and policy reach of their proposal by designing a systematic research agenda to explore the capacity of American police organizations to adopt hot spots policing. More generally, evidence-based criminology can benefit from blending insights from criminology and organizational science in an effort to understand not only whether interventions reduce crime, but whether agencies are capable of implementing and sustaining those interventions.

REFERENCES

Bichler, G. & Gaines, L. (2005). An examination of police officers' insights into problem identification and problem solving. Crime and Delinquency 51, 53-74.

Braga, A. & Weisburd, D. (2006). Problem-oriented policing: The disconnect between principles and practice. In D. Weisburd & A. Braga (Eds.), Police Innovation: Contrasting Perspectives, (pp. 133-152). Cambridge: Cambridge University Press.

Cordner, G. & Biebel, E.P. (2005). Problem-oriented policing in practice. Criminology & Public Policy, 4, 155-180.

Damanpour, F. (1991). Organizational innovation: A meta-analysis of effects of determinants and moderators. Academy of Management Journal, 34, 555-590.

Downs, Jr., G.W. & Mohr, L.B. (1976). Conceptual issues in the study of innovation. Administrative Science Quarterly, 21, 700-714.

Dopson, S., Locock, L., Gabbay, J. Ferlie, E. & Fitzgerald, L. (2003). Evidence-based medicine and the implementation gap. Health: An Interdisciplinary Journal for the Social Study of Health, Illness, and Medicine, 7(3), 311-330.

Eisenberg J.M. (2000). Quality research for quality healthcare: The data connection. Health Services Research, 35, 12-17.

Goldstein, H. (1990). Problem-Oriented Policing. New York: McGraw-Hill.

Institute of Medicine (2001). Crossing the Quality Chasm: A New Health System for the 21st Century. Washington, DC: National Academy Press.

King, W.R. (2000). Measuring police innovation: Issues and measurement. Policing: An International Journal of Police Strategies and Management, 23, 303-317.

Meyer, M.W. & Zucker, L.G. 1989. Permanently Failing Organizations. Newbury Park, CA: Sage Publications.

Moore, M.H., Sparrow, M. & Spelman, W. (1997). Innovations in policing: From production lines to job shops. In A.A. Altshuler & R.D. Behn (Eds.), Innovation in American Government, (pp. 274-298). Washington, DC: Brookings Institution Press.

Rosenbaum, D.P. (2006). The limits of hot spots policing. In D. Weisburd & A. Braga (Eds.), Police Innovation: Contrasting Perspectives, (pp. 245-266). Cambridge: Cambridge University Press.

ENDNOTES

[i] King (2000) treated the four categories used by Moore and his colleagues as a point of departure for his own research on police innovation. King chose the term "radical" as a substitute for "strategic." He also split the "technological" category into two categories: line technical and management technical.

[ii] King (2000:310) characterizes line-technical innovations as those that would be used primarily by street officers as opposed to other people in police organizations. King argues that line-technical innovations that "are perceived by line police officers to enhance their law enforcement image will be more readily adopted" than technical innovations that do not enhance the law enforcement image.

Hot Spots Do Not Exist, and Four Other Fundamental Concerns About Hot Spots Policing

Ralph B. Taylor

Mastrofski, Weisburd and Braga's (2009) policy proposal (MWB hereafter), comes from three of the most respected policing researchers in the discipline. Among them they share far over half a century of policing research and policy expertise. Their research and the advice they have given police departments have done much to shape policing in the U.S. and elsewhere. They propose a national policy supporting hot spots policing (hereafter HSP).

Despite the sagacity, individually and collectively of the team, this work suggests such a proposal is premature because fundamental questions about and misunderstandings of hot spots or hot spots policing have not yet been resolved. Further, the proposed policy may create adverse side effects.

Readers should bear in mind three points. First, this author has never claimed to be a policing researcher, nor have police departments ever sought his advice. (Nor, after this piece, are they likely to in future!). Second, given space limitations the points here are delivered unadorned. This may create a more callow impression than intended. Third, the intent here is to stimulate debate, not be gratuitously critical.

MWB are to be toasted for developing their bold proposal, for opening the debate on whether we need a national policing policy and for asking would it look like. The ideas proposed deserve serious attention. What types of initiatives could serve as national policing templates is a most worthy topic for national debate.

My comments here raise the following concerns:
1. Hot spots do not exist in the real world. To believe they do is to commit the logical fallacy of reification.
2. The most important abstract quality of hot spots may **not** be that they are hot spots. To believe so is to commit the logical fallacy of misplaced concreteness.
3. There is no one set definition of the policies and procedures that constitute HSP. We know where this places police, but no consensus has emerged about what police do next. In short, there may not yet be a coherent set of policies, procedures, practices and strategies most would agree represent the core of HSP.
4. Advancing HSP as a national policing policy over and above other plausible initiatives is at best premature. Even if we disagree on the merits of the above three points, the sound scientific basis for establishing the significantly superior effectiveness and cost effectiveness of HSP *relative* to other potential national policing policies

does not exist. We do not have the requisite corpus of scientific work documenting its relative superiority.

5. Advancing HSP as a national policy may generate potentially adverse impacts including (a) police jettisoning key elements in their overall mission, (b) further isolating U.S. policing innovations from policy innovations in other countries, (c) overlooking important emerging new understandings about the roles of police in security and governance, (d) accelerating further the retreat from co-producing public safety which has been underway in American policing for at least the two last decades, and (e) further undermining the legitimacy of police and other public institutions.

Some of the points made here overlap to some degree with comments made earlier, either by myself or others, about hot spots policing (Buerger, Cohn & Petrosino, 1995; Rosenbaum, 2005; Taylor, 1998; Taylor, 2001) or policing more broadly (Mazerolle & Ransley, 2005, 2006)

CORE CONCEPTUAL CONFUSIONS

Despite an impressive 170 citations from scholars around the world in numerous disciplines to one of the key early publications on hot spots (Sherman, Gartin & Buerger, 1989), and enormous interest in HSP among police departments in many countries, two core confusions about hot spots have yet to be resolved.

To state the first confusion: assuming a stance of hypothetical realism, hot spots exist in the data world but not the real world (Taylor, 1994), unless you study geology (Taylor, 1998). There are types of places which exist in both social scientists' data world and the real world: places like land use parcels (Hirschfield & Bowers, 1997) or behavior settings (Wicker, 1979) or street blocks (Taylor, 1997) are some examples. To conclude that hot spots are free standing entities existing in the real world is to commit the logical fallacy of reification (Gould, 1981). It is in part because of this fallacy that it is so hard to operationally identify and bound hot spots using agreed upon, replicable, scientific criteria (Buerger, Cohn & Petrosino, 1995).

Rather, hot spots are amalgams of different types of locations. As MWB tell us: "they are addresses, buildings, block faces, street segments, or clusters of addresses" (p. 2). Because crime or arrest or calls for service data points cluster more densely on a map, relative to the surround, does not make the area within those points a specific type of entity. In short there is a core unresolved construct validation question.

This confusion surfaces when, in specific studies, researchers and police personnel must move from the maps to the streets. In the process of operationalizing hot spots so that police personnel can work with them, idiosyncratic adjustments are made to each hot spot (Buerger, Cohn &

Petrosino, 1995). To take just one recent example, in describing their Lowell (MA) randomized trial of hot spots policing Braga and Bond (2008: 583) report: "Qualitative data on place characteristics, local dynamics, and Lowell Police Department (LPD) patrol officer perceptions of crime problems were used to determine hot-spot area boundaries."

Consider this. Suppose that researchers started finding that 70 percent of shootings in a number of large cities took place within about 1/10th of the hours in a typical week (9 pm – 3 am, Friday, Saturday and Sunday evenings: 18/168). They then proposed that these times deserved special recognition and policing strategies, and labeled them "hot hours."

Where reification is about making mistakes going from the abstract to the concrete, a related fallacy involves focusing selectively on concrete qualities as one abstracts. The abstraction may overlook other potentially important qualities. This is the fallacy of misplaced concreteness: "the accidental error of mistaking the abstract for the concrete" (Carolan, 2009; Whitehead, 1967: 50-51)." 'Where does the misplacement come in?' Prima facie it seems as though at best there is the suppression of important detail in the definition; at worst the crux of the matter has been ignored." (Lawrence, 1953) This error is potentially dangerous because it draws our attention away from other potentially critical features of these locations. Such features might be critical for advancing our scientific understanding of crime dynamics. In short, there may be numerous hitherto overlooked features of this crime patterning, relevant for advancing our scientific understanding, that the hot spots label has led to our overlooking.

Turning to hot spots policing activities, although MWB talk about adding problem oriented policing elements, and other discussions of hot spots have talked about introducing components of a co-produced model (Braga & Bond, 2008), all of which is helpful, there is no set of agreed *activities* which we all agree are HSP.

Broad agreement about *what activities* police will do does not exist, and varies from place to place. All that we know is that police will be present more, or doing more in these locations than they will be in other non-hotspot locations.

SHOULD HSP HOLD A PRIVILEGED POSITION IN THE POLICY DEBATE?

Why is hot spots policing privileged to be forwarded as a possible national policy? Yes, it is true the recent National Academy report spoke well of geographically targeted policing (Skogan & Frydl, 2004). But we have extensive empirical research on other policing strategies, including third party policing (Mazerolle & Ransley, 2006) and intelligence led policing (Ratcliffe, 2008), for example.

Most importantly, as yet, we have no solid *comparative* research testing *various* policing innovations against one another, and providing compelling rigorous scientific evidence that HSP has emerged as the winner. We need a *cadre* of careful studies, preferably using randomized trials (Weisburd, 2000), across a range of cities and departments, which test HSP not against business as usual, but against *other policing innovations*. In part because of sub-optimal funding for policing innovation research in the U.S. in the last few years, the requisite evidence base is just not there.

RISKS

All policy proposals have potentially adverse side effects, and the national HSP proposal is no exception. Five are discussed below. It is hoped that drawing attention to them stimulates policy planners to think about policy features which might minimize them.

(a) In such initiatives (see for example, Braga & Bond, 2008: 584-584) what police actually do is likely to be dominated either by disorder reduction strategies or aggressive enforcement. Social service interventions and "deep" information gathering for problem solving are unlikely. Hot spots policing is basically about law enforcement (Weisburd & Eck, 2004: Figure 1). Service and reassurance functions of police diminish in importance and are engaged in less (see Weisburd & Eck's (2004) contrast of HSP with community policing). The service component of policing is at risk of being lost.

(b) Second, this initiative is at variance with other recent national policing policy initiatives undertaken in other countries. To take just one example, following the work on signal disorders and signal crimes (Innes, 2004b), the United Kingdom implemented a national reassurance policing policy (Innes, 2004a). What reassurance policing is and isn't, and where it would work best, and how it can be co-opted by ongoing police organizational traditions all make for interesting debates (Fielding & Innes, 2006; Herrington & Millie, 2006; Innes, 2005; Williamson, Ashby & Webber, 2006). But the key point here is that the policy explicitly seeks to make police more visible and available to local citizens and business personnel, and to increase communication between the police and the public. "Reassurance policing … places an emphasis on police visibility, familiarity and accessibility" (Millie & Herrington, 2005: 41). It is about decreasing the distance between officers and the public. Hot spots policing, especially if intensive enforcement predominates, is likely to increase that distance.

New Zealand, to take another example, has moved toward an intelligence led policing model (Ratcliffe, 2008: 206). This is a revised, geographically-aware evolution of problem oriented policing model (Goldstein, 1993). Intelligence analysts in police departments play leading roles.

(c) HSP views police departments as agencies with more solo responsibility for security than they have in some situations. More recent policy initiatives like third party policing (Mazerolle & Ransley, 2005, 2006) recognize that police operate within a complex web of organizations, and examine how to most effectively embed police work within that broader web. This type of innovation is in line with an emerging policy framework in security studies emphasizing shared governance dynamics (Wood & Shearing, 2007). This emerging perspective recognizes hybrid governance operative in many situations and considers how agencies can most effectively operate when governance around security is distributed across a public or public/private mix of groups. A focus on hot spots policing seems at the least to overlook the increasing prevalence of and recognition of hybrid governance around security issues.

(d) Embracing HSP may mark another step in American policing's retreat from reform. Initiatives emerging in the U.S. following the civil disorders of the 1960s sought to create more understanding between police and the policed (Taylor, 2005). Somewhere between 1980 and 1990 these series of reforms (community relations councils, team policing, geographic policing, community crime prevention, community policing, incivilities reduction policing) morphed into strategies that instead further alienated the police from the public (quality of life policing, zero tolerance policing) and collapsed the harm principle (Harcourt, 2001).

The reforms intended initially to create co-produced public safety and increased police responsiveness (Ostrom, Parks, Whitaker & Percy, 1979; Ostrom & Whitaker, 1973) ended up doing the opposite. "Security is unlikely to be produced by institutional actions undertaken in isolation. Security must be co-produced, with publics playing their part in enacting informal modes of social control that interlock with the more formal actions of the police and partner agencies" (Innes, 2004a: 162).

(f) HSP if formally endorsed seems likely to continue this retreat from a co-production reformist model. Another potential consequence follows if this happens. Because the police activities most likely in the hot spots policed – most likely because this is what has generally been done in the bulk (but not all) of the works cited by those promoting this approach (Sherman, 1989, 1995; Sherman et al., 1989; Sherman & Weisburd, 1995) – has been aggressive enforcement. If so, then given what we know about procedural justice, HSP seems likely to further decrease the perceived procedural justice of police actions, especially in communities of color (Tyler, 2004; Tyler & Wakslak, 2004).

I recognize that MWB talk about integrating problem solving activities into HSP, and this has occurred to some degree in some studies (Braga & Bond, 2008). I seriously question, however, whether on the ground in most settings aggressive enforcement would not dominate (McArdle & Erzin, 2001)

CLOSING COMMENTS

It is premature to promote a national policy favoring hot spots policing. Literally, hot spots do not exist; we do not yet know what the most important scientific attributes are of hot spots and their variations; there is no agreement on what defines hot spot policing behaviors, we do not have a corpus of comparative empirical work clearly indicating the superiority of this approach relative to other policing innovations, the approach makes governance assumptions about police agencies that appear increasingly unrealistic, and the policy carries with it serious potential liabilities for how the public views police and public agencies more broadly.

MWB's proposal is enormously valuable, however, for three reasons. First, it gets us started on thinking about important issues. Should there be a national policing policy and if so what would it be? Other countries like the U.K. and New Zealand have moved recently in this direction. Second, MWB endorse reviving locally initiated research partnerships (LIRPs) between police and local researchers. These were last promulgated in the mid-1990s with varying success (McKewen, 1999). Let's revisit and update that model based on what we have learned so that the second generation of LIRPs can be more cost effective and more useful for police. Third, their call will hopefully stimulate not only policy debate, but meta-analyses of recent U.S. and non-U.S. policing research, deeper examinations of innovations in other countries, and most important of all a raft of high quality new policing studies which can provide us with more information about the *relative* effectiveness and relative cost effectiveness of a range of policing innovations, including co-production models involving citizens (Ostrom et al., 1979) and other agencies (Mazerolle & Ransley, 2006), and how relative innovation return rates might be shaped by the local crime, political, cultural, and organizational climates.

REFERENCES

Braga, A.A. & Bond, B.J. (2008). Policing crime and disorder hot spots: A Randomized controlled trial. *Criminology, 46,* 577-607.

Buerger, M.E., Cohn, E.G. & Petrosino, A.J. (1995). Defining the 'hot spots of crime': Operationalizing theoretical concepts for field research. In J.E. Eck and D. Weisburd (Eds.), *Crime and Place* (pp. 237-257). Monsey, NY: Criminal Justice Press.

Carolan, M.S. (2009). Process sub-politics: Placing empirical flesh on Whiteheadian thought. *Ethics, Place & Environment, 12,* 187-203.

Fielding, N. & Innes, M. (2006). Reassurance policing, community policing and measuring police performance. *Policing & Society, 16,* 127-145.

Goldstein, H. (1993). *The New Policing: Confronting Complexity.* Washington, DC: National Institute of Justice.

Gould, S.J. (1981). *The Mismeasure of Man.* New York: Norton.

Harcourt, B.E. (2001). *Illusion of Order: The False Promise of Broken Windows Policing.* Cambridge, MA: Harvard University Press.

Herrington, V & Millie, A. (2006). Applying reassurance policing: Is it "business as usual"? *Policing & Society, 16,* 146-163.

Hirschfield, A. & Bowers, K.J. (1997). The development of a social, demographic and land use profiler for areas of high crime. *British Journal of Criminology, 37,* 103-120.

Innes, M. (2004a). Reinventing tradition?: Reassurance, neighborhood security and policing. *Criminal Justice, 5,* 151-171.

Innes, M. (2004b). Signal crimes and signal disorders: notes on deviance as communicative action. *British Journal of Sociology, 55,* 335-355.

Innes, M. (2005). Why 'soft' policing is hard: On the curious development of reassurance policing, how it became neighbourhood policing and what this signifies about the politics of police reform. *Journal of Community & Applied Social Psychology, 15,* 156-169.

Lawrence, N. (1953). Single location, simple location, and misplaced concreteness. *The Review of Metaphysics, 7,* 225-247.

Mastrofski, S.D., Weisburd, D. & Braga, A.A. (2009). *Rethinking Policing: The Policy Implications of Hot Spots of Crime.* Policy Proposal essay submitted to the American Society of Criminology.

Mazerolle, L.G. & Ransley, J. (2005). The Case for third-party policing. In D. Weisburd and A.A. Braga (Eds.), *Police Innovation: Contrasting Perspectives* (pp. 191-206). Cambridge: Cambridge University Press.

Mazerolle, L.G. & Ransley, J. (2006). *Third-party Policing.* Cambridge: Cambridge University Press.

McArdle, A. & Erzin, T. (Eds.). (2001). *Zero Tolerance: Quality of Life and the New Police Brutality in New York City.* New York: New York University Press.

McKewen, T. (1999). NIJ's locally initiated research partnerships in policing: Factors that add up to success. *NIJ Journal, January(238),* 2-10.

Millie, H. & Herrington, V. (2005). Bridging the gap: Understanding reassurance policing. *The Howard Journal, 44,* 41-56.

Ostrom, E., Parks, R.B., Whitaker, G.P. & Percy, S.L. (1979). The public service production process: A framework for analysing police services. In R. Baker and F.A. Meyer, Jr. (Eds.), *Evaluating Alternative Law Enforcement Policies* (pp. 65-73). Lexington, MA: DC Heath.

Ostrom, E. & Whitaker, G. (1973). Does local community control of police make a difference?: Some preliminary findings. *American Journal of Political Science, 17,* 48-76.

Ratcliffe, J.H. (2008). *Intelligence-Led Policing.* Cullompton, Devon: Willan Publishing.

Rosenbaum, D.P. (2005). The limits of hot spots policing. In D. Weisburd and A.A. Braga (Eds.), *Police Innovation: Contrasting Perspectives* (pp. 245-263). Cambridge: Cambridge University Press.

Sherman, L.W. (1989). Repeat calls for service: Policing the "hot spots". In D.J. Kenney (Ed.), *Police and Policing: Contemporary Issues* (pp. 150-165). New York: Praeger.

Sherman, L.W. (1995). Hot spots of crime and criminal careers of places. In J.E. Eck and D. Weisburd (Eds.), *Crime and Place* (pp. 35-52). Monsey, NY: Criminal Justice Press.

Sherman, L.W., Gartin, P.R. & Buerger, M.E. (1989). Hot spots of predatory crime: Routine activities and the criminology of place. *Criminology, 27,* 27-56.

Sherman, L.W. & Weisburd, D. (1995). General deterrent effects of police patrol in crime 'hot spots': A randomized, controlled trial. *Justice Quarterly, 12,* 625-649.

Skogan, W.G. & Frydl, K. (2004). *Fairness and Effectiveness in Policing: The Evidence.* Washington, DC: National Academies Press.

Taylor, R.B. (1994). *Research Methods in Criminal Justice.* New York: McGraw Hill.

Taylor, R.B. (1997). Social order and disorder of streetblocks and neighborhoods: Ecology, microecology and the systemic model of social disorganization. *Journal of Research in Crime and Delinquency, 33,* 113-155.

Taylor, R.B. (1998). Crime in small scale places: What we know, what we can do about it. In *Crime and Place: Plenary Papers of the 1997 Conference on Criminal Justice Research and Evaluation* (pp. 1-20). Washington, DC: National Institute of Justice.

Taylor, R.B. (2001). *Breaking Away from Broken Windows: Evidence from Baltimore Neighborhoods and the Nationwide Fight Against Crime, Grime, Fear and Decline.* New York: Westview Press.

Taylor, R.B. (2005). Incivilities reduction policing, zero tolerance, and the retreat from coproduction: Weak foundations and strong pressures In D. Weisburd and A.A. Braga (Eds.), *Police Innovation: Contrasting Perspectives* (pp. 98-114). Cambridge: Cambridge University Press.

Tyler, T. (2004). Enhancing police legitimacy. *Annals of the American Academy of Political and Social Science, 593,* 84-99.

Tyler, T & Wakslak, C. (2004). Profiling and police legitimacy: Procedural justice, attributions of motive, and acceptance of police authority. *Criminology, 42,* 253-281.

Weisburd, D. (2000). Randomized experiments in criminal justice policy: Prospects and problems. *Crime & Delinquency, 46,* 181-193.

Weisburd, D. & Eck, J.E. (2004). What can police do to reduce crime, disorder, and fear? *Annals of the American Academy of Political and Social Science, 593,* 42-65.

Whitehead, A.N. (1967). *Science and the Modern World.* New York: Free Press.

Wicker, A.W. (1979). *Introduction to Ecological Psychology.* Monterey, CA: Brooks/Cole.

Williamson, T., Ashby, D.I. & Webber, R. (2006). Classifying neighborhoods for reassurance policing. *Policing & Society, 16,* 189-218.

Wood. J. & Shearing, C. (2007). *Imagining Security.* Cullompton, Devon: Willan.

THE U.S. NEEDS A NATIONAL POLICE UNIVERSITY

GARY CORDNER

The body of scientific and professional knowledge about policing has expanded greatly over the past three decades, as has knowledge about crime, crime prevention, and related topics. It might be hoped, even expected, that police executives would be masters of this knowledge, but they are not. Our fragmented and extremely thin system of police higher education leaves most police executives substantially uninformed about the research, knowledge, and evidence that should form the basis of police strategies and programs. We lack an effective system by which police leaders might keep up with the latest knowledge in their field. The existing executive development institutes and professional police associations all suffer from significant limitations. None of our universities is willing or able to make a truly substantial and long-term commitment to police higher education. The only viable solution is the creation of a brand new national institution – a national police university – not for entry-level police officers, but for commanders and chief executives.

A LOT OF CHIEFS

The American police system is extremely fragmented. There are almost 18,000 separate and distinct law enforcement agencies in the country, of which 88.3% are local police departments and sheriff's offices, 11.1% are special jurisdiction police and investigative agencies, and the remaining 0.6% are primary state police or federal law enforcement agencies (Reaves, 2006; 2007). In this federal system, the vast majority of police agencies are locally operated and controlled. With these 18,000 separate agencies come 18,000 police CEOs – chiefs, sheriffs, commissioners, superintendents, directors, etc. Most of these CEOs are in charge of pretty small operations, but the number of sizeable agencies is not insignificant:

- 1,000+ full-time sworn officers – 93 agencies
- 250-999 full-time sworn – 318 agencies
- 50-249 full-time sworn – 1,993 agencies
- 0-49 full-time sworn – 15,537 agencies

There are no national requirements or standards for police CEOs, and few state requirements. Typically, in order for a chief or sheriff to have sworn status, which is traditionally expected in most jurisdictions, he or she must meet the state's police officer training requirements, although some states exempt sheriffs on account of their elected and constitutional status.

279

Generally, the only legal limitations on civilian (non-sworn) police CEOs are that they lack the police powers of arrest, search, detention, and use of force. Their formal managerial authority vis-à-vis their police organization and employees is not usually derived from state law or affected by sworn vs. civilian status, although informal and symbolic authority may be a different story.

Some states impose specific training requirements on police CEOs – for example, Ohio requires new sheriffs to complete a three-week training program (Ohio Revised Code, 1997). More commonly, sworn police CEOs must meet the same training requirements as other police officers – they can choose to meet these requirements by attending leadership/management courses or other approved police training. In Illinois, police chiefs and deputy police chiefs must complete at least 20 hours of approved training each year related to "law enforcement, management or executive development, or ethics" (Illinois Law Enforcement Training & Standards Board, 2006). In Kentucky, special courses are offered for new chiefs and sheriffs, and a variety of command, management, and leadership courses are offered for incumbent CEOs, but a chief or sheriff can still choose any approved courses to meet the state's annual 40 hour police training requirement. Among many courses offered each year, CEOs can take the annually updated and revised "Police Executive Command Course" or "Patrol Shotgun" (Department of Criminal Justice Training, 2009).

As a result of fragmentation and lax regulation, there is little standardization or consistency in the preparation of police CEOs in the U.S. There are no standards that all CEOs must meet nor any courses that all must complete. Rather, 14,000 of them are appointed by mayors, city managers, or similar governing officials who have almost complete leeway to set their own criteria, while the other 4,000 or so are elected by voters based on even more nebulous considerations. The vast majority are then free to choose their own paths for personal and professional development.

JEFFERSON WOULD BE PROUD

In spite of all this fragmentation and lack of regulation, or maybe because of it, good things have sprouted across the country. Many of today's police CEOs are experienced, well-trained, and highly educated. It is now common for police chiefs to have college degrees, many have master's degrees or law degrees, and a few have doctoral degrees. Indicative of this situation, of 21 police executive positions advertised in May 2009 on the International Association of Chiefs of Police (IACP) "Discover Policing" website (www.theiacp.org/Jobs/tabid/73/Default.aspx), 19 required a minimum of a bachelor's degree. This is a significant change from educational requirements in place in earlier decades (Greene & Cordner, 1980).

Another significant change has been the development of police executive training institutes and courses. Prior to 1980, few states offered any substantial training courses or programs on police leadership and management for police commanders and CEOs. At the regional and national levels, the FBI National Academy, the Southern Police Institute's Administrative Officers Course, and Northwestern University's School of Police Staff and Command were most noteworthy among a small set of programs. This situation has now changed substantially. Several states, including California, Florida, Texas, Kentucky, Massachusetts, and North Carolina offer menus of police management development courses including some type of capstone executive leadership course. At the national level, the Police Executive Research Forum's Senior Management Institute for Police and the FBI's National Executive Institute have been added to the mix. A few universities have also become serious contributors, including Johns Hopkins University's Police Executive Leadership Program and John Jay College's new Leadership Academy. Even a few individual law enforcement agencies have taken the plunge – such as the Los Angeles Police Department Leadership Program.

THE MONSTER THAT ATE POLICE EDUCATION

With all these highly educated and trained police commanders and CEOs, a high level of professional expertise should be in place. But the current situation is not as good as it should be. One problem is that, for all their formal education, few police executives have seriously studied policing. They typically have not read the classic works in the field, such as Varieties of Police Behavior (Wilson, 1968), Justice Without Trial (Skolnick, 1966), The Functions of the Police in Modern Society (Bittner, 1970), or Policing a Free Society (Goldstein, 1977). They are enmeshed in (and responsible for) police organizations, but probably have not read Police Leadership in America (Geller, 1985), The Strategic Management of Police Departments (Moore & Stephens, 1991), The Bottom Line of Policing (Moore & Braga, 2003), or Leadership in the LAPD (Reese, 2005). They almost certainly know about broken windows and community policing, but have not read Problem-Oriented Policing (Goldstein, 1990), Situational Crime Prevention (Clarke, 1997), Fairness and Effectiveness in Policing (Skogan & Frydll, 2004), or Police Innovation (Weisburd & Braga, 2006). It is highly unlikely that they are familiar with evidence-based policing or the Campbell Collaborative.

How could such well-educated professionals be so poorly read about their own business? The answer is criminal justice. There has been less and less police education going on in American universities since the 1970s – programs that once offered degrees in police administration or police science have disappeared, replaced by degree programs in criminal justice. These criminal justice programs typically started out with a heavy dose of police courses, but the clear trend has been to shift away from police-centric curricula. Because criminal justice is such a broad field with a rapidly expanding knowledge base, the police share of the educational enterprise has been steadily shrinking. It is common now for an undergraduate criminal justice curriculum to include just one required policing course, supplemented by a small number of elective courses. Police administration, once the center of the curriculum, no longer exists in many criminal justice programs, and appears only as an elective in others. The situation is largely the same at the graduate level.

Too Many Highly Effective Habits

Perhaps this vacuum in police education has been filled by the surge in police executive training institutes and courses? Undoubtedly this has occurred to some degree. Police managers going through the Southwestern Law Enforcement Institute (now the Institute for Law Enforcement Administration) used to call their lead instructor, Gary Sykes, "son of Bittner." The SPI's AOC course, the FBINA, and Kentucky's School of Strategic Leadership, among others, have significant academic components. The California Command College emphasizes future perspectives, while Johns Hopkins emphasizes ethics. In general, however, the police executive training world has been hijacked by the powerful and popular leadership/management training "airport-bookstore-industrial-complex." The COPS Office embraced the Covey program, PERF went with "Good to Great," and IACP adopted the West Point model (the 1970s version).

These programs certainly have their merits, but none seems to have made any systematic or serious effort to inform their generic products with the last 40 years of research on police administration, police organizations, police cultures, or police strategies. It is enough of a problem that the half-life of the latest leadership fad (i.e., airport book) is about three months. More importantly, police work and police tasks have their particular characteristics, the environment of police organizations is not much like the environment of GM or GE or Google, research on what works and does not work in the realm of police programs and strategies is largely ignored, and so on. When police management and leadership training is divorced from critical features of policing and police organizations, it becomes about as useful as most generic products.

Why The Disconnect?

On one hand, we have 40 years of research and knowledge-building about policing. On the other hand, precious little of that is incorporated in the higher education or executive training of police commanders and CEOs. What gives?

On the academic side, police studies has been overwhelmed and dwarfed by criminal justice. Criminal justice has been the fastest growing major in the liberal arts and social sciences for 20 years – there are plenty of students. Criminal justice faculty tend to be trained as social scientists. Their doctoral training emphasizes the study of crime more than the study of criminal justice institutions – if you say theory, they think criminological theory, not organization theory. If they have studied police at all, they have studied police deviance and police abuses, not police strategy or police administration. Most importantly, the driving force in criminal justice higher education for 30 years has been to establish the discipline's legitimacy within academia. This has meant the elimination of any courses that reminded anyone of the old days when the field defined itself as police science and police administration.

Another factor on the academic side is that there was a debate 30 years ago about the proper form of undergraduate police education, and the winner was liberal arts/social science (Sherman, 1978). At the time, the choice was framed between a narrow technical education focused on police operations or a broad-based liberal arts education. Easy choice. The way that criminal justice education has evolved since then, however, has mostly squeezed out history of police, theory of police, sociology of police, police research – all good liberal arts/social science matter, but there is no room in the curriculum for it. Nor is there any room for criminal investigation, police administration, police strategies, or a host of other deserving professional topics.

It also comes down to finances. The typical academic criminal justice program has 5-10 faculty, including on average one or none who specialize in policing. Why so few? Some programs would like more, but the pool of well-qualified police academics is not very deep. Also, because criminal justice is so broad, programs need lawyers and criminologists, plus faculty to teach courses on research methods, statistics, courts, corrections, juvenile justice, crime prevention, ethics, race, gender, and more. This higher education reality stands in the way of developing the kinds of rich, deep, serious police education courses and programs that could provide mid-career police, police commanders, and police CEOs with the knowledge about their business that they presently lack. The police journals continue to fill up, and the National Institute of Justice continues to fund police research, but little of it makes it into the consciousness of criminal justice students or police executives.

So students who get bachelor's degrees in criminal justice (or other subjects) and then join police departments do not have much knowledge about policing. A few years later, some of them decide to pursue graduate degrees. By far the most common option is a master's in criminal justice, probably followed in distant second by a master's in public administration. For many of the same reasons noted above, master's degree programs in criminal justice usually lack any serious focus on police – lack of faculty with policing expertise, a desire to cover all the many bases in the broad field of criminal justice, and an inclination toward the abstract, theoretical, and sociological aspects of criminal justice rather than professional and applied aspects. Another limiting factor at the graduate level is that, except in a few places like New York and the Baltimore-Washington metropolitan area, there probably are not enough mid-career police interested in graduate study to support and sustain a police-focused program, even if some university and its faculty were willing and capable of producing such a program.

Police executive training institutes, as opposed to universities, are more inclined to focus on providing professional police knowledge, but they suffer from several disadvantages. One is that their instructors are rarely engaged in research themselves, may not themselves be steeped in the literature and knowledge base of policing, and may be tied to the classroom to such an extent that it is impossible for them to keep up with an expanding knowledge base. Also, the learning cultures of their institutions may not support making students (trainees) read complex material, making them write, or making them engage in critical analysis and reflection. In many police training settings, the culture and tradition is that you show up, you listen, you get your ticket punched, and you leave. These classes often don't use textbooks, much less journal articles.

Another disadvantage faced by many police executive training programs is that they are fairly short and not integrated with university degree programs. Some are as short as two days or a week, others as long as a semester. The short format, unless it is repeated periodically in some kind of coordinated schedule (i.e., one week a month for several months), tends to mitigate against reading, writing, and reflection. Recently, some of these institutes have married up with on-line degrees, so that graduates of the executive training programs have a degree-completion opportunity. Typically, though, the on-line degree is in criminal justice, so the bulk of the students' educational experience is, once again, focused on subjects other than police studies.

THE FIX

What we need to fix this situation is a National Police University (NPU) – not a West Point for pre-career police, but a graduate-level finishing school for mid-career police. The NPU would be the one place where a critical mass of expert police faculty could focus on disseminating research-based and profession-based knowledge to serious and committed police students. The NPU should offer an accredited master's degree in police studies or police administration to students from all over the country who would actually be expected to master the knowledge base of the field.

Putting political and fiscal considerations aside for a moment, this should be a no-brainer. We have 100 years of evidence that no existing university has the capacity or commitment to create such a program that would serve the whole nation – only a few have even tried to do it for their local region. We also have plenty of evidence that this crucial gap in professional development cannot be effectively filled by POSTs or other state entities – some have created reputable programs, but they cannot produce the combined academic and professional focus that is required, and they are inevitably restricted by state interests and state resources. The major national police associations (IACP, PERF, NSA, NOBLE, NAWLEE, FOP) do not have the membership support or the portfolio for this kind of effort.

A National Police University authorized and funded by Congress could do what none of these other institutions have been able to do – create and deliver high-quality, up-to-date, academically-legitimate, professionally-relevant graduate education in police studies. Imagine a master's degree program with 10 or 12 courses, all focused on policing and all taught by the most competent police scholars well-grounded in practical policing, police administration, and contemporary police issues. Students graduating from this program would be on top of current knowledge about the field and, equally important, would know how to sustain that mastery as the knowledge base expands over the rest of their careers.

The National Police University should fulfill a few other roles besides the penultimate educational one. The NPU would have more expert police faculty than any other institution – consequently, it should be engaged in the acquisition and production of knowledge, the synthesis of knowledge, and the dissemination of knowledge to other audiences besides students. It should be a resource of expertise for Congress, federal agencies, and public officials (e.g., mayors, city managers, state legislators). Simply put, the NPU should take the responsibility for producing and compiling knowledge about policing and making it available to all those who need it. To make this possible, NPU faculty will need time to do more than just teach, although teaching will be their fundamental role. The NPU will also need research fellows and executives-in-residence who collaborate with the faculty in both teaching and knowledge building.

This may sound a bit grandiose, but it is not. The U.S. police field employs over one million people (Reaves, 2007) and the country spends over $100 billion annually for police protection (Bureau of Justice Statistics, 2008). A line item in the annual federal budget on the order of $25 million would be a tiny price to pay for a National Police University that would elevate the police field to an entirely different professional and scientific level.

The bigger challenge will be politics. The idea of a national police university may scare some police and political leaders, since local control is a hallmark of the U.S. police system. However, Congress has federalized various aspects of crime control over the past 20-30 years (as a supplement to local and state efforts, not to replace them), so creating a national university would not be any deviation from current trends. Most importantly, attendance at the university would certainly be voluntary and federally-financed, which should alleviate many local concerns. No outcry emerged when a top-level homeland security graduate program, targeted largely at state and local officials, was implemented at the Naval Postgraduate School. Doing something similar to dramatically raise the bar for police administration should not be perceived as any threat to local control of policing.

Who might feel threatened are the FBI, FLETC, IACP, PERF, John Jay, and other established interests in the worlds of professional policing and police leadership. A National Police University would need to be independent of all these existing institutions, if for no other reason than they presently compete with each other, and would not tolerate one of their siblings being picked over them. All of these institutions should be invited to collaborate with the National Police University, though, as they have considerable experience and important constituencies.

The National Police University will need to be independent, yet connected. It should provide its education and services to police from federal, state, and local agencies, but it should not be an arm of any of them, for obvious reasons. An ideal administrative arrangement might be within the Office of Justice Programs in the U.S. Department of Justice – along with NIJ, BJS, and other agencies that traditionally have operated with a degree of independence (managed by a presidential appointee) – or even directly under the Attorney General. Physically, placement at a current or former military base might be most practical, as these facilities have existing classrooms, offices, and sleeping quarters. Of course, the National Police University needs to be civilian, not military, but the most relevant model might be the National Defense University, and logistically, it should not be necessary to fund any new bricks and mortar when adequate facilities already exist.

What should it look like? It is premature to delve deeply into curriculum or pedagogy, but I would envision a blended-learning one-year program of 12 courses – one a month. A mid-career police official taking the program might take the first four courses by distance, then take the next four courses in-residence (a four-month stay), then complete the final four courses again by distance. The program should be rigorous and thought-provoking, and it should genuinely integrate academic and professional content and orientation. It should be possible to graduate 150-300 police commanders and executives per year, which would dramatically upgrade the knowledge and professionalism of U.S. police leaders in short order and would take American policing to a new level. Creating a National Police University is the smart thing to do and now is the right time to do it.

REFERENCES

Bittner, E. (1970). *The Functions of the Police in Modern Society.* Washington, DC: Government Printing Office.

Bureau of Justice Statistics. (2008). *Justice Expenditure and Employment Abstracts. Bureau* of Justice Assistance. Available online: http://www.ojp.usdoj.gov/bjs/glance/exptyp.htm.

Clarke, R. V. (Ed.). (1997). *Situational Crime Prevention: Successful Case Studies (2nd ed.).* Guilderland, NY: Harrow and Heston.

Department of Criminal Justice Training. (2009). *2009 Training Schedule.* Richmond, KY: Kentucky Department of Criminal Justice Training.

Geller, W. A. (Ed.). (1985). *Police Leadership in America: Crisis and Opportunity.* New York: Praeger.

Goldstein, H. (1977). *Policing a Free Society.* Cambridge, MA: Ballinger.

Goldstein, H. (1990). *Problem-Oriented Policing.* New York: McGraw-Hill.

Greene, J. R. & Cordner, G. (1980). Education and police administration: A preliminary analysis of impact. *Police Studies, 3,* 12 23.

Illinois Law Enforcement Training & Standards Board. (2006). *Public Act 94-354.* Available online: http://www.silec.org/forms_20hourchiefs.pdf.

Moore, M. H. & Braga, A. (2003). *The Bottom Line of Policing: What Citizens Should Value (and Measure) in Police Performance.* Washington, DC: Police Executive Research Forum.

Moore, M. H. & Stephens, D. (1991). *Beyond Command and Control: The Strategic Management of Police Departments.* Washington, DC: Police Executive Research Forum.

Ohio Revised Code. (1997). *Basic Training Course for Sheriffs – Continuing Education. Chapter 109, Section 80.* Available online: http://codes.ohio.gov/orc/109.80.

Reaves, B. A. (2006). *Federal Law Enforcement Officers, 2004.* Washington, DC: Bureau of Justice Statistics.

Reaves, B. A. (2007). *Census of State and Local Law Enforcement Agencies, 2004.* Washington, DC: Bureau of Justice Statistics.

Reese, R. (2005). *Leadership in the LAPD: Walking the Tightrope.* Durham, NC: Carolina Academic Press.

Sherman, L. W. & The National Advisory Commission on Higher Education for Police Officers. (1978). *The Quality of Police Education.* San Francisco, CA: Jossey-Bass.

Skogan, W. & Frydll, K. (Eds.). (2004). *Fairness and Effectiveness in Policing: The Evidence.* Washington, DC: National Research Council.

Skolnick, J. H. (1966). *Justice Without Trial: Law Enforcement in a Democratic Society.* New York: John Wiley.

Weisburd, D. & Braga, A. (Eds.). (2006). *Police Innovation: Contrasting Perspectives. Cambridge,* UK: Cambridge University.

Wilson, J. Q. (1968). *Varieties of Police Behavior: The Management of Law and Order in Eight Communities.* Cambridge, MA: Harvard University.

THE MANAGEMENT OF POLICE EDUCATION AND TRAINING

GEOFFREY P. ALPERT

Gary Cordner has suggested that the United States has such diverse police training and applications that in order to create best practices, "The only viable solution is the creation of a brand new national institution – a national police university – not for entry-level police officers, but for commanders and chief executives." It is hard to argue with a proposal that would require our chiefs and sheriffs to learn together about command, management and leadership from an evidence-based perspective. Cordner's point is that most police executives are not aware of research findings and how the results of good quality research could improve their efficiency and effectiveness.

One of his best arguments for the formation of a National Police University is the fragmentation of policing in the United States and the fact that we have so many small agencies with commanders who may not know about innovations in policing. While he doesn't explore the various international models for such a university, Cordner does provide us with reasons why we have reached a point in our history where such a uniform program would be welcome and why it may be necessary to share research findings to guide best practices and evaluations of what works in policing. It is a bit odd that countries such as the Philippines, India, Korea and Sweden, among others, have a national police university yet one does not exist in the United States. One would hope that these national universities operate on sound research findings and shared experiences, similar to the way Professor Cordner suggests the American model would function. Without a national police university or something similar, police decision makers are left to their own methods of determining proper organizational mandates.

While many chief officers can gain knowledge and share experiences with other managers in a variety of schools, courses and institutes, there is no set curriculum or even a list of topics that are covered. Students are exposed to critical issues or high liability items but rarely spend sufficient time understanding the police as an institution, structure or process. In many cases, difficult management or supervisory skills are not addressed as they are not the topics of "de jour" that generate interest or popular sound bites. Curricula in the current academies or institutes are often limited to topics that may be motivating and appealing but the accountability for learning and understanding the "big-picture" issues in policing has been compromised. First, most classes are silent on topics that deal with such essential but mundane issues as how to make assignments or how to design and implement shifts. It is rare that a class is available on how to determine and manage the proper number of officers available on a given shift at a specific time. Are chiefs given instruction on the best ways to reduce officer-created jeopardy, how to save officer's lives or reduce car crashes? The generic leadership courses may offer very good suggestions but are too often not linked to empirical findings from sound research. Further, command-level officers may not be familiar with proper ways to share resources or to receive assistance from other criminal justice agencies. Second, it is unlikely that chiefs are tested, held formally responsible or graded on the materials provided. Finally, where do police chiefs learn how to think and learn to think not always like police chiefs? Where are these individuals challenged to come up with solutions to everyday and unique problems?

In other words, there are multiple reasons that a national policing university should be developed and supported, and professor Cordner has done an excellent job making these arguments. His idea is to have in place "A National Police University ... (to) create and deliver high-quality, up-to-date, academically-legitimate, professionally-relevant graduate education in police studies." He might add to his vision the idea of using this knowledge in a department that can be seen as a teaching police department similar to the model of a teaching hospital. Although the idea of a teaching police department has been around for many years and recently touted by the Providence, Rhode Island Police Department, the maturity of an agency where officers and managers can learn what really works in policing has not been realized.

THE VEILED THREATS

Professor Cordner noted some threats to a National Police University, specifically those agencies and institutions that provide advanced training to police managers. While a federally funded university would supplant some of the current providers, the ones run by entrepreneurs could find a niche and survive. Another threat is the large number of police chiefs and their differences in education, philosophy and experience. In other words, the talent pool may differ significantly between the larger, better paying agencies and the smaller ones. As we all know, the talent pool differs significantly within most agencies, regardless of size! Although a threat, this diversity could be turned into a strength where the most capable agency executives could share valuable information and experiences with those who have less experience. It is difficult to envision a better training ground for future chief executives than a National Police University. For example, the National Advocacy (NAC) is operated by the Department of Justice and trains local, state and federal prosecutors in advocacy skills and management of legal operations. Although the NAC administers relatively short courses, it brings together attorneys with various backgrounds who practice throughout the United States. In these courses, attorneys from numerous jurisdictions who encounter different problems and prospects are able to discuss alternatives and solutions to their various challenges. In addition, the FBI's National Academy does an excellent job of providing cutting-edge training for state and local police officers but does not achieve the breadth and scope of education and training as suggested by the development of a national police university. Both the National Advocacy Center and the National Academy provide excellent models that could be used in the development of a national police university.

A REAL THREAT

Perhaps the most serious threat to a National Police University is the same problem faced by those who teach graduate courses in policing; finding sufficient materials for evidence-based policing. A review of the literature in policing shows more rhetoric than evidence and more philosophy than empiricism. What we know about policing is based on more experiential and anecdotal information than good quality research findings. Most of the good research has been conducted in large departments that have more resources than smaller agencies and with administrators who are truly interested in learning what works and have the confidence to allow researchers into their agencies to look around and explore their behaviors and practices. These administrators welcome investigators and permit them to review files and find out what really happens on a day-to-day basis.

Perhaps a National Police University would interest smaller agency executives to open their doors and allow researchers to investigate the activities of their departments. Perhaps chief executives would share evidence-based decisions, and policing in America would be improved. We currently have a host of good senior-level schools, institutes and courses. Unfortunately, the courses are not well connected and not normally based on research findings. Many police chiefs, like other executives, do not like numbers and do not appreciate how policies and practices can be improved by empirical research findings. While the development of a National Police University will not stop criminal behavior and will not make good administrators out of bad police officers, it could go a long way to improve policing in America by developing talent for the future, teaching the importance of collaborative work and building relationships between decision makers and the research community.

RESPONSE TO CORDNER

DAVID BAYLEY

Gary Cordner proposes creating a U.S. national police university that offers "high-quality, up-to-date, academically-legitimate, professionally-relevant graduate education in police studies." In my judgment, he's dead right. His paper is appropriately provocative, insightful, and intelligent. It is also short, which inevitably leaves a great deal to discuss, not necessarily here.

His paper is a *cri de coeur* with which many of us who have observed American policing close-up would agree. Namely, that "Our fragmented and extremely thin system of police higher education leaves most police executives substantially uninformed about research, knowledge, and evidence that should form the basis of police strategies and programs" (page 1). Frustrated about the ineffectiveness of current mechanisms for disseminating knowledge about the standard police strategies, Cordner says, "We lack an effective system by which police leaders might be kept up with the latest knowledge in the field" (1). This issue has arisen at every conference I've ever attended about research and policing. Again in Cordner's words, "The police journals continue to fill up, and the National Institute of Justice continues to fund police research, but little of it makes it into the consciousness of criminal justice students or police executives." (8)

The ironic fact is that the training of senior police officers is light-years behind the training of senior military officers. Ironic, I say, because the police job is more complicated than the military's. Police possess the unique authority to lay hands on the bodies of Americans at home, not foreigners abroad, to hold, incarcerate, and, sometimes, hurt and kill. Moreover, they exercise this awesome authority individually, without benefit of close supervision and direction.

The United States is also behind most developed democracies in developing specialized training for its police executives. The English-speaking democracies of Britain, Ireland, Scotland, and New Zealand all have national police colleges (respectively, Bramshill, Templemore, Tulliallan, and the Royal New Zealand College near Wellington). So do Sweden and the Netherlands, who, like the United States, have decentralized police systems. All but two of the world's six largest federal democracies have national police colleges for senior executives - Australia, Canada, Germany, and India. Only Brazil and the United States do not. In short, countries like ours are well down the road to standardizing education for senior police executives. The United States doesn't need to reinvent the wheel; there is lots of experience to draw on from countries very like ours.

Designing specialized training for senior executives is part of a larger problem of police education that many other countries are addressing ahead of the U.S., namely, the integration of *basic* training for all police officers with tertiary qualifications. Although there are no current national estimates of the proportion of American police who are college graduates, it is probably rising with many having some college experience (Cordner, private communication). Training in American police academies does increasingly earn credit toward college degrees and some states have salary-incentive programs for serving officers based on college attendance. Cordner, however, is not impressed - "...higher education reality stands in the way of developing the kinds of rich, deep, serious police education courses and programs that could provide mid-career police, police commanders, and police CEOs with the knowledge about their business that they presently lack" (8).

In making his case for a national police university, Cordner makes some claims that may well be true but for which evidence is lacking.

(1) What do senior police executive actually know about the evidence-based literature on police crime-prevention and control? Have they read as little as Cordner claims?

(2) What do recruits, not just executives, know about what works in policing? Does their academy training encourage critical thinking about the moral as well as the strategic issues of policing?

(3) What exactly is being offered in American training programs for senior police managers? At the federal level by the FBI, FLETC, and perhaps the ILEAs (International law Enforcement Academies); by states for promoted officers (CA, LF, TX, MY, MA, NC); by NGOs, such as PERF, IACP, the Southern Police Institute; and by university graduate programs, such as the Kennedy School, John Jay, and Northwestern.

(4) Is it true that undergraduate criminal justice programs have increasingly slighted criminal justice administration in favor of criminology? Is scholarship about criminal justice, especially the evaluation of programs, regarded as being below the academic salt? Does participation in the ASC mean more professionally than participation in the ACJS?

These questions constitute an implicit research agenda for people interesting in exploring the need for standardized training for American police CEOs.

Because Cordner's paper is an invitation to a discussion rather than the presentation of a blueprint, there are several issues that will have to be addressed in constructing a national police university.

First: what level of police officer should be encouraged to attend? Not just their rank level, but should the target audience be officers already promoted to senior posts or officers who are potentially promotable?

Second: where should they come from - any American police department, agencies over some threshold of size, or only a few of largest and most influential? Cordner's own suggestion is that they be selected from the 93 agencies with more than 1000 full-time sworn employees.

Third: what exactly should senior executives be taught at a national university? Cordner suggests theoretical and evidence-based studies of police strategy. He is adamantly opposed to "airport" how-to-manuals on police management. I would add that normative issues fundamental to policing, not simply empirical ones, should also be part of a CEO's education – privacy and surveillance, transparency and accountability (including relations with the media), diversity inside and outside police organizations, human rights and police powers, and the management of integrity.

Fourth: how much training would be required and what should be the mix of distance with residential learning?

Fifth: how should a police university go about promoting research? Cordner suggests its faculty should do cutting-edge research. What sort of research would be most useful - the kind undertaken by university-based scholars, by consultants to police agencies, or by practitioners about problems arising in their agencies? The national police academies I know are weak in generating worthwhile research. They have not become centers of research excellence.

What's the likelihood that what Cordner recommends, and I support, will occur? The obstacles are obvious: America's history of police development from the bottom up; political distrust of federal impositions and control; and special interests protecting their own investment in management training, universities as well as NGOs. The United States is caught in a classic Catch-22: because there is no national corporate ownership of policing, there are few advocates for generalized executive training, but because there is no generalized executive training, there is no national corporate ownership of policing.

Sadly, I suspect that the United States will continue its practice of muddling through rather than explicitly confronting this problem, proving once again that a fundamental element of American exceptionalism is its unwillingness to learn from others.

Provide Justice For Prostituted Teens: Stop Arresting and Prosecuting Girls

Linda M. Williams

This essay presents the policy argument that we should stop arresting prostituted (commercially sexually exploited) teens[i] who are trafficked domestically in the United States. The essay relies on a growing body of empirical evidence to support the policy of no arrest for prostituted teens because as juveniles they are the victims and not the offenders, in the exchange of sex with an adult for money or other goods. Current policies focused on control of the teen fall short in addressing the offending behavior of the pimps and "johns" or customers and are based on misconceptions about the relationship between the pimps and the prostituted teens and the pathways to youth prostitution. There is no evidence that a pro-arrest policy directed at juvenile victims is a successful crime control approach. Such an approach also ignores remediation of underlying social factors that propel teens into prostitution. Achieving justice and social control of prostitution is more likely with a law enforcement focus on the purveyors of sex with a child—the so-called "pimps"—and the "customers" or "johns" who engage in criminal sexual conduct with the teens -- and not on arrest and enhanced social control of juveniles. Ceasing the practice of arrest of prostituted juveniles is not a simple task, however, because it requires a major shift in the way law enforcement approaches this crime.

Despite some important research on child and teen prostitution[ii] and other commercial sexual exploitation (CSE) in the U.S., for a number of reasons, the sexual victimization of youth via prostitution has, until relatively recently, received little attention. Commercial sexual exploitation (in which a youth engaged or agreed or offered to engage in sexual conduct in return for a fee, food, or clothing; stripped or was filmed or photographed doing sexual acts; or loitered for the purpose of engaging in a prostitution) may have escaped attention in large part because of the secrecy of the behaviors, the youth and vulnerability of the victims and the use of a variety of tactics by the perpetrators (including violence, fear, force, and "grooming"). Further contributing to the neglect of the crimes perpetrated against these youth is the fact that often the children who are prostituted are "thrownaways," or are poor, minority, runaway or drug-involved and garner little sustained public concern or attention because they are not empowered constituencies. Although there have been some new approaches, consistent with the notion that these teens are victims and not offenders, implemented in a number of states or local jurisdictions, to date these approaches have developed and refined further a rationale for the increased social control of girls while usually offering minimal consideration of or funding for support to help them escape the social circumstances that contributed to their vulnerability to exploitation, and have devoted remarkably little focus and coordinated resource deployment directed toward arrest of the adult perpetrators.

More attention has recently been paid to CSEC (Albanese, 2007; Cooper et al., 2005; Curtis et al., 2008; Estes & Weiner, 2001; Friedman, 2005; Gragg et al., 2007) and it is more likely today to be challenged on the local, national and international levels in an attempt to reduce the numbers of victimized children and the manner and severity of the harm inflicted on them. In recent decades, evidence has been mounting that commercially sexually exploited youth have been repeatedly victimized in a variety of destructive and damaging ways, including: physical (Widom & Kuhns, 1996), emotional (Kidd & Krall, 2002) and sexual abuse (Brannigan & Gibbs Van Brunschot, 1997; Forst, 1994; Silbert & Pines, 1981; Simons & Whitbeck, 1991); and drug abuse (Inciardi et al., 1991) and social marginalization (Farrow et al., 1992; Inciardi et al., 1991). As one might expect, children and youth exposed to the cumulative destructive factors of child maltreatment and CSE have many and deep harms and coincident needs. Both the anecdotal and, increasingly, the more systematic or empirically-based profiles of these prostituted teens (Curtis, et al., 2008; Friedman, 2005; Gragg et al., 2007) show patterns of involvement in multiple service-based systems (children and youth or child protective services, mental/behavioral health, juvenile/criminal justice, and physical health), because of their multiple, cumulative, and long-lasting needs. The best evidence we have to date is that, with a few notable exceptions, these agency involvements are, usually, not tailored to the needs of CSE youth and are usually short lived, uncoordinated, and unsupported by professional best practices (whether expert- or evidence-based models) (Clawson & Grace, 2007; Estes & Weiner, 2001).

Today in response to the prostitution of children, there is evidence that many of the same rationalizations offered 30 years ago to deflect attention from the criminal aspects of perpetration of intra-familial child sexual abuse are employed. The arguments that the girl "asked" for it, "enjoyed" it or "seduced" the male or that he did not know she was under the age of consent are used to defend policies that focus on arrest and control of the prostituted juvenile and release of the customer or "john" who often could be charged with rape of a minor. These approaches reflect justifications which rationalize and neutralize the culpability of the person who pays to have sexual intercourse with a child or underage teen (Estes & Weiner, 2001; Flowers, 2001). While it is true that in the 1970s and 1980s children who were victims of intra-familial child sexual abuse (CSA) were not commonly arrested or prosecuted as happens with CSE victims today, it is useful to recall that in the early stages of the discovery of CSA (Herman, 1981) it was common for the young teen to be the one removed from the home and viewed as "incorrigible" or as a person in need of supervision based on her alleged "misbehaviors" (Chesney-Lind & Sheldon, 2004). In the 1970s it was not unheard of for the authorities to place female teen victims of incest in youth detention settings ostensibly for the purpose of "protecting" these victims while avoiding "contamination" of other "wards of the state" who resided in group homes and community settings. In truth this was a means of controlling these teens. The incest survivor was feared for her advanced sexual knowledge and "promiscuity" suggesting once again that, for girls, victimization is one short step in a pathway to the juvenile justice system (Chesney-Lind & Sheldon, 2004).

Although they often may find themselves kept in secure detention, recent research indicates that minors involved in the sex trade or trafficking who come into contact with the police are as likely to be viewed as victims as offenders (Halter, 2009). Our available social and legal responses to commercially sexually exploited children and youth, however, often make such an assessment of little practical difference for the teen victim. Even when this occurs it has been reported that because of their demeanor and behavior, prostituted girls and boys may be held in great distain by social service providers and the community in general (Friedman, 2005). Indeed, in the U.S. minors who are found to have traded sex for money may also be arrested and charged in criminal courts or even when viewed as victims they may be threatened with such charges if they do not cooperate with the authorities. Recent research reveals that U.S. law enforcement personnel are inconsistent in their treatment of juveniles involved in prostitution (Finkelhor & Ormrod, 2004; Halter, 2009). This inconsistency may reflect the conflict between law enforcement driven criminalization of prostituted youth and application of other statutes and regulations that define sexual contact by an adult with a person under 18 as a reportable act of child maltreatment. Indeed child, welfare agencies may place responsibility on the offending adults or on other adults who failed to protect the youth.

Service providers and potentially sympathetic law enforcement officers may be confused by teens' assertions that they are 'doing what they want' or (for girls) that they love the pimp and do not view themselves as the victims. We know that teen girls who are prostituted may believe that they are earning their own money and thus determining their own life path, although in the most common scenario for "pimp involved" girls, the pimp controls and does not allow them and direct access to the money they receive (Albanese, 2007; Estes & Weiner, 2001). While it has been reported that both girls and boys are insidiously drawn to "the life" by the lies of those who recruit them, the lure of the parties and drugs, or even the simple shelter and food that they may also get as part of the payment barter (Williams, Powell, & Frederick, 2008), and the rationalizations that they control their fate (Friedman, 2005), few have placed this discussion of how teens get drawn in to prostitution in the context of their attempts to escape extremely destructive and violent families or the extreme poverty and hunger they have encountered in their young lives. In addition, objectively viewed, the behaviors of prostituted teens arguably can be understood as survival-based coping (Albanese, 2007; Goodman et al., in press; Williams, in press). There is also an unwillingness to approach the possibility that as part of a survival strategy youth may "prostitute themselves," that is, they may trade sex for money without involvement of a pimp. These youth are less likely to be viewed as victims and are either ignored or criminalized, with scant attention to the adults who have paid for sex with these minors.

Once "captured" by the system, these youth may be confined in juvenile detention facilities where the victimization they experienced is minimized; traditional methods of preserving order and asserting authority may result in re-traumatization and/or re-victimization and lead to attempts to return to the "life" they know on the street or with the pimp wherever he is located. The focus is on using the law and threat of prosecution to "encourage" them to provide evidence that can be used against the "pimp." The criminal justice system in the U.S. no longer finds it necessary to use such techniques to "persuade" youth to testify against family members who have sexually assaulted them and this approach today with prostituted teens is equally indefensible. Those who are deemed to have not been pimp-involved are more likely to be viewed as offenders and treated as such (Halter, 2009).

The empirical evidence about the criminal justice interactions with prostituted teens and the impact of the system response on these youth is scant. Until such research is conducted, we must turn to evidence related to practice with teens charged with other types of offenses. We have seen evidence that increased criminalization of youth and application of harsh sanctions has garnered political support generally in the U.S. But research (Frazier, Bishop & Lanza-Kaduce, 1999) has shown that not only do such policies generally not deter these individuals, in many cases, these juveniles go on to commit more frequent and more serious crimes. In addition, prosecution is likely to be disproportionately applied to minority youth. Although the prosecution of prostituted teens had not been studied empirically, qualitative research has suggested that it is similarly unlikely that such action will have a significant deterrent effect on the behaviors of the teen.

Some have argued that recent changes in prosecutorial policies or family court statutes that allow prostituted teens to escape prosecution will be a boon for the pimps who, as a result, will find that such changes make it easy to quickly get those identified by police as under-age back out "on the streets" with no consequences or interruption of profit. Others suggest that the pimps may even become more inclined to target and recruit teens, knowing these teens will not be prosecuted. But this argument misses the point that with a pro-prosecution of teen victims' policy in place, under-age girls are most likely to hide their age from law enforcement. Unfortunately, such under-age females then often see the pimp as the one person who can protect her from the "system" and likely incarceration. In addition, the threat of prosecution of a juvenile may increase the likelihood that during all interactions with the police the teen will try to hide her young age and, when arrested, attempt (often successfully) to pass herself off as an adult (Williams, Fernandez, & Frederick, 2009). Interestingly, once under-age teens have been entered into the criminal justice system and fingerprinted as "adults" the pimps find it easier to manage their movement as *de facto* adults through the revolving door of arrests, minimal fines and release back on the streets. This makes it clear how important it is for police to learn how to detect the juveniles amongst those persons they arrest for prostitution. An arrest that provides a teen who has presented fake ID with an adult identity backed up by her own fingerprints would seem to most casual observers to be just the opposite of what a juvenile arrestee wants. But this mistake by law enforcement means that in future arrests for prostitution this teen will more easily pass as an adult and be summarily treated as such. On the other hand, removing the threat of prosecution (along with changes in the supports provided to teens who leave this "life") may instead increase the likelihood that teens will admit their correct ages or even come forward and seek assistance of law enforcement and eventually provide assistance in the prosecution of the perpetrators. Once teens become aware they will not be prosecuted but will be offered reasonable and age appropriate protection and this information becomes known and is seen as credible on the streets it will be more difficult for the pimp (or other exploiter) to convince them that he or she is their only protection from lockup. In most communities such promises of no prosecution of 16 and 17 year old or even younger victims are rare and, in addition, useful services for these youth are unavailable to help them exit the "life" of teen prostitution, and to stop the violence they experience at the hands of the pimps and the customers (Clawson & Grace, 2007).

While youth and social service agencies may be aware of the acute problem of prostitution of children and teens in their communities, few have the resources to design comprehensive programs to prevent it or to assist teens exiting prostitution (Priebe & Suhr, 2005). In most cases, assistance is needed from a variety of resources including but not limited to, health professionals, counselors, youth agencies, schools, and law enforcement. A lack of trust of authorities inhibits the youth's ability to seek out these services, thus increasing the apparent need of coordinated efforts (Clawson & Grace, 2007; Clawson, Salomon, & Grace, 2008).

Based on findings from the Pathways Study (Williams, 2008; in press) the inability to meet the needs of these youth can be attributed, in part, to failure to develop ways to reach, build and maintain connections with and support for youth on the streets; lack of coordination of and training for services across multiple jurisdictions; reluctance to provide means by which youth can be free of destructive families; and failure to provide appropriate interventions for those with complex trauma.

Justice calls for more arrests and serious charges lodged against the "pimps" and "johns." Achieving justice and social control of prostitution requires a law enforcement focus on the purveyors of sex with a child—the pimps—and also on the demand side focusing on the customers or "johns." Evidence suggests that customers' decisions to engage in prostitution are more free and consensual than those of prostitutes (Monto, 2004). More research is needed on strategies to reduce the demand side of prostitution. Recommitting law enforcement efforts to arrest of perpetrators should be easy; however, prosecuting the pimps is not unlike interdiction in the drug trade where finding the kingpins or bosses requires resources for investigations that are likely to cross state and even national boundaries. Thus far in most jurisdictions the major law enforcement strategy has been to "clean up" prostitution through a focus on arrests of prostitutes and customers, often using sting operations. When these mostly street or internet-based sting operations occur it is unlikely that the third party exploiters, the pimps and purveyors of sex are apprehended. More coordinated time consuming coordination of law enforcement and prosecution efforts are required to reach the individuals and networks. These coordinated efforts do not achieve the immediately visible results that politicians and communities seek to "clean up" visible evidence of prostitution. Sustained and coordinated efforts applied by a law enforcement focus on pimps are likely necessary before more meaningful success will be achieved.

In consideration of many of the concerns raised in this essay, some jurisdictions have decided not to eliminate the prosecution of prostituted teens but to make it a rarely used option, offering teens the "opportunity" to escape prosecution. In these jurisdictions there are many difficulties faced in an attempt to encourage the teens to regain trust the authorities. To that end, anecdotal experience in cities such as Boston have shown that it is important that the justice system not *renege* on promises too quickly and that prosecutors, judges, law enforcement, and social service providers understand the complexities of the prostituted teens' victimization experiences and connection to the pimp or others in "the life." Exiting the web of relationships and social problems that contribute to a youth's vulnerability to commercial sexual exploitation is likely to be a process that requires some second chances. These second chances may not be forthcoming unless the juvenile and criminal justice system actors are educated about these matters. The success of these approaches requires careful evaluation and documentation.

Complications are likely to arise in NY State with the passage of the "Safe Harbor Act" pertaining to petitions of delinquency (Family Court Act, Article 3, Section 311.4) which will provide for arrested prostituted teens under the age of 16 to instead be certified as "in need of supervision" and not be adjudicated as "delinquent." This new law also does not apply to 16 and 17 year old juveniles. The courts will be able to have a petition of delinquency reinstated if the juvenile refuses counseling or does not cooperate with court requirements, such as, testifying against and avoiding all other contact with the sex traffickers. Juveniles with prior prostitution adjudications will not be eligible. While this "Safe Harbor" act is viewed as an important opportunity for those who are 15 years of age or younger to escape prosecution, if this act leads in practice to a "one strike and you are out" approach it may not provide safe harbor for most prostituted teens who will once again be treated as offenders and not victims.

A review of the family background and experiences of many prostituted teens reveals a long history of highly destructive families fraught with violence and dysfunction. Many of the teens have been in numerous foster care settings or have lived on the streets or with no permanent home for months and even years. They often have little trust in the child welfare systems that some of them have encountered first hand or heard about from others. Their experiences and survival based coping skills suggest a successful strategy for care and support of these youth may be achieved only through the development of meaningful partnerships between the youth and social services (Williams, in press). Without such partnerships that provide the youth a pathway to achieve freedom from incarceration and some meaningful control over their lives (including in many cases freedom from their families) (Bittle, 2002) there may be little likelihood of success. Such new partnerships need to be implemented and carefully evaluated. The narratives of teens who have been prostituted underscore the urgency of this need but also must be balanced against the complexity of making necessary policy changes to put appropriate empowering supports in place.

It is not enough to develop such programs for youth and to change the way they are treated in the criminal and juvenile justice systems, approaches to stopping prostitution of teens require a broader societal focus. Such an approach should address the social conditions that propel teens into prostitution including family violence, lack of financial and material resources, and sexual socialization of males that feeds demand for teen prostitution and supports patriarchal social relations that facilitate pimps having power over teen girls. Meaningful partnerships are needed between youth and social services to help the teens regain control over their lives (Rabinovitch & Strega, 2004). Committing law enforcement efforts to arresting the perpetrators, though challenging, may actually be the easy part. Ceasing the practice of arresting juveniles who engaged, agreed or offered to engage in sexual conduct in return for a fee, food, or clothing; have stripped or been filmed or photographed doing sexual acts; or have loitered for the purpose of engaging in a prostitution offense, however, is not a simple task because it requires a shift in the way we understand social control of youth and how we view the relationship between the state, teens and their families.

REFERENCES

Albanese, J. (2007). *Commercial Sexual Exploitation of Children: What Do We Know and What Do We Do About It?* Washington, DC: National Institute of Justice

Bittle, S. (2002). When protection is punishment: Neo-liberalism and secure care approaches to youth prostitution. *Canadian Journal of Criminology*, *44*, 317-350.

Brannigan, A. & Gibbs Van Brunschot, E. (1997). Youthful prostitution and child sexual trauma. *International Journal of Law and Psychiatry*, *20*, 337-354.

Chesney-Lind, M. & Shelden, R.G. (2004). *Girls, Delinquency and Juvenile Justice.* Belmont, CA: Wadsworth.

Clawson, H. & Grace, L. (2007). *Finding a Path to Recovery: Residential Facilities for Minor Victims of Domestic Sex Trafficking.* Washington, DC: U.S. Department of Health and Human Services.

Clawson, H.J., Salomon, A. & Grace, L. (2008) *Treating the Hidden Wounds: Trauma Treatment and Mental Health Recovery for Victims of Human Trafficking.* Washington, DC: U.S. Department of Health and Human Services.

Cooper, S., Estes, R., Giardino, A., Kellogg, N. & Vieth, V. (2005).*Medical, Legal, and Social Science Aspects of Child Sexual Exploitation: A Comprehensive Review of Pornography, Prostitution, and Internet Crimes Against Children.* St. Louis, MO: GW Medical Publishing.

Curtis, R., Terry, K., Dank, M., Dombrowski, K., Khan, B., Muslim, A., Labriola, M. & Rempel, M. (2008). *The Commercial Sexual Exploitation of Children in New York City.* Report to the National Institute of Justice. New York, NY: Center for Court Innovation and John Jay College of Criminal Justice.

Estes, R.J. & Weiner, N.A. (2001). *The Commercial Sexual Exploitation of Children in the U.S., Canada, and Mexico.* Philadelphia, PA: University of Pennsylvania, Center for the Study of Youth Policy.

Farrow, J.A., Deisher, R.W., Brown, R, Kulig, J.W. & Kipke, M.D. (1992). Health and health needs of homeless and runaway youth. *Journal of Adolescent Health*, *13*, 717-726.

Finkelhor, D. & Ormrod, R. (2004) *Prostitution of Juveniles: Patterns from NIBRS Office of Juvenile Justice and Delinquency Prevention*. Washington, DC: U.S. Department of Justice.

Flowers, R.B. (2001). *Runaway Kids and Teenage Prostitution.* Westport, CT: Greenwood Press.

Forst, M.L. (1994). Sexual risk profiles of delinquents and homeless youths. *Journal of Community Health*, *19*, 101-114.

Frazier, C., Bishop, D. & Lanza-Kaduce. L. (1999) 'Get tough' juvenile justice reforms: The Florida experience. *Annals of the American Academy of Political and Social Science, 564,* 167-184.

Friedman, S. (2005). *How the System Fails Sexually Exploited Girls in the United States: Examples from Four American Cities.* Brooklyn, NY: End Child Prostitution And Trafficking.

Gragg, F., Petta, I., Bernstein, H., Eisen, K. & Quinn, L. (2007). *New York Prevalence Study of Commercially Sexually Exploited Children Final Report.* Westat, MD: Rockville.

Goodman, L.A., Smyth, K.F., Borges, A.M. & Singer, R. (in press). When crises collide: How intimate partner violence and poverty intersect to shape women's mental health and coping. *Trauma, Violence and Abuse: Special Issue on the Mental Health Implications of Violence Against Women.*

Halter, S. (2009). *Youth Engaging in Prostitution: The Social Construction of the Child Sexual Abuse Victim by Law Enforcement.* Paper presented at the annual meeting of the American Society of Criminology, Atlanta, Georgia.

Herman, J. (1981). *Father-Daughter Incest.* Cambridge, MA: Harvard University Press.

Inciardi, J.A., Pottieger, A.E., Forney, M., Chitwood, D. & McBride, D. (1991). Prostitution, IV drug use, and sex-for-crack exchanges among serious delinquents: Risks for HIV infection. *Criminology, 29,* 221-235.

Kidd, S. & Krall, M.J. (2002). Suicide and prostitution among street youth: A qualitative analysis. *Adolescence, 37,* 411-430.

Monto, M. A. (2004). Female prostitution, customers, and violence. *Violence Against Women, 10,* 160-188.

Priebe. A. & Suhr, C. (2005). *Hidden in Plain View: The Commercial Sexual Exploitation of Girls in Atlanta.* Atlanta, GA: Atlanta Women's Agenda.

Rabinovitch, J. & Strega, S. (2004). The PEERS story: Effective services sidestep the controversies. *Violence Against Women, 10,* 140-159.

Silbert, M.H. & Pines, A.M. (1981). Sexual child abuse as an antecedent to prostitution. *Child Abuse and Neglect, 5,* 407-411.

Simons, R.L. & Whitbeck, L.B. (1991). Sexual abuse as a precursor to prostitution and victimization among adolescent and adult homeless women. *Journal of Family Issues, 12,* 361-379.

Widom, C.S. & Kuhns, J.B. (1996). Childhood victimization and subsequent risk for promiscuity, prostitution, and teenage pregnancy: A prospective study. *American Journal of Public Health, 86,* 1607-1612.

Williams, L.M. (2008). *Terror and Trauma for Homeless and Prostituted Street Youth: How Can Mental Health and Societal Response be Improved?* Paper presented at the annual meeting of the International Society for Traumatic Stress, Chicago, Illinois.

Williams, L.M. (in press). Harm and resilience among prostituted teens: Broadening our understanding of victimization and survival. *Social Policy and Society, 9.*

Williams, L.M., Fernandez, J. & Frederick, M. (2009). *Pathways Into and Out of Commercial Sexual Exploitation: Law Enforcement Role in Finding*

  Justice for Prostituted Teens. Paper presented at the annual meeting of
  the Academy of Criminal Justice Sciences, Boston, Massachusetts.
Williams, L.M., Powell, A. & Frederick, M. (2008). *Pathways Into and Out of
  Commercial Sexual Exploitation: Preliminary Findings and Implications
  for Responding to Sexually Exploited Teens.* Report by Department of
  Criminal Justice and Criminology, University of Massachusetts Lowell
  and Fair Fund, Inc.

ENDNOTES

[i] Most of the research and law enforcement activity has been about prostituted females. Commercial sexual exploitation of boys, a serious issue (see Curtis et al. 2008), needs attention and further study.

[ii] Discussion of this issue is fraught with problems of nuances of language and word choice. Writing the words "child or youth prostitute" or "youth involved in prostitution" may suggest to some a willingness or voluntary involvement on the part of the youth. Some prefer the term "prostituted child" or "prostituted teen" that makes more clear that the prostitution or other CSE is at the hands of someone else —the customer, client (or some would call this person the rapist, john or trick) or the third party exploiter (also called the pimp, panderer, or procurer) who benefits from the acts and takes the money.

THE CSEC POPULATION IN NEW YORK CITY: SUPPORTING THE ARGUMENT TO ABOLISH PROSECUTING PROSTITUTED TEENS

KAREN TERRY

MEREDITH DANK

Commercially sexually exploited children (CSEC) are those juveniles, usually under the age of 18, who perform sexual acts in exchange for money, drugs, food or shelter. The youth can be male, female or transgendered, heterosexual or homosexual, and they may be controlled by "pimps" or engage in the CSEC market on their own for survival. In nearly all states the act of accepting money or goods in exchange for sex is illegal, regardless of the age of the offender. As Linda Williams explains, however, such policies as applied to youth are harmful and go against the goals of the very system through which they are processed. Prosecution of these youth can and likely will lead to further entrenchment in the criminal justice system. A recent study of the CSEC population in New York City (Curtis et al., 2008) supports her assertions and provides an example of why the resources currently used to prosecute CSEC youth would be better allocated to assisting these youth with stable housing, intensive counseling, educational and job opportunities, reducing substance dependency, and escaping abusive situations in the home.

Though often ignored, the CSEC population in cities such as New York City, Atlanta and Las Vegas is quite high and there are few resources devoted to this population. Curtis et al (2008) estimated the CSEC population in New York City to be 3,946 youth, with nearly equal percentages of male and female youth. The high rate of male CSEC youth is not always acknowledged, though the respondent-driven sampling techniques employed in this study allowed for the identification of this often-hidden population. Curtis et al. (2008) also found that three quarters of the CSEC population in the city are African American, Caucasian, or Hispanic, and just over half were born in the city – not runaways from the Midwest, as has often been reported, though many are homeless and / or products of the foster care system. These youth have disproportionately high rates of sexual, physical and emotional abuse, many have mental health problems, most use drugs and have had extended substance abuse problems, and few have graduated from high school or have any other vocational skills. As such, many trade sex as a means of survival or because they feel they have no other option or way to leave "the life." To do so, they said they would need stable employment, housing and education.

Importantly, most CSEC youth want to leave "the life" (87% of the CSEC youth interviewed by Curtis et al., 2008) and say they would do so if they had other means to support themselves or legitimate opportunities for work. There is a discrepancy, however, between the needs of the CSEC population and the resources allocated to it; only one agency in New York City is devoted specifically to this population. This agency, the Girls Education and Mentoring Services (GEMS), only serves the CSEC population of pimped girls and there are no programs or agencies committed to aiding boys and transgender youth. One reason for this is that most previous studies have focused on pimped girls and the dangers to them, and, thus, the city focuses its resources on this population. However, Curtis et al. (2008) found that only 8% of the youth in their study were recruited into the market by a pimp and 10% were subsequently under the control of a pimp. This low percentage, however, may be due to the methodology employed for the study, which may have resulted in an under-estimate of this particular sub group – pimped girls. Yet, the findings showed that the most common way in which male, female and transgendered youth became involved in "the life" was through friends (46%, 44%, and 68% respectively). Once involved in "the life", the teens developed an extensive CSEC network, with more than half of the CSEC population knowing 10 or more other youths in this population.

Recognizing the need to do more for this population, the Safe Harbor for Exploited Youth Act was recently passed through the New York Assembly and is awaiting signing by the governor. This Act would decriminalize first acts of prostitution for youth 16 and under, would classify these youth as "persons in need of supervision" (PINS), and provide services to exploited youth under the age of 18. Despite this promise of services, however, the Safe Harbor Act would provide few additional resources to the CSEC population and would instead rely primarily on existing services. Dank (2008, p. 89) makes the following policy recommendations based upon the findings of the Curtis et al. (2008) study. These support the assertions of Williams, though they look beyond the needs just of the prostituted girls.

- More services need to be available to boys and transgender youth, who make up a significant portion of the CSEC population. These services should include emergency shelter, long-term housing, intensive counseling, medical services, educational opportunities, life-skills and job training and employment opportunities.

- Use social networks to deliver services. Mandating youth, either through the court system or by law enforcement, to partake in services is not likely to be effective at helping youth exit the life. As Curtis et al. (2008) demonstrated, prostituted youth are often times influenced by their peers, whether it is through recruitment into the market or reasons to remain in the life, and infiltration of these social networks can be instrumental in effectively delivering services. One possible way to do this is to find, with the help of existing youth agencies, individuals with the largest and most diverse CSEC network and have them conduct outreach to their peers.

▪ Properly train staff who work with the CSEC youth. Training youth agency staff and law enforcement is necessary in order to gain the trust of prostituted youth. Without the proper training, agency staff and law enforcement officials could discourage a youth from ever seeking help again. Almost, if not, all sexually exploited youth have severe, deep-seeded issues with adults and authority, and if they are not approached with a non-judgmental and empathetic ear, they will see no reason to leave the life.

An additional factor to consider is the role and definition of a "pimp". Curtis et al (2008) found that many individuals played a role in facilitating the payment for sexual acts with a minor. In fact, they used the term "market facilitator" to describe these individuals since they were variously traditional pimps, friends who arranged meetings, and local businesses, such as bodega owners. They exhibited various levels of control, from a simple meeting between the prostituted youth and potential clients, to full control over the youth. Thus, while Williams recommends increased sanctions for pimps and johns, it is necessary to further clarify the definition of the pimp.

The move towards the elimination of prosecution for prostituted youth is a necessary first step towards reducing the tragedy of exploiting youth. However, it is not enough. Cities must provide services for the youth so that they will choose to, and be able to, leave the life. Without other viable options in regard to both services and social networks, CSE youth will not choose to leave the life, even if they would like to do so.

REFERENCES

Curtis, R., Terry, K.J., Dank, M., Kahn, B., and Dombrowski, K. (2008). *The Commercial Sexual Exploitation of Children in New York City.* Report to the National Institute of Justice. Washington, D.C.: NIJ.

Dank, M. (2008). The Safe Harbor for Exploited Youth Act: Recognizing that Sexually Exploited Children Are Not "Offenders". *Sex Offender Law Report, 9(6)*, 81-96.

M.H. Silbert & Pines, A.M. (1982). Entrance into prostitution. *Youth & Society, 13(4),* 471-500.

C.S. Widom & Kuhns, J.B. (1996). Childhood victimization and subsequent risk for promiscuity, prostitution, and teenage pregnancy: A prospective study. *American Journal of Public Health, 86(11),* 1607-1612.

Ban Juvenile Transfer to Adult Court in Homicide Cases: Brain Development and the Need for a Blended Sentence Approach[*]

Carrie Pettus-Davis
Eric Garland

The prevalence of juvenile transfer stems from public intolerance for the almost 200% jump in juvenile violence during the last two decades of the 20th century (DiCataldo & Everrett, 2008; Fox, 1996). Through widespread adoption of juvenile transfer laws, policymakers abandoned the traditional structure of the juvenile court designed to respond to youth problems and instead placed responsibility for adjudication with adult courts. However, committing a crime, no matter how illicit, does not developmentally transform a juvenile into an adult. Transferring a juvenile to adult criminal court for the purpose of adjudicating severe sentences capable of nullifying the presumably mature criminality of the youth in question ignores findings from developmental science, neuroscience, and conventional wisdom - youth are inherently different from adults and are in a critical period of formative change. The transfer of juvenile homicide offenders to the adult court system hinders the development of an appropriate societal and legal response to juvenile violence.

In a first step to reversing this misguided trend, the transfer of juvenile homicide cases to adult criminal court should be abolished for those who commit offenses prior to their 18th birthday. Instead, States should adopt a blended sentence approach that allows juvenile courts and adult courts to work in concert to impose developmentally appropriate punishments. Although juvenile transfers are not limited to youth homicide offenders, juvenile homicide offenders are at the greatest risk of the consequences of transfer because of the severity of the crime and related penalties. Furthermore, if a blended sentence approach is successful with juvenile homicide offenders, it naturally follows that a similar approach would be effective with less serious juvenile offenders. This essay draws on neuroscientific evidence to argue for a ban of juvenile transfers for homicide cases and proposes an alternative blended sentence approach.

---

[*] Acknowledgment: A special thanks to Joseph E. Kennedy, Associate Professor of Law at the University of North Carolina at Chapel Hill for his critical insights and feedback.

JUVENILE HOMICIDE

Between 1978 and 1993, juvenile murder rose 177% while adult murders only increased by 7% (Levitt, 1998). Currently, juveniles account for one in every ten murder arrests (Synder, 2008). The increased use of guns instead of fists and knives as weapons in youth violence is a leading explanatory factor for the dramatic increase in youth homicide (Shumaker & McKee, 2001). While killing with all other weapons has remained constant since the 1980's, the number of juvenile killings with handguns quadrupled (Fox, 1996). In the well cited Cornell study of 72 juvenile murderers in Michigan, more than 60% reported use of a gun to kill their victim (Cornell, Benedek & Benedek, 1987). In a more recent study of a random sample of violent juvenile offenders, of those juveniles with homicide cases, 67.7% used guns on their victims, whereas only 21.1% of the violent juvenile offenders with nonhomicide cases used firearms (DiCataldo & Everett, 2008). Contrary to expectations, non-homicidal offenders had longer and more extensive delinquent careers, as well as greater problems with anger control and antisocial characteristics than homicidal juveniles. However, the homicidal youths were differentiated from non-homicidal youths in that they had more immediate access to guns and were more likely to report intoxication during the time of the offense (DiCataldo & Everett, 2008). The resulting combination of guns and drugs may overwhelm limited impulse control among youths and increase the likelihood of fatal outcomes during instances of juvenile violence. Overall, national statistics indicate that adolescent males between the ages of 16 to 19 display the highest rates of violence and that a high percentage of males participate in violence during their teenage years and then desist in adulthood (Berkheiser, 2005).

JUVENILE TRANSFER

The process of transferring youths from the juvenile court to the adult court occurs through a waiver, bindover, removal, or transfer (Siegel, Welsh & Senna, 2006). For the purposes of this essay, the term juvenile transfer will be used to describe the removal of a youth from juvenile court jurisdiction to adult court jurisdiction. The minimum age specified for transferring juveniles to adult court varies by State; in twenty-three states and the District of Columbia there is no minimum age for juvenile transfer (Siegel et al., 2006). Thus, in 23 states, an 8 year-old boy who shot and killed his father and his father's friend in November of 2008 (Dougherty & O'Connor, 2008) could be tried, and sentenced as an adult. Fifteen states have a minimum juvenile transfer age of either age 14 or age 15, and in ten states the minimum age ranges from age 10 to age 13 (Siegel et al., 2006).

The frequency of juvenile transfers has varied over time. In 1994, juvenile transfers peaked at 12,100 cases (Siegel et al., 2006) coinciding with a 177% increase in juvenile homicide offenses during that same time-period (Levitt, 1998). In 2003, there were 7,100 juvenile transfer cases (Siegel et al., 2006) and in 2004 approximately 7% of juvenile arrests were referred directly to adult criminal court (Synder, 2006). The decision to transfer is based on many factors including the manner in which the crime was committed, the offender's prior delinquent record, maturity of the offender, seriousness of the offense, and likelihood for rehabilitation (Horowitz, 2006). Although theoretically each of these factors is considered, in practice juvenile homicide cases are usually transferred to adult court jurisdiction (Grisso, 1996). Transfer alters the legal experience of the minor wherein the adult criminal court takes on a much more adversarial model than the cooperative model likely to be used in the juvenile court (Steinberg & Cauffman, 1999).

LEGAL AND EMPIRICAL PRECEDENCE FOR DIFFERENTIAL TREATMENT OF JUVENILES AND ADULTS

The appropriateness of adult criminal prosecution and sentencing of juveniles has been debated extensively over the past three decades. In 2005, the Roper v Simmons ruling declared the unconstitutionality of the juvenile death penalty. The U.S. Supreme Court held that it was cruel and unusual punishment to sentence a juvenile to death who was under the age of 18 at the time of offense. The Court cited sociological, developmental, and neurological evidence in partial support of the ruling stating that juveniles do not possess the same level of maturity and responsibility of adults (Siegel et al., 2006). Furthermore, the adult standard for punishment contradicts the age of majority in almost every other area of nonpenal law (Zimring, 2000). For example, all States bar minors from voting, sitting on the jury, drinking alcohol, or smoking (Horowitz, 2006).

Consistent with conventional wisdom, results from empirical research in developmental psychology describe adolescence as time when individuals have diminished decision making capacities, are less able to resist coercive influence, and are still undergoing personality change (Steinberg & Scott, 2003). Researchers in child development describe adolescence as a highly malleable and transformative period in human development (Steinberg & Schwartz, 2000). This period is a unique time in the human life trajectory when individuals are most easily influenced by external factors such as peers or a problematic home life (Steinberg & Cauffman, 1999). Recent neuroscience findings provide biological evidence for these theoretical propositions.

NEUROSCIENCE EVIDENCE:
DIFFERENCES BETWEEN JUVENILES AND ADULTS

Cognitive neuroscience research of adolescent and adult brains using behavioral tasks coupled with neuroimaging technologies (e.g., structural and functional magnetic resonance imaging, or MRI) support collective wisdom that juveniles are neurologically immature, have poor impulse control, and a diminished ability to understand consequences relative to adults. The often substantial cognitive and behavioral disparities observed between children and adults may result from differences in the structure and function of their brains (Beckman, 2004).

As the brain develops, neurons are covered in a sheath of insulating tissue, called myelin (which appears white in a MRI scanner, thus termed "white matter"), leading to faster transmission of neural impulses. In childhood much of the brain is comprised of grey matter, that is, unmyelinated neural tissue. The ratio of grey to white matter changes across brain areas over the course of development. During the first several years of life, neurons of the sensory and motor areas of the brain become fully myelinated, whereas neurons of the prefrontal cortex and its widespread connections throughout the brain continue to develop myelin sheaths throughout adolescence. As grey matter density declines while white matter increases, the speed of signal processing in the brain is enhanced, resulting in improved ability to coordinate thoughts and behaviors, make decisions, and delay gratification (Blakemore & Choudhury, 2006). Development of the prefrontal cortex and its linkages to other brain areas leads to further differentiation and integration of brain structures that subserve response inhibition, assessment of risk and rewards, and emotion regulation (Spear, 2000; Steinberg, 2005).

Cortical maturation occurs gradually throughout adolescence as distant brain structures become assembled into neural circuits that function more efficiently as white matter density increases. During this integrative process, the prefrontal cortex takes on an executive function, coordinating the inhibition or disinhibition of activity in various brain structures. Executive function does not fully develop until well into late adolescence and early adulthood (Beckman, 2004; Giedd, 2004; Steinberg, 2005).

As prefrontal cortical regions become increasingly coupled with the amygdala, a brain structure implicated in the processing of emotions, activation of central executive structures reciprocally inhibits strong emotional reactions (Oschner & Gross, 2005). In other words, as the adolescent matures he or she becomes better able to regulate his or her feeling states and act with forethought rather than impulsivity. However, pubertal increases in emotional arousal occur prior to the maturation of the prefrontal cortex; thus, adolescent behavior is impelled by emotions without the benefit of fully developed self-regulatory competence (Steinberg, 2005).

Risky adolescent behavior may result from pubertal increases in emotional reactivity (Spear, 2009). Adolescents exhibit greater hypothalamic-pituitary-adrenal axis and autonomic nervous system responses to stressors than children (Stroud et al., 2009), and, relative to prepubertal children, evidence heightened sensitivity to both pleasant and aversive emotional stimuli (Quevado, Benning, Gunnar & Dahl, 2009). During emotion regulation tasks, adolescents show exaggerated amygdala activity compared to children and adults (Hare et al., 2008). It appears as if emotional reactivity increases during pubescence while prefrontal regions devoted to self-regulation remain immature until adulthood, resulting in the inability to regulate increasingly strong emotions in the face of stressful circumstances.

The developmental increase in psychophysiological activation to emotionally-distressing events observed among adolescents may be exacerbated by difficulties recognizing and understanding emotional experience. Children are less able than adults to correctly identify emotions when viewing facial expressions (Baird et al., 1999). This inequality in emotion recognition may be subserved by differential patterns of brain activation between children and adults during emotion recognition tasks. Functional magnetic resonance imaging studies have shown that child participants viewing emotional faces (e.g., faces of persons grimacing in sadness) exhibit greater amygdala activation during emotion recognition than adults, who show more prefrontal cortical activation when performing the same task (Baird et al., 1999). Emotion recognition deficits may manifest in the misreading of social cues, which can ultimately result in antisocial, violent behavior among adolescents, who may impulsively respond to perceived threats and rebuffs without regard to the consequences of their actions.

This developmental disjunction between emotional-motivational and executive function systems in the brain can be assessed with the Iowa Gambling Task, a behavioral task used to evaluate decision making ability. Participants are presented with four decks of cards and are told that drawing cards can either result in a gain or loss of money. The decks vary in terms of their ratio of rewards to losses. Two "bad" decks offer high rewards but frequent moderate or occasional large losses; drawing from either of these decks results in a net loss of money over time. The other two "good" decks offer low rewards but either frequent small or sporadic moderate rewards that lead to net gain of money over time. Healthy adults initially draw from the decks at random but gradually over time choose more cards from good decks while decreasing draws from bad decks. Hooper, Luciana, Conklin and Yarger (2004) administered this test to children and adults and found that while adults (ages 18-25) choose cards from good decks 75% of the time, participants under the age of 18 draw cards from good decks on slightly more than 50% of trials. The researchers attributed this disparity in decision-making ability to the differential maturity of prefrontal cortical structures in children and adults. Differences in brain development may lead children to favor risky choices that offer the possibility of immediate high rewards in spite of potential long term consequences. Real-world examples of impulsive decision-making include criminal activities such as stealing, substance use, and violent behavior, choices marked by an emphasis on immediate gratification without regard for risk. The consequences of these actions are more likely fatal when youth have easy access to guns.

In sum, brain maturation is incomplete during adolescence (Reyna & Farley, 2006). Differences between children and adults in impulsivity, sensation seeking, and thrill seeking can be attributed to fundamental changes in brain structure and function throughout the developmental process. Simply put, the neuro-cognitive functions required for lawful behavior begin to mature around age 17 (Beckman, 2004).

Conclusion

Juvenile transfers change the legal process for an adolescent by moving the minor from a juvenile court system created to consider the unique cognitive-emotional characteristics of youths to an adult court that assumes maturity and adjudication competence (Myers, 2003). Proponents of juvenile transfer argue that adult courts can address the needs of juveniles through consideration of age, coercion from peers, or mitigated sentences by reducing the level of offense charged through plea bargaining or special sentencing provisions. The evidence suggests that mitigation related to age does not commonly occur. Studies show that juveniles are sentenced equally to or more harshly than adult offenders with similar crimes in adult criminal courts (see Redding, 1999). In circumstances of heinous crimes, those juveniles with the most compelling cases are likely the only ones truly to benefit from the mitigating circumstances of age.

Proponents of juvenile transfer further argue that adult penalties for youth crimes serve as a deterrent for violence (Bilchik, 1998). There is little evidence that transfer policies lower juvenile crime (Redding, 1999). In contrast, recent research demonstrates that once released, transferred juveniles have a higher recidivism rate than their counterparts who remained in juvenile courts (Myers, 2003).

As legal precedent, biopsychosocial research, and conventional wisdom converge and demonstrate that juveniles do not manifest the same impulse control, emotional regulation, and decision making capabilities as adults. Juvenile transfer practices should therefore be reconsidered. Clearly, procedures are needed that ensure appropriate punishment for juvenile homicide offenders. These procedures should prevent assignment of these offenders to a juvenile detention center only for youths to be automatically released back to communities at age 18 or 21 with the potential to cause more harm. However, the current dearth of legal procedures to address youth violence in developmentally appropriate ways does not validate the continued pursuit of unjust responses to young offenders.

A ban on the transfer of all juvenile homicide offenders who commit the crime prior to their 18th birthday should be paired with a state mandate to adopt a blended sentence approach. Using blended sentencing, three states (Connecticut, Kentucky, and Minnesota) have addressed the balance of punishment and rehabilitation. In these states, juveniles are first assigned to the juvenile justice system with the option of transferring an individual to the adult correctional system if the youth does not show significant progress in rehabilitation (Siegel et al., 2006). Similarly, under the proposed blended sentence approach, juveniles would be tried and convicted in a juvenile court and serve the first years of their sentence in juvenile facilities. During this period, the juvenile would by psychologically evaluated and required to attend therapy, social and cognitive skills training, and other related rehabilitative programming. As the offender aged into adulthood (defined as age 21 or older), he or she would be assessed by a multidisciplinary team for rehabilitative progress and potential for dangerousness. Blended sentences preserve the role of punishment and retribution in the deterrence of future crime while addressing the diminished culpability of juveniles due to developmental and neurological immaturity.

In sum, because of advancements in science, research supports what any parent knows to be common knowledge. Children and adolescents are less able than adults to foresee the consequences of their actions, to regulate their emotions, to manage their impulses, to delay instant gratification, and to independently make critical choices about their well-being. Throughout the maturation process from adolescence to adulthood, the prefrontal cortex of the brain undergoes dramatic development. During this developmental period there is a radical reorganization and coordination of neural structures which results in improved decision making, better awareness of consequences, and enhanced inhibition of urges and emotional reactions (Giedd, 2004). Criminal behaviors stemming from the lack of such capabilities result in punitive legal judgments, and yet these brain functions do not begin to mature until around age 17 (Beckman, 2004). Given this incongruity between legal expectation and biological capacity, justice cannot truly be served. A ban on juvenile transfer for homicide cases is the first step in a more just response to American youth.

REFERENCES

Baird, A.A., Gruber, S.A., Fein, D.A., Maas, L.C., Steingard, R.J., REnshaw, P.F., Cohen, B.M. & Yurgelun-Todd, D.A. (1999). Functional magnetic resonance imaging of facial affect recognition in children and adolescents. *Journal of the American Academy of Child and Adolescent Psychiatry, 38,* 195-199.

Beckman, M. (2004). Crime, culpability, and the adolescent brain. *Science, 305,* 596-599.

Berkheiser. M. (2005). Capitalizing adolescence: Juvenile offenders on death row. *University of Miami Law Review, 59,* 135-202.

Bilchik, S. (1998). A juvenile justice system for the 21st Century. *Crime & Delinquency, 44,* 89-101.

Blakemore, S.J. & Choudhurry, S. (2006). Development of the adolescent brain: implications for executive function and social cognition. *Journal of Child Psychology and Psychiatry, 47,* 296-312.

Cornell, D.G., Benedek, E.P., & Benedek, D.M. (1987) Characteristics of adolescents charged with homicide: Review of 72 cases. *Behavioral Sciences & the Law, 5,* 11-23.

DiCataldo, F. & Everett, M. (2008). Distinguishing juvenile homicide from violent juvenile offending. *International Journal of Offender Therapy and Comparative Criminology, 52,* 158-174.

Dougherty, J. & O'Connor, A. (2008, November 11). Prosecutors say boy methodically shot his father. *The New York Times,* A19.

Fox, J.A. (1996). *Trends in Juvenile Violence.* Washington DC: Bureau of Justice Statistics.

Giedd, J.N. (2004). Structural Magnetic Resonance imaging of the adolescent brain. *Annals of New York Academy of Sciences, 1021,* 77-85.

Grisso, T. (1996). Society's retributive response to juvenile violence: A developmental perspective. *Law and Human Behavior, 20,* 229-247.

Hare, T., Tottenham, N., Galvan, A., Voss, H.U., Glover, G. & Casey, B.J. (2008). Biological substrates of emotional reactivity and regulation in adolescence during an emotional go-nogo task. *Biological Psychiatry, 63,* 927-934.

Hooper, C.J., Luciana, M., Conklin, H.M. & Yarger, R.S. (2004). Adolescents' performance on the Iowa Gambling Task: Implications for the development of decision-making and ventromedial prefrontal cortex. *Developmental Psychology, 40,* 1148-1158.

Levitt, S.D. (1998). Juvenile crime and punishment. *Journal of Political Economy, 106,* 1156-1185.

Myers, D.L. (2003). The recidivism of violent youths in juvenile and adult court: A consideration of selection bias. *Youth Violence and Juvenile Justice, 1,* 79-101.

Ochsner, K.N. & Gross, J.J. (2005). The cognitive control of emotion. *Trends in Cognitive Science, 9,* 242-249.

Quevedo, K., Benning, S.D., Gunnar, M.R. & Dahl, R.E. (2009) The onset of puberty: Effects on the psychophysiology of defensive and appetitive motivation. *Development and Psychopathology, 21,* 27-45.

Redding, R. (1999). Juvenile offenders in criminal court and adult prison: Legal, psychological, and behavioral outcomes. *Juvenile and Family Court Journal, 50,* 1-15.

Reyna, V.F. & Farely, F. (2006). Risk and rationality in adolescent decision making: Implications for theory, practice, and public policy. *Psychological Science, 7,* 1-44.

Shumaker, D.M. & McKee, G.R. (2001). Characteristics of homicidal and violent juveniles. *Violence and Victims, 16,* 401-409.

Siegel, L.J, Welsh, B.C. & Senna, J.J. (2006). *Juvenile Delinquency: Theory, Practice, and Law.* Belmont, CA: Thomson Wadsworth.

Spear, L. (2009). Heightened stress responsivity and emotional reactivity during pubertal maturation: Implications for psychopathology. *Development and Psychopathology, 21,* 87-97.

Spear, P. (2000). The adolescent brain and age-related behavioral manifestations. *Neuroscience & Biobehavioral Reviews, 24,* 417-463.

Steinberg, L. (2005). Cognitive and affective development in adolescence. *TRENDS in Cognitive Sciences, 9,* 70-74.

Steinberg, L. & Cauffman, E. (1999) A developmental perspective on serious juvenile crime: When should juveniles be treated as adults? *Federal Probation, 63,* 52-57.

Steinberg, L. & Schwartz, R.G. (2000). Developmental psychology goes to court. In T. Grisso & R.G. Schwartz (Eds.), *Youth on Trial: A Developmental Perspective on Juvenile Justice* (pp. 9-32). Chicago: University of Chicago Press.

Steinberg, L. & Scott, E.S. (2003). Less guilty by reason of adolescence: Developmental immaturity, diminished responsibility, and juvenile death penalty. *American Psychologist, 58,* 1009-1019.

Stroud, L., Foster, E., Handwerger, K., Papandonatos, G.D., Granger, D., Kivlighan, K.T., et al. (2009). Stress response and the adolescent transition: Performance versus peer rejection stress. *Development and Psychopathology, 21,* 47-68.

Synder, H.N. (2006). *Juvenile Arrest 2004.* Washington, DC: Office of Juvenile Justice and Delinquency Prevention.

Synder, H.N. (2008). *Juvenile Arrest 2006.* Washington, DC: Office of Juvenile Justice and Delinquency Prevention.

Zimring, F.E. (2000). Penal proporationality for the young offender: Notes on immaturity, capacity, and diminished responsibility. In T. Grisso and R.G. Schwartz (Eds.), *Youth on Trial: A Developmental Perspective on Juvenile Justice* (pp. 9-32). Chicago: University of Chicago Press.

IN DEFENSE OF WAIVER AND YOUTHFULNESS AS A MITIGATING FACTOR IN SENTENCING

BARRY C. FELD

Increases in youth violence, crimes with firearms, and homicide in the late-1980s and early-1990s prompted states to "get tough," to transfer more and younger juveniles to criminal court, and to shift discretion from judges in a waiver hearing to prosecutors making charging decisions (Torbet et al 1996; Feld 1998; 1999; 2000; 2003a; Snyder and Sickmund 2006; Griffin 2008). Responding to that punitive over-reaction, Pettus-Davis and Garland draw on recent neuroscience research to argue for a complete ban on transfer of juveniles charged with homicide to criminal court. They propose instead that states adopt blended sentencing for young murderers and, by extension, to use it in lieu of waivers for less serious offenders as well.

I have four concerns with their proposal. First, there is a legitimate place for a properly structured judicial waiver process to try some young offenders in criminal court (Feld 2000; Zimring 2000). Second, recent neuroscience findings simply confirm what behavioral scientists and parents long have observed – "kids are different" – but it does not provide a normative basis to make judgments about criminal responsibility (Morse 2006). Third, blended sentencing threatens the rationale for a separate juvenile court and produces "net-widening" that consigns less serious youths to criminal incarceration (Zimring 2000; Podkopacz and Feld 2001). Fourth, whether through waiver or blended sentences, judges will sentence some youths in criminal court and we need a means to incorporate youthfulness as a mitigating factor (Feld 1999; 2008).

1. Waiver as "Safety Valve"

Although juvenile courts attempt to rehabilitate offenders, successful treatment of older delinquents convicted of serious crimes may not be feasible during their remaining minority years (Podkopacz and Feld 1996). Their serious offenses conflict with the perceived immaturity and lesser culpability of most young offenders (Scott and Steinberg 2008). Retaining them as juveniles could negatively affect less sophisticated youths and divert scarce resources from more tractable juveniles. The political reality is that highly visible, serious offenses committed by youths evoke community outrage or fear that only a punitive response can mollify.

A mechanism to prosecute some offenders as adults functions as a safety valve to respond to political pressure and to preserve the juvenile system for the vast majority of youths (Zimring 2000). Without transfer mechanisms, pressures to lower the maximum age of juvenile court jurisdiction could prove irresistible (Zimring 1998; 2000). Transfer to criminal court is appropriate when a youth's record of persistence and serious present offense warrant minimum lengths of confinement substantially longer than the maximum term for which a judge could sentence a delinquent (Feld 2000; Scott and Steinberg 2008; Zimring 1998). Because juvenile judges may impose sentences of two or three years or more, waiver criteria should identify combinations of serious present offense, offense history, culpability, and other aggravating and mitigating factors that deserve minimum sentences substantially longer than those available in juvenile court (Zimring 2000; Feld 2000; Scott and Steinberg 2008).

2. *Roper v. Simmons, Neuroscience and Diminished Responsibility*

Roper v. Simmons (2005) prohibited states from executing offenders for crimes committed when younger than eighteen years of age. The Court conducted a proportionality analysis and concluded that juveniles' immature judgment, susceptibility to negative peer influences, and transitory personality development reduced their criminal responsibility. Significantly, *Roper* did *not* cite any neuroscience research and concluded only that states could not equate the culpability of adolescents with adults (Feld 2008). Although differences between adolescents' and adults' judgment and self-control seem intuitively obvious – "as any parent knows" – *Roper* did not cite social science research to bolster its intuition (Denno 2006). Moreover, adolescents' diminished responsibility does not prevent states from finding them criminally responsible or punishing them, but only barred their execution.

Despite the appeal of neuroscience advances, the research does not provide a basis to make normative judgments about criminal responsibility or deserved punishment (Morse 2006). Neuroscience may provide a hard-science explanation for social scientists' observations about youths' immature behavior and limited self-control, but we knew that long before magnetic resonance imaging. Neuroscience has not established a direct link between adolescents' immature brain structure and function and their real-life decisions and behavior under stressful conditions, nor does it provide a basis to individualize among young offenders on the basis of brain development. The neuroscience simply enhances our understanding of how and why juveniles think and behave differently from adults (Morse 2006). Their impaired judgment and behavior – impulsivity, poor risk assessment, and emotional volatility – provide the bases for assessments of criminal responsibility and justify mitigating punishment (Feld 2008).

3. *Perils of Blended Sentencing – Eroding Juvenile Courts' Rationale and Net-Widening*

Although Pettus-Davis and Garland favorably cite Minnesota's blended sentencing law, as an architect of that policy (Feld 1995), I long since have abandoned my enthusiasm for it (Podkopacz and Feld 2001). In theory, blended sentencing is a non-exclusive strategy to increase the punitive powers of juvenile courts (Redding and Howell 2000). It increases the sentence lengths available in juvenile courts to the point that they may become as disfiguring and debilitating as those criminal courts impose (Zimring 2000). Endorsing punishment blurs and confuses the purpose and functions of rehabilitative juvenile courts (Zimring 1998). It intrudes criminal sanctions into juvenile courts, places juvenile judges in the role of imposing criminal sentences, and erodes courts' rehabilitative mission with spill-over effects on other delinquents (Redding and Howell 2000). Finally, blended sentencing exacerbates the manifold procedural deficiencies of juvenile courts (Feld 2003b).

Although analysts endorse blended sentences as an alternative to waiver, juvenile court judges do not use them in lieu of transfer but instead impose them on less serious offenders (Redding and Howell 2000; Podkopacz and Feld 2001). Minnesota's blended sentencing law provides a clear example of "net-widening." "Net widening" occurs when reformers introduce a new sanction to be used in lieu of another, more severe sanction – e.g. blended sentencing in lieu of transfer – but which judges then use on those who previously would have been treated less severely than the new sanction permits (Podkopacz and Feld 2001). Judges in Minnesota continued to transfer the same numbers and types of youths whom they previously waived *and* imposed blended sentences with a stayed criminal sentence on many younger delinquents with less extensive prior records. They sentenced more severely youths whom they previously dealt with as delinquents, rather than those who previously were bound for prison. More than one-third of those youths subsequently failed during their juvenile treatment, primarily for probation violations rather than serious new offenses. Blended sentences widened the net and moved younger, less serious youths into the adult correctional system through the "back-door" of probation revocation proceedings rather than through waiver hearings (Podkopacz and Feld 2001). Finally, prosecutors use the threat of transfer as leverage to coerce youths to plead to blended sentences, to waive their procedural rights, and to risk exposure to criminal sanctions.

4. Youthfulness as a Mitigating Factor in Sentencing – Virtues of a "Youth Discount"

States should apply the principle of youthfulness as a mitigating factor as part of a just and fair youth sentencing policy. Recognizing youthfulness as a mitigating factor holds youths accountable for their crimes and simultaneously recognizes their diminished responsibility (Scott and Grisso 1997; Feld 2008). Even when youth cause the same harms as adults, their crimes are not the moral equivalents because of reduced culpability. We should protect them from the full penal consequences of immature decisions (Zimring 2000; Scott and Steinberg 2008).

Roper treated adolescents' diminished responsibility categorically and used age-as-a-proxy for culpability because no better or more accurate bases exist on which to individualize responsibility. Culpability is a normative valuation, rather than an objective thing. Proportioning sentences to culpability involves a moral judgment about deserved punishment. Clinicians lack tools with which to assess impulsivity, foresight, or preference for risk, to relate them to maturity of judgment and criminal responsibility, or to calibrate how much culpability a young offender possesses (*Roper* 2005; Scott and Steinberg 2008). *Roper* feared that efforts to individualize culpability assessments would introduce a systematic bias because of the inability to fairly weigh an abstraction – youthfulness as a mitigating factor – against the reality of a horrific crime.

All adolescents share the developmental characteristics of immature judgment, impulsiveness, and lack of self-control that systematically reduces their culpability, and all young offenders should receive categorical reductions of adult sentences (Feld 1997; Morse 1997; Scott and Steinberg 2008). Recognizing youthfulness as a mitigating factor represents a moral and criminal policy judgment that no child deserves to be sentenced as severely as an adult who caused the same harm. Other area of law uses age-based lines to approximate the maturity required for particular activities – e.g., voting, driving, and consuming alcohol – and restricts youths because of their immaturity and inability to make competent decision (Zimring 2000). I long have advocated (Feld 1997; 1999; 2008), and others have endorsed, my proposal for a "youth discount" that provides adolescents with fractional reductions in sentence-lengths based on age-as-a-proxy-for culpability (Scott and Steinberg 2008; Tanenhaus and Drizin 2004). A "youth discount" represents a sliding scale of diminished responsibility that gives the largest sentence reductions to the youngest, least mature offenders. On a sliding scale of diminished responsibility that corresponds with developmental differences, a fourteen-year-old offender might receive a sentence that is twenty-five percent of the length an adult would receive and a sixteen-year-old might receive a sentence no more than half the adult length. The deeper discounts for younger offenders correspond with their greater developmental differences in maturity of judgment and self-control (Zimring 2000; Feld 2008).

Roper also emphasized that juveniles' personalities are more transitory and less-fixed, and their crimes provide less reliable evidence of moral depravity and a greater likelihood that they can be reformed. A youth discount enables young offenders to survive serious mistakes with a semblance of their life chances intact. We can hold juveniles accountable, manage the risks they pose to others, and provide them with "room to reform" without extinguishing their lives (Zimring 1998; 2000). Because they eventually will return to the community, the state bears a responsibility to provide them with resources with which to reform as they mature.

REFERENCES

Denno, D.W. (2006). The scientific short-comings of *Roper v. Simmons*. *Ohio State Journal of Criminal Law* 3, 379 – 396.

Feld, B.C. (1995). Violent youth and public police: A case-study of juvenile justice law reform. *Minnesota Law Review*, 79, 965-1128.

Feld, B.C. (1997). Abolish the juvenile court: Youthfulness, criminal responsibility, and sentencing policy. *Journal of Criminal Law and Criminology*, 88, 68 – 136.

Feld, B.C. (1998). Juvenile and criminal justice systems' responses to youth violence. *Crime & Justice, 24*, 189-261.

Feld, B.C. (1999). *Bad Kids: Race and the Transformation of the Juvenile Court.* New York, NY: Oxford University Press.

Feld, B.C. (2000). Legislative exclusion of offenses from juvenile court jurisdiction: A history and critique. In J.E. Fagan & F.E. Zimring (Eds.), *Changing Borders of Juvenile Justice: Transfer of Adolescents to the Criminal Court* (pp. 83-144). Chicago, IL: University of Chicago.

Feld, B.C. (2003a). Race, politics, and juvenile justice: The Warren Court and the conservative 'backlash'. *Minnesota Law Review, 87*, 1447.

Feld, B.C. (2003b). The constitutional tension between *Apprendi* and *McKeiver*: Sentence enhancements based on delinquency convictions and the quality of justice in juvenile courts. *Wake Forest Law Review*, 38, 1111-1224.

Feld, B.C. (2008). A Slower form of death: Implications of *Roper v. Simmons* for juveniles sentenced to life without parole. *Notre Dame Journal of Law, Ethics, & Public Policy* 22, 9-65.

Griffin, P. (2008). *Different from adults: An updated analysis of juvenile transfer and blended sentencing laws, with recommendations for reform.* Pittsburgh, PA: National Center for Juvenile Justice and John D. and Catherine T. MacArthur Foundation.

Morse, S.J. (1997) Immaturity and irresponsibility. *Journal of Criminal Law and Criminology.* 88, 15 – 55.

Morse, S.J. (2006). Brain Overclaim Syndrome and criminal responsibility: A diagnostic note. *Ohio State Journal of Criminal Law* 3, 397-412.

Podkopacz, M. & Feld, B.C. (1996). The end of the line: An empirical study of judicial waiver. *Journal of Criminal Law and Criminology* 86, 449 – 492.

Podkopacz, M. & Feld, B.C. (2001). The back-door to prison: Waiver reform, "blended sentencing," and the law of unintended consequences." *Journal of Criminal Law and Criminology,* 91. 997-1071.

Redding, R.E. & Howell, J.C. (2000). Blended sentencing in American juvenile courts. In J. Fagan & F.E. Zimring, (Eds.), *The Changing Borders of Juvenile Justice: Transfer of Adolescents to the Criminal Court.* Chicago: University of Chicago Press.

Roper v. Simmons (2005). 543 U.S. 1.

Scott, E.S. & Grisso, T. (1997). The evolution of adolescence: A developmental perspective on juvenile justice reform. *Journal of Criminal Law and Criminology,* 88, 137 – 183.

Scott, E.S. & Steinberg, L. (2008). *Rethinking Juvenile Justice.* Cambridge, MA: Harvard University Press.

Snyder, H. & Sickmund, M. (2006). *Juvenile Offenders and Victims: 2006 National Report.* Washington D.C.: Office of Juvenile Justice and Delinquency Prevention.

Torbet, P., Gable, R., Hurst IV, H., Montgomery, I., Szymanski, L. & Thomas, D. (1996). *State Responses to Serious and Violent Juvenile Crime: Research Report* Washington, D.C.: Office of Juvenile Justice and Delinquency Prevention.

Zimring, F.E. (1998). *American Youth Violence.* New York: Oxford University Press.

Zimring, F.E. 2000. The punitive necessity of waiver. In J. Fagan & F.E. Zimring (Eds.), *The Changing Borders of Juvenile Justice: Transfer of Adolescents to the Criminal Court.* Chicago: University of Chicago Press.

Public Health is Public Safety: Revamping the Correctional Mission[i]

Faye S. Taxman
Liz Ressler

Today, the unanticipated impact of the economic recession is that it has forced us to re-examine the incarceration binge of the last three decades where confinement and churning have dominated crime control policies. With an expanding correctional landscape of over eight million adults and adolescents under correctional control, these incarceration-focused punitive policies have contributed to unhealthy people and communities by increasing the very same risk factors that advocates of punishment believed would deter criminal behavior. Instead, involvement in the criminal justice system is now considered a normal part of the lifecycle for many adults and children, particularly minorities. Criminal justice involvement is no longer considered a novelty; instead prison and incarceration are frequently glamorized in the culture through television shows and fashionable clothing. The challenge before us is not to merely alter sentencing goals or adopt evidence-based rehabilitation programming. Neither will serve to fundamentally change the social institutions that manage society's undesirable citizens, or affect the perception that offenders are second-class citizens. We must recognize that unhealthy offenders will not become productive, law abiding citizens until their unmet and detrimental physical, psychological and social behaviors are addressed. It is now incumbent that we recognize that correctional agencies must be transformed to be service providers with a primary goal to concurrently address public health and safety goals. Public health is public safety. To make this shift will require a revamping of correctional agencies to have the tools and personnel to reduce the same risk factors that promulgate criminal behavior.

A widely unaddressed fact is that offenders are among the unhealthiest on most major measures of wellbeing. Offenders tend to die early (Binswanger et al., 2007; Teplin, Abram, McClelland, Dulcan & Mericle, 2002) and suffer from nearly all chronic and acute health conditions--physical, mental health and substance abuse. As such, their need for care is not only high, but it is also critical gap to building the prospects for a productive, law abiding future. Research suggests that justice-involved people are medically underserved prior to sentencing (Feinstein et al., 1998), during periods of confinement (Chandler, Fletcher & Volkow, 2009; Gallagher & Dobrin, 2006; Gallagher, Dobrin & Douds, 2007; Taxman, Perdoni & Harrison, 2007; Young, Dembo & Henderson, 2007), and during periods of community supervision (Taxman et al., 2007). Unhealthy people are unlikely to become law-abiding citizens, particularly if they perceive their health and well-being as inconsequential to the correctional system. A focus on basic (survival) needs often results in continued behaviors that contribute to involvement in the criminal justice system.

Health care falls low on the priority list of most correctional agencies, since health is not squarely rooted in the core mission of safety (or punishment, incapacitation or deterrence). Health care is difficult, expensive and perceived to be inconsequential to the mission and goals of a correctional agency. Except for constitutionally mandated medical care provided in prisons and jails--which often translates into minimal, crisis driven services--correctional agencies do not perceive their role to be a service provider. The protective role of public safety rarely encompasses the provision of basic medical and psychological services to facilitate obedience to the norms and laws. In security driven milieu, the medical and psychological services are frequently viewed as too "rehabilitation-oriented," and are abandoned in favor of other priorities. Any health care, including mental and substance abuse services, is often considered a tertiary goal at best.

It is unreasonable to expect that the deficits in physical and psychological health will have no impact on lawful or criminal behavior. Offenders can become law-abiding, productive members of society. We cannot sidestep that the provision of health care will provide an important bridge to offender change. Attending to the physical and mental health needs of this population will serve to: 1) help offenders become healthy members of society; and, 2) overcome the perception and recent evidence that the criminal justice system is merely a net to trap the offender, his/her family, and community in the cycle of incarceration and criminal justice involvement. Providing services that address the legitimacy of the punishment process, society (at large) and correctional agencies (in particular) should focus on incorporating physical and mental health services into the basic incarceration and community corrections services. Criminologists should affirm the importance of transforming correctional agencies from bureaucratic security oriented or compliance monitors to active care providers that recognize humane treatment as a cornerstone to behavior change. Transforming these organizations will have the greater benefit of creating safe and healthy communities, workplaces, and people. We present three rationales for offering this radical shift that focuses on public health goals.

1: Offenders Have Copious Unmet Health Needs

With over 8 million adults and 650,000 youth under the control of the American correctional system (Taxman, Young, Wiersema, Rhodes & Mitchell, 2007), the system directly impacts 4.5% of all 18-65 year olds and 3.9% of all 12-17 year olds. Minorities are over-represented in the criminal justice system, with black men 5.7 to 8.5 times more likely to be incarcerated as compared to white men (Sabol, Minton & Harrison, 2007).

The ripple effects of incarceration on communities as well as the lives of the families and children of individuals who are in the criminal justice system are not included (Thomas, Levandowski, Isler, Torrone & Wilson, 2008; Thomas & Torrone, 2006; Wilbur et al., 2007). Educational deficits exist with nearly half of the population failing to achieve a high school degree or GED as compared to 18% of the general population (Harlow, 2003). While prisons and jails have constitutional mandates to attend to the health needs of offenders, it is often pursued as a band-aid rather than a means of reducing risk factors. Since the general population does not view preventative health care as an important issue, it is not surprising that preventative health care services are not provided to offenders to address their health needs and criminal risk factors.

A few examples illustrate the importance of addressing unmet health needs of offenders (see Taxman, Cropsey, Perdoni & Gallagher, 2009 for an expansive discussion including estimates of the number of offenders that can receive health services). Correctional populations have much higher rates of infectious diseases compared to the general population. Rates of Chlamydia are approximately 18-50 times higher in adult prisoners and 8-13 times higher in juvenile justice inmates compared to the general population (Center for Disease Control, 2005, 2006b). Rates of gonorrhea are 18-32 times higher in adult offenders and 5-9 times higher among juvenile inmates than the general population (Center for Disease Control, 2005, 2006b). Approximately 3.7% of male and 5.2% of female inmates test positive for Syphilis compared to less than .001% of adults in the general population (Center for Disease Control, 2005, 2006b). Rates of Human Immunodeficiency Virus (HIV) and confirmed Acquired Immunodeficiency Syndrome (AIDS) are about 3 times higher in adult correctional populations compared to adults outside of correctional facilities (Glynn & Rhodes, 2005; Maruschak, 2007), although among juveniles, HIV infection rates are similar between the correctional and general populations.. Active or latent tuberculosis (TB) infections are also higher; approximately 20-25% of inmates test positive to at least latent TB, while only about .0048% of the general population tests positive for TB (Baillargeon, Black, Pulvino & Dunn, 2000; Center for Disease Control, 2006a). Up to about a third of prisoners are infected with Hepatitis C infection, while rates within the general adult population are less than 2% (Center for Disease Control, 2002, 2008).

The saga of unmet needs continues with mental health and substance abuse disorders. Rates of mental illness are approximately 2-3 times higher in correctional adult and juvenile populations compared to general populations (James & Glaze, 2006; Mental Health America, 2008; National Institute of Mental Health, 2008; Otto, Greenstein, Johnson & Freidman, 1992; Teplin et al., 2006). Suicide rates are approximately 2-4 times higher among incarcerated adults and juveniles compared to similar non-incarcerated populations (Gallagher & Dobrin, 2006). Analogous to rates of mental illness, substance abuse rates are also four times higher among adult and juvenile correctional populations compared to the general population (Karberg & James, 2002; Mumola, 1997; Substance Abuse and Mental Health Services Administration, 2006).

Tobacco smoking rates among adult and juvenile prisoners are approximately three to four times higher than the general populations and about twice as high among juveniles (Cropsey, Eldridge & Ladner, 2004; Cropsey, Eldridge, Weaver, Villalobos & Stitzer, 2006; Cropsey & Kristeller, 2003, 2005; Cropsey, Linker & Waite, 2008). High rates for smoking are likely the result of high co-morbidity of psychiatric and substance use disorders in this population (Cropsey et al., 2004, 2008) and are partly responsible for the high rates of other medical conditions observed among incarcerated individuals (Maruschak & Beck, 2001).

Suffice it to say, unhealthy people are focused on alleviating pain and suffering. Without treating these disorders, it is unlikely that self-medication, self-actualization, or manipulative, self-centered behaviors will stop.

2 Inadequate, Incompetent Services Reinforce Unhealthy Behaviors

Over the last two decades a defined set of principles for effective systems of care and treatment services has evolved from the research literature, referred to as "what works" or "evidence-based practices". A number of consensus panels confirm the value of these principles, and the science community continues to reinforce the importance of evidence-based practices. The principles appear in many different forms but deal with system issues as well as adequacy of clinical program, but generally they embrace the following three principles: 1) standardized risk and needs assessment tools are used to identify risk factors, followed by assigning offenders to appropriate programs and services to address their needs; 2) evidence-based treatments (e.g. cognitive behavioral therapy, motivational enhancement therapies, therapeutic communities) are offered; and 3) graduated sanctions and incentives (contingency management) are used to address compliance issues. A fourth, slowly evolving area, is that the working alliance between the offender and the agent of the state (i.e. correctional officer, probation officer, judge, etc.) is important to promoting improved outcomes through a supportative, empowering position (Taxman, 2008). In fact, as Moos (1976) raised the issues regarding whether the total institution nature of the correctional milieu provides an environment where offender change can occur. The punitive, churning policies of the past three decades are not the type of supportive, therapeutic environment that contributes to better outcomes. These evidence-based practices are widely disseminated through the National Institute of Corrections (NIC) (NIC, 2004), National Institute on Drug Abuse (NIDA) (Chandler et al., 2009; NIDA, 2006), and other common resources, as well as abundant research literature (Andrews & Bonta, 1998; Andrews, Bonta & Hoge, 1990; MacKenzie, 2000; Taxman, 1999). However, despite the consensus and wide dissemination, a tension exists between the research literature and practice. Consider the following:

Correctional Agencies are Slow to Adopt Evidence Based Practices. Recent surveys of the practices of correctional agencies has demonstrated that the average correctional agency adopts less than 5 of 15 evidence-based practices and treatments or to provide a system of offender process model to match offender to appropriate care (Friedmann, Taxman & Henderson, 2007; Henderson, Taxman & Young, 2008)[ii]. Even when adoption occurs (i.e. the agency indicates that they use the practice), it is not widely implemented across the system. An example is that 30 percent of the correctional agencies reported using a standardized risk assessment tool, but the risk tool was not used for more than half of the population (Taxman, Cropsey, Young & Wexler, 2007; Taxman, Perdoni & Harrison, 2007).

Correctional Services are Inadequate to Meet the Needs of Offenders. The sad reality is that when correctional agencies offer services, they are most often unlikely to meet the needs of the offender, and therefore unlikely to serve the goals of public health or safety. The National Criminal Justice Treatment Practices Survey documented the types of services and programs offered (in 2004-2005). Take substance abuse programs for adults, of which one-third of the male population and one-half of the females are likely to need intensive services to address substance dependency problems (see Belenko & Peugh, 2005). Yet, drug and alcohol education and outpatient counseling are the most prevalent services offered as the mainstream of substance abuse treatment. Three-quarters of prisons offer drug and alcohol education, as do 53% of community agencies, and 61% of jails. Just over half (55%) of prisons provide under 4 hours of group counseling per week, as do 47% of community agencies, and 60% of jails. For the most part, these services do not employ the recommended cognitive therapy and/or behavioral interventions. Nor do the services use manualized treatments or role playing that are noted as quality control measures. Intensive services—those that are time-intensive and involve various clinical stages of care—are more likely to reduce substance abuse disorders, but are infrequently offered (Taxman, Perdoni & Harrison, 2007). Instead of minimal low intensity services it is recommended that treatment services should be offered in more rigorous programs such as intensive outpatient (5 or more hours a week), therapeutic community, and drug treatment courts. These would all be more appropriate for the population given the severity of disorders. Twenty percent of prisons provide therapeutic communities, as do 26% of jails, and 3% of community correctional agencies.

Besides offering the inappropriate treatment programs, the dosage or length of services is generally too short to affect behavioral change. The average substance abuse education and/or treatment program in the U.S. is around 60 days which is a far shy from the recommended program length of 90 days or more. The 90 days plus has been found to be sufficient to change offender behavior based on the research literature (Hser et al., 2001; Hubbard et al., 1989; Simpson, Joe & Brown, 1997). The National Criminal Justice Treatment Practices (NCJTP) found that both adult and juvenile offenders are generally exposed to inadequate programs that are not structured to alter behavior (see Taxman, Perdoni & Harrison, 2007, for adults; Young, Dembo & Henderson, 2007, for youth). A therapeutic jurisprudence principle is that services should be offered that can ameliorate problem behaviors; otherwise the legal system should not mandate that offenders participate in services that offer a false pretense to promote behavioral change. If this principle was uphold, many of the substance abuse and mental health services would not meet this threshold. The all-too infrequent physical health services would also not be offered.

The capacity is too limited to influence the correctional culture as well as offender behavior. Not only did the NCJTP uncover that many services are inappropriate given the needs of offenders (Chandler et al., 2009), a major problem is the limited capacity to serve the population. In 2004-2005, drug treatment programs available to offenders could serve less than 9.2% of offenders on any given day, with the reach to offenders in the community much smaller. A small portion of the offender population receives an appropriate level of treatment, and low intensity programs dominate the available programs. For example, in prisons, close to 875,000 of the 1.2 million offenders in prisons need some form of clinical substance abuse treatment, but the actual number receiving care is estimated to be from 164,000 to 196,000. In jails, around 531,000 of the 745,765 inmates in U.S. jails are in need of some level of treatment services on any given day, but only about 71,586 (14%) of jail inmates have access to treatment daily, with the annual participation rate ranges from 131,000 to 160,500. The access to services is even more limited in the probation and parole systems. Of the estimated 4.2 million offenders in community correctional settings that are in need of clinical treatment services, around 213,600 offenders can access treatment services (5%) with an annual flow of 301,000 to 362,000 offenders (Taxman & Perdoni, 2009). To illustrate the gap in appropriate levels of care, an estimated 25,300 probationers/parolees complete high intensity services annually as compared to the more than 4 million that need that level of care.

Despite the overwhelming need for services as indicated by the unmet health needs, society, the criminal justice system, and correctional institutions do not recognize the role of service provider (Taxman, Henderson, & Belenko, in press). Studies have shown that the availability of and access to treatment while involved in the justice system is minimal. The previously discussed National Criminal Justice Treatment Practices Survey furnishes a wealth of information on the nature and availability of treatment services across all correctional settings. These findings show that substance abuse treatment services are sparse, and when they are provided, they tend to be inadequate for dealing with the severity of the problems presented. More importantly, the survey findings show that intensive treatment services are rarely offered and are available to a lower proportion of offenders. To a large extent the survey did point out the obvious that the punitive policies of the past have negatively affected the ability to offer quality services that can improve health and well-being while simultaneously reducing recidivism. As shown in a series of articles on organizational factors that affect adoption of evidence based practices among correctional agencies (see Taxman, Henderson, & Belenko, in press, and related articles in a special edition of *Drug and Alcohol Dependence* to be published in the summer of 2009), attention to the correctional culture, skill sets of staff, state and federal policy, interagency collaborations, and other factors must be addressed to turn the tide to providing services that have been shown to be effective in the adoption of evidence-based practices.

3: A Tipping Point is needed to Advance Productive Behaviors

Marginal services, inadequate access, and a system driven to punish characterize the current correctional environment even with the well-intended, well-focused efforts undertaken by many individuals and agencies to improve the quality of services and programs offered. Part of the adoption-related issues is affected by the need to reorient the culture of correctional agencies away from a devotion to punishment, standards of conduct that even law-abiding citizens may not be able to meet (i.e. 15 or so standard conditions of probation), and therefore promotion of churning through the system, and the attitude (propagated by resource constraints) that "some services" for more offenders are better than no services. Gladwell's "tipping point" suggests that a critical point must be reached to create a force to overcome brick walls or constraining factors that prevent a change to occur (2000). This notion of a "tipping point" suggests that organizationally attention needs to be given to the issues of capacity and nature of the existing services. That is, the low prevalence of substance abuse treatment services (less than 10% of offenders a day can access services) or other types of services (Taxman, Perdoni & Harrison, 2007), coupled with the inadequate nature of these services suggests that change cannot occur until more momentum is devoted to the issues of delivering health-changing care. The notion of a tipping point is that there must be sufficient energy and "space" devoted to service provision within the environment. The tipping point would be to convert from a current security and monitoring culture (where few programs are offered) to an emphasis on a therapeutic milieu where offenders gain needed skills and health care to reduce unhealthy behaviors, to address risk factors, and to become a productive member of society.

PUBLIC HEALTH IS PUBLIC SAFETY

Modest changes of adding a few more programs or services are unlikely to make the great strides in reducing risk factors that promulgate criminal behavior and continued involvement in the justice system or to create the synergy to advance a focus on improving the health and well-being of one of society's unhealthiest members (offenders, their families, and communities). Reaffirming that rehabilitation is the goal of sentencing is unlikely to make this large shift in focus and attention. Nor, will a continued commitment to adopt evidence-based practices and treatments when resources become available. The research literature has reinforced that adoption of evidence-based practices is a long-term endeavor. While it is recognized that organizations are slow to shift their focus and attention and the momentum for organizational change is difficult to maintain given the socio-political environment, the challenge is that the shift must not be incremental but rather swift and monumental. Health must be a primary mission of the correctional agencies since it serves to promote safety and well-being. This transformation would recognize that correctional agencies are part of the family of the "helping" professions that includes education, somatic health care, and mental health care.

The question is how we get there. The Institute of Medicine, in their recent quality chasm series, documents a series of steps to improve the quality of health care for mental and substance abuse conditions (Institute of Medicine, 2006). By adapting the Institute of Medicine's aims for high-quality health care, the correctional setting would change their focus from a punitive setting to focusing on the needs of the offenders. The Table below articulates these principles and adapts them for the correctional settings.

THE SIX AIMS OF HIGH-QUALITY HEALTH CARE

Safe-avoiding injuries to patients from the care that is intended to help them. The focus should be on services and programs that will not create "false hopes" of recovery or advancement but rather provides an important effort to address unhealthy behaviors that result in negative care.

Effective-providing services based on scientific knowledge to all who could benefit and refraining from providing services to those not likely to benefit. Using the evidence-based practices and treatment literature will advance the use of programs and services that are focused on risk reduction and healthy behavior change.

Patient-centered-providing care that is respectful of and responsive to individual patient preferences, needs, and values and ensuring that patient values guide all clinical decisions. For the correctional system, this would involve a movement away from authoritarian models of care to more patient-centered, shared decision making models of care.

Timely-reducing waits and sometimes harmful delays for both those who receive and those who give care. This tenets focus on providing services not as a "crisis" point (i.e. suicide, critical care, etc.) but focusing attention on prevention and immediate attention to promote healthy behaviors.

Efficient-avoiding waste, in particular of equipment, supplies, ideas, and energy. Like any system, the focus needs to be on efficiency and in this case, efficiency may mean that the delivery of "correctional services" is offered in other settings such as primary care centers. Co-location with other organizations would require correctional staff to work on issues of efficient delivery of services rather than placing the burden on offenders to acquire their own services.

Equitable-providing care that does not vary in quality because of personal characteristics such as gender, ethnicity, geographic location, and socioeconomic status.

The emphasis on public health for justice-involved individuals will require fundamental changes in the nature and structure of services. To move this agenda along, three critical steps should be taken.

1. Measure success to include prevention of unhealthy behaviors. The focus on proximal measures of improved well-being at both the individual level and at the population level will alter how the correctional agency is evaluated by the public, and change the expectations of outcomes. For example, an emphasis on reduced drug use and improved mental health status will improve violation rates. Additionally, a focus on reducing STDs will create individuals that are unlikely to spread infectious diseases or require additional care due to diseases. Defining a set of measures will reshape the goals of the agency to focus on these efforts. Besides serving a symbolic message, the articulation of new measures of success will resonate that the agency's goals are shifting. Along with the provision of these services, this will serve to alter the culture.

2. Staff for correctional agencies should dramatically shift to include those from the "helping professions" including nurses, social workers, and health educators that can help offenders understand how to care for themselves, as well as how to become managers of their own behavior. Existing correctional staff of probation, parole, correctional and other security based staff will benefit from the co-existence of the helping professions. This will change the focus to focus to principles of patient-centered care, and the notion that behavior change consists of incremental steps. While physical space is always an issue, the emphasis on co-locating correctional facilities with other routine care facilities can shift the environment. This is probably most easily accomplished in the community, where probation and parole could be joined with primary care centers, hospitals, community clinics, community college educational centers, and so on. Enhancing the staff for correctional facilities will result in more collaboration and integrated services that have been found to improve adoption of evidence-based practices (see Lehman, Fletcher, Wexler & Melnik, in press). The goal should be to create a tipping point with staffing

where the infusion of helping professions will focus the attention on providing care, then merely security and control issues. Given that the NCJTP found that most correctional agencies have less than 5 percent of their staff in the helping professions, a six-fold increase would shift the agencies focus.

3. Use organizational incentives for correctional agencies to transform their attention to addressing educational, health, and vocation deficits by providing additional funding for those agencies that are focused on new types of performance. Organizational incentives are well recognized as a tool to change the culture of organizations by reaffirming the values that improving the health and well being of offenders matter. McLellan, Kemp, Brooks and Carise (2008) recently found that a pay-for-performance system used in outpatient programs in Delaware improved utilization of program slots by nearly 100% and improved patient participation in treatment by over 30% due to the financial incentives provided to providers. The incentives can be shaped around achievement of target goals, much like they have been used in substance abuse treatment settings where organizational incentives are used to improve length of stay in drug treatment programs. The incentives here could model the United Kingdom's National Health Care System where the emphasis is on prevention, and clinics that achieve greater utilization of prevention services and reduced chronic care are offered incentives such as enhanced resources and recognition. This model is critical to altering the mindset of correctional agencies and reinforcing that the societal expectation is that punishment systems will result in healthier behavior (instead of contributing to unhealthier and more criminal behavior).

These steps will advance the notion that correctional agencies are part of the circle of helping agencies designed to reduce the risk factors that promote unhealthy behaviors. The Surgeon General's 2010 Healthy People is focused on risk factors that promote disease. The two overarching goals of the Healthy People 2010 are to increase "years and quality of life" by eliminating racial and ethnic disparities in health. As shown above, offenders fit appropriately into the goals but the report does not specifically mention the need to address the unmet needs of offenders. A reorientation where correctional agencies are service providers will ensure that larger societal initiatives (such as health care reform) recognize that the offender population, which is no longer a small subset of the population, is included in the total initiative. This will only occur by moving forward with a revamping of the mission to be oriented toward public health.

To this end, Catherine Gallagher and I formed the *Network for Justice Health* (http://njh.thelloydsociety.org/index.php) devoted to addressing the unmet health needs of offenders, families, and communities. The aims are to facilitate and coordinate the synthesis and open-access availability of knowledge, and to move towards evidence-based guidelines for providing care to this medically complex and typically underserved population. The Network will: 1) Provide practitioners, policy makers and researchers with free, web-based interaction tools to disseminate research evidence on key clinical and organizational issues; 2) Collaborate with Cochrane and Campbell Collaborations to ensure state-of-the-art techniques to develop knowledge about effective clinical and system practices; 3) Identify effective interventions in non-justice settings that may be adapted and imported into the justice setting; 4) Design mapping techniques of knowledge and gaps; 5) prioritize areas for knowledge development; and, 6) Develop training methodologies for policy makers, practitioners, researchers, and students on how to incorporate evidence into decision-making. An open invitation is extended to join The Network for Justice Health as part of an international collaboratory of researchers, policy makers, and practitioners to pursue public health goals for offenders, their families, and their communities. The Network for Justice Health focuses on the notion that health care is part of the solution to shift the focus of corrections from sentencing goals to societal goals of justice, well-being, and citizenship.

REFERENCES

Andrews, D.A. & Bonta, J. (1998). *Psychology of Criminal Conduct (2ndEdition)*. Cincinnati, OH: Anderson Publishing Co.

Andrews, D.A. Bonta, J. & Hoge, R.D. (1990). Classification for effective rehabilitation. *Criminal Justice and Behavior, 17,* 19-52.

Baillargeon, J., Black, S.A., Pulvino, J. & Dunn, K. (2000). The disease profile of Texas prison inmates. *Annals of Epidemiology, 10,* 74-80.

Belenko, S. & Peugh, J. (2005). Estimating drug treatment needs among state prison inmates. *Drug and Alcohol Dependence, 77,* 269-281.

Binswanger, I.A., Stern, M.F., Deyo, R.A., Heagerty, P.J., Cheadle, A., Elmore, J.G. & Koepsell, T.D. (2007). Release from prison-a high risk of death for former inmates. *New England Journal of Medicine, 356,* 157-165.

Center For Disease Control. (2002). *Viral Hepatitis and the Criminal Justice System.* Atlanta, GA: U.S. Department of Health and Human Services, CDC.

Center For Disease Control. (2005). *Hospitalization by First Diagnosis, All Ages: U.S., 2002-2004.* Atlanta, GA: U.S. Department of Health and Human Services, CDC.

Center For Disease Control. (2006a). *Reported Tuberculosis in the United States, 2005.* Atlanta, GA: U.S. Department of Health and Human Services, CDC.

Center For Disease Control. (2006b). *Sexually Transmitted Disease Surveillance 2005 Supplement.* Atlanta, GA: U.S. Department of Health and Human Services, CDC.

Center For Disease Control. (2008). *Hepatitis C Fact Sheet.* Atlanta, GA: U.S. Department of Health and Human Services, CDC.

Chandler, R.K., Fletcher, B.W. & Volkow, N.D. (2009). Treating drug abuse and addiction in the criminal justice system: Improving public health and safety. *Journal of American Medical Association, 301,* 183-190.

Cropsey, K.L, Eldridge, G. D. & Ladner, T. (2004). Smoking among female prisoners: An ignored public health epidemic. *Addictive Behaviors, 29,* 425-431.

Cropsey, K.L., Eldridge, G.D., Weaver, M.F., Villalobos, G.C. & Stitzer, M.L. (2006). Expired carbon monoxide levels in self-reported smokers and non-smokers in prison, *Nicotine & Tobacco Research, 8,* 653-659.

Cropsey, K.L. & Kristeller, J.L. (2003). Motivational factors related to quitting smoking among prisoners during a smoking ban. *Addictive Behaviors, 28,* 1081-1093.

Cropsey, K.L. & Kristeller, J.L. (2005). The effects of a prison smoking ban on smoking behavior and withdrawal symptoms. *Addictive Behaviors, 30,* 589-594.

Cropsey, K.L., Linker, J.A. & Waite, D.E. (2008). An analysis of racial and sex differences for smoking among adolescents in a juvenile correctional center, *Drug and Alcohol Dependence, 92,* 156-163.

Feinstein, R., Lampkin, A., Lorish, C.D., Klerman, L.V., Maisiak, R. & Oh, K. (1998). Medical status of adolescents at time of admission to a juvenile detention center. *Journal of Adolescent Health, 22,* 190-196.

Friedmann, P.D., Taxman, F.S. & Henderson, C. (2007). Evidence-based treatment practices for drug-involved adults in the criminal justice system. *Journal of Substance Abuse Treatment, 32,* 267-277.

Gallagher, C.A. & Dobrin, A. (2006). Deaths in juvenile justice residential facilities. *Journal of Adolescent Health, 38,* 662-668.

Gallagher, C. A., Dobrin, A. & Douds, A.S. (2007). A national overview of reproductive health care services for girls in juvenile justice residential facilities. *Women's Health Issues, 17,* 217-226.

Gladwell, M. (2000). *The Tipping Point.* Lebanon, IN: Little, Brown and Company.

Glynn, M. & Rhodes, P. (2005). *Estimated HIV Prevalence in the United States at the End of 2003.* Paper presented at the National HIV Prevention Conference, Atlanta, Georgia.

Harlow, C.W. (2003). *Education and Correctional Populations.* Washington, DC: Bureau of Justice Statistics.

Henderson, C., Taxman, F.S. & Young, D. (2008). A Rasch model analysis of evidence-based treatment practices used in the criminal justice system. *Drug and Alcohol Dependence, 93,* 163–175.

Hser, Y. Grella, C.E., Hubbard, R.L., Hsiesh, S.C., Fletcher, B.W., Brown, B.S. & Anglin, M.D. (2001). An evaluation of drug treatment for adolescents in 4 US Cities. *Archives of General Psychiatry, 58,* 689-695.

Hubbard, R. Marsden, M., Rachal, J., Harwod, H., Cavanaugh, E. & Ginzburg, H. (1989). *Drug Abuse Treatment: A National Study of Effectiveness.* Chapel Hill, NC: University of North Carolina Press.

Institute of Medicine. (2006). *Improving the Quality of Health Care for Mental and Substance-Use Conditions.* Washington, DC: The National Archives Press.

James, D.J. & Glaze, L.E. (2006). *Mental Health Problems of Prisons and Jail Inmates.* Washington, DC: Bureau of Justice Statistics.

Karberg, J.C. & James, D.J. (2002). *Substance Dependence, Abuse, and Treatment of Jail Inmates, 2002.* Washington, DC: Bureau of Justice Statistics.

Lehman, W., Fletcher, B., Wexler, H. & Melnick, G. (in press). Organizational factors and collaboration and integration activities in criminal justice and drug abuse treatment agencies. *Drug and Alcohol Dependence.*

MacKenzie, D.L. (2000). Evidence-based corrections: Identifying what works. *Crime and Delinquency, 46,* 457-471.

Maruschak, L.M. (2007). *HIV in Prisons, 2002.* Washington, DC: Bureau of Justice Statistics.

Maruschak, L.M. & Beck, A.L. (2001). *Medical Problems of Inmates, 1997.* Washington, DC: Bureau of Justice Statistics.

McLellan, A., Kemp, J., Brooks, A. & Carise, D. (2008). Improving public addiction treatment through performance contracting: The Delaware experiment. *Health Policy, 87,* 296-308.

Mental Health America. (2008). *Prevalence of Mental Disorders Among Children in the Juvenile Justice System.* Available online: http://www1.nmha.org/children/justjuv/prevalence.cfm

Moos, R.H. (1976). Evaluating and changing community settings. *American Journal of Community Psychology, 4,* 313-326.

Mumola, C.J. (1997). *Substance Abuse and Treatment, State and Federal Prisoners.* Washington, DC: Bureau of Justice Statistics.

National Institute of Corrections. (2004). *Implementing Evidence-based Practice in Community Corrections: The Principles of Effective Interventions.* Washington, DC: Community Corrections Division.

National Institute on Drug Abuse. (2006). *Principles of Drug Abuse Treatment for Criminal Justice Populations: A Research-Based Guide.* Washington, DC: National Institutes of Health.

National Institute of Mental Health. (2008). *Statistics.* Available online: http://www.nimh.nih.gov/health/topics/statistics/index.shtml.

Otto, R.K., Greenstein, J.J., Johnson, M.K. & Friedman, R.M. (1992). Prevalence of mental disorders among youth in the juvenile justice system. In J.J. Cocozza (Ed.), *Responding to the Mental Health Needs of Youth in the Juvenile Justice System* (pp. 7-48). Seattle, WA: National Coalition for the Mentally Ill in the Criminal Justice System.

Sabol, W.J., Minton, T.D. & Harrison, P.M. (2007). *Prison and Jail Inmates at Midyear 2006.* Washington, DC: Bureau of Justice Statistics.

Simpson, D.D., Joes, G.W. & Brown, B.S. (1997). Treatment retention and follow-up outcomes in the Drug Abuse Treatment Outcome Study (DATOS). *Psychology of Addictive Behaviors, 11,* 294-307.

Substance Abuse and Mental Health Services Administration. (2006). *Results from the 2005 National Survey on Drug Use and Health: National Findings.* Rockville, MD: Office of Applied Studies

Taxman, F.S. (1999). Unraveling "what works" for offenders in substance abuse treatment services. *National Drug Court Institute Review, 2,* 93-134.

Taxman, F.S. (2008). No illusion, offender and organizational change in Maryland's proactive community supervision model. *Criminology & Public Policy, 7,* 275-302.

Taxman, F.S., Cropsey, K.L., Gallagher, C. & Perdoni, M. (2009). *Size and Scope of the Correctional Population in the US.* Working Paper at George Mason University.

Taxman, F.S., Cropsey, K.L., Young, D. & Wexler, H. (2007). Screening, assessment, and referral practices in adult correctional settings: a national perspective. *Criminal Justice and Behavior, 34,* 1216-1234.

Taxman, F.S., Henderson, C.E. & Belenko, S. (in press). Integration of drug treatment in correctional agencies: Organizational factors. *Drug and Alcohol Dependence.*

Taxman, F.S. & Perdoni, M.L. (2009). Considering Options for Handling Offenders: Applying Risk-Need Concepts in Practice. Under Review.

Taxman, F.S., Perdoni, M.L. & Harrison, L.D. (2007). Drug treatment services for adult offenders: The state of the state. *Journal of Substance Abuse Treatment, 32,* 239-254.

Taxman, F.S., Young, D.W., Wiersema, B., Rhodes, A. & Mitchell, S. (2007). The national criminal justice treatment practices survey: multilevel survey methods and procedures. *Journal of Substance Abuse Treatment, 32,* 225-238.

Teplin, L.A., Abram, K.M., McClelland, G.M., Dulcan, M.K. & Mericle, A.A. (2002). Psychiatric disorders in youth in juvenile detention. *Archives of General Psychiatry, 59,* 1133-1143.

Teplin, L.A., Abram, K.M., McClelland, G.M., Mericle, A.A., Dulcan, M.K. & Washburn, J.J. (2006). *Psychiatric Disorders of Youth in Detention.* Washington, DC: Office of Juvenile Justice and Delinquency Prevention.

Thomas, J.C., Levandowski, B.A., Isler, M.R., Torrone, E. & Wilson, G. (2008). Incarceration and sexually transmitted infections: A neighborhood perspective. *Journal of Urban Health, 85,* 90-99.

Thomas, J.C. & Torrone, E. (2006). Incarceration as forced migration: effects on selected community health outcomes. *American Journal of Public Health, 96,* 1762-1765.

Wilbur, M.B., Marani, J.E., Appugliese, D., Woods, R., Siegel, J.A., Cabral, H.J. & Frank, D.A. (2007). Socioemotional effects of fathers' incarceration on low-income, urban, school-aged children. *Pediatrics, 120,* 678-685.

Young, D.W., Dembo, R. & Henderson, C.E. (2007). A national survey of substance abuse treatment for juvenile offenders. *Journal of Substance Abuse Treatment, 32,* 255-266.

ENDNOTES

[i] Acknowledgments: We appreciate the contributions of Catherine Gallagher, Kate Zinsser, Jennifer Lerch, Carolyn Watson, Anne Rhodes, Karen Cropsey, Anne Douds, Kimberly Mehlman-Orozco to this essay.

[ii] The components included in this inventory of evidence based practices and treatments are based on the research literature and consensus among scholars and practitioners. The list includes: (1) standardized risk assessment; (2) standardized substance abuse assessment and treatment matching, (3) use of techniques to engage and retain clients in treatment; (4) use of therapeutic community, cognitive-behavioral, or other standardized treatment orientation; (5) a comprehensive approach to treatment and ancillary needs; (6) addressing co-occurring disorders; (7) involvement of family in treatment; (8) a planned treatment duration of 90 days or longer; (9) integration of multiple systems to optimize care and outcomes; (10) continuing care or aftercare; (11) use of drug testing in treatment; (12) use of graduated sanctions and (13) incentives to encourage progress; (12) availability of qualified treatment staff, (13) assessment of treatment outcomes; (14) use of role play in treatment sessions; and (15) small group treatment size (i.e., small client to counselor ratio). Note that the NCJTP created an index to define adoption (Friedman, Taxman & Henderson, 2007).

REVAMPING THE MISSION: OBSTACLES AND ISSUES

DORIS L. MACKENZIE

As I finished Taxman and Ressler's essay on "Revamping the Correctional Mission" I was left with a major question: How could we make this happen? The authors ask us to re-examine the incarceration binge and our crime control policies. Instead of continuing to pass more draconian laws resulting in sending more people to prison and keeping them in longer we should consider taking a public health perspective on public safety. They argue correctional agencies have problems -- they are slow to adopt evidence-based practices, services are inadequate and the capacity to address the needs of offenders is limited. According to them, the safe, effective, patient-centered, timely, efficient, and equitable aims of high quality health care will go a long way towards addressing the problems in our correctional system. Success in this endeavor will take fundamental changes in the nature and structure of services. The proposal is ambitious. As I said at the start my interest is in how this could be made to happen. However, from the beginning it behooves us to be aware of the obstacles that will be in the path of successful implementation.

WILL THIS SELL IN PEORIA?

I want to start by examining what I see as the obstacles to this proposal and I see many. I don't want to throw a wet blanket on the suggestion; however, any acceptance of these ideas must be done with an awareness of the difficulties that will be confronted as people try to implement the proposal. I see several areas of concern. In the following paragraphs I discuss the type of hurtles supporters of the proposal with have to overcome. Overall my concerns relate to public perspectives about criminals, simplistic ideas, sound bites and buzz words. So I begin by expressing my concerns and the reasons the authors' ideas will have a tough uphill battle to even be heard let alone be accepted by policy makers and the public. On the other hand, I am excited about the proposal, many of the ideas they espouse are not just limited to a public health perspective, many practitioners and researchers who have been supportive of providing services and rehabilitation for offenders will agree with the type of changes the authors want to see occur (see for instance, Clear 2007: MacKenzie 2006; Andrews and Bonta 2003).

One of my first concerns is with the complexity of the idea. This is not a program that will easily be grasped by policymakers and the public. Traditionally, many popular criminal justice ideas promoted by policy makers – at least those popular with the public and policy makers are simplistic ideas easily captured by media sound bites and buzzwords. Take for instance the correctional boot camps (MacKenzie & Styve-Armstrong 2004). After the first camps opened, the idea rapidly spread across the nation, first in corrections and then for at-risk children, and now there are exercise boot camps, boot camps for the obese and more. The correctional boot camps "felt right" to policymakers. Some remembered how their own experiences in military boot camp changed them for the better. They forgot after they completed military boot camp, they had years in the military when they had paid employment and time to practice the skills they had learned. Others viewed boot camps as effective because they thought the programs would instill discipline in young unruly men. For various reasons people supported the idea of correctional boot camps.

It was not only that people believed such camps would change young peoples' lives but also the idea of the camps could be captured in sound bites for the media. I was researching the boot camps in the early 1990s and I could hardly keep up with the media requests for information and interviews. The camps made great media. Drill sergeants confronting inmates, drill and ceremony, obedient responses to requests, rigorous early morning exercise regimes, and uncomfortable living conditions made great visuals for TV. As I repeated many times in these interviews, research did not demonstrate success in reducing recidivism. Given the popularity of the programs, some correctional administrators used the programs to obtain money to support rehabilitation programs within the daily schedule of activities. Others looked for goals that could be achieved even if the programs didn't reduce recidivism (MacKenzie and Souryal 1995). For example, New York State used the programs as an early release mechanism for drug-involved offenders. Certainly, the media attention was paramount in influencing the rapid increase in the number of boot camps.

Buzz words are popular in corrections and they play well in correctional policy. Words like "boot camps," "war on drugs," and "three-strikes" capture simple concepts that can be easily repeated, are media friendly and demonstrate a tough-on-crime perspective. Politicians seem to believe they need a quick and easy summary of the newest fad for being tough on crime. The complexity of the ideas combined with the lack of buzz words and media attractiveness (e.g., sound bites) means this proposal will have difficulty when it is presented to the public. Can this idea be "revamped" to include buzz words and simple sound bites? This would greatly improve the chances this proposal will be accepted and acted upon.

"CRIMINALS ARE DIFFERENT FROM ME AND MINE"

The proposal will also have difficulty because it appears soft on crime. Many people seem to believe: "Criminals are different from me and mine." This statement reflects the beliefs of many of the policymakers and public. They see themselves as the "good" guys who will not impacted by strict laws. Those "others" deserve long prison sentences. There is little sympathy for the young people whose lives are so negatively influenced by convictions and long sentences. With little evidence to support the idea, many were willing to accept the notion of young "super predators" who, according to Dilulio (1994) grew up with no socialization and presented serious dangers for the community. Policymakers are fearful of showing compassion for offenders and delinquents because they would be accused of being "soft" on crime. How we can change these attitudes so people are willing to view public health as public safety?

I have always believed part of the draconian perspective on punishing offenders in the United States reflects a type of racism. The increased punishments have fallen most dramatically on minority populations. Some inner city neighborhoods have been decimated (Clear 2007). In some urban areas, the majority of young men have spent time in prison; their lives are negatively impacted from then on. It might be "malign neglect," not overt racism but we should have known who were going to be the recipients of the increased punishments (Tonry 1995). In any case, I believe many policy makers and the public view prisons and prisoners as something they and their loved ones will never have to encounter. In their views, the punishments are deserved and they are given to "the others"— the dangerous ones, members of the underclass who need to be controlled and contained (Feeley and Simon 1992). One wonders what public outrage would result if we were incarcerating a comparable number of white middle class boys.

The proposal to move correctional agencies into the circle of helping agencies requires a major change in the public's views of criminals, crime and corrections. It will not be easy to sell this idea to the community. Furthermore, it assumes the public will accept the new concept of correctional agencies as part of helping agencies and such a change will have direct benefit for the public. It will necessitate a change from a "we-them" mentality to an "us" mentality. No longer will offenders be considered and treated as dangerous outsiders; instead they will be viewed as people with health problems. This will be a monumental change in thinking.

FIRST STEPS

If the problem of persuading people to accept the idea of viewing public safety as a public health problem can be overcome then we will need several things to occur in the short term. First, to my knowledge, no prospective well-thought out study has been done examining the impact of the proposed change in perspective. A rigorous research study demonstrating the effectiveness of this program would go a long way toward its acceptance. It will be important to show the proposed emphasis on public health had a significant impact on society well being and costs.

In this public health scenario, administrators will have to be willing to be held responsible for outcomes and many administrators are reluctant to accept such responsibility. This was a strongly held view during the time after Martinson's (1974) article lead to the mantra of the "nothing works" philosophy. Prison administrators argued they should not be held accountable for outcomes because correctional programs were not effective in changing offenders. Many agreed with Logan's (1992) assertions that prisons should be responsible for "well-kept" prisoners -- keeping them inside, keeping them busy and keeping them healthy. If nothing worked to change delinquents and offenders then prison administrators and staff could not be held accountable for what they did in the future.

Despite the fact we now have evidence to show correctional programs and strategies can effectively reduce recidivism, many correctional authorities balk at being held responsible for the outcomes of their charges (MacKenzie 2006). It is shocking how little data is available about prisons, juvenile facilities, delinquents and prisoners, particularly in this time of computerization. For example, we did a national study of juvenile correctional facilities and studied approximately 50 facilities with over 5,000 juveniles (MacKenzie, Wilson, Armstrong and Gover 2001). When we asked facility administrators what happened to the juveniles after they were released, they did not know. Most did not know if the youth returned to school or their families or began working. A surprising number had no idea whether the children were later returned to a facility for a new adjudication or were convicted as adults. One wonders how they designed programs within the facilities if they knew so little about the future of the youth and had no feedback on whether they were having an impact on the young people in the future. Transforming correctional agencies by using new organization incentives will require the facilities to collect the type of data that will demonstrate the effectiveness of the new policies.

The proposal will require the collection of data on the public health of those admitted to facilities and follow up data on the outcomes. Not only will prison administrators have to begin accepting responsibility for outcomes but also policymakers in legislatures and at the highest levels of correctional decision making will have to provide support for administrators to obtain the data necessary to determine the level of health problems and also changes that occur as the result of programming to reduce health problems. In the study of juvenile facilities we conducted, facility administrators were shocked when we asked them about the outcomes of the youth, they did not know how they could obtain the data. I think they were correct. Collecting such data entails a considerable commitment of time and money. This is a problem at the highest levels of decision making and must be a commitment to cover the costs incurred. If this proposal is accepted, there will be substantial costs to obtaining sufficient data on health and health outcomes.

The latest buzz words in corrections seem to be "evidence-based." Everyone claims to be using evidence-based programming, yet what they mean exactly by these words is not entirely clear. Researchers have coined the term to refer to programs that have been studied with sufficiently rigorous research and enough research has been completed to provide evidence the programs are effective in achieving the desired outcome (MacKenzie 2001). What policy makers mean by research often differs tremendously from what social science researchers mean by the term. Many policy makers are trained a lawyers. The term research is used very different from its use in social science. Legal research examines past precedents and opinions of authorities. Anecdotal information can be critical is demonstrating support for a position. Law is adversarial. Legal researchers search for support for their side of the argument. This is very different from social science where scientists collect empirical data in order to understand some phenomenal. Social science research is designed to minimize the influence of subjective factors and maximize objectivity. Decision makers will have to understand the premise of this proposal and the importance of social science research showing that punishment systems can result in healthier behavior "instead of contributing to unhealthier and more criminal behavior."

REVAMPING THE MISSION OF CORRECTIONS

As I first read this proposal I thought: "These people are dreaming." The proposal is too ambitious! How can we make such a dramatic change in people's perspectives? But I know these authors – they are not just dreamers – they are movers and shakers. They can make this happen. Certainly there are many hurtles to overcome if this new perspective is to have an impact. On the other hand, there are many people including researchers, policy makers, and correctional personnel who will gladly support a new vision of corrections. The old version is not working. Perhaps the idea of a "Network for Justice Health" proposed by the authors will be the instrument to educate people about the potential for a new perspective and how it would improve all our lives.

REFERENCES

Andrews, D.A. & Bonta, J. (2003). *The Psychology of Criminal Conduct.* Cincinnati, OH: Anderson Publishing Company.

Clear, T.R. (2007). *Imprisoning Communities: How Mass Incarceration Makes Disadvantaged Neighborhoods Worse.* Oxford, UK: Oxford University Press.

DiIulio, J. (1994). The question of Black crime. *The Public Interest,* Fall, p.3.

Feeley, M.M. & Simon, J. (1992). The new penology: Notes on the emerging strategy of corrections and its implications. *Criminology. 30,* 449-474.

Logan, C.H. (1992). Well kept: Comparing quality of confinement in private and public prisons. *The Journal of Criminal Law and Criminology, 83,* 577-613.

MacKenzie, D.L. (2006). *What Works in Corrections? Reducing the Criminal Activities of Offenders and Delinquents.* Cambridge, UK: Cambridge Press.

MacKenzie, D.L. (2005). The importance of using scientific evidence to make decisions about correctional programming. *Criminology & Public Policy,* 4(2), 249-258.

MacKenzie, D.L. 2001. Corrections and sentencing in the 21st century: Evidence-based corrections and sentencing. *The Prison Journal,* 81(3), 299-312.

MacKenzie, D.L. & Armstrong, G.S. (Eds.), (2004). *Correctional Boot Camps: Military Basic Training as a Model for Corrections.* Thousand Oaks, CA: Sage Publications.

MacKenzie, D. L. & Souryal, C. (1995). A "Machiavellian" perspective on the development of boot camp prisons: A debate. University of Chicago Roundtable. Chicago, IL: University of Chicago Press.

MacKenzie, D.L., Wilson, D.B., Armstrong, G.S., & Gover, A.R. (2001). The impact of boot camps and traditional institutions on juvenile residents: Perception, adjustment and change. *Journal of Research in Crime and Delinquency,* 38(3), 279-313.

Martinson, R. (1974). What works? Questions and answers about prison reform. *Public Interest,* 10, 22-54.

Tonry, M. (1995). *Malign Neglect: Race, Crime, and Punishment in America.* N.Y.: Oxford Univ. Press.

Improving the Health of Current and Former Inmates: What Matters Most?

Michael Massoglia
Jason Schnittker

We are delighted to respond to the thoughtful and important essay by Taxman and Ressler (T&R hereafter). Against the backdrop of the expansion of the penal system, the risk to health posed by incarceration is an important issue that has received surprisingly little attention. The essay by T&R helps to shed light on the issue and proposes some compelling policy solutions. It also brings considerable reform-minded passion to the debate.

T&R offer an overview of the health needs of current inmates and the capacity of correctional agencies and institutions to service those needs. It is clear that inmates have unique health-care needs and that many correctional institutions are woefully underprepared to address those needs. T&R note that even when penal institutions have active health care programs, the quality of those programs is often inadequate. T&R encourage policy makers to improve the quality of care in our nation's prisons and jails. And we agree with T&R's central thesis: our prisons and jails could do better.

Yet we also believe the problem is more complex and that this complexity makes it unclear how best to promote inmate health and, ultimately, who is responsible for the health of inmates. T&R's essay begins by emphasizing the inadequacies of prison health care, but then quickly segues into the quality of the American health care system in general. This progression is important to appreciate, as we believe it elides some important distinctions. We believe the quality of prison health care may be less than the quality of health care in the United States more generally, but it is also the case that the quality of health care in the U.S. suffers because of the large and growing population of uninsured and underinsured persons. This makes issues surrounding health care quality perhaps less important than simple health care access, especially among former inmates. This does not make the reform of prison health care any less important, but it does suggest that improving the health of current and former inmates requires much more than simply improving the quality of services provided while behind bars.

This distinction can be pushed further. In our research, we find that incarceration has very different short and long-term effects on health (Massoglia 2008, Massoglia and Schnittker 2009; Schnittker and John 2007). In our work, we attempt to specify the causal effect of incarceration on health using a variety of methods. Causality is important to this debate insofar as it is important to understand what kinds of illnesses prisoners bring with them to the institution, what illnesses they acquire while serving time, and what kinds of risks they face following release. We find that incarceration has a lasting negative effect on health, irrespective of initial risk, but that this effect is largely driven by what happens following release. While behind bars, an inmate's health often improves.

Although at odds with some of the ideas discussed in T&R, this finding is not all that surprising once we consider where inmates tend to come from. As T&R notes, prisoners tend to come from unusually disadvantaged backgrounds, with respect to family, economic resources, neighborhoods, and health care. Relative to these circumstances, the prison environment is, in some ways, an improvement. Incarceration provides, at a minimum, the basic necessitates for good health, including nutritious meals, a warm and covered place to sleep, and, in most cases, the opportunity for regular exercise. The prison environment also provides reasonable protection. Homicide, a leading cause of premature mortality among African-American men, is lower in institutional settings than in many African-American communities. Furthermore, while not completely absent from the prison environment, drug and alcohol use is usually much more difficult to sustain within prison than outside.

In addition, of course, inmates are provided with health care, which, by statute and legal mandates, must be commensurate with that provided in the general community. As T&R argue, the quality of this care leaves much to be desired—it is not clear if prison health care is always commensurate with community standards. Yet relative to what many inmates had before the health care available in prison is, in many respects, an improvement. Many inmates had little or no regular care prior to incarceration. In addition, the care provided in prison may be more comprehensive than what they experienced before in the sense that inmates are evaluated for a variety of health problems as part of ordinary prison intake, rather than for presenting complaints, as would be the case in a typical outpatient physician visit. T&R focus on institutional barriers to quality improvement, but it is not entirely clear whether low-quality care in prison is the result of the institution or the population being treated. As T&R make clear, inmates have unusually high rates of infectious disease and psychiatric problems. Inmates are also unusual in their high levels of comorbidity. The treatment of highly comorbid conditions is difficult in even the best health care facilities.

In any event, improving the quality of prison care will do little to improve the post-release environment. We believe the larger problem with respect to inmate health lies with their poor reintegration prospects. T&R see health as a barrier to reintegration, whereas we see poor health as more as an outcome of poor reintegration. Former inmates often live on the fringes of the labor market, have unstable marriages, live in poverty for extended periods of time, and face the discrimination associated with their stigmatized status. All these factors are strongly related to the risk of poor mental and physical health. At the same time, many inmates lose the opportunity for health care following release. In the United States, the biggest barrier to adequate health care is being uninsured. The majority of Americans get their insurance through an employer, a partner, or by purchasing a private policy. Former inmates are less likely than others to secure insurance through any of these sources, leading to unusually high levels of uninsurance. Surely even poor care is better than no care at all. Compounding the problem, even former inmates who are able to secure some form of health insurance are unlikely to receive treatment for pre-existing conditions, some of which could have been acquired while behind bars. Even if former inmates received the best possible treatment while in prison, that treatment is typically short-lived. According to 2004 Bureau of Justice Statistics numbers, the average sentence length is around five years, meaning individuals spend a relatively small part of their lives behind the prison walls.

Our focus on post-release conditions is more than a simple matter of emphasis; it implies a different focus. If, as T&R suggest, prisoners often enter prison with disease, and prisons usually fail to adequately address their problems, then the issue is providing appropriate health care while in prison in order to prevent further deterioration following release. If, as we contend, the issue lies in failed reintegration, then the remedy lies in doing more to ease reentry. Reintegration can be improved both by providing services within prison, but also by changing the environment following release. This includes, among other things, eliminating legal discrimination, providing more opportunities for ex-inmates, and doing more to insure access to some form of health care. Although rarely thought of as health policies, these social policies can have a demonstrable impact on health. Such policies also address reintegration directly, whereas T&R's proposals address reintegration only insofar as reintegration is affected by health. We agree that broad reform is important, but the goals of such reform efforts can be as broad as the policies themselves.

To be sure, T&R's health proposals are not lacking for ambition. Indeed, their goal seems to be no less than the reform of the entire U.S. health care system. T&R end their essay by discussing the Institute of Medicine's Quality Chasm report. Here, too, we agree there is much room for improvement, and that much of this improvement lies in focusing on evidence-based medicine, but it's important to not make the best the enemy of the good, especially if one's motivating concern is with improving the circumstances of an unusually disadvantaged group. In this regard, a focus on the quality chasm seems misplaced. Research consistently shows that those without health insurance forego care, even when their need for care is clear, as it is for individuals with chronic conditions such as diabetes. The research discussed in The Quality Chasm concerns the gap between what the typical health care consumer receives and what best-practice evidence recommends. This gap is large, to be sure, but it is unclear whether it's as large as the gap between the insured and uninsured. At the same time, if one is interested in improving the health of former inmates, it is perhaps just as important to improve their social environment as it is to improve the quality of services they might receive. This pertains both to the prison environment and the environment former inmates encounter following release. There is no doubt that the conditions in many prisons are now intolerable, including with respect to health care delivery, but this may have less to do with services per se than with overcrowding and other structural problems. If prisons were not filled far beyond their capacity, the human resources within prisons—including medical staff—could be put to better use. A focus on prison overcrowding, as well as other issues pertaining to prison administration, is perhaps also more politically attractive than a focus on prison health care. Political feasibility is not an unimportant consideration. In the current political climate, it may be much easier to expand prison capacity than to, say, take explicit steps to provide inmates with higher quality care. The correctional system is, after all, a legal institution whose primary function is social control.

T&R argue that the health of inmates is related to public safety insofar as unhealthy inmates are less able to become productive citizens. Although framing inmate health as a matter of public safety is attractive for a number of reasons, we question the strength of this connection. Inmates face many other barriers to reentry. As a result, even a perfectly healthy former inmate is likely to face discrimination in, for example, labor and housing markets. A criminal justice system that neglects the health care needs of inmates may, as T&R suggest, exacerbate their sense of being marginalized citizens, but certainly other factors contribute to that sense as well. We believe the health of current and former inmates should be an important concern irrespective of its connections with public safety. Medical sociologists regularly note that health depends on more than health care. We believe the same lesson should be applied to inmate health. In our assessment, the best hope for breaking the incarceration-health connection rests with providing opportunities and resources that help inmates move beyond their incarceration experience and successfully reintegrate back into the community.

REFERENCES

Massoglia, M. & Schnittker, J. (2009). No real release: The health effects of incarceration. *Contexts, 8*, 38-42.

Massoglia, M. (2008). Incarceration, health, and racial disparities in health. *Law & Society Review, 42*, 275-306.

Schnittker, J. & John, A. (2007). Enduring stigma: The long-term effects of incarceration on health. *Journal of Health and Social Behavior, 48*, 115-130.

MAKING PRISONS SAFER: POLICIES AND STRATEGIES TO REDUCE EXTREMISM AND RADICALIZATION AMONG U.S. PRISONERS[i]

BERT USEEM
OBIE CLAYTON

Starting in 2006, we undertook a study of the radicalization of U.S. prison inmates. We came into the study expecting, like many others, to find that prisons were systematically generating a radical orientation among inmates which, at a later date, would lead to terrorism. The general claim should be distinguished from the assertion that prisons harbor radicals, whose political orientation would be similar if not behind bars. For example, testifying before the United States Senate, Michael Waller (2003) stated that radical Islamist groups "dominate Muslim prison recruitment in the U.S. and seek to create a radicalized cadre of felons who will support their anti-American efforts." Along the same lines, a university-based taskforce issued a report based on testimony of law enforcement, homeland security, and corrections experts. The taskforce noted that, "Prisons have long been places where extremist ideology and calls to violence could find a willing ear, and conditions are often conducive to radicalization" (Cilluffo et al., 2006: i).

Our expectations were not met. We found that prisons do not appear to be fertile grounds for radicalization and terrorist recruitment (Useem & Clayton, 2009). This finding needs to be carefully qualified, as we suggest further below. For the study, we conducted interviews in ten state departments of corrections and one municipal jail system during the 2006-2009 calendar years. We visited 27 medium- or high-security prisons for men. In each jurisdiction (with two exceptions), we interviewed prison officials in the central office, prison officials in each prison facility, and inmates in each prison facility visited.

Inmates were asked to report their observations of radicalization of prison inmates; none reported any significant signs. Moreover, inmates expressed considerable collective solidarity against terrorism. In part, this appeared to reflect inmate loyalty to the country. While inmates may be out for themselves, as evidenced by the crimes that put them in prison, they remain loyal to the country to the extent that they do not seek to damage the country at high personal risk (death or imprisonment).

It is possible that inmates who harbored anti-state positions refused to talk to us and those who did, dissembled about the low levels of inmate radicalization in the prisons. Prison officials, however, including intelligence personnel at both the facility- and central office-levels, reported few signs of radicalization. We believe they had little incentive to understate the extant threat.

Four factors seemed most important in explaining this finding. First, over the last 20 years, U.S. prisons have been able to restore order and improve inmate safety. The rates of disorder – as measured by the rates of individual and collective violence – have fallen significantly. A byproduct of this restoration of order is that the appeals of radicalization are reduced. Prisons are successful, not failed, states. Second, in every agency we visited, corrections officials are aware of the threat of inmate radicalization. Correctional leadership (at both the agency and prison-level) has infused into the organization the mission of observing signs of inmate radicalization. They are not sitting ducks, waiting to the picked off by radicalizing groups.

Third, the educational backgrounds of male inmates helps explain the finding of low levels of jihad radicalization in prisons. Both foreign and domestic terrorists tend to have relatively high levels of education (Krueger, 2007). In contrast, inmates tend to have low levels of education. Fourth, we would expect that Islamic inmates would be more disposed to radicalization if the Muslim community outside of prisons perceived its treatment as unfair, and if radical values existed in that external community. However, the contrary is the case. There are an estimated to 2.3 to 3 million Muslims in America. For the most part, Muslim Americans are solidly middle class, both in their economic standing (median income a little above the national average) and their political views.

Our core argument, then, is that U.S. prisons are not systematically generating a terrorist threat to the U.S. homeland. They are not the perfect storm. This conclusion does not imply that we should write down the probability to zero. In our earlier paper, we discussed a plot that emerged from the California State Prison at Sacramento. Inmate Kevin James formed Jam'iyyat Ul-Ilsam Is-Saheeh ("JIS," the Authentic Assembly of God), which later planned a three-person attack on U.S. military recruitment offices, the Israeli Consulate, and synagogues in the Los Angeles area. The plan was to kill as many people as possible at each site. The effort was thwarted by law enforcement in its early stages. The difficult judgment to make is whether Kevin James, had he been on the streets rather than behind bars, would have been equally inclined but more capable of leading a terrorist strike. The evidence suggests this conclusion.

The purpose of this paper is to further develop the policy implication of our analysis. We begin by discussing recent work on inner city life, and then turn to a second deviant case.

RACE AND CLASS IN THE UNITED STATES

As already noted, our earlier paper argued that one reason that inmates are not being recruited to terrorism is that U.S. Muslims are not the objects of strong enmity by other American and are generally well integrated. U.S. society has been relatively open to American Muslims and Muslim immigrants. As a result, the hostility that might otherwise brew in minority group enclaves, disconnected with little opportunity, has not been present in the United States. There is little sense of injustice among the external Muslim community, which could otherwise be "imported" to prison.

We had little to say, however, about the communities from which inmates themselves originate and their economic standing and their attitudes toward politics. Since our main concern is the recruitment of African American inmates to jihadist-type radicalism, it is useful to consider recent scholarship on those communities. That is, what it is like to be "black and poor in the inner city," to draw on the subtitle of William Julius Wilson's most recent book?

Recent studies of inner city African Americans – by Elijah Anderson (1999), Sudhir Venkatesh (2006), and Wilson (2009) – lead to a similar set of conclusions. All three authors argue that primary weight for explaining the economic conditions of inner city African Americans should be given to structural factors, such as collapse of the job market for low-wage earners, poorly performing schools, and housing segregation. However, all three authors contend that structural forces produce a cultural residue which, in turn, becomes its own causal force. Wilson (2009, p. 134) states: "Even though [cultural] codes emerge under conditions of poverty and racial segregation, once developed they display a degree of autonomy in the regulation of behavior." If so, we should expect this cultural residue to be "imported" into prison, possibly to inhibit or to facilitate radicalization. Which is it?

Three features of this cultural residue are especially important. One is strong adherence to conventional political morality. Wilson (2009: 83) reports that, in a large random survey of inner city blacks, respondents "spoke unambiguously in support of American values concerning individual initiative." In open ended interviews, according to Wilson, "participants overwhelmingly endorsed the dominant American belief system concerning poverty."

Second, all three authors gives little hint of a political dimension of the "code of the streets." African American men, in particular, are foremost concerned with issues of personal respect and disrespect. Wilson describes this concern, while having a structural root, as "negative" in nature. In the absence of conventional means of gaining respect (e.g., good jobs), black males "devise alternative ways to gain respect that emphasize manly pride, ranging from simply wearing brand-name clothing to have the 'right look' and talking the right way, to developing a predatory attitude toward neighbors" (2009, p. 18). These cultural attitudes would seem not to be fertile grounds for jihadist recruitment, if that means ideological conversion to traditional jihadist ideology.

Third, working at cross current with the first two points, the cultural patterns of inner city residents obstruct their integration into the boarder society. The code of the streets makes possible a thriving underground economy, with its own set of norms. But it does not provide a stepping stone to conventional opportunities. For example, Venkatesh (2006) points out that work in the underground economy cannot be mentioned to conventional employers as evidence of a work ethic and learned skills. The underground economy becomes a trap.

Thus, on the one hand there seems little natural ideological affinity between code of the streets and jihadist ideology. The code of the street is not a politicized code. On the other, the alienation from the economy may provide the basis of recruitment, in the sense that ex-offenders are "available" for recruitment to jihadist causes. As inmates are released from prison they may be drawn to terrorist causes due to lack of attachment to conventional institutions. In 2007, 725,000 inmates were released from federal and state prisons (West & Sabol, 2008: 3).

CASE ANALYSIS: EL RUKNS

In November, 1987 five members of a Chicago-based gang, El Rukns, were convicted of conspiring to blow up government buildings and assassinate U.S. public officials in exchange for $2.5 million from the Libyan government.[ii] The plan was orchestrated by Jeff Fort, the gang leader, who was then serving a sentence in a federal prison in Texas.

The El Rukns started in the 1960s in Chicago as the Blackstone Rangers. The Rangers became involved in political and community activities. For example, they mobilized efforts to increase voter turnout and elect candidates. When riots broke out following the assassination of Martin Luther King, they helped prevent rioting in their neighborhoods. These political activities notwithstanding, hundreds of gang members were convicted of serious crimes, including murder, and were assigned to one of three maximum security prisons in Northern Illinois.

In the early 1970s, the gang became knows at the Black P. Stone Nation. In 1977, Fort declared his conversion to Islam and claimed that his gang was a religious organization in the tradition of the Moorish Science Temple of America. He changed its name to the El Rukns, which means "The Foundation" in Arabic. In 1983, Fort was convicted of drug trafficking charges and sentenced to 13 years at the Federal Correctional Institution at Bastrop, Texas. Even from here, however, Fort maintained leadership of the El Rukns through frequent conversation from the Bastrop prison to gang headquarters in Chicago. Fort was on the phone as many as 18 hours a day.

While in federal prison, Fort learned that that Louis Farrakhan, had received $5 million from the Libyan government. Apparently, this led Fort to believe that the Libyan government would employ the El Rukns to conduct terrorist activities in the United Sates. He decided to offer El Rukns' services to Libya for $1 million a year. On March 11, 1986, three El Rukns traveled to Libya to meet with Libyan military officials. After their return, Fort developed a plan to demonstrate to the Libyans their commitment and capabilities to carry out terrorist acts. They considered blowing up a government building, shooting down a commercial airplane, killing a Milwaukee alderman, and executing "a killing here and a killing there" (914 F.2d 934). Fort, however, initially concluded that it would be simpler and easier to lay claim to acts of violence conducted by others. Newspaper stories of unsolved violent crimes throughout the United States were clipped and placed in a file for submission to Libyans. The El Rukns would claim responsibility for the violence reported in the clips. In addition, Fort decided to make a video tape of El Rukns pretending to be from other cities to impress the Libyans with the breadth of the gang. Under Fort's direction the videotape was delivered to the Libyan government in a meeting in Panama in May of 1986.

In June, 1986, Fort decided that the Libyans would only be truly impressed by the use of powerful explosives. He instructed two members to acquire a hand-held LAW rocket -- a weapon designed to destroy armored tanks and can penetrate a concrete bunker. The plan, however, was detected by the FBI. An agent sold to the El Rukns an inoperative LAW, in which a radio transmitter had been hidden. Tracing the LAW to a building owned by the El Rukns, the FBI found the LAW rocket, along with 32 firearms, including a machine gun with several rounds of armor-piercing bullets, as well as hand grenades. Five El Rukns, including Jeff Fort, were indicted with conspiracy to commit terrorist acts. On November 24 1987, a jury found all five defendants guilty. They were given lengthy sentences.

This case study is instructive in several regards. First, our central argument, in this and previous work, has been that that there is a weak association between prison and terrorism. This claim does not imply that prisoners cannot become involved in terrorist acts. Plainly, they can and have – as the case study illustrates. Thus, while we affirm that prisons are not a breeding ground for terrorism, but neither are they an inoculation against it. Second, El Rukns involvement in planning for terrorist activities may have been in spite of, rather than because of, imprisonment. Had the same actors been on streets, they may have been equally disposed toward terrorism, and possibly more capable of acting on that disposition

Third, ideology plays an ambiguous role in leading the El Rukns toward terrorism. On the one hand, the El Rukns appear to have been motivated mainly by the goal of financial gain. This is supported by the fact that the El Rukns first decided to fabricate evidence of their destructive acts to present to Libyan officials. The appearance of damaging the country was enough, if it would bring forth Libyan payment. The El Rukns turned to explosives only when they believed more had to be done to gain the respect of their Libyan contacts. On the other hand, the Islamic ideology, as it was understood by the El Rukns leadership, may have provided a rationalizing framework for choosing to attack the country. In our earlier paper we pointed out prison inmates tend, in their own way, to be patriotic. The El Rukn ideology may have played a necessary role in neutralizing patriotism. Perhaps both financial gain and ideology were important, though we do not know their relative weights.

WHY THE FOCUS ON PRISONS

If our analysis is correct – prisons thus far have not been a breeding ground for terrorism – why have so many argued that we should anticipate otherwise? We believe the answer is three-fold. One is that the position has face plausibility. One aspect of that plausibility is that terrorism and violent crime share a common feature of using violence to obtain desired ends. A person willing to use violence to harm another would more readily, than a non-violent type, use violence against society. However plausible the argument, we should insist on evidence before drawing conclusions. This has not always been done.

A second reason for a willingness to accept the prison-breeds-terrorism argument (absent supporting evidence) is our stereotypes of prisoners. Writing about the U.S. prison buildup, economist Glenn Loury argues that has been a historic shift in how we think about criminal offenders. He states that with the buildup, "we have created scapegoats, indulged our need to feel virtuous, and assuaged our fears. We have met the enemy, and the enemy is them" (Loury, 2008: 25). If Loury is correct, perhaps we are reacting to our own stereotypes, at least in part.

Consider the response to the release of a recent report by the Department of Homeland Security (DHS) on the recruitment of military personnel to right-wing terrorist groups. The report states that rightwing extremists will attempt to recruit and radicalize returning veterans in order to exploit their skills and knowledge learned in military training and combat. It is argued that a small percentage of military personnel joined extremists groups during the 1990s because they were disgruntled, disillusioned, or suffering from the psychological effects of war. This is being replicated today (DHS Office of Intelligence and Analysis, 2009).

Revealing is the political reaction to the DHS report – opposition without an evidence-based assessment. For example, House Minority Leader John Boehner (R- Ohio) disparaged the DHS report. "To characterize men and women returning home after defending our country as potential terrorists is offensive and unacceptable." We would like to see the evidence.

To move away from rhetoric, consider the numbers of veterans in state and federal prison. In 2004, 10 percent of state and federal prisoners were veterans, down from 20 percent in 1986 (Noonan & Mumola, 2007). While, in 2004, the rate of incarceration of male veterans (630 per 100,000 male residents) was lower than of non-veterans (1,390 per 100,000 male residents), the absolute numbers is non trivial – 140,000 inmates. More than half of the veterans in state prisoners were serving time for a violent offense (57 percent), including 15 percent for homicide and 23 percent for sexual assault. Among non-veterans, 47 percent had committed a violent offense; 12 percent were serving prison time for homicide and 9 percent for sexual assault.

Another data point: Joshua Freilich and Steven Chermak collected open source data on crimes committed since 1990 by adherents of far-right ideologies, such as fierce nationalism, anti-globalization, and exaggerated reverence for civil liberties (START 2009). Freilich and Chermak found only a small minority – 6.7 percent – were veterans. However, as they point out, the actual percentage may be higher, because the open source material may have not disclosed veteran status. Since 1990, far rightists have killed 42 law enforcement officers in 32 incidents, and perpetrated another 275 homicides in 36 states. Again, one should not mistake rates for absolute number which, here, are significant. Veteran status should be celebrated; but it does not inoculate against anti-social behavior.

Third, one does not need to be a Foucauldian to argue that the level of effective surveillance in prisons has greatly improved over the last two decades. Security threat groups are tracked by staff dedicated to that task; telephone calls (at least in most states) and visiting rooms are closely monitored; television cameras are omnipresent; corrections coordinates and shares information with external law enforcement agencies. Al Qaeda has proclaimed that they seek to recruit prison inmates to their cause. The obstacles to doing so are, thankfully, very great. This point has been missed by those who predict that prisons will pour out domestic terrorists.

In sum, predicting where domestic-based terrorism may arise entails a high degree of uncertainty. It is like looking for a needle in the haystack. Our preconceptions, our theories, even our ideology, can provide useful leads to where to look. One must start somewhere, one haystack or another. Much to our surprise, prisons populations are less of a threat than anticipated. Prisons may both facilitate and inhibit radicalization. With the current regime, the balance appears in favor of the latter.

FUTURE CHALLENGES

A principle finding of our research study is that corrections has responded with a sense of urgency to the threat of radicalization. When we arrived in central offices and facilities, we did not surprise anyone by raising the issue of prisoner radicalization. Their antennae were already up. Correctional leadership has fashioned, staffed, and energized the effort to defeat radicalization. Several areas of concern remain.

One is the sustainability of the effort over time. The claim that prisons will generate scores of terrorists spilling out on to the streets of our cities – the position described at the opening of this paper – appears to be false, or at least overstated. This false positive, however, can far too easily morph into a false negative: prisons are never the breeding ground for radicalization, even in small numbers. Nothing in this work supports this claim. Thus, corrections should maintain a high level of vigilance. This is increasingly difficult, the further away in time we are from exemplars of the threat.[iii]

Second, a surprising finding coming out of our inmate interviews is the presence of inmate solidarity against jihadist radicalization coming out of a positive identification with the country – patriotism. While this level of patriotism may not be cause for civic celebration, it does suggest corrections should view inmates as an ally in the fight against prisoner radicalization. They should employ that ally.

Third, another source of inmate solidarity against jihadist terrorism is prison order and safety. American prisons have made significant strides over the last two decades in achieving legitimate order. A thankfully unintended consequence of increased order has been that prisoners are less susceptible to the appeals of radicalization. Corrections should continue to advance its successful effort to build legitimate order behind bars.

Finally, at year end 2007, over two-third (69.8 percent) of 7.3 million adults under correctional supervision were supervised in the community, either probation or parole (Glaze & Bonczar, 2008). Might these populations contribute to the threat of jihad radicalization? And how can the institutions of probation and parole curb radicalization? We know of no effort to explore these issues.

REFERENCES

Anderson, E. (1999). *Code of the Street: Decency, Violence, and the Moral Life of the Inner City*. New York: W.W. Norton.

Cilluffo, F., Saathoff, G. et al. (2006). *Out of the Shadows: Getting Ahead of Prisoner Radicalization.* Report by George Washington University Homeland Security Policy Institute and University of Virginia Critical Incident Analysis Group. Available online:
    http://www.gwu.edu/~dhs/reports/rad/Out%20of%20the%20shadows.pdf

Department of Homeland Security, Office of Intelligence and Analysis. (2009). *Rightwing Extremism: Current Economic and Political Climate Fueling Resurgence in Radicalization and Recruitment.* Available online:
    http://www.fas.org/irp/eprint/rightwing.pdf

Glaze, L.E. & Bonczar, T.B. (2008). *Probation and Parole in the United States, 2007.* Washington, DC: Bureau of Justice Statistics.

Kruger, A.B. (2007). *What Makes a Terrorist: Economics and the Roots of Terrorism.* Princeton, NJ: Princeton University Press

Kushner, H.W. (2002). *Encyclopedia of Terrorism.* Thousand Oaks, CA: Sage.

Loury, G.C. (2008). *Race, Incarceration, and American Values.* Cambridge, MA: MIT Press.

Noonan, M.E. & Mumola, C.J. (2007). *Veterans in State and Federal Prison, 2004.* Washington, DC: Bureau of Justice Statistics.

START. (2009). Background Information: Far-Right Attacks on U.S. Law Enforcement. Available online:

http://www.start.umd.edu/start/announcements/announcement.asp?i
d=140

Useem, B. & Clayton, O. (2009). Radicalization of U.S. inmates. *Criminology &
Public Policy.* Forthcoming.

Useem, B. & Kimball, P.A. (1989). *States of Siege: U.S. Prison Riots, 1971 –
1986.* New York: Oxford University Press.

Venkatesh, S.A. (2006). *Off the Books: The Underground Economy of the
Urban Poor. Cambridge,* MA: Harvard University Press.

Waller, M. (2003, October 14). Testimony Before the Subcommittee on
Terrorism, Technology and Homeland Security, Senate Committee
on the   Judiciary. Available online: http://judiciary.senate.gov/
testimony.cfm?id=960&wit_id=2719

West, H.C. & Sabol, W.J. (2008). *Prisoners in 2007.* Washington, DC: Bureau
of Justice Statistics.

Wilson, W.J. (2009). *More than Just Race: Being Black and Poor in the Inner
City.* New York: W.W. Norton.

CASES CITED

*United States Court of Appeals, Seventh Circuit. United States of America,
Plaintiff-Appellee, v. Leon McAnderson, Roosevelt Hawkins, Jeff Fort, Alan
Knox and Reico Cranshaw, Defendants-Appellants.* 914 F.2d 934.

ENDNOTES

[i] Funded by the National Institute of Justice, U.S. Department of Justice and the
Department of Homeland Security/START, University of Maryland.

[ii] The following account is based on these sources: 914 F.2d 934; Kushner
(2002: 121); Useem and Kimball (1989).

[iii] This essay was completed before four ex-prisoners were charged with plotting
to bomb two New York City synagogues and to shoot down U.S. military
planes.

A Response to Useem & Clayton's Making Prisons Safer

Bill Wakefield
Scott Chenault

Useem and Clayton have provided a very timely and important perspective on a topic currently generating significant response from the academic community—a simple click on *Google* immediately provides a list of more than 70 pages of articles, etc., containing more than 326,000 words related to this topic(June, 2009). Like the authors, we must admit that upon first reading the title a similar expectation of reviewing one more article supporting the contention that prisons are *systematically* influential in providing a context and environment supporting a move by prisoners, during time served, which could lead toward terrorism(p. 1). The authors speak of the misperception that prisons "harbor radicals" and provide a "willing ear, and conditions are often conducive to radicalization"(Cilluffo et al, 2006:i). Thus, it was particularly refreshing and enlightening to continue to read of the authors' claim that "prisons do not appear to be fertile grounds for radicalization and terrorist recruitment"(Useem and Clayton, 2009).

Utilizing a self-report methodology involving interviews with representatives from all components of a prison system—administrators, prison officials, and inmates—Useem and Clayton were able to get a sense of the attitudes of how these "front line" people feel about radicalization of prisoners and the role prisons play in developing extremism and terrorism idcologies. In this brief response, we will focus on what we perceive to be the strengths of Useem and Clayton's position as well as what we might consider to be some possible limitations. We take this approach with the intent of pointing to areas requiring focus and further attention in order to construct a more solid argument supporting further development of the "policy implications" purpose of their research.

STRENGTHS

It is intellectually rewarding to reflect on two sociologists who do not hesitate to point out some basic structural observations regarding current prison systems in the U.S.:

- Inmates do not perceive *themselves* to be 'radicals' and actually display a sense of solid opposition to terrorism.
- In the past two decades, our prisons have made great progress in improving safety and order in the prisons.

- Prison officials are more knowledgeable today about radicalization threats and appear to be more sensitive to any inmate radicalization threats in their own institutions.

The low educational level of inmates, in general, almost serves as a shield against the more complex ideologies typical of foreign and domestic terrorists. These individuals are more educated and idealistic than the inmates serving time today. This would appear to be commensurate with the more highly educated and middle class U.S. Muslim community on the outside. This condition is not conducive to recruitment of the "typical" inmate currently doing time.

In support of the above findings, Useem and Clayton undertake a solid discussion of race and class in the U.S. and the realistic state of African-American men in our society--whether inmate or on the outside where "there seems to be little natural ideological affinity between code of the streets and jihadist ideology" — a cogent point! Therefore, inmates would not be *the most* fertile population for recruitment to radical causes and terrorism. In actuality, male, African American, inmates may be *the least* amenable target for recruitment. In support of this position, Useem and Clayton cite and discuss the case of the Chicago-based El Rukins gang from 1960-1987 and their extremist and terrorist activities to reinforce the argument *against* a strong association between prison and future inmate terrorism.[i]

AREAS OF CONCERN

While we agree in principle with the main thrust of the essay there are three main areas of concern that we have with the argument put forth. First, the article focuses solely on the possibility of black inmates being radicalized into militant Islamic groups. While this has been the focus of much terrorism research in the post 9-11 world, it is certainly not the only ground for extremist recruitment. In fact when Cilluffo et al (2007) argue that prisons are historically fertile recruiting grounds for extremists they use the Aryan Nations, and The Order(two white power groups) as primary examples (Cilluffo, Cardash, & Whitehead). Further, the Aryan Nations has sponsored a "prison ministry" which serves as a *de facto* recruiting service since the 1970's (Anti-Defamation League, 2009). This represents a formalized attempt to recruit white inmates into extremist groups.

Second, the essay was written primarily based on research conducted in 10 state departments of correction and one municipal jail. There is no mention of research conducted at the federal level. While the federal system typically resembles the aggregate of state systems on this issue, there is the possibility that an important difference may exist between state and federal level inmates. It is a reasonable possibility that inmates imprisoned by the federal government may hold more anti-government attitudes than those convicted at the state level. These attitudes could then lead to a greater likelihood of radicalization among these inmates. Additionally, research indicates that federal level inmates, in general, display a higher educational level versus state level inmates(Harlow, 2003).

Finally, while we agree with the general tenet of the essay that prisons are not generating scores of terrorists it seems to perhaps be a "bit of a leap of faith" to make such an assertion based on data collected in just 20% of the country. It is quite possible that the states chosen are simply not representative or, more likely, that there are regional differences between departments of corrections on this issue. Regional differences could result in certain areas of the country having prisons which might serve as radicalizing agents while other areas do not. The authors lend credence to this when they argue that part of the reason prisons are not breeding grounds for radicalization is that "prisons are successful, not failed, states"(p.2). They point to the reduction in both individual level and collective violence within prisons as evidence of this. While this reduction is present across state systems, there is still a great deal of variance in the level of violence from state-to- state and region-to-region (Byrne, Hummer, & Taxman 2008).

CONCLUSION

In conclusion, the authors present a timely essay which serves as a significant contribution to the literature. With the recent closing of the Guantanamo Bay detention facility and the announcement that those political prisoners previously held there will soon be transferred to domestic prisons it is important to revisit this issue. We would also like to commend the authors on presenting an argument contrary to some popularly held beliefs regarding prisons as "hot-beds of radicalization".

While the ideas and argument presented in this paper are strong and commendable the methodology should be refined if the authors intend to draw conclusions conducive to policy implications. As mentioned above, the methodology should incorporate a more representative approach to account for potential regional differences as well as potential differences between state and federal level inmates. Such a revised methodology will allow the authors to more confidently assert policy implications stemming from the research.

With a change in the methodology we believe the research could produce meaningful policy implications for departments of corrections nationwide. One potential policy implication is to extend the sensitivity toward radicalization, which the authors found at the administrative level, to line-level prison staff. Line-level staff have far more contact with, and knowledge of, inmates in any given institution than administrative personnel. Therefore, providing line level staff with training that sensitizes them to the potential for radicalization of inmates would only strengthen the "sustainability of effort over time" that the authors point to as an area of concern.

REFERENCES

Anti-Defamation League. (2009). Dangerous convictions: An introduction to extremist activities in prison. Available online: http://www.adl.org/learn/Ext_Terr/dangerous_convictions.pdf

Byrne, J., Hummer, D., & Taxman, F. (2008). *The Culture of Prison Violence.* Pearson, Boston: MA.

Cilluffo, F., Cardash, S., & Whitehead, A. (2007). Radicalization: Behind bars and beyond borders. 13 (2), (113-122).

Cilluffo, F., Saathoff, G., et al. (2006). *Out of the Shadows: Getting Ahead of Prisoner Radicalization,* A report by George Washington University, Homeland Security Policy Institute and University of Virginia, Critical Incident Analysis Group.

Harlow, C. (2003). Education and Correctional Populations. Bureau of Justice Statistics Special Report. Washington, DC: U.S. Government Printing Office.

United States Court of Appeals, Seventh Circuit. United States of America, Plaintiff-Appellee, v. Leon McAnderson, Roosevelt Hawkins, Jeff Fort, Alan Knox and Reico Cranshaw, Defendants-Appellants. *914 F.2d 934.*

Useem, B. & Clayton, O. (2009). Radicalization of U.S. inmates. *Criminology & Public Policy,* forthcoming.

Useem, B. & Kimball, P.A. (1989). *States of Siege: U.S. Prison Riots, 1971 – 1986.* New York: Oxford University Press.

ENDNOTES

[i] See *914 F.2d 934*; *Encyclopedia of Terrorism* (2002); Useem and Kimball (1989).

Searching for a Needle in the Haystack: A Look at Hypotheses and Explanations for the Low Prevalence of Radicalization in American Prisons

Vincent J. Webb

Bert Useem and Obie Clayton have done social science and public policy a great favor through their research and with this paper on extremism and radicalization among U.S. prisoners. Although the title of their paper is somewhat misleading since there is very little in the paper about making prisons safer, the central finding presented comes across loud and clear; they found no evidence of prisoner jihad radicalization and that... "U.S. prisons are not *systematically* generating a terrorist threat to the U.S. homeland". They offer four explanations for why American prisons are not centers for radicalization churning out a stream of terrorists, all of which warrant serious consideration. First, they argue that violence in American prisoners has been greatly reduced and consequently the potential for prison violence as the basis for prisoner radicalization has been greatly reduced. Prison violence still exists, and some prisons are more violent than others, but overall they are correct in asserting that American prisons are much safer places than they were one or two generations ago. But what has this to do with radicalization and terrorism? They maintain that reduced violence or conversely, increased prison safety makes radicalization less attractive to inmates, which in part accounts for the apparent absence of significant numbers of radicalized prisoners in American prisons. This is an interesting claim that is best thought of as a working hypotheses; however it is a hypotheses that might not be testable.

The second explanation for the absence of prisoner radicalization offered by Useem and Clayton is that prison officials are on top of things and have an eye out for the signs of prisoner radicalization. It is probably the case that prison systems and the officials that run them are more focused on the need to be aware of and have better systems for identifying and tracking the signs of prisoner radicalization. This focus is probably the result of the increased concern about homeland security in the U.S. on the part of all public safety sector officials since September 11, 2001. With regard to prison officials, improvements in the identification and monitoring of Security Threat Groups (STGs) are one example of an opportunity for detecting such signs. Useem and Clayton have provided some convincing empirical evidence to support the hypothesis of increased awareness and observation of potential radicalization by prison officials, even though their sample of prisons and officials is somewhat limited.

The third explanation is that in contrast to domestic and foreign terrorists, the vast majority of American prison inmates have relatively low levels of education, with the implication being that radicalization occurs most frequently among those who have higher levels of education. Although it is generally a sensible claim, it needs some fine tuning if it is to be generalized to all forms of radicalization. This claim requires empirical verification and in the case of American domestic terrorists, there is evidence in both directions with some terrorists being highly educated and others being much less so. One need only to recall the U.S. radical movements of the late 1960's and early 1970's to be reminded that many of the most radical leaders were highly educated. At the same time, a review educational histories of those involved in the 1995 Oklahoma City bombing results in a profile of terrorists with educational achievement levels similar to most prison inmates. It should be noted Useem and Clayton seem to want to limit this claim to those Muslim inmates who might be more susceptible to jihad radicalization.

The fourth explanation has to do with the general characteristics of the American Muslim community described by Useem and Clayton as being solidly middle class and non-supportive of radicalization. Their argument is that inmates would be more prone to radicalization if they perceived the larger Muslim community to be supportive of radicalization. This is another interesting hypothesis, but it is just that, a hypothesis in need of empirical verification.

Taken together, these four explanations serve as a set of interesting hypotheses that along the other ideas presented in the Useem and Clayton essay can provide guidance to both the academic/research and policy communities. With regard to the academic/research community, even though Useem and Clayton reporting finding no evidence that American prisons are the breeding grounds for terrorists, there still exists an important need to make systematic inquiry into this possibility. Even though, as the authors point out, it is the proverbial search for the needle in a haystack, it is nevertheless an important search. In criminological terms, researchers working in this area still need to identify the *prevalence*, as small as it might be, of prison radicalization. Useem and Clayton's research, while extensive, is limited to a sample of 27 medium or high security prisons and ten state department of corrections plus one municipal jail. This leaves forty other systems and hundreds of other prisons untouched. Useem and Clayton's research needs replication with additional samples.

Their work also highlights the need not only to study *prevalence*, but also to study specific *incidents* (not incidence in the criminological sense) of the radicalization of prison inmates, which is a daunting task. There is a difference between studying terrorist in prison and the radicalization of inmates who then leave prison with the potential to engage in terrorism upon release. While it is logical to study the *process of radicalization* by using known and imprisoned terrorists as subjects, evidence from such studies should not be interpreted as necessarily bearing on the question of whether or not prisons are the caldrons in which ingredients of radicalization are brought together to produce radicals and subsequently terrorists.

Clayton and Useem offer three reasons why there has been a focus on prisons as breeding groups for terrorism. First, violent crime and terrorism share a common dimension – violence. When we look for violent people, we look at the places where we know they reside, i.e. prisons. The logic is that since terrorists are violence-prone we will find them in the same places as other violence-prone people. Their second argument is that the stereotypes of prisoners are such that they become the scapegoats for many of society's post 9-11 terrorism-related concerns. One might also argue that in the fog of the war on terror knowing where your next terrorists are, brings a sense of comfort and security. A focus on prisons might bring such a sense even though it might be a false sense of comfort and security. The third reason for the focus on prisons as breeding grounds for terrorism given by Useem and Clayton is murky and even seems out of place. They argue that there have been improvements in surveillance within prisons of security threat groups, inmate phone calls and visitors, and that prison intelligence is shared with external law enforcement agencies. It seems reasonable that increased surveillance and better intelligence are instrumental in detecting radicalization and related post-imprisonment plans, but it is not clear how this has increased the focus on prisons as breeding grounds for terrorisms. Instead, it can be argued that increased surveillance is in response to the focus on prisons. Perhaps such an increase can be thought as part of a recursive process where because it is thought that prisons are breeding grounds for terrorism more resources are dedicated to surveillance and intelligence sharing. More resources dedicated to the problem means there is a problem and therefore more resources are required to address the problem.

There has been substantial increase in criminological and social science research on terrorism post 9-11. The research and scholarly focus on prisons as a pathway to terrorism is itself a part of the larger focus on prisons as the breeding grounds for terrorism. If research requires terrorists as subjects and the only access to terrorists is in prisons, then researchers will go to prisons and in doing so contribute to the focus on prisons. Research on the pathways to terrorism is extremely important and such efforts need to be increased. However, care needs to be taken so that findings on the radicalization of imprisoned terrorists are not misused to gauge the prevalence of inmates who become radicalized while imprisoned. Contemporary research on the pathways to terrorism would do well to use a much longer historical perspective than post 9-11. In fact, what we might learn is that college campuses are a much more profitable focal location for understanding radicalization than are prisons.

In sum, Clayton and Useem have done academics and policymakers a huge favor by conducting research leading to findings which challenge some fairly deeply entrenched beliefs about the role of prisons in radicalizing inmates and producing tomorrows terrorists. They offer some interesting explanations for their central finding that U.S. prisons are not producing terrorists, explanations that can serve as guiding hypotheses for other researchers. Their work epitomizes one of the most important functions of social science, debunking commonly held, but ill-founded beliefs that influence social policy. For this they are to be applauded.

SUBSTANTIALLY REDUCE MASS INCARCERATION BY SENTENCING FOCUSED ON COMMUNITY WELL-BEING

DOUGLAS THOMSON

During the past decade, criminologists have devoted increasing attention to the problem of mass incarceration in the United States of America. They have described its magnitude, trends, and dimensions and explored its impacts. They have attempted to explain its sources. This paper briefly summarizes and synthesizes this literature as prequel to proposing research-based policy for eventually ending mass incarceration. In particular, it focuses on a curiously neglected venue for a strategy of impact: the courtroom. The analysis identifies empirical research that provides guidance for a policy of substantially reducing mass incarceration by relying on sentencing focused on community well-being.

Three bodies of empirical research, in addition to related theory work, support this proposed policy change: 1) the dimensions, sources, and impact of mass incarceration; 2) the courtroom and courthouse dynamics of sentencing; 3) system and public receptivity to such a policy shift. While the second body of research serves as the central focus for this essay and this proposal, the first provides important support in terms of the internal realities of mass incarceration and the third some external support for moving more fully to community well-being sentencing.

As we shall see, the empirical record shows that mass incarceration is harmful in various ways. That demonstrates a need for policy change to heal or prevent those harms. Extensive, and highly reliable, documentation of the size and growth of mass incarceration testifies to the magnitude and urgency of the problem. Research also indicates sources of mass incarceration, and hence possible points for political, legal, and social intervention. All of this demonstrates the need for change and some directions for going about it.

Nevertheless, the growing research literature on the problem of mass incarceration has given short shrift to one important part of this policy puzzle: the dynamics of sentencing. This essay brings this part of the empirical record more fully into the discussion, and suggests explicit policy directions in which it points.

The Problem of Mass Incarceration

Criminologists have written an impressive amount of compelling critical material on the problem of mass incarceration. While empirical work regarding remedies has lagged behind, research has convincingly documented the size, scope, and trends characterizing the growth of prison, jail, and juvenile institutions from about 1975 to the present. Variously denominated as mass imprisonment (Garland, 2001b), the justice

371

juggernaut (Gordon, 1990), the imprisonment binge (Irwin & Austin, 1994), the prison build-up (Useem & Piehl, 2008), the carceral state (Wacquant, 2001; Gottschalk, 2006), the prison industrial complex (Christie, 1993), over-incarceration (Thomson, 1990a), and mass incarceration (Tonry, 2007), the phenomenal expansion of incarceration in the USA during the last quarter of the 20th century and throughout the first decade of the 21st century stands as one of the most significant developments in criminal justice policy in our time and a marker of our politics. It has elicited searching critiques from many criminologists as an abuse of state power, a degradation of the criminal sanction, a malignancy for families, communities, the polity, and the economy, and an accelerant for divisions of inequality and oppression in our society. To some extent, it serves as a potential or nascent rally point for community resistance and social action (West & Morris, 2000; Davis, 2003).

Some of the key indicators, frequently presented, include the following: growth in the imprisonment rate from a highly stable rate around 110 per 100,000 adult population from 1925-1975 to 476 per 100,000 in 2007; wide racial/ethnic disparities, e.g., ratios such as 7:1 African-American young men compared with European-American young men; increases each year; concomitant increases in costs (Christie, 1993; Garland, 2001a; Tonry, 2008; Useem & Piehl, 2008). Eight years ago, Zimring (2001) predicted – correctly thus far – that the imprisonment juggernaut would continue unabated. His pessimism about any subsequent significant reversal of "the new politics of punishment" only recently begins to show signs of challenge (Jacobson, 2006).

Sources of Mass Incarceration

What causes mass incarceration? We know that it has little to do with crime rates. The well-documented crime drop of the 1990s (Zimring, 2007) followed a pattern of fluctuation prior to that, along with some discordant patterns depending on whether National Crime Victimization Survey or Uniform Crime Reports data provided the basis of description. Fear of crime and the politicization of crime and nationalization of crime control interest appear as stronger factors. Politics, read one way or another, misleading 1970s and 1980s academic and government research and commentary, the resulting turn from the rehabilitative ideal and the emergence or strengthening of mandatory incarceration sentencing and wars against drugs, along with sublimated or overt racism have been offered in the mix of sources (Garland, 2001a; Pattillo, Weiman, and Western, 2004; Gottschalk, 2006; Western, 2006; Clear, 2007; Tonry, 2008; Useen & Piehl, 2008). Jacobs (2001) reminds us that the growth of mass incarceration strongly implicated liberal Democratic leaders, apparently trying to keep up with the perceived popular appeal of the get tough rhetoric and punitive policies and larger social control agenda of conservative Republican leaders.

Consequences of Mass Incarceration

Research indicates that mass incarceration has multiple consequences, many of them negative (Clear, 2007; Mauer & Chesney-Lind, 2002; Hagan & Dinovitzer, 1999; Murray & Farrington, 2008). It tears apart families and further devastates struggling communities. It disenfranchises citizens and depletes the polity. It violates the norm of proportionality in sentencing. It threatens the legitimacy of the legal order and the political order (Reiman, 2007). While it appears to have led to some short-term gains in reducing crime, it has eroded the deterrent value of the criminal sanction by making incarceration commonplace, routine, and even a rite of passage (Doob & Webster, 2003). The social, cultural, economic, legal, and political costs of mass incarceration fall especially heavily on African-Americans and their neighborhoods and communities (Braman, 2004; Pattillo et al., 2004; Roberts, 2004; Manza & Uggen, 2006; Tonry, 1995; Mauer, 1999; Tonry, 2008; Western, 2006).

Community Well-Being Sentencing to Reduce Mass Incarceration

The preceding brief review summarizes the substantial literature that convincingly demonstrates that the contemporary USA has a serious problem of mass incarceration and describes the scope and dimensions of that problem and its consequences. The remainder of this essay demonstrates that a substantial empirical record points toward viable policies to end mass incarceration. It particular, it advances a sentencing policy seeking community well-being.

Strategies advanced thus far for ending mass incarceration tend to fall into several areas: decriminalization, or legalization, of drugs, i.e., ending the War on Drugs (Mauer, 1999; Garland, 2001a; Moskos, 2008); altered policing practices (Moskos, 2008); expanded community corrections options (Petersilia, 1997, 1999); fiscal strategies (Jacobson, 2005); early prison release policies/shortened sentences (Austin & Irwin, 2001); downsizing prisons (Jacobson, 2005); right-sizing prisons (Useem & Piehl, 2008); sentencing reform (Tonry & Hatlestad, 1997; Clear, 2007; Zimring, 2007); community justice (Clear, 2007); restorative justice (Thomson, 2004; Tonry, 2006). While each of these strategies has merit, and a comprehensive approach to ending mass incarceration would do well to rely on most or all of them, the effort needs to pay more attention to what happens in the courtroom. In short, we should direct our attention again to the courtroom workgroup (Eisenstein & Jacob, 1977) that imposes criminal sentences every day in thousands of courthouses across the nation, making the mundane decisions (Lipsky, 1980) that add up to millions of people in prison. Moreover, the proposed policy would rely on increased knowledge of contemporary sentencing options and impacts, and of growing elite and popular receptivity, to what we know about how sentencing decisions are made.

Sentencing focused on community well-being, as the term denotes, would attend primarily to the benefits that a particular sentence would bring to the affected community. As such, it would need to counter powerful organizational tendencies to merely process cases or satisfy the needs of the courtroom work group and the courthouse community, as described below. It also would benefit from a restorative justice perspective (Sullivan & Tifft, 2005; Braithwaite, 1999) that emphasizes involvement of all central lay parties – offender, victim, and affected community – in repairing the harm caused by the offense via a collaborative process that stresses accountability and prevention of future harm. It also could benefit from a community justice perspective (Clear, 2007) that seeks to build community capacity for well-being by concentrating on ensuring public safety in local neighborhoods.

Courtroom Workgroups, the Guilty Plea Process, Going Rates, and Sentencing

Much of what we know about sentencing dynamics emerged from the spate of courthouse studies that began in the 1970s. Eisenstein & Jacob's (1977), *Felony Justice: An Organizational Analysis of Criminal Courts*, provides the concept of the courtroom workgroup and of its problematic grounding in sponsoring organizations and political/legal and task environments.   It shows how variations in courtroom stability and familiarity affect case review, prosecution, plea bargaining and sentencing practices in three urban criminal courts.   Subsequent work (Eisenstein, Flemming, and Nardulli, 1988), in this genealogical line, provides empirical replication while extending the conceptualization to courts as communities that feature the guilty-plea process and the social construction of sentencing.

Rosett & Cressey's (1976) classic work on plea bargaining paved the way.   Heumann (1978), Mather (1979), Feeley (1979), McIntyre (1987), and Thomson (1990b) provided ethnographic and other empirical detail. Much more recently, Bogira's (2005) investigative journalism examined the ecological, social, and political context of one urban criminal courthouse, echoing similarities in court behavior over the decades.

Criminal Sentencing: Routinization, Fear, and the Glorification of Guesswork

The aforementioned studies of criminal sentencing within courtrooms and in courthouses, along with many others, identify the work of judges, prosecutors, and defenses attorneys as street-level bureaucratic work (Lipsky, 1980) but with a certain mystique. Courtrooms serve as sanctuaries of judgment. Like other forms of public service discretionary work (Maynard-Moody & Musheno, 2003), the court's work makes justice in everyday decisions.   But the court's decisions, including sentencing, appear publicly and bask in a mythology of justice featuring fairness, equality, individualization, due process, and equal protection (Scheingold, 2004 [1974]). No institution or person could live up to such claims, and numerous sociological explorations have revealed the organizational dynamics of the mundane work. Yet the precision of the criminal sentence, especially under determinate sentencing, generates expectations that defy the capabilities of human cognition. Hence, we find an institution characterized by routine adjudication and sentencing, a context of fear of damage to public safety, and a glorification of guesswork. This institutional description does not demean the work of the intelligent and dedicated legal professionals and their colleagues who struggle daily to do justice within a framework of consciousness that leaves them, as well as other constituencies, largely dissatisfied with the results in the large (Rosett & Cressey, 1977; Feeley, 1979; Heuman, 1978; McIntyre, 1987; Bogira, 2005).

In his well-known sentencing memorandum, *United States v. Bergman* (416 F. Supp. 496 [S.D.N.Y. 1976]), Judge Marvin Frankel explicitly acknowledged the extraordinary difficulty of 'measuring' a sentence. After carefully considering whether Bernard Bergman merited a sentence to incarceration, under principles of rehabilitation, incapacitation, specific deterrence, general deterrence, and desert, Frankel noted that "the setting of a term ... is a subject even more perplexing, unregulated, and unprincipled." Moreover: "Days and months and years are countable with a sound of exactitude. But there can be no exactitude in the deliberations from which a number emerges." Judge Frankel thus lays bare for us what those working in criminal courtrooms every day must know: the guesswork involved in the ambiguity and uncertainty of sentencing. Yet as he then continues: "Without pretending to a nonexistent precision, the court notes at least the major factors." So also must we. This paper proposes that the guesswork of sentencing points, together with considerations of liberty and equality, toward our erring on the side of avoiding incarceration whenever possible. This constitutes a significant part of the common good in sentencing.

The Criminal Justice Mystique and the Mask of Overprediction

The criminal justice mystique refers to an ideology that privileges the views of criminal justice system insiders, and more broadly to the cultural and political hegemony of the mythology of the criminal justice system. As exhibited in the USA in the late twentieth century and early 21st century, it has contributed to the growth of mass incarceration and operates as a nearly insurmountable obstacle to ending it. The concept of the criminal justice mystique synthesizes the work of a host of criminologists, as evidenced in the work of Rosett & Cressey (1976) on "the subculture of justice within the courthouse", Heumann (1978) on socialization of newcomers to the criminal court, Mather (1979) on the dynamics of plea bargaining, and McIntyre (1987) on "the myth of incompetence" and "stigma of ineptitude" in facilitating the survival of the public defender institution.

Under the criminal justice mystique, the meaning and salience and the lost liberty of incarceration receive scant attention. The assumption seems to be that more is better. But what conception of individualized justice informs such sentences? What sentencing purpose, what public good, does a fifteen year prison sentence for robbery serve that a ten-year, five-year, or one-year prison sentence, or a community sentence could not have served? Both the adversarial ideal and community restorative justice tend to receive scant attention in sentencing under the criminal justice mystique that dominates the courthouse landscape in the USA.

The criminal justice mystique echoes concepts such as the aforementioned Rosett & Cressey's "subculture of justice within the courthouse", Bouza's (1990) "police mystique", Christie's (1993) "prison industrial complex", Eisenstein and Jacob's (1977) "courtroom workgroup" and "going rates", Garland's (1990) "penality", and more broadly, Scheingold's (2004 [1974]) "myth of rights". But the concept of criminal justice mystique promises to pull together the dynamics behind mass incarceration and the obstacles that prevent ending it. The following section highlights these earlier contributions to the concept of the criminal justice mystique, and then explains what more it contributes to our understanding of criminal justice policy, especially with regard to the problem of mass incarceration.

How the criminal justice mystique helps to explain sources of mass incarceration

The literature on mass incarceration points to various contributing factors, including: the war on drugs, racism, the punitive impulse, fear, political symbolism, and exploitation (Tonry, 2008). Explanations of the origins and persistence of mass incarceration, however, have not paid sufficient attention to the mundane realities of criminal court ideology and processes in prosecuting and sentencing persons to prison. The criminal justice mystique provides the cover within which "the mask of overprediction" (Morris, 1974) and "judicial prudence" (Scheingold, 1991: 146-161) can operate. The concept of the criminal justice mystique can help us to theorize more effectively about this part of the puzzle, and in so doing, to better move from research to policy formulations.

The concept derives from a basic sociological perspective, the social construction of reality (Berger and Luckmann, 1967), which long ago infused scholarly and now public discourse. We all live in social worlds constituted by shared definitions of the situation. These worlds enable our action, lend meaning to our collective lives, and reinforce what we find real and important. They also create boundaries to membership and participation and to understanding. Each local criminal justice system functions as a social world. As with other social worlds, we need to do more than analyze the social processes of constituent agencies. We need to understand the taken-for-granted understandings by which the criminal justice system -- locally and nationally – and criminal court communities (Eisenstein et al., 1988) constitute this part of the political order (Scheingold, 2004 [1994]).

Support for Community Well-Being Sentencing

Having briefly reviewed sentencing dynamics and having explored how they can be better aligned with sentencing focused on community well-being, an important question remains: what would influence large numbers of judges to alter their sentencing practices in this direction? The predominance of the guilty plea process immediately raises the corollary concern of how to change the plea bargaining practices of attorneys, i.e., prosecutors and defense attorneys, who play key roles in crafting sentencing (Feeley, 1979). To a lesser degree, probation officers may influence sentencing in their responsibilities for presentence investigations (Rosecrance, 1985, 1987) and in responding to violations of probation (Clear, 2007).

In short, this question and its corollaries return us to the centrality of the courtroom work group as gatekeeper to mass incarceration and hence to its reduction. Yet courtroom workgroup theory and research immediately turns our attention to the impact of sponsoring organizations and of task and political environments, and to their prospective role in reform.

Clearly, a full answer to what would move courtroom work groups toward sentencing for community well-being and hence away from mass incarceration lies well beyond the scope of this paper with its focus on the empirical basis for such a policy shift. Nevertheless, the centrality of the question calls for some preliminary observations drawn from a related part of the political record. In short, distilled from that literature, we find some promising support for such movement. Public opinion research during the past twenty-five years has offered a revisionist view of the people's sentiments with regard to criminal sentencing that strongly challenges assumptions underlying mass incarceration. In addition, mass incarceration fatigue appears to be setting in, further preparing the stage for community well-being sentencing. (Jacobson, 2006; Blumstein & Piquero, 2007). The challenge of the impossibility of justifying individual sentences (Wilkins, 1969; Zimring and Hawkins, 1991), suggests that we err in favor of liberty and community well-being. This in turn requires changing the culture, countering the criminal justice mystique.

Restorative Justice, Modest Retributive Justice, Communities of Care, and Positive Youth Development

The contemporary restorative justice movement (Zehr, 1990; Sullivan & Tifft, 2005; Sullivan & Tifft, 2006; Harris, 2006; McCold, 2006), despite cooptation and internal divisions (Thomson, 2004), has at least become part of the discourse in criminal justice. Although still largely confined to diversion efforts in the USA, restorative justice may be developing a critical mass sufficient to supporting community well-being sentencing with which considerable congruence of principle and practice could exist (Tonry, 2006). This especially should occur if popular perception of compatibility between restorative justice and retributive justice (Gromet & Darley, 2009) facilitates a prudent synthesis. Hence, the progressive justice model's emphasis on moderation in punishment (McAnany, Thomson, and Fogel,

1984), pursued mournfully (Christie, 1993), and in conjunction with restorative justice perspective would provide community well-being sentencing with solid grounding in traditional jurisprudence with regard to purposes of sentences while limiting the criminal sanction in favor of genuine community stewardship.

Public Opinion Support and the Deceleration of the Justice Juggernaut

A growing body of empirical research over the past quarter of a century has documented a broad reservoir of public opinion support for moderation in criminal sentencing (Thomson & Ragona, 1987; Roberts, 1992; Cullen, Fisher, and Applegate, 2000; Roberts & Stalans, 2000). Moderation in public opinion extends to support as well for juvenile rehabilitation (Nagin, Piquero, Scott, and Steinberg, 2006). Public opinion speaks with two voices with regard to the people's sentiments about criminal sentencing. Hence, it serves as resource as well as obstacle, depending on how it is constructed. Community well-being sentencing would do well in an environment of public opinion deliberativeness.

Such deliberative public opinion might thrive in the context of other promising developments for ending mass incarceration. They include: the reemergence of community organizing; the current economic crisis; examples of incarceration reductions/policy shifts thus far, e.g., California (Jacobson, 2005); weariness with and skepticism about mass incarceration (Jacobson, 2006); growing support for ending the war on drugs, including recent popular articles by mainstream influentials such as Senator Jim Webb; as well as longstanding harm reduction advocacy efforts. All such factors remind us of the salience of political and task environments for shaping the justice done in criminal courtrooms by their workgroups (Eisenstein & Jacob, 1977; Eisenstein, et al., 1988). These scholars remind us that prioritizing a courtroom work group's major goals – doing justice, disposing of the caseload, maintaining group cohesion, reducing uncertainty – depends on external as well as internal forces. With the growth of a restorative justice movement with potential to affect such decision-making, against the backdrop of increased receptivity for ending mass incarceration, an enabling public context exists for moving toward sentencing focused on community well-being. Yet it would have to develop locally in the court communities that always face sentencing issues locally.

The anticipated social movement (Merry and Milner, 1993; Gottschalk, 2006; Braithwaite, 2007; Butler, 2009) – and attendant involvement of a new group of cause lawyers (Sarat, 2001) – would elicit and nurture individual and small-scale collective action locally. Every citizen or resident of the USA has a local criminal courthouse. Hence, everyone can act for sentencing for community well-being, for sentencing for the common good: for the end of mass incarceration, the building of community, the prevention of violence, and the expansion of democracy.

REFERENCES

Austin, J. & Irwin, J. (2001). *It's About Time: America's Imprisonment Binge.* Third Edition. Belmont, California: Wadsworth.

Berger, P. & Luckmann, T. (1967). *The Social Construction of Reality: A Treatise in the Sociology of Knowledge.* London: Penguin.

Blumstein, A. & Piquero, A.R. (2007). Restore rationality to sentencing policy. *Criminology & Public Policy.* 6 (4), 679-688.

Bogira, S. (2005). *Courtroom 302: A Year Behind the Scenes in an American Criminal Courthouse.* New York: Knopf.

Bouza, A.V. (1990). *The Police Mystique: An Insider's Look at Cops, Crime, and the Criminal Justice System.* New York: Plenum.

Braithwaite, J. (1999). Restorative justice: assessing optimistic and pessimistic accounts. In M. Tonry (Ed.), *Crime & Justice: A Review of Research, Vol. 25.* (pp. 1-70). Chicago: University of Chicago Press.

Braithwaite, J. (2007). Encourage restorative justice. *Criminology & Public Policy,* 6 (4), 689-696.

Braman, D. (2004). *Doing Time on the Outside: Incarceration and Family Life in Urban America.* Ann Arbor: University of Michigan Press.

Butler, P. (2009). *Let's Get Free: A Hip-Hop Theory of Justice.* New York: New Press.

Christie, N. (2000). *Crime Control as Industry: Towards Gulags, Western Style.* Third Edition. New York: Routledge.

Clear, T.R. (2007). *Imprisoning Communities: How Mass Incarceration Makes Disadvantaged Neighborhoods Worse.* New York: Oxford University Press.

Cullen, F.T. (2007). Make rehabilitation corrections' guiding paradigm. *Criminology & Public Policy,* 6 (4), 717-728.

Cullen, F. T. & Gilbert, K. (1982). *Reaffirming Rehabilitation.* Cincinnati: Anderson.

Davis, A.Y. (2003). *Are Prisons Obsolete?* New York: Seven Stories Press.

Doob, A.N. & Webster, C.M. (2003). Sentence severity and crime: Accepting the null hypothesis. In M. Tonry (Ed.), *Crime and Justice: A Review of Research, Volume 30.* (pp. 143-194). Chicago: University of Chicago Press.

Eisenstein, J. & Jacob, H. (1977). *Felony Justice: An Organizational Analysis of Criminal Courts.* Boston: Little, Brown.

Eisenstein, J., Flemming, R.B., & Nardulli, P.F. (1988). *The Contours of Justice: Communities and their Courts.* Boston: Little Brown.

Feeley, M. (1979). *The Process Is the Punishment: Handling Cases in a Lower Criminal Court.* New York: Russell Sage.

Garland, D. (1990). *Punishment and Modern Society: A Study in Social Theory.* Chicago: University of Chicago Press.

Garland, D. (2001a). *The Culture of Control: Crime and Social Order in Contemporary Society.* Chicago: University of Chicago.

Garland, D. (Ed.). (2001b). *Mass Imprisonment: Social Causes and Consequences.* Thousand Oaks, California: Sage.

Gordon, D.R. (1990). *The Justice Juggernaut: Fighting Street Crime, Controlling Citizens.* New Brunswick, New Jersey: Rutgers University Press.

Gottschalk, M. (2006). *The Prison and the Gallows: The Politics of Mass Incarceration in America.* New York: Cambridge University Press.

Gromet, D.M. & Darley, M. (2009). punishment and beyond: achieving justice through the satisfaction of multiple goals. *Law & Society Review,* 43, 1-38.

Hagan, J. & Dinovitzer, R. (1999). Collateral consequences of imprisonment for children, communities, and prisoners. In M. Tonry & J. Petersilia (Eds.), *Prisons.* (pp.121-162). Chicago: University of Chicago Press.

Heumann, M. (1978). *Plea Bargaining: The Experiences of Prosecutors, Judges, and Defense Attorneys.* Chicago: University of Chicago Press.

Irwin, J. & Austin, J. (1994). *It's About Time: America's Imprisonment Binge.* Belmont, California: Wadsworth.

Jacobs, J.B. (2001). Facts, Values, and Prison Policies: A Commentary on Zimring and Tonry. In D.Garland (Ed.), *Mass Imprisonment: Social Causes and Consequences.* (pp. 165-170). Thousand Oaks, CA: Sage.

Jacobson, M. (2005). *Downsizing Prisons: How to Reduce Crime and End Mass Incarceration.* New York: New York University Press.

Jacobson, M. (2006). Reversing the punitive turn: The limits and promise of current research. *Criminology & Public Policy,* 5, 277-284.

Lipsky, M. (1980). *Street-Level Bureaucracy: Dilemmas of the Individual in Public Service.* New York: Russell Sage Foundation.

Manza, J. & Uggen, C. (2006). *Locked Out: Felon Disenfranchisement and American Democracy.* New York: Oxford.

Mather, L. (1979). *Plea Bargaining or Trial? The Process of Criminal-Case Disposition.* Lexington, MA: Lexington.

Mauer, M. (1999). *Race to Incarcerate.* New York: The New Press.

Mauer, M. & Chesney-Lind, M. (Eds.). (2002). *Invisible Punishment: The Collateral Consequences of Mass Imprisonment.* New York: The New Press.

McAnany, P., Thomson, D., & Fogel, D. (1984). *Probation and Justice: Reconsideration of Mission.* Boston: Oelgeschlager, Gunn & Hain.

Maynard-Moody, S. & Musheno, M. (2003). *Cops, Teachers, Counselors: Stories from the Front Lines of Public Service.* Ann Arbor: University of Michigan.

McCold, P. (2006). The recent history of restorative justice: Mediation, circles, and conferencing. In D. Sullivan & L. Tifft (Eds.) *Handbook of Restorative Justice: A Global Perspective.*(pp. 23-51). New York: Routledge.

McIntyre, L. (1987). *The Public Defender: The Practice of Law in the Shadows of Repute.* Chicago: University of Chicago Press.

Merry, S.E. & Milner, N. (1993). *The Possibility of Popular Justice: A Case Study of Community Mediation in the United States.* Ann Arbor: University of Michigan Press.

Morris, N. (1974). *The Future of Imprisonment.* Chicago: University of Chicago Press.

Moskos, P. (2008). *Cop in the Hood: My Year Policing Baltimore's Eastern District.* Princeton, New Jersey: Princeton University Press.

Murray, J. & Farrington, D. (2008). The effects of parental imprisonment on children. In M. Tonry (Ed.), *Crime and Justice: A Review of Research, Vol. 37,* (pp 133-206). Chicago: University of Chicago Press.

Nagin, D.S., Piquero, A.R., Scott, E.S., & Steinberg, L. (2006). Public preferences for rehabilitation versus incarceration of juvenile offenders: Evidence from a contingent valuation survey. *Criminology & Public Policy,* 5, 627-652.

Pattillo, M., Weiman, D., & Western, B. (eds.). (2004). *Imprisoning America: The Social Effects of Mass Incarceration.* New York: Russell Sage Foundation.

Petersilia, J. (1997). Probation in the United States. In M. Tonry (Ed.), *Crime and Justice: A Review of Research. Vol. 22* (pp. 149-200). Chicago: University of Chicago Press.

Petersilia, J. (1999). Parole and prisoner reentry in the United States. In M. Tonry & J. Petersilia (Eds.), *Prisons.* (pp. 479-529). Chicago: University of Chicago Press.

Reiman, J. (2007). *The Rich Get Richer, and the Poor Get Prison: Ideology, Class, and Criminal Justice.* 8th edition. Boston: Pearson/Allyn & Bacon.

Roberts, D. (2004). The social and moral cost of mass incarceration in african american communities. *Stanford Law Review,* 56, 1271-1305.

Roberts, J.V. (1992). Public opinion, crime, and criminal justice. In M. Tonry (ed.), *Crime & Justice: A Review of Research, Vol. 16* (pp. 99-180). Chicago: University of Chicago Press.

Roberts, J.V. & Stalans, R.J. (2000). *Public Opinion, Crime, and Criminal Justice.* Boulder, Colorado: Westview Press.

Rosett, A. & Cressey, D. (1976). *Justice By Consent: Plea Bargains in the American Courthouse.* Philadelphia: Lippincott Press.

Rosecrance, J. (1985) The probation officers' search for credibility: ballpark recommendations. *Crime & Delinquency* 31: 539-554.

Rosecrance, J. (1988). Maintaining the myth of individualized justice: probation presentence reports. *Justice Quarterly* 5.

Sarat, A. (2001). State transformation and the struggle for symbolic capital: cause lawyers, the organized bar, and capital punishment in the United States. In A. Sarat & S. Scheingold (eds.), *Cause Lawyering and the State in a Global Era.* (pp 186-210). New York: Oxford University Press.

Scheingold, S.A. (2004/1974). *The Politics of Rights: Lawyers, Public Policy, and Political Change.* 2nd Ed. Ann Arbor: University of Michigan Press.

Scheingold, S.A. (1991). *The Politics of Street Crime: Criminal Process and Cultural Obsession.* Philadelphia: Temple University Press.

Sullivan, D. & Tifft, L. (Eds.) (2006). *Handbook of Restorative Justice: A Global Perspective.* New York, New York: Routledge.

Sullivan, D. & Tifft, L. (2005). *Restorative Justice: Healing the Foundations of Our Everyday Lives. 2nd Ed.* Monsey, New York: Willow Tree Press.

Thomson, D. (1990a). The changing face of probation in the USA. In J.K. Harding (Ed.), *Probation in the Community*, (pp. 101-125). London: Tavistock.

Thomson, D. (1990b). How plea bargaining shapes intensive probation supervision policy goals. *Crime & Delinquency* 36, 146-161.

Thomson, D. (2004). Can we heal ourselves? transforming conflict in the restorative justice movement. *Contemporary Justice Review,* 107-116.

Thomson, D. & Ragona, A. (1987). Popular moderation versus governmental authoritarianism. *Crime & Delinquency* 33, 337-357.

Tonry, M.. (1995). *Malign Neglect: Race, Crime, and Punishment in America.* New York: Oxford University Press.

Tonry, M. (2006). Purposes and functions of sentencing. In M. Tonry (Ed.), *Crime and Justice: A Review of Research,* Vol. 34. (pp. 1-53). Chicago: University of Chicago Press.

Tonry, M. (2008). Crime and human rights – how political paranoia, protestant fundamentalism, and constitutional obsolescence combined to devastate black america: The American Society of Criminology 2007 Presidential Address. *Criminology,* 46, 1-34.

Tonry, M. & Hatlestad, K. (eds.). (1997). *Sentencing Reform in Overcrowded Times: A Comparative Perspective.* New York: Oxford University Press.

Useem, B. & Piehl, A.M. (2008). *Prison State: The Challenge of Mass Incarceration.* New York: Cambridge University Press.

Wacquant, L. (2001). Deadly symbiosis: When ghetto and prison meet and mesh." In D. Garland (Ed.), *Mass Imprisonment: Social Causes and Consequences.* (pp. 82-120). Thousand Oaks, California: Sage.

West, W.G. & Morris, R. (eds.). (2000). *The Case for Penal Abolition.* Toronto: Canadian Scholars' Press.

Western, B. (2006). *Punishment and Inequality in America.* New York: Russell Sage Foundation.

Wilkins, L.T. (1969). *Evaluation of Penal Measures.* New York: Random House.

Zimring, F. (2001). Imprisonment rates and the new politics of criminal punishment. In D. Garland (Ed.), *Mass Imprisonment: Social Causes and Consequences.* (pp. 145-149). Thousand Oaks, CA: Sage.

Zimring, F. (2007). *The Great American Crime Decline.* New York: Oxford.

Zimring, F. & Hawkins, G. (1991). *The Scale of Imprisonment.* Chicago: University of Chicago Press.

Zimring, F. & Frase, R. (Eds.). (1980). *The Criminal Justice System: Materials on the Administration and Reform of The Criminal Law.* Boston: Little, Brown.

Zehr, H. (1990). *Changing Lenses.* Akron, Pennsylvania: Herald Press.

CASE CITED

United States v. Bergman 416 F. Supp. 496 (S.D.N.Y. 1976), in Zimring and Frase.

OPPORTUNITIES FOR REDUCING AMERICA'S PRISON POPULATIONS

JAMES AUSTIN

Doug Thomson's essay has many good points to consider. First and foremost, he correctly places a major source of "mass incarceration" on the courts and the various people who work as public defenders, prosecutors, judges and probation officers. They do indeed form a community where their daily interactions and decisions directly determine how many people will go to prison, long they will remain incarcerated, and whether they will be returned to prison for probation and parole violations. These agencies and the people they employ do enjoy a fair amount of discretion in the law in how they make these decisions. So it follows that if these agents of social control could somehow be persuaded to lower prison disposition rates and shorten prison terms, the prison population would start receding. The problem is whether these people can be so persuaded.

Professor Thomson believes they can and provides an impressive array of public opinion data and other developments that suggest change is about to come. The public is open to more progressive approaches and may be tiring of the constant drumbeat of more prisons. But it is not clear that these opinions are changing over time with the exception of the death penalty.

One force that I believe will have a far more reaching effect is the current recession and the opportunities it has produced for prison population reductions. Spellman (2009) uses complex statistical analysis to point out the obvious that the economic surge over the past two decades helped fund the massive prison expansion.

Several states are now embarking on such a course simply because they no longer can afford their current level of imprisonment. We are likely to witness a major reduction in California's 170,000 prisoner population simply because the state is broke. Traditionally conservative and low tax states like Mississippi and Nevada recently passed laws that allow prisoners to earn more good time and serve shorter prison terms. They did so not because they had a change of heart or because they attended a conference on evidence based practices. No it was because they were running out of money.

New York is a state that actually reduced it prisoner population from 71,000 to 63,000 and the New York City Jail population declined from 21,000 to 13,000. According to Jacobson (2005) these reductions did not occur because of some change in sentencing reform or a new sentencing ideology by the courts. Rather it occurred because the New York City police altered their arrest policies by focusing on misdemeanor quality of life crimes. But the public would not have supported this shift in policy if it

383

were not accompanied by dramatic declining crime rates. In fact it seems that the declines in New York were a secondary and indirect effect of the dual forces of declining crime rates and the shift to an arrest policy that was proportional to the offenses being committed.

THE LIMITS OF COMMUNITY WELL BEING SENTENCING AND "EVIDENCE BASED" REFORMS

We know that crime rates and incarceration rates and other forms of social control vary dramatically by and within states. And we know that the states with the lowest crime rates also have the lowest incarceration rates. Further, low crime rate and low incarceration rate states tend to be small states with homogeneous populations. Even within a state, the same pattern exists. For example, in Illinois, the so-called collar counties that surround Chicago's Cook County have drastically lower crime and incarceration rates (Illinois Criminal Justice Authority, 2004). So it's not so much that all of America has these exorbitant incarceration rates but that certain states and places within these states fuel the high incarceration rates.

Thomson's concept of "community well-being sentencing" has great theoretical promise. And there is some evidence that it may be working its way into the criminal justice culture. Perhaps the best example of the concept in practice is the burgeoning number of drugs courts and the associated effort to decriminalize marijuana. My own theory is that these drugs-related reforms (as limited as they may be) took hold because many of the current lawmakers and criminal justice officials (and their families) have experimented with drugs themselves. In a sense they form a community based on the knowledge that drug use and marijuana in particular is not harmful, does not often lead to a career in crime and is not worthy of criminal justice sanctions or harsh prison terms. This is not unlike the explanation that prison sentences are quite short in the Netherlands because many of the judges or their families experienced incarceration during the occupation of the Nazis in World War II.

A recent publication by Listwan, Jonson, Cullen and Latessa (2008) also supported Thomson's belief that help is on the way. They also claimed that public sentiment now favors reform and that we have sufficient evidence to justify a moderate penal policy. But as Zimring (2008) and Webster and Doob (2008) point out, there is less evidence that any reform will occur on a voluntary basis due to the unique political and cultural structure of the United States. I would add that the claim that we now (or will) have the capacity to dramatically reduce recidivism rates by launching a massive infusion of treatment programs is both naïve and counterproductive to a decarceration movement.

But the other reality is that the same "community" that makes the laws and funds the legislators and other public officials are from a very different "community" from those who are arrested and sentenced by the courts on a daily basis. The upper class community believes that the current criminal justice system is functioning just fine and is cost-effective. Transforming this socio-economic class's perspective would be quite an unlikely accomplishment.

Finally, we have to recognize that over $200 billion a year is being spent on the criminal justice system that employs a large work force. Taking this system apart will require an equally large task for relocating jobs of for the hundreds of thousands of people who make a decent living in criminal justice (including many state universities and community colleges). It would require another federal bailout which hopefully will not occur.

IS THERE A WAY OUT?

Prison populations are the product of admissions and length of stay (LOS). For a state to lower its population it must reduce one or both of these factors. Both admissions and lengths are stay are driven by policy and law. For example, over 60% of prison admissions are probation and parole violators. The ability to send someone to prison for violating the terms of probation or parole is provided by law and then further refined via agency policy. Similarly how long someone is incarcerated is predicated on the sentences length as provided by law and then mitigated by pretrial and good time credits also determined by law and again mitigated by agency policy. The dramatic rise in prison populations (as well as all forms of correctional supervision) was based on changes in law and to a lesser degree by agency policy. So it's clear that in order to lower the size of the correctional system, the same laws that fueled the increase must repealed and setback to where they were.

While prison admissions were a major contributor to the prison increases, another major source was an increase in the length of stay. As shown in Table 1, there has been a 5-8 month increase in the LOS since 1993. This increase has not been fueled by longer prison sentences, but rather by people being required to serve a greater proportion of the imposed sentence. More specifically, the longer LOS is the result of lower parole grant rates and less good time being awarded to prisoners.

In a recent paper prepared for the U.S. Department of Justice, I tried to show mathematically what it would take to substantially reduce the entire correctional system (Austin 2009). This exercise was based on an earlier effort by a number of criminologists to reach a consensus on how and why it must be done. (Austin et al., 2007). These exercises were based on policies that are in existence now in some states or were recently in practice in most states. The point was to show that it can done safely and produce sizeable savings to taxpayers.

A key recommendation was that the current LOS be returned to what it was in 1993. For example, reducing the nation's prison population by 1/3rd (that's over 500,000 prisoners) can be simply accomplished by returning to the length of stay (LOS) in prison that existed in 1994. We have further considerable evidence that altering the LOS on prisoners by these amounts

(4-8 months) has no impact on public safety or statewide crime rates. So the science supports this reduction (Austin et al., 2007). But will it happen?

The perfect storm of lower crime rates and a prolonged economic recession will force the reduction in prison population and other forms of correctional social control that Thomson and others so desire. Such reductions will require a change in sentencing laws and practices which are not likely to come easily or voluntarily from those who now profit and benefit from the current system of punishment and treatment. Rather it must come from elected policy makers who have the power to change existing law and agency policies. Their change of heart will be driven by the economic recession and not evidence-based practices although it will be useful to have such evidence to justify the reforms.

Just like the unpleasant reforms now being instituted to avoid further financial turmoil and an unsupportable standard of living, we will be required by the long-term economic recession to "take a hair cut" and trim back the level of punishment (especially shorter prison terms) currently being handed out (Talbott, 2008). As America is forced to live within its economic means, we will be forced to punish within our means and in proportion to the harm inflict by people who commit crimes.

Table 1: Sentence Lengths, Time Served, and Length of Parole Supervision for Released Prisoners, 1993 – 2003

Length of Supervision	1993	2003	Change
Sentence			
Median	48 months	36 months	- 12 months
Mean	66 months	62 months	-4 months
Average Time			
Median	12 months	17 months	+5 months
Mean	21 months	29 months	+ 8 months
Average Parole	19 months	26 months	+9 months
Total Time	40 months	55 months	+15 months

Sources: U.S. Department of Justice, Office of Justice Programs, Bureau of Justice Statistics, Prison Statistics. Online. Available: http://www.ojp.usdoj.gov/bjs/prisons.htm. Accessed: December 22, 2008.

REFERENCES

Austin, J. (2009). *Reducing America's Correctional Populations: A Strategic Plan.* Concept paper prepared for the National Institute of Corrections, US Department of Justice, Washington, DC.

Austin, J., Clear, T.R., Duster, T., Greenberg, D.F., Irwin, J., McCoy, C. Mobley, A., Owen, B. & Page, J. (2007). *Unlocking America: Why and How to Reduce America's Prison Population.* Washington, DC: JFA Institute.

Jacobson, M. (2005). *Downsizing Prisons: How to Reduce Crime and End Mass Incarceration.* New York: New York University Press.

Illinois Criminal Justice Information Authority (2004). *The Extent and Nature of Drug and Violent Crime in Illinois' Counties.* Chicago, IL: ICJIA.

Listwan, S.J., Jonson, C.L., Cullen, F.T., & Latessa, E.J. (2008). Cracks in the penal harm movement. *Criminology & Public Policy, 7,* 423- 466.

Spellman, W. (2009). Crime, cash and limited options: Explaining the prison boom. *Criminology & Public Policy, 8,* 29-78.

Talbott, J.R. (2008). *Contagion: The Financial Epidemic that is Sweeping the Global Economy...and how to Protect Yourself from It.* Hoboken, New Jersey: John Wiley & Sons, Inc.

Webster, C.M. & Doob, A.N. (2008). America in a larger world: The future of the penal harm movement. *Criminology & Public Policy 7,* 473-487.

Zimring, F.E. (2008). Public sentiment, political action, and governmental crime policy – On the origins and significance of mixed feelings. *Criminology & Public Policy, 7,* 467-472.

PRISONER REENTRY PLANNING AND PROGRAMMING MUST ADDRESS FAMILY REUNIFICATION, RELATIONSHIP CONFLICT, AND DOMESTIC VIOLENCE

WILLIAM OLIVER

Research on prisoner reentry and parole recidivism has primarily focused on how unemployment, substance abuse, and inadequate housing among recently released prisoners adversely impact successful prisoner reentry (Petersilia, 2000; Travis, Solomon & Waul, 2001; Visher & Travis, 2003). As such, very little attention has been devoted to examining the relationship between prisoner reentry, relationship conflict, domestic violence and recidivism. Currently, most efforts to address the response to domestic violence by criminal justice practitioners and domestic violence service providers occur at the front end of the criminal process. That is, to focus on examining the effectiveness of mandatory arrest policies for batterers (Maxwell, Garner, & Fagan, 2001), developing specialized domestic violence courts (Karan, Kelitz, & Denard, 1999), the effectiveness of mandatory batterer's intervention (Gondolf & Williams, 2001), and linking battered women and their children to shelter and advocacy services (Shepard & Pence, 1999). However, public policy must also address domestic violence as a feature of comprehensive prisoner reentry planning and programming in order to enhance the safety of women currently involved and/or formerly involved with returning offenders. Furthermore, an enhanced focus on prisoner reentry and domestic violence will serve to facilitate a less problematic transition from prison to the community for returning offenders and their female partners.

THE PRISONER REENTRY CHALLENGE

What we know about prisoner reentry and recidivism is that upwards of 650,000 prisoners are returning to communities throughout the United States annually (Travis et al., 2001). However, only 45% of parolees will successfully complete their parole term (Langan & Levin, 2002). It has been reported that within 3 years, 67% of returning prisoners are rearrested for a serious offense and 52% returned to prison for a new criminal offense (Langan & Levin, 2002).

Furthermore, returning offenders are often confronted by a broad range of obstacles that hinder their capacity to make a smooth transition from prison to the community. For example, given that offenders tend to lack of education and vocational training and the reluctance of employers to hire ex-offenders, it is difficult for returning offenders to secure employment. Securing employment is further compounded by state laws which ban convicted felons from certain occupations (e.g. airport personnel, unarmed security guards, barbers, nurse's aids, and taxi drivers). Moreover, federal laws banning ex-offenders with felony drug-related convictions from receiving federal Pell grants to attend college, and aggressive enforcement of the collection of child support from non-custodial fathers (Holzer, Offner, & Sorensen, 2004) also serve as reentry barriers. Consequently, the poor economic prospects of returning offenders have the potential to erode already weakened bonds between incarcerated men and their female partners during a critical turning point in a couple's relationship.

DOMESTIC VIOLENCE AND THE PRISON POPULATION

While very little is known about the number of parolees or ex-offenders who are returned to prison as a result of domestic violence or the number of parolees who become involved in relationship conflicts that lead to parole revocation (Petesilia, 2000; Travis et al., 2001), what we do know is that incarcerated populations are disproportionately represented among persons with a history of domestic violence offending and victimization experiences (Harlow, 1999). For example, Greenfeld and Snell (1999) found that nearly 6 in 10 women in State prisons had experienced physical or sexual abuse in the past; just over a third of imprisoned women had been abused by an intimate in the past; and just under a quarter reported prior abuse by a family member.

Most incarcerated women with a history of abuse report that their abusers were current or former male romantic partners. In addition, women convicted of domestic homicide disproportionately report high rates of intimate partner violence. In a 1998 study of 150 incarcerated women in the general population of Bedford Hills Maximum Security Correctional Facility in New York, 75% of all respondents reported severe physical abuse by intimate partners in adulthood. In addition, over one-third (35%) reported experiencing marital rape or being forced to participate in other sexual activity (Browne, Miller & Maguin, 1999). Incarcerated men also report high rates of intimate partner battering. For example, White, Gondolf, Robertson, Goodwin, and Caraveo (2002) have reported that 1 in 3 men incarcerated in federal prisons for low risk crimes acknowledged recent physical violence against intimate female partners and 1 in 10 reported severe violence toward women.

INCARCERATION, REENTRY AND RELATIONSHIP CONFLICT

Marital and romantic relationships are severely strained and frequently terminate during imprisonment as a consequence of the stresses associated with enforced separation (Hairston, 1998). For example, many prisoners are housed a great distance from their families. Furthermore, the cost of visitation and the rigid visitation rules of correctional facilities (e.g., limited visitation hours, lack of privacy, and restrictions on physical contact) may function to erode already strained relationships (Fishman, 1990; Hairston, 1998). A source of conflict that emerges early in a man's incarceration pertains to the demands of men that women visit them more often and that women be attentive to their material needs as a means of assisting them mitigate the pains of imprisonment (Fishman, 1990; Nurse, 2002). Moreover, research indicates that conflict between incarcerated men and their current or former female partners is a central concern of most male offenders when asked to describe their current family relations (Tripp, 2003). In addition, a study of the social-psychological processes affecting recidivism and desistance from crime found that interpersonal conflict with heterosexual partners was a common problem mentioned by recidivists (Zamble and Quinsey, 1997).

A major source of relationship conflict occurring between incarcerated men and their female partners is the men's obsession with the fidelity of their female partners and accusations of unfaithfulness (Oliver & Hairston, 2008; Nurse, 2002). It is has been reported that it is not uncommon for incarcerated men to engage in a variety of tactics (e.g. issuing demands as to who is allowed to visit their partner's residence, expecting their female partners to be available to receive collect calls, requiring the partner to avoid social settings in which other men will have an opportunity to pursue a relationship with them, and informing the partner that relatives or friends of the incarcerated man are monitoring her activities) as a means of controlling the mobility and availability of their wives and girlfriends during their period of imprisonment (Fishman, 1990; Hairston & Oliver, 2006). Moreover, issues of fidelity and unfaithfulness are often not resolved and tend to emerge as sources of relationship conflict during reentry (Hairston & Oliver, 2006).

The reality is that many women opt to terminate romantic relationships with incarcerated men. As such, women's decision to terminate relationships with incarcerated men and to move on to new relationships often serve as a major source of conflict during and following a man's incarceration, particularly when the returning offender is unwilling to accept change (Nurse, 2002; Oliver & Hairston, 2008). Furthermore, the emotional stability of incarcerated men and men returning to the community are often compounded by the intersections of untreated substance abuse and mental health issues (Glaze & Maruschak, 2008), concerns about the well being of their children, and worrying about being replaced in their children's lives by the new boyfriends/husbands of their children's mothers (Hairston, 1998; Nurse, 2002).

CORRECTIONS AND DOMESTIC VIOLENCE COLLABORATION

There is a major need for collaboration and partnership between institutional corrections, community corrections, and the domestic violence service delivery network relative to addressing the intersection of prisoner reentry and domestic violence. Research indicates that returning offenders who assume conventional roles within their families have greater success in their transition from prison (Maruna, 2001; Sampson & Laub, 1990). Among the problems hindering a coordinated response to prisoner reentry and domestic violence is it is not clear who owns the problem (Bobbitt, Campbell & Tate, 2006; Petersilia, 2000). Historically, correctional systems, particularly state correctional institutions, have not regarded the problem of domestic violence offending or victimization as their responsibility to address beyond the requirement of incapacitating those batterers or victims who have been sentenced to a period of incarceration (Buzawa & Buzawa, 2003). Hence, batterers and/or victims of domestic violence sentenced to prison on charges directly related or un-related to domestic violence have not had sufficient access to institution based program interventions (e.g. batterers intervention programs or support groups for victims) to address domestic violence (Bobbitt et al., 2006).

Furthermore, the lack of a history of collaboration between institutional corrections, community corrections, and the domestic violence service delivery network around this issue tends to preclude consideration of the need to partner with agencies outside of the criminal justice system to address prisoner reentry and domestic violence (Bobbitt et al., 2006). While domestic violence service providers tend to recognize the value of providing domestic violence awareness and intervention services to men in prison and those who have returned to the community they have major concerns with regard to how partnerships with correctional agencies have the potential to threaten the safety of battered women; particularly correctional interventions that involve bringing incarcerated men or men on parole and their former or current partners together to enhance parenting skills, to construct a method of effective co-parenting and/or strengthening marital relationships (Bobbitt et al.; RTI., 2008).

Because partnerships involving corrections and the domestic violence service delivery network are new, these partnerships must be cultivated for the long term safety and benefit of the intimate partners of offenders and for the long-term benefit of returning offenders who seek to re-establish relationships with intimates and to remain crime free. As such, in order for there to be progress in addressing the intersection of prisoner reentry and domestic violence there needs to be an ongoing dialogue involving key stakeholders (e.g. institutional corrections, community corrections, domestic violence service providers and battered women) about the challenges associated with addressing domestic violence during the transition from prison to the community. Hence, incarcerated men and returning offenders need services and interventions that will assist them in developing the capacity to reunite with female partners who desire to reunite with them. However, where their female partners have terminated the relationship following the man's incarceration, many men will need to be exposed to institution and community-based interventions that assist them in accepting change in their pre-incarceration relationships and where there are children, developing the skills to successfully co-parent with the mothers of their children (Hairston & Oliver, 2006; RTI, 2008).

Community reentry is not an individual affair but rather a family matter. When men go to prison and return home, their wives and girlfriends, as well as children, are deeply impacted (Braman, 2007; Nurse, 2002). As such, it is imperative that comprehensive reentry programs be designed to reduce recidivism and support safe and healthy connections with family and community. Some situations may require temporary or permanent separation from intimate partners to achieve safety. Others may require appropriate supports to help families safely reconnect. To meet the goals of reducing recidivism and domestic violence during reentry, correctional agencies and domestic violence service providers must develop interventions that consider the unique circumstances of offenders returning to the community and women who have an interest in maintaining their personal safety (Hairston & Oliver, 2006).

Domestic violence victim advocates can play a crucial role in partnering with correctional agencies to develop institution and community-based interventions designed to help maintain family safety as men are released from prison. In addition, given the high rate of domestic violence among incarcerated women, domestic violence service providers must begin to engage in more proactive outreach to women returning to the community following a period of incarceration. To do so victim advocates must develop non-traditional outreach strategies to reach women in need through partnerships with corrections, parole and community-based prisoner/family support programs (Hairston & Oliver, 2006). Furthermore, in communities experiencing a high rate of offender return, domestic violence organizations must expand and orient their programs and services toward the wives and girlfriends of returning offenders. While domestic violence advocacy agencies have primarily focused on helping women seek safety through separation, they should reconsider how to help women – both women involved with male offenders returning to the community and returning female offenders who have a history of domestic violence victimization-who desire to reunite with their partners Practitioners can also help women assess their own risk for violence during reentry by partnering with correctional case workers and parole departments to develop assessment tools and reentry safety checklists (Hairston & Oliver, 2006).

Policies and protocols based on the explicit goal of supporting prisoners' safe and successful transition back to family living are needed to guide correctional practice both within correctional facilities and upon return to the community (RTI, 2008). As such, comprehensive reentry planning must include several components in order to address issues associated with prisoner reentry and domestic violence. First, prisoners need preparation to resume living in a family setting in much the same way that they need preparation for successful adaptation to a changing job market. Family life preparation and domestic violence prevention should be basic components of pre-release programs. Incarcerated men and women need support programs that will help them deal with their feelings about changes that are taking place in their relationships and instruction and resources to help handle conflict constructively and manage new family roles and responsibilities without resorting to abuse (Nurse, 2002; RTI, 2008). Women who are involved with men who are returning home need similar assistance to help them prepare themselves and their children for the man's return home and the changes that will bring in their normal routines. The usual family support and violence prevention programs may not adequately prepare families for reunification given that incarceration and parole supervision present unique challenges for correctional agencies and domestic violence service providers. Therefore, corrections should collaborate with traditional community based programs to educate them about the challenges of reentry to extend the resource network for returning prisoners and their families. Similarly, correctional case workers and others involved in assisting offenders prepare for reentry would benefit from participating in cross trainings provided by community based domestic violence service providers in order to enhance their understanding and response to men who batter and women who are battered.

CONCLUSION

Comprehensive prisoner reentry planning requires the inclusion of programs and interventions that assist returning offender's mange conflict, manage new family roles and responsibilities, and provide information that will assist them in accessing community resources that will be useful in efforts to address personal and interpersonal challenges. Reentry planning and programming should not be considered comprehensive unless some attention is devoted to assisting prisoners and their families strengthen their relationships and develop the capacity to negotiate conflict and change.

REFERENCES

Braman, D. (2007). *Doing Time on the Outside: Incarceration and Family Life In Urban America.* Ann Arbor, MI: University of Michigan Press.

Bobbitt, M., Campbell, R. & Tate, G. (2006). *Safe Return: Working Toward Preventing Domestic Violence When Men Return from Prison.* New York: Vera Institute of Justice.

Browne, A., Miller, B. & Maguin, E. (1999). Prevalence and severity of lifetime physical and sexual victimization among incarcerated women. *International Journal of Law and Psychiatry, 22,* 301-322.

Buzawa, E.S. & Buzawa, C.G. (2003). *Domestic Violence-The Criminal Justice Process* (3rd Edition). Thousand Oaks, CA: Sage Publications.

Fishman, L.T. (1990). *Women at the Wall: A Study of Prisoners' Wives Doing Time on the Outside.* Albany, NY: State University of New York Press.

Glaze, L.E. & Maruschak, L.M. (2008). *Parents in Prison and their Minor Children.* Washington, DC: Bureau of Justice Statistics.

Gondolf, E.W. & Williams, O.J. (2001). Culturally focused batterer counseling for African American men. *Trauma, Violence, & Abuse, 2,* 243-295.

Greenfeld, L.A. & Snell, T.L. (1999). *Women Offenders.* U.S. Department of Justice.

Hairston, C.F. (1998). The forgotten parent: Understanding the forces that influence incarcerated fathers relationships with their children. *Child Welfare, 77,* 617-639.

Hairston, C.F. & Oliver, W. (2006). *Domestic Violence and Prisoner Reentry: Experiences of African American Women and Men.* New York: Vera Institute of Justice.

Harlow, C.W. (1999). *Prior Abuse Reported by Inmates and Probationers.* Washington, DC: U.S. Department of Justice.

Holzer, H., Offner, P. & Sorrenson, E. (2004). *Declining Employment Among Young Black Men: The Role of Ex-offenders and Child Support, Working Paper.* Washington, DC: George Washington University Public Policy Institute and Urban Institute.

Karan, A., Keilitz, S. & Denard, S. (1999). Domestic violence courts: What are they and how should we manage them? *Family and Juvenile Court Journal, 50,* 75-86.

Langan, P. & Levin, D. (2002). *Recidivism of Prisoners Released in 1994.* Washington, DC: Bureau of Justice Statistics.

Maruna, S. (2001). *Making Good-How Ex-Convicts Reform and Rebuild Their Lives.* Washington, DC: American Psychological Association.

Maxwell, C., Garner, J. & Fagan, J. (2001). *The Effects of Arrest on Intimate Partner Violence: New Evidence from the Spouse Assault Replication Program.* Washington, DC: U.S. Department of Justice.

Nurse, A. (2002). *Fatherhood Arrested – Parenting from within the Juvenile Justice System.* Boston, MA: Northeastern University Press.

Oliver, W. & Hairston, C.F. (2008). Intimate partner violence during the transition from prison to the community: Perspectives of incarcerated African American men. *Journal of Aggression, Maltreatment & Trauma, 16,* 258-276.

Petersilia, J. (2000). *When Prisoners Return to the Community: Political, Economic, and Social Consequences.* Washington, DC: U.S. Department of Justice.

RTI International. (2008). *Incarceration and the Family-A Review of Research and Promising Approaches For Serving Fathers and Families.* Washington, DC: U S. Department of Health and Human Services.

Sampson, R.J. & Laub, J.H. (1990). Crime and deviance over the life course: The salience of adult social bonds. *American Sociological Review, 44,* 465-508.

Shepard, M.F. & Pence, E. (1999). *Coordinated Community Response to Domestic Violence: Lessons from Duluth and Beyond.* Thousand Oaks, CA: Sage Publications

Travis, J., Solomon, A.L. & Waul, M. (2001). *From Prison to Home: The Dimensions and Consequences of Prisoner Reentry.* Washington, DC: The Urban Institute.

Tripp, B. (2003). Incarcerated African American fathers: Exploring changes in family relationships. In O. Harris & R. Miller (Eds.), *Impacts of Incarceration on the African American Family,* (pp. 17–31). New Brunswick, NJ: Transaction Publishers.

Visher, C.A. & Travis, J. (2003). *Transitions from Prison to Community: Understanding Individual Pathways.* Washington, DC: The Urban Institute.

White, R.J., Gondolf, E.W., Robertson, D.U., Goodwin, B.J. & Caraveo, L.E. (2002). Extent and characteristics of women batterers among federal inmates. *International Journal of Offender Therapy and Comparative Criminology, 46,* 412-426.

Zamble, E. & Quinsey, V.L. (1997). *The Criminal Recidivism Process.* New York: Cambridge University Press.

THE MULTI-PRONGED POTENTIAL EFFECTS OF IMPLEMENTING DOMESTIC VIOLENCE PROGRAMS IN MEN'S PRISONS AND REENTRY PROGRAMMING

JOANNE BELKNAP

William Oliver provides a powerful and compelling point with his essay on the need to address domestic violence recidivism as a component of male prisoners' reentry into their communities. Clearly, not every incarcerated man has an official domestic violence criminal record, but Oliver documents that such a record is disproportionately high among incarcerated men. Moreover, it is likely that some of the incarcerated men without official domestic violence offending records have perpetrated domestic violence in cases where there were no arrests, including when criminal legal system officials never even knew about the abuse (it was unreported), and some of these men who might self-refer to a prison domestic violence program may be the ones most likely to change (see Roffman et al., 2008).

Not only have many incarcerated men committed domestic violence, but it is likely that many of both those male prisoners who have committed and not committed domestic violence have witnessed it, including as children. Thus, providing even a domestic violence awareness (as opposed to an intervention) program in prison could be a powerful healing experience for such men. At the same time, participating in such programming might result in these men becoming more intrinsically invested in being nonviolent, and to be more than simple bystanders when witnessing other men (e.g., brothers, neighbors, and so on) committing domestic violence when back in their communities post-prison. In short, whether they have a domestic violence record or not, incarcerated men's improved awareness about the dynamics and effects of domestic violence might reduce their own abusive treatment of current and former women partners when they leave prison, and make them more willing to stand up against domestic violence and other sexist behaviors they witness in their families and communities upon their release.

It is worth acknowledging an overall poor performance of batterer intervention programs (BIPs) (e.g., Day et al., 2009; Buttell & Carney, 2008). However, it is equally noteworthy that these assessments note the unusually poor attendance/compliance by the court-ordered offenders, and that longer programs tend to be more effective, as do the cases where individuals had higher attendance. Prisons are an ideal place to offer BIPS in that they provide, quite literally, a captive audience. Moreover, boredom is a daily and prevalent problem most prisoners face. Thus, implementing BIPS in men's prisons is ideal not only for the disproportionately high rate

397

of domestic violence offending by incarcerated (as compared to community) men as Oliver so effectively documents, but also because prison is a place where these men are likely most uniquely willing to participate (there is little to do). Even if they do not want to willingly participate, enforcing their participation in prison is far easier than enforcing it once they are in the community. And if these in-prison BIPs can be coordinated to work with reentry programs for incarcerated men, they could be even more impactful. For example, if a man takes part in a BIP while incarcerated, and when returning to the community is able to meet regularly with, or at least have access to a BIP provider, this would likely provide powerful continuance in his work to become non-abusive to his intimate partner and a better father and role model to his children.

In sum, Oliver's proposal for domestic violence programs as part of incarcerated men's reentry to communities is a meaningful way to enhance women's safety as well as deter some portion of the revolving-door aspect of incarceration (the same individuals repeatedly in and out of prison). This essay presents two additional potentially positive aspects of the implementation of domestic violence awareness and intervention programs in men's prisons: (1) the potential to increase children's safety, emotional well-being, and their likelihood of discontinuing the cycle of domestic violence in their adult lives; and (2) re-framing domestic violence as "men's problem."

THE POTENTIALLY POSITIVE IMPACTS
ON THE CHILDREN OF ABUSIVE MEN

In his essay, Oliver focuses on the safety of the women partners, but does not acknowledge the numerous potentially powerful impacts of domestic violence awareness and BIPs for incarcerated men on their children. First, a growing body of research documents the extreme emotional hardship for children exposed to witnessing and hearing their mothers' victimizations by the children's fathers (or other male partner of the mothers) (e.g., Kitzmann et al., 2003). Clearly, anything that limits children's exposure to their mothers' victimizations, such as Oliver's proposed BIPs, could have a huge impact on the well-being of the children of men returning home from prison.

Also, there is the potential to intervene in the intergenerational transmission of violence: the belief that children who witness parental domestic violence are more likely to grow up to think that it is acceptable or even expected behavior. Thus boys witnessing domestic violence are more likely to become abusers and girls witnessing are more susceptible to believing this is normal husband/boyfriend behavior, and then may be more likely to date, marry, have children, and stay with abusive male partners than some women not having these childhood exposures of domestic violence or even abuse partners themselves (see McKinney et al.,

2009; Wareham, Boots, & Chavez, 2009). Therefore, domestic violence programs in men's prisons could be effective in breaking the intergenerational transmission of domestic violence in some families.

Finally, if the programming for the incarcerated men returning to their communities includes the impact of domestic violence on children (which it should), the implementation of such programming will likely improve the chances of healthier parenting by these fathers, and subsequently, stronger and healthier bonds between these men and their children, regardless of whether the men are still in intimate relationships with the mothers of their children. Taken together, these three potential benefits impacted upon children through domestic violence programs in men's prisons and upon reentry to their communities, could be truly momentous.

REFOCUSING DOMESTIC VIOLENCE AS A PROBLEM WITH MEN/ABUSERS

An additional benefit of implementing domestic violence programming for imprisoned men during incarceration and reentry is the reframing of domestic violence as "men's problem." Violence against women is typically labeled as "women's problem." Many women's prisons offer programs, at least irregularly, on domestic violence (usually focusing on the women's victimization, not offending). While this can be incredibly helpful and healing for the many incarcerated women who have been victims directly or had mothers, sisters, daughters and others as victims of domestic violence, it cannot work to deter domestic violence in the way that programs for men/abusers can. Certainly, domestic violence programs for incarcerated women can be extremely useful in providing them with ways to look for signs of potential abusers, to not blame themselves (and to shift blame to the batterers), and to learn some empowering skills and access some resources. But these domestic violence programs for incarcerated women cannot stop men from abusing. Thus, Oliver's proposal offers a profound way to focus domestic violence as "men's problem." Again, this is not to deny the significant lethal, emotional, physical, and financial harm that domestic violence abusers have wreaked on their current and former partners and the need for programs and treatment for domestic violence victims, particularly in prison. Rather it is to stress that meaningful deterrence focuses on the offenders, not the victims.

CONCLUSION

I am close to embarrassed to admit I never thought about implementing domestic violence programs in men's prisons. I have certainly read and heard about, and even participated in some domestic violence programming (based on women's victimization not offending) in women's prisons. William Oliver's idea is brilliant. Such implementation holds significant potential for women's safety and slowing the revolving door to men's prisons. Additionally, domestic violence programming in men's prisons is also a potentially powerful tool to enhance children's safety and well-being, deter the intergenerational transmission of violence, improve incarcerated men's parenting, and help to re-frame domestic violence as men's problem. Of course, any domestic violence program must have integrity, including and addressing the correct areas with good facilitators to be effective (e.g., Day et al., 2009).

REFERENCES

Belknap, J. & Potter, H. (2006). Intimate partner abuse. In C. Renzetti, L. Goodstein, & S. Miller (Eds.), *Women, Crime, and Criminal Justice (2/e)*, (pp. 168-184) Roxbury Publishing.

Buttell, F.P. & Carney, M.M. (2008). A large sample investigation of battering intervention program attrition. *Research on Social Work Practice, 18(3),* 177-188.

Day, A., Chung, D., O'Leary, P. & Carson, T. (2009). Programs for men who perpetrate domestic violence: An examination of the issues underlying the effectiveness of intervention programs. *Journal of Family Violence, 24(3),* 203-212.

Healey, K., Smith, C. & O'Sullivan C. (2001). The causes of domestic violence: From theory to intervention. In H.M. Eigenberg (Ed.), *Woman Battering in the United States,* (pp. 161-179). Prospect Heights, IL: Waveland.

Kitzmann, K.M., Gaylord, N.K., Holt, A.R., & Kenny, E.D. (2003). Child witnesses to domestic violence: A meta-analytic review. *Journal of Consulting and Clinical Psychology, 71,* 339–352.

McKinney, C.M., Caetano, R., Ramisetty-Mikler, S. & Nelson, S. (2009). Childhood family violence and perpetration and victimization of intimate partner violence: Findings from a national population-based study of couples. *Annals of Epidemiology, 19(1),* 25-32.

Roffman, R.A., Edleson, J.L., Neighbors, C., Mbilinyi, L. & Walker, D. (2008). The men's domestic abuse check-up: A protocol for reaching the nonadjudicated and untreated man who batters and who abuses substances. *Violence Against Women 14(5),* 589-605.

Scully, D. (1990). Understanding Sexual Violence. Boston: Unwin Hyman.

Wareham, J., Boots, D.P. & Chavez, J.M. (2009). A test of social learning and intergenerational transmission among batterers. *Journal of Criminal Justice, 37(2),* 163-173.

THE IMPORTANCE OF FAMILY REUNIFICATION IN THE PRISONER REENTRY PROCESS

JOHNNA CHRISTIAN

In the United States, more than 2 million people are incarcerated in prisons and jails and 600,000 return to their communities every year (Sabol, Couture, & Harrison, 2007; Travis, 2005). This scale of imprisonment and reentry into communities gives researchers and policy makers a sense of urgency to develop programs and policies that will facilitate successful transitions from prison to communities (National Research Council, 2008; Petersilia, 2003). Indeed, a host of national and local efforts—such as the Serious and Violent Offender Reentry Initiative, the Department of Labor's Prisoner Reentry Initiative, the Council of State Government's Reentry Policy Council, and passage of the Second Chance Act— are aimed at identifying the needs of prisoners released to the community, implementing model programs, and ultimately enhancing public safety by reducing recidivism.

Although these efforts traditionally emphasize needs such as addiction, mental illness, job training, and housing (Visher & Travis, 2003), and former prisoners themselves place a high priority on such needs (Visher & Lattimore, 2007), growing evidence indicates that strengthening family relationships is a crucial component of reentry policy and programming (Naser & LaVigne, 2006; see Herman-Stahl, Kan & McKay [2008] for a thorough review of recent research). Yet, as Oliver (2009, this volume) suggests, family reunification presents specific challenges, which are shaped by pre-incarceration relationships (Visher & Travis, 2003), the demands of maintaining family connections with incarcerated individuals (Christian, 2005; Comfort, 2008), and shifting family dynamics upon a prisoner's return to the family and community (Arditti, 2005; Fishman, 1990; Hairston & Oliver, 2006).

Hairston (1988) proposed that the family relationships of the incarcerated and formerly incarcerated were central to curbing criminal activity because of the potential for family members to provide social support to those released from prison. Further, she wrote that family relationships "provide opportunities for nurturing and sustain morale and a sense of security and well-being. They provide a reassurance of worth and attest to an individual's competence in a social role" (p. 50). These functions are particularly salient in light of research about the narrative process of desistance, which unfolds in conjunction with changing perceptions of self, generated through interactions with supportive social networks (Maruna, 2001), and the potential for social relationships to provide "hooks for change" (Giordano, Cernkovich, & Rudolph, 2002) that lead to desistance.

Unfortunately, these important family support processes are likely to be damaged, or perhaps missing entirely, for some former prisoners. As Oliver (2009) outlines, these issues have not received adequate attention, yet failure to address them has serious consequences for the safety of returning prisoners and family members, and the potential for support offered by family members to minimize offending (Foster & Hagan, 2009; Mills & Codd, 2008).

FAMILY RELATIONSHIPS AND PRISONER REENTRY

Criminological theory points to the role of informal social ties and supports in encouraging people to desist from crime (National Research Council, 2008; Sampson & Laub, 1993; see Bales & Mears [2008] for an application to incarcerated individuals' ties to family members). Importantly, the protective functions provided by social ties also serve specific and immediate instrumental functions for released prisoners. For example, Farrall's (2004) research with probationers in the United Kingdom found that social capital, used when family members offered information and provided contacts for potential jobs, helped people on probation secure employment. These findings indicate that family members' efforts in the desistance process likely overlap with the steps taken by criminal justice officials, and that there are ways to integrate the supports provided by formal and informal systems of social control (Mills & Codd, 2008; Wolff & Draine, 2004).

In addition, while we know that former prisoners rely on family members for support upon release from prison, we also know that support exchanges are contextualized by residence (Martinez & Christian, 2009), the former offender's perceptions of the future (Maruna, 2001), and the nature of the relationship prior to (Visher & Travis, 2003), and during (LaVigne, Naser, Brooks, & Castro, 2005) incarceration. These situations indicate both strengthening and delimiting factors in the family relationships of formerly incarcerated people, with specific implications for Oliver's (2009) timely and compelling call to address family reunification, relationship conflict, and domestic violence in prisoner reentry planning and programming.

Such initiatives must account for the variety of complicating factors in family relationships, including the recognition that reunification is not in the best interest of all families (Codd, 2007; Hairston & Oliver, 2006) and that scant empirical evidence is available about how to make decisions regarding reunification planning and placement (Herman-Stahl, Kan, & McKay, 2008). Oliver's (2009) proposal highlights one of the most problematic aspects of research about prisoner family relationships: We study, and therefore understand best, the family members with at least minimal connections to current and former prisoners, thereby neglecting the family members who by choice or necessity completely sever relationships.

Therefore, I see two emerging bodies of research and policy development with important implications for Oliver's (2009) proposal. First, evidence about prisoners' expectations for life upon release from prison suggests both potentially problematic situations and possible points for interventions to strengthen family relationships and supports. Individuals recently released from prison have high expectations of receiving a range of supports from family members, including assistance in finding employment, pocket money, and a place to live (Martinez & Christian, 2009; Naser & LaVigne, 2006). In a study of men returning from prison to Baltimore and Chicago, Naser and LaVigne (2006) found that, in a pre-release survey, 69 percent of prisoners expected to live with family members after release, and that, in a post-release interview, 86 percent of respondents indicated they were living with at least one family member. Moreover, although 55 percent of prisoners anticipated that family would be an important component of their success after release from prison, in post-release interviews, 80 percent reported that this was actually the case.

Similarly, prisoners incarcerated in Texas predicted that they would live with their children after their release from prison at even higher rates then they actually lived with them prior to incarceration (Foster & Hagan, 2009). These findings indicate that prisoners have expectations that family relationships and circumstances will improve during incarceration and be better upon release than they were in the pre-incarceration period. When relationships have been plagued by conflict and violence, however, this potentially unrealistic expectation may exacerbate problems and place family members at risk.

Following a strengths-based reentry framework (Maruna & LeBel, 2003), Foster and Hagan's (2009) findings also highlight offenders' willingness to repair fractured relationships, even if driven by an anticipation of their needs upon release from prison and the likelihood that they must call upon family members to fulfill some of these needs. This suggests a window of opportunity to address the family situations that Oliver (2009) describes.

We must think carefully about how best to implement the policies outlined by Oliver. Although family reunification is becoming a higher priority for correctional officials (National Institute of Corrections, 2002), there is little precedent for programs that specifically address family conflict and domestic violence (Hairston & Oliver, 2006). The intersections of race, class, and gender are central in this regard (Christian & Thomas, 2009), as mass imprisonment disproportionately impacts African Americans and Hispanics, the family support systems of male and female inmates differ greatly (Casey-Acevedo & Bakken, 2002), and women of color who have been subjected to intimate partner abuse face cultural norms and expectations, as well as structural disadvantage, that put them at greater risk of abuse (Potter, 2008).

Thus, we must ask critical questions about how female prisoners, already facing "gender entrapment" in their own routes to offending

(Richie, 1996), are further stigmatized and marginalized upon their release from prison, and how this status increases, rather than decreases, their risk for victimization. In the same vein, the female partners of incarcerated men face similarly disadvantaged statuses and also require special attention in the development of programs and policies (Christian & Thomas, 2009). For example, female visitors to men's prisons have been targeted for HIV preventive education because they are a high risk population for HIV infection, and their partners' incarceration is viewed as an opportunity to reach them. Such efforts, however, require dedicated collaboration across multiple systems (see Grinstead, Zack, & Faigeles, 1999).

I close with several cautionary points about potential unintended consequences of making family reunification an element of reentry planning and programming. First, few authors, other than Codd (2007), have explicitly applied a critical framework to delineate the multiple ways family members may be harmed by reunification efforts that mobilize the social capital (Mills & Codd; 2008; Wolff & Draine, 2004) of families that are stigmatized already (Braman, 2004) and socially and economically marginalized (Christian, Mellow & Thomas, 2006; Clear, 2007; Western, 2006). Second, to depend on these families to supplement the assistance that the criminal justice system provides for former prisoners without providing appropriate supports to these family members themselves further perpetuates their social exclusion (Codd, 2007). Finally, there is the danger of an insidious form of net-widening, in which under the guise of helping offenders, family members become labeled, monitored, and even stigmatized further. Recognizing that Oliver's (2009) suggestions to address family reunification, relationship conflict, and domestic violence in reentry planning are vital, we must implement them with appropriate planning, care, and consideration.

REFERENCES

Arditti, J.A. (2005). Families and incarceration: An ecological approach. *Families in Society: Journal of Contemporary Social Services, 86,* 251–260.

Bales, W.D., & Mears, D. P. (2008). Inmate social ties and the transition to society: Does visitation reduce recidivism? *Journal of Research in Crime and Delinquency, 45,* 287–321.

Braman, D. (2004). *Doing time on the outside: Incarceration and family life in urban America.* Ann Arbor: University of Michigan Press.

Casey-Acevedo, K., & Bakken, T. (2002). Visiting women in prison: Who visits and who cares? *Journal of Offender Rehabilitation, 34,* 67–83.

Christian, J. (2005). Riding the bus: Barriers to prison visitation and family management strategies. *Journal of Contemporary Criminal Justice, 21,* 31–48.

Christian, J., Mellow, J., & Thomas, S. (2006). Social and economic implications of family connections to prisoners. *Journal of Criminal Justice, 34,* 443–452.

Christian, J. & Thomas, S. (2009). Examining the intersections of race, gender, and mass imprisonment. *Journal of Ethnicity in Criminal Justice* 7, 69–84.

Clear, T. R. (2007) *Imprisoning Communities: How Mass Incarceration Makes Disadvantaged Neighborhoods Worse.* New York: Oxford University Press.

Codd, H. (2007). Prisoners' families and resettlement: A critical analysis. *Howard Journal of Criminal Justice, 46,* 255–263.

Comfort, M. (2008). *Doing Time Together: Love and Family in the Shadow of the Prison.* Chicago: University of Chicago Press.

Farrall, S. (2004). Social capital and offender reintegration: Making probation desistance focused. In S. Maruna & R. Immarigeon (Eds.), *After Crime And Punishment: Pathways To Offender Reintegration,* (pp. 57–82). Portland, OR: Willan Publishing.

Fishman, L. T. (1990). *Women at the Wall: A Study of Prisoner's Wives Doing Time on the Outside.* Albany: State University of New York Press.

Foster, H., & Hagan, J. (2009). The mass incarceration of parents in America: Issues of race/ethnicity, collateral damage to children, and prisoner reentry. *Annals of the American Academy of Political and Social Science, 623,* 179–194.

Giordano, P.C., Cernkovich, S.A, & Rudolph, J.L. (2002). Gender, crime and desistance: Toward a theory of cognitive transformation. *American Journal of Sociology, 107,* 990–1064.

Grinstead, O.A., Zack, B. & Faigeles, B. (1999). Collaborative research to prevent HIV among male prison inmates and their female partners. *Health Education and Behavior, 26,* 225–238.

Hairston, C.F. (1988). Family ties during imprisonment: Do they influence future criminal activity? *Federal Probation, 52,* 48–52.

Hairston, C. F. & Oliver, W. (2006). Domestic violence and prisoner reentry: Experiences of African American women and men. New York: Vera Institute of Justice.

Herman-Stahl, M., Kan, M.L., & McKay, T. (2008). Incarceration and the family: A review of research and promising approaches for serving fathers and families. Washington, DC: U.S. Department of Health and Human Services.

LaVigne, N.G., Naser, R.L., Brooks, L.E., & Castro, J.L. (2005). Explaining the effects of incarceration and in-prison family contact on prisoners' family relationships. *Journal of Contemporary Criminal Justice, 21,* 314–335.

Martinez, D.J., & Christian, J. (2009). The familial relationships of former prisoners: Examining the link between residence and informal support mechanisms. *Journal of Contemporary Ethnography, 38,* 201–224.

Maruna, S. (2001) *Making Good: How Ex-Convicts Reform and Rebuild Their Lives.* Washington, DC: American Psychological Association.

Maruna, S., & LeBel, T.P. (2003). Welcome home? Examining the "reentry court" concept from a strengths-based perspective, *Western Criminology Review, 4,* 1–7.

Mills, A., & Codd, H. (2008). Prisoners' families and offender management: Mobilizing social capital. *Probation Journal, 55,* 9–24.

Naser, R.L., & LaVigne, N.G. (2006). Family support in the prisoner reentry process: Expectations and realities. *Journal of Offender Rehabilitation, 43,* 93–106.

Naser, R.L., & Visher, C.A. (2006). Family members' experiences with incarceration and reentry. *Western Criminology Review, 7,* 20–31.

National Institute of Corrections. (2002). *Services for families and their children* (Bureau of Justice Statistics Special Report). Longmont, CO: National Institute of Corrections Information Center.

National Research Council. (2008). *Parole, Desistance from Crime, and Community Integration.* Committee on Community Supervision and Desistance from Crime. Committee on Law and Justice, Division of Behavioral and Social Sciences and Education. Washington, DC: National Academies Press.

Oliver, W. (2009). Prisoner reentry planning and programming must address family reunification, relationship conflict, and domestic violence. This volume.

Petersilia, J. (2003). *When Prisoners Come Home: Parole and Prisoner Reentry.* New York: Oxford University Press.

Potter, H. (2008). *Battle Cries: Black Women and Intimate Partner Abuse.* New York: New York University Press.

Richie, B. (1996). *Compelled to Crime: The Gender Entrapment of Battered Black Women.* New York: Routledge.

Sabol, W. J., Couture, H., & Harrison, P. M. (2007). *Prisoners in 2006.* Bureau of Justice Statistics Bulletin. Washington, DC: Office of Justice Programs.

Sampson, R.J. & Laub, J.H. (1993). *Crime in the Making: Pathways and Turning Points Through Life.* Cambridge, MA: Harvard University Press.

Travis, J. (2005). *But They All Come Back: Facing The Challenges of Prisoner Reentry.* Washington, DC: Urban Institute Press.

Visher, C.A., & Lattimore, P.K. (2007). Major study examines prisoners and their reentry needs. *National Institute of Justice Journal, 245,* 30–33.

Visher, C.A., & Travis, J. (2003). Transitions from prison to community: Understanding individual pathways. *Annual Review of Sociology, 29,* 89–113.

Western, B. (2006). *Punishment and Inequality in America.* New York: Russell Sage Foundation.

Wolff, N., & Draine, J. (2004). The dynamics of social capital of prisoners and community reentry: Ties that bind? *Journal of Correctional Health Care 10,* 457–490.